Emily Dickinson and Her Culture

This exotic Victorian "Still Life" by the great British photographer Roger Fenton can serve as a symbolic portrait of Emily Dickinson's art. An albumen print of about the year 1857, Fenton's photograph delights in exploring the tactile values of diverse objects that are both rare and strange—coral beads, artificial flowers, Chinese embroideries—yet are also bound together by a seductive and harmonious chiaroscuro. At the left we note the presence of one of Dickinson's favorite fabrics, diaphanous folds of tulle, and at the center of the whole meticulous composition, an enigmatic locked box of heavily carved ivory. Yet to the right of this focal point there is a conspicuous technical flaw, most probably caused by damage to the negative from an accidental spill of fluids during the long process of fixing the image. That Fenton signed and exhibited the finished print in spite of this idiosyncrasy is a tribute to his pride in his own work and to his audience's tolerance for the limitations as well as the possibilities of a new aesthetic medium. The more retiring Dickinson chose to preserve the materiality of her culture in a way decidedly more private, but no less hauntingly beautiful. (Reproduced by permission of the Museum of Art, Rhode Island School of Design.)

Emily Dickinson and Her Culture

The Soul's Society

BARTON LEVI ST. ARMAND

Department of English
Brown University

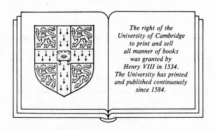

The right of the
University of Cambridge
to print and sell
all manner of books
was granted by
Henry VIII in 1534.
The University has printed
and published continuously
since 1584.

CAMBRIDGE UNIVERSITY PRESS

Cambridge

London   New York   New Rochelle

Melbourne   Sydney

MAR   1986

ELMHURST COLLEGE LIBRARY

Published by the Press Syndicate of the University of Cambridge
The Pitt Building, Trumpington Street, Cambridge CB2 1RP
32 East 57th Street, New York, NY 10022, USA
296 Beaconsfield Parade, Middle Park, Melbourne 3206, Australia

First published 1984

Printed in the United States of America

Library of Congress Cataloging in Publication Data
St. Armand, Barton Levi.
Emily Dickinson and her culture.
(Cambridge studies in American literature and culture)
Includes index.
1. Dickinson, Emily, 1830–1886 – Criticism and in-
terpretation. I. Title. II. Series.
PS1541. Z5S7 1984 811'.4 84–3188
ISBN 0 521 26267 4 (U.S.)

Part of Chapter 4 was first published in *American Quarterly* 29, no. 1 (Spring 1977):55–78, © 1977, Trustees of the University of Pennsylvania, and part of Chapter 5 first appeared in *Topic 31: Studies in American Literature* 17 (Fall 1977):3–19.

Quotations from the poems of Emily Dickinson are reprinted by permission of the publishers and the Trustees of Amherst College from *The Poems of Emily Dickinson*, edited by Thomas H. Johnson, Cambridge, Mass.: The Belknap Press of Harvard University Press, © 1951, © 1955, 1979, 1983 by the President and Fellows of Harvard College; and from *The Complete Poems of Emily Dickinson*, edited by Thomas H. Johnson, © 1914, 1929, 1935 by Martha Dickinson Bianchi, © renewed 1942 by Martha Dickinson Bianchi, © renewed 1957, 1963 by Mary L. Hampson. By permission of Little, Brown and Co. in association with the Atlantic Monthly Press.

Lines and passages from *Emily Dickinson Face to Face* by Martha Dickinson Bianchi, © 1932 by Martha Dickinson Bianchi, © renewed 1960 by Alfred Leete Hampson, and from *Life and Letters of Emily Dickinson* by Martha Dickinson Bianchi, © 1924 by Martha Dickinson Bianchi, © renewed 1952 by Alfred Leete Hampson, are reprinted by permission of Houghton Mifflin Co. Quotations from Dickinson's letters are reprinted by permission of the publishers and the Trustees of Amherst College from *The Letters of Emily Dickinson*, edited by Thomas H. Johnson, Cambridge, Mass.: The Belknap Press of Harvard University Press, © 1958 by the President and Fellows of Harvard College.

Appendix A, "The Books of Revelation," by Martha Dickinson Bianchi, is printed here for the first time by the kind permission of Mary L. Hampson.

To
my mother,
Josephine Mackiewicz,
who saw me through,
spiritually and materially,
this book is lovingly dedicated.

The Soul selects her own Society –
Then – shuts the Door

CONTENTS

ACKNOWLEDGMENTS

In the ten years that it has taken me to try to measure what Henry James called "the immeasurable power of culture," I have contracted many unpaid and outstanding debts. First among these is a debt to my mentors, and any tribute to them should rightfully be carved in marble or, like ancient imperial proclamations, graven in bronze. Good teaching is such an ephemeral thing, however, that paper is perhaps the most appropriate medium for this kind of commemoration, and so in antique style I begin by saluting three great teachers of Brown University:

John Shroeder,
who taught the hardest kind of looking;

Hyatt Waggoner,
who taught the highest kind of seeing;

and

S. Foster Damon,
who taught that "Fear & Hope are – Vision."
(Blake, *For the Gates of Paradise*)

To Mrs. Mary L. Hampson, of the Evergreens, I will forever be grateful for sharing with me the treasures of paintings, artifacts, and manuscripts housed in her Amherst home, objects that give a rich sense of the material culture of the Dickinson family.

Although I take issue with him in these pages, I wish to acknowledge Austin Warren as friend, intellectual father, and American Scholar par excellence.

I commiserate with those friends, colleagues, and editors who read the manuscript in various states of revision – George Monteiro, Laurence Goldstein, Mary Trigg, David Cody, and Albert Gelpi – and thank them, as Dickinson did, for "the surgery." Like her, I found it not so painful as I supposed, and in every case sure, sensitive, professional, and, ultimately, lifesaving. I am equally obliged to those who aided through advice and good counsel, especially my colleagues David Hirsch, George Landow, and Elmer Blistein. Richard Gid Powers first pointed out the real significance of the Dickinson–Higginson relationship in graduate school, and I remain grateful for his pioneering scholarship, his continuing encouragement, and his loyal friendship. My research assistants, Susan Donaldson, David Williams, and Paul Fees, tracked down many an elusive and hermetic fact in many a quaint and curious volume of half-forgotten lore.

I am personally obliged to John Stanley, Rosemary Cullen, and the staff of the John Hay Library at Brown, and to John Lancaster, Archivist of the Amherst College Library, for their help and expertise. Sean B. Tarpey, Curatorial Assistant at the Mead Art Museum, provided me with prompt information about Amherst College's art collections, and Rodris Roth, Curator of the Division of Domestic Life at the National Museum of American History, Smithsonian Institution, helped me to track down a serviceable photograph of Bergonzoli's sculpture at the Free Library of Philadelphia. I am equally obliged to the head of that institution's Print and Picture Department, Robert F. Looney, for his cordiality in supplying me with a copy of the photograph. In the cool depths of the Providence Athenaeum Library, I discovered numerous cultural analogues, while breathing in its unsurpassed Victorian atmosphere. My profound thanks are due to its unfailingly generous staff. Richard Hurley of the John Carter Brown Library expertly photographed the paintings at the Evergreens and produced reproductions of other photographic materials used here. Louann M. Skorupa, Keeper of Photographs at the Rhode Island School of Design Museum in Providence, arranged for the reproduction of the Roger Fenton still life that serves as a frontispiece to this book, and Franklin W. Robinson, Director, gave his kind permission to use it. Candy Pezzera, Deborah Johnson, and Christopher Monkhouse of the museum staff aided me with supporting information.

The typists who worked on various drafts of the manuscript are pearls above price. The late Dody Giletti made typing the best kind of English composition course; Rheta Martin exhibited the perseverance of the saints; and Sandy Norman triumphantly met the computer on its own grounds. To Ruth Oppenheim and the efficient staff of the Brown English Department I am indebted for much clerical aid, comfort, and support. Arnold Sanders undertook the task of final corrections at short notice, and accomplished them with dispatch and finesse.

A departmental Bronson Fellowship in 1973 helped me get the whole project started, and a timely grant from the Brown University Faculty Development Fund allowed me to finish it up.

Finally, I wish to thank my students at Brown, both graduate and undergraduate, who over the years had to live with my obsession, humored it, and even now ask after it with affectionate concern. If Nathaniel Hawthorne had known them as I do, he would not have lamented the passing of that "genial personage," the "Gentle Reader," in his 1859 Preface to *The Marble Faun*.

Harrisville, Rhode Island   B.L.S.

ABBREVIATIONS

FF   Martha Dickinson Bianchi, *Emily Dickinson Face to Face: Unpublished Letters with Notes and Reminiscences* (Boston: Houghton Mifflin, 1932).

J   Thomas H. Johnson, ed., *The Poems of Emily Dickinson*, 3 vols. (Cambridge: Harvard University Press, 1955); numbers cited are Johnson's poem numbers.

L   Thomas H. Johnson and Theodora Ward, eds., *The Letters of Emily Dickinson*, 3 vols. (Cambridge: Harvard University Press, 1958).

LED   Richard B. Sewall, *The Life of Emily Dickinson*, 2 vols. (New York: Farrar, Straus & Giroux, 1974).

MP   John Ruskin, *Modern Painters*, 5 vols. (New York: Wiley, 1886).

MW   Harriet Beecher Stowe, *The Minister's Wooing*, intro. by Sandra R. Duguid (Hartford: Stowe-Day Foundation, 1978).

ODP   T. W. Higginson, *Out-Door Papers* (Boston: Ticknor & Fields, 1863).

TWH   Mary Thacher Higginson, *Thomas Wentworth Higginson: The Story of His Life* (Boston: Houghton Mifflin, 1914).

YH   Jay Leyda, *The Years and Hours of Emily Dickinson*, 2 vols. (New York: Archon Books, 1970).

APOLOGIA

An Art of Assemblage

Art is an embalmer, a magician . . . It prolongs, it preserves, it consecrates, it raises from the dead.

Henry James

Writing two years after the landmark publication of Thomas Johnson's variorum edition of Emily Dickinson's poems, the eminent critic Austin Warren declared that only when an artist did ostensibly "bad" work should we look for an explanation in biography or culture. "When a good poet writes inferior poems," he argued, "we are concerned with the reason for the badness, in order to leave inviolate, the goodness of the other poems. But the 'goodness' is not so to be explained."[1] Yet what is good or bad, superior or inferior about poetry is a matter not only of personal judgment but of the temper of the times and the texts that are "raised" by that temper. Personality (temperament) and general culture (temper) enter into any aesthetic judgment, and now at the distance of over twenty-five years we can see that Warren's noble attempt to relegate "bad" poetry to the sphere of biography and elevate "good" poetry to the sphere of elite commentary was itself a product of New Critical dogmatics, especially T. S. Eliot's self-defensive dictum that poetry is an escape from, or continual extinction of, the poet's own personality.[2] Although few today would agree with Warren when he maintains that "what is biographically peculiar to the empirical person is not relevant to the 'good poems,' those intelligible to and valued by competent readers" (i.e., orthodox New Critics), we yet must heed his caveat that "biographical studies and culture-histories – for those who practice them, ends in themselves – are to be used by a critic with caution and delicacy" ("Emily Dickinson," 109).

In this study I have tried to write as both critic and cultural historian, each role being not an end in itself but an attempt to restore and appreciate Dickinson's art rather than to deconstruct it or explain it

1

away. In doing so, I feel that I have written (with caution, if not with delicacy) not simply a cultural biography but a biography of American Victorian culture, related in its own special way to what is current in my own unique intellectual climate. I see parallels to what I am doing in contemporary French historiography and to a so-called *histoire de mentalité* like Philippe Ariès's *The Hour of Our Death* (1981) as well as to structuralism's concern with "coding" and what Roland Barthes has called the *Studium* of a work of art, its cultural context.[3] But unlike these theorists, I come to the problem of the interaction between text and context with no set methodology, no ready-made rhetoric, and no monolithic ideological axe to grind. More important is what I come out of: a training in American studies and a belief that every deep consideration of a work of art must develop an approach to that art which is interdisciplinary as well as unique; that is, "organic" in the largest and perhaps most romantic sense. In an overly cerebral and technical age of theory, modern scholarship needs a holistic approach to literary texts as much as modern medicine needs a holistic approach to the human body. Such an approach, however, does not preclude judgment of a particular work; in this matter I find Warren's oft-expressed discrimination between the scholar and the critic to be especially misleading. For in his essay on Emily Dickinson, Warren concludes that "scholarship as such restricts a great poet to her own time, place and empirical self. Criticism must delicately 'clear' the poems for present use and evaluation – show what is for our time, or more grandiosely, what is for all times" (109).

On the contrary, I feel that scholarship can free rather than restrict our view of a great poet, that like art it can magically "raise" as well as "embalm," to borrow the words of Henry James's essay on Daumier that I use as an epigraph to this preface.[4] In this sense, "raise" takes on the meaning expressed (perhaps too grandiosely) in the epitaph engraved on Michelet's tomb at Père Lachaise: "History is Resurrection." For sometimes in "clearing" poems for "present use and evaluation," criticism may act more as a snowplow than as a delicate agent of quality control. Can we really judge what is classic, what is for all times? Characteristically, Warren "felt the immediate need to reduce the one thousand, seven hundred and seventy-five poems in Johnson's edition to three hundred or less" ("Emily Dickinson," 101). Dickinson's first editors felt a similar need, and no doubt her editors a hundred years hence will discover a like impulse, but will they always agree on the same three hundred poems? Only with the rise of feminist criticism has "My Life had stood – a Loaded Gun – " (J 754) become an indisputable part of this shifting canon, so much so that its explication is well-nigh obligatory among my contemporaries. We cannot predict which poems by Dickinson are reserved for future renovation, rehabilitation, or resurrection, but we can at the very least (to invoke James again) prolong, preserve, and consecrate what we have.

We can also now see that much of the initial interest in Dickinson's work was based more on cultural serendipity than on critical cogency. When she was published even in normalized form in the 1890s, there was a renewed vogue for New England "antiquities" of all kinds, and so Dickinson was hailed as the last fading flower of American Puritanism. What might have been considered childish, profane, or meretricious by her true contemporaries was discovered to be refreshingly piquant by a new generation, which had not fought the battles, learned the lessons, or read the books that she had. Being "old-fashioned" was suddenly in fashion, and I suspect that if Dickinson had been persuaded to publish a volume of her verses in the 1850s or 1860s, she would have received much the kind of review that Herman Melville's *Battle-Pieces* of 1866 received from Charles Eliot Norton, though without Norton's tolerance for Melville's early popular success. Writing in the *Nation,* Norton lamented that it was impossible not to read Melville "with a certain melancholy," because

> nature did not make him a poet. His pages contain at best little more than the rough ore of poetry. Here and there gleams of imaginative power shine out like the grains of gold in a mass of quartz. But, accustomed as we have been of late, in certain works professing to be poetry, to astonishing crudity and formlessness, we yet cannot refrain from expressing surprise that a man of Mr. Melville's literary experience and cultivation should have mistaken some of these compositions for poetry, or even for verse. There are some of them in which it is difficult to discover rhythm, measure, or assonance of rhyme. The thought is often involved and obscure. The sentiment is weakened by incongruous imagery . . .
>
> It would seem that only a writing medium could mistake such stuff as this for poetry.[5]

Interestingly, mediumship was one of the few professions open to sensitive and intelligent women in the nineteenth century, and Dickinson toyed with this sibylline role, though eventually she opted for the more conventional vocation of spinster aunt.[6] But if Norton's review of Melville can give us some indication of the place Dickinson's poetry, as cultural artifact, most probably would have assumed among her peers if she had indeed "gone public," it also raises the question what place it actually did hold as a personal and private book of revelation. That is, a comparative study of Dickinson's culture demonstrates that her art did have a place, that it was part of a recognizable genre, and that Thomas

Wentworth Higginson correctly classified it when in his preface to the 1890 *Poems* he wrote that her verses "belong emphatically to what Emerson has long since called 'the Poetry of the Portfolio.' "[7]

Emerson had examined portfolio verses in an essay entitled "New Poetry" published in the influential Transcendentalist periodical the *Dial* for October of 1840, and no greater contrast could be found between his late romantic liberalism and Charles Eliot's Norton's mid-Victorian formalism. For what Emerson's "The Poet" is to the poetry of Walt Whitman, his review of the "manuscript inspirations, honest, great, but crude" of an unknown youth is to the poems of Emily Dickinson: both a prelude and a prophecy. Ascribing the proliferation of such a private art to the rise of democracy, which has spurred a "like revolution in literature" that "is now giving importance to the portfolio over the book," he asks:

> Is there not room then for a new department in poetry, namely, *Verses of the Portfolio?* We have fancied that we drew greater plea-sure from some manuscript verses than from printed ones of equal talent. For there was herein the charm of character; they were confessions; and the faults, the imperfect parts, the fragmentary verses, the halting rhymes, had a worth beyond that of a high finish; for they testified that the writer was more man than artist, more earnest than vain; that the thought was too sweet and sacred to him, than that he should suffer his ears to hear or his eyes to see a superficial defect in the expression.[8]

In speaking of "finish," it is significant that Emerson should use a term that was equally applicable to painting or literature, and so point to the visual roots of this genre. The early works of the American landscapist George Inness were also accused of lacking suf-ficient "finish," though only one of the two merits that Emerson sees as distinguishing this new "department" really can be ascribed to the burgeoning Hudson River school artist. These merits were "fine-ness of perception; and the poet's trust in his own genius to that degree, that there is an absence of all conventional imagery, and a bold use of that which the moment's mood had made sacred to him, quite careless that it might be sacred to no other, and might even be slightly ludicrous to the first reader" ("New Poetry," 141). Late in his life, when he was recognized as America's foremost artist of the native scene, Inness managed to achieve this latter boldness and un-orthodoxy by means of an idiosyncratic tonalism. Emily Dickinson was unorthodox in execution nearly from the start of her poetic career, and this merit – so much a ludicrous defect to her early edi-tors – combined with a constant emphasis on the visual to yield the special equation that in turn created the "amazing sense" (J 448) of her art. That art, to use another phrase from Emerson's review, was never "filed or decorated for the eye that studies surface" (147).

Dickinson's poetry was in fact in the popular tradition of the portfolio or sketchbook, pioneered by Washington Irving through his persona as Geoffrey Crayon, author of *The Sketch Book* (1819), and epitomized by such mid-nineteenth-century best-sellers as Sarah Parton's *Fern Leaves from Fanny's Portfolio* (1853). As late as 1884, Helen Hunt Jackson wondered in a letter to Dickinson about "what portfolios of verses you must have" and scolded, "It is a cruel wrong to your 'day & generation' that you will not give them light" (L 3:841). But Dickinson's reticence underscored the essentially private nature of the portfolio genre, its function as a loose repository of musings, views, portraits, copies, caricatures, and "studies from nature" that made it truly an idiosyncratic "Book of the Heart." The portfolio, although it derived from the pictorial mode, had close affinities with the schoolgirl exercises of the album, the herbarium (in which Dickinson was adept), and the scrapbook,[9] and it is more than ironic that this largely female art form found its fullest contemporary realization in Walt Whitman's lusty *Leaves of Grass* of 1855.[10]

A new age of popular journalism, made possible largely by innovations in print technology, rapidly transformed the private and the domestic into common public property. It did this in order to make personal contact with its readers, creating general mythologies that few, including Emily Dickinson, could ignore. The portfolio tradition, however, was a means of preserving the secret self in the face of such growing technological exposure, and its cursive privatism explains why Dickinson wrote to Higginson, "I smile when you suggest that I delay 'to publish' – that being foreign to my thought, as Firmament to Fin" (L 2:408). What marked the unpublished portfolio as unique was its very eclecticism and nature as a repository or sourcebook whose sketches could be worked up into more finished products when the occasion demanded. Until that time – if it ever came – the portfolio was meant to be a closely guarded and thoroughly "sealed" volume, open only to the scrutiny of intimate friends and family members. Even Emerson was "loath to see the wholesome conventions . . . broken down by a general incontinence of publication, and every man's and woman's diary flying into the bookstores" ("New Poetry," 139). Another indication of the depth of intimacy associated with this mode is the episode in Charlotte Brontë's *Jane Eyre* (1847) where Rochester demands to see Jane's portfolio, but only "if you can vouch for its contents being original," since "I can recognize patchwork." Jane obliges, and after viewing the dreamlike and Blakean watercolors secreted therein, Rochester has to admit that "the drawings are, for a school-girl, peculiar."[11] (135). But a closer analogue to Dickinson's practice than this exists, one fully American and undoubtedly as well known to her as Brontë's fictional model.

Oddly enough it is also fictional, for Emerson's real example in his 1840 review-essay wrote verses that strike us today as far too imitative of Wordsworth to be truly original, outstanding, or even arresting. In the series entitled *The Professor at the Breakfast-Table,* which Oliver Wendell Holmes published in the *Atlantic Monthly* in 1859, the poetic heroine is a young "golden-*blonde*" named Iris. Iris is significantly gifted with second sight (Jane Eyre's art, too, turns out to be prophetic), and she is the jealous guardian of a locked portfolio consisting of striking "sketches" in various media, including music and poetry as well as watercolors. Fascinated by both Iris and her portfolio, the professor gradually gains enough of the young girl's confidence to be entrusted with the key to this mysterious book, feeling, when he opens it, that "I held the heart of Iris in my hand." In her prefatory poem entitled "Iris, Her Book," he is startled to find that she has a dark and haunted side that finds full expression only in her fugitive art:

> She knew not love, yet lived in maiden fancies, –
> Walked simply clad, a queen of high romances,
> And talked strange tongues with angels in her trances.
>
> Twin-souled she seemed, a twofold nature wearing, –
> Sometimes a flashing falcon in her daring,
> Then a poor mateless dove that droops despairing.
>
> Questioning all things: Why her Lord had sent her?
> What were these torturing gifts, and wherefore lent her?
> Scornful as spirit fallen, its own tormentor.[12]

Although Iris's verse form is vaguely Tennysonian, the sentiments are firmly Dickinsonian, especially the manic-depressive doubleness of emotion and the anguished questioning of the deity. It is not what we would expect from a stereotypical Victorian blonde maiden, and the professor exhibits a Hawthornesque scrupulosity in reading a book "so full of the heart's silent language, so transparent that the heart itself could be seen beating though it" (289). Such "self-revelations" instead should be "whispered by trembling lips, under the veil of twilight, in sacred confessionals . . . which I cannot look at in the light of day without a feeling of wronging a sacred confidence" (287–8). But look the professor does anyway, without any compulsions of guilt, since in her poetry of the portfolio Iris "did not know how fearfuly she had disclosed herself," simply because "she was too profoundly innocent."

Hawthorne himself was to deal with these ambiguities in his *Marble Faun* of 1860 and center them on the character of Hilda, but whereas Hilda is a public and professional artist (albeit a "copyist"), Iris remains a divinely gifted amateur:

> Her soul was no more ashamed than the fair shapes that walked in Eden without a thought of over-liberal loveliness. Having nobody to tell her story to, – having, as she said in her verses, no musical instrument to laugh and cry with her, – nothing, in short, but the language of pen and pencil, – all the veinings of her nature were impressed on these pages, as those of a fresh leaf are transferred to the blank sheets which inclose it. [288]

Who touches this book, then, touches the woman who is Iris, a woman who differs from Dickinson in being unconscious of her rebellion as both child of nature and sinless child. Where Iris is prelapsar.an, Dickinson cultivated her art after the Fall, though her spotless white gown was (among many other things) a tangible symbol of her patent guiltlessness in causing a Fall in the first place. Like Iris, Dickinson was not dissuaded from practicing her art by the lack of a suitable musical instrument:

> Bind me – I still can sing –
> Banish – my mandolin
> Strikes true within –   [J 1005]

While Iris is a real orphan, Dickinson was a spiritual one, whose only playmate was poetry and who wrote to Higginson in August of 1862, "I had no Monarch in my life, and cannot rule myself, and when I try to organize – my little Force explodes – and leaves me bare and charred – " (*L* 2:414). Isolated from family, friends, and that lover she referred to in both poems and letters of the late 1850s and early 1860s as "Master," Dickinson acted like the trance-prone Iris in allowing the professor who was T. W. Higginson to examine her portfolio and pronounce upon it. Both professors agreed that there was undeniable genius in these portfolios, the one fictional and the one actual, but also that there was no place for them in a world that exalted talent but deprecated originality.

The scruples of American Victorianism again prevailed, in contrast to the romantic voice of Emerson, who had breezily declared almost twenty years before that "the prescription which demands a rhythmical polish may be easily set aside; and when a writer has outgrown the state of thought which produced the poem, the interest of letters is served by publishing it imperfect, as we preserve studies, torsos, and blocked statues of the great masters" ("New Poetry," 139). To use a phrase applied to one of Higginson's protégées who did go public, Iris as well as Dickinson was "A Flaming Fire Lily Among the Pale Blossoms of New England,"[13] and the only solution that Holmes's professor could propose was to pack her off to Italy, that congenial aesthetic climate full of grand fragments and sanctified by the melodramatic elopement of the Brownings. Dickinson longed for such an escape herself in many poems, but foreign travel was as much an impossibility for her as it was for Iris, and each poet had to explore the exotic as well as the erotic through the only means possible – the armchair adventurousness of the portfolio genre.

When we consider the common culture that nurtured such an art, it is not surprising that a striking similarity of subject matter and approach should characterize the manuscript books of Iris and of Emily. Thus the soul of Iris is embodied sometimes in a poem and sometimes in a drawing – an "angel, arabesque, caricature, or mere hieroglyphic symbol of which I could make nothing," as Holmes's professor remarks (294). Here he echoes the Higginson who compared Dickinson's handwriting (and by implication, the cryptics of her poetry) to the famous fossil bird tracks in Amherst College's natural history museum. Dickinson took delight in identifying herself with wayside wild flowers, even to the point of calling herself "Daisy" in her love poems to Master, and in Iris's portfolio we find a similar penchant for studies of common weeds like buttercups and dandelions, as well as dead birds and odd sky effects: "A rag of cloud . . . with a streak of red zigzagging out of it across the paper as naturally as a crack runs through a China bowl" (294). We see, besides pages of "emblematic traceries" and comic grotesques, lone landscapes that are Turneresque or even Friedrichesque in their proto-symbolism:

> Above, a long monotonous sweep of waves, leaden-hued, anxious and jaded and sullen, if you can imagine such an expression in water. On one side, an Alpine *needle,* as it were, of black basalt, girdled with snow. On the other a threaded waterfall. The red morning-tint that shone in the drops had a stange look, – one would say the cliff was bleeding; – perhaps she did not mean it. Below, a stretch of sand, and a solitary bird of prey, with his wings spread over some unseen object. [296]

But in spite of such vertiginous foreign prospects, above all there is a tendency to sacramentalize the signs and seasons of the New England year. In a poem memorializing the death of a beautiful young girl, Iris writes:

> When, turning round their dial-track,
> Eastward the lengthening shadows pass,

Her little mourners, clad in black
   The crickets, sliding through the grass,
   Shall pipe for her an evening mass.   [320]

In a poem memorializing the death of a season itself, Dickinson writes
with an ear just as acute, but with much greater succinctness:

Further in Summer than the Birds
Pathetic from the Grass
A minor Nation celebrates
It's unobtrusive Mass.   [J 1068][14]

   Given such similarities of theme and content, the very eclecticism of
the art of the portfolio as practiced by Boston's Iris and Amherst's
Emily raises a larger formal question. It is a scholarly question that has
continued to plague the discussion of those fascicles or manuscript
books which served as Dickinson's version of the portfolio: the question of order. For neither the fictional book of Iris nor the actual literary
remains now at Harvard seem to exercise much reason in the placement
of their rhymes. Even Ralph Franklin's meticulous reassemblage of
Dickinson's manuscripts has revealed, save for a few early fascicles
largely devoted to gatherings of flower poems, no ostensible dramatic
or dynamic sequence of images, motif, or ideas.[15] What strikes us rather
is the emotional intensity of the individual fragments combined with a
seemingly random or patchwork pattern, such as that which Rochester
warned Jane Eyre about. Poems are entered in order to use up blank
spaces rather than to augment or modify a narrative. Narrative there
certainly is, as William Shurr has ably argued and as I also argue here – a
narrative of an undeniably romantic nature.[16] But in spite of Shurr's
demonstration that this narrative contains both consistency and development, it is also true that the narrative often seems to be cut up and
"bordered" very unromantically by poems that have little to do with
Dickinson's central "myth" – what I will later call "The Romance of
Daisy and Phoebus."
   These facts return us to the question of genre and impress me, in my
role as an American scholar, as important clues to the kind of art that
Dickinson was practicing. This art was not exclusively literary in nature
but originated in Dickinson's situation as a nineteenth-century woman
who was a part of a community where many nonliterary or nonacademic arts were practiced. Whereas the art of the portfolio is manifestly
an elite pursuit, the art of quilting offers an alternative model for coher-
ence and design. May not Dickinson's art also be an art of assemblage,
a "quilting" of elite and popular ideas onto a sturdy underlying folk
form, frame, or fabric? As Jonathan Holstein writes of pieced quilt
designs, they are

usually geometric, the parts of each block working in close relation to those surrounding it to make the larger forms and arrangements of line and color. These formal relationships are maintained
by the meticulous care with which the parts are measured, cut,
and sewn, so that they will link perfectly when joined. Very often
the ways in which the individual blocks will combine to form the
overall design are extremely complicated, and it is sometimes impossible to envision, without elaborate computations, the finished
quilt design from a single block. The tops of so-called "crazy"
quilts are made by fitting together pieces of cloth of random sizes
and shapes. In both appliqué and pieced quilts the quilting is often
done in patterns which add secondary, textual motifs, or, following the designs of the top, enhances those.[17]

I am not maintaining that there is necessarily any "finished quilt
design" in Dickinson's overall work other than the romantic narrative
embedded in the fascicles; her art may simply be part crazy quilt, part
scrapbag. But I would maintain that it is still far too early in the history
of Dickinson criticism to declare that there is no other design at all, no
mega-motif that makes the whole comprehensible. The pieced quilt
provides us with an alternative model or metaphor for Dickinson's art
that is visual rather than verbal, yet that was also as firmly a part of her
own culture as the elitist love relation that is Elizabeth Barrett Browning's *Sonnets from the Portuguese*. The discipline of the pieced quilt is just
as rigorous as that of the sonnet, but at the same time it is even more
abstract, and when we examine only one "cluster" of Dickinson poems, the closeness of the "blocks" may prevent us from seeing any
unified vision.[18] As Holstein reminds us, the planning of quilts involved
a myriad of aesthetic decisions: "Which among the literally hundreds of
existing patterns, should be chosen? Should a new one be invented, or a
variation made on a standard one? How big should each block be? What
colors should be used, and what textures? Should the blocks be sewn
together, or separated by strips? Should there be a border or borders?"
As he concludes, "It is obvious that the possibilities were infinite, and
that within the framework of the technique each woman had full freedom to make aesthetic decisions" (*American Pieced Quilts,* 14). If it is
true that these women "painted" with colors and fabrics, then how are
we to evaluate Dickinson's varied use of emotional color and more
neutral "borders" of flower and nature poems?

Only the elaborate computations of future scholars and an openness
to visual as well as verbal structures will allow us to settle such points
once and for all. In the meantime, what I propose to do here is to
examine the general fabric of the culture from which Dickinson cut out

her "blocks," refashioning them in her own unique way. Because any master design that may govern her work is at present still latent, obscure, and beyond our reach, I will choose not the quilt but the scrapbook, cousin-german of the portfolio, as a constituting metaphor to examine the chintzes, cassimeres, and calicoes that attracted her eye and that seem so startling when we view them abstracted from the wholecloth bolts out of which they were snipped. Of necessity I must deal with fragments, and the result of my "restoration" may itself seem sometimes fragmentary and episodic. Such an approach can never hope to match the ideological unity that informs a great summation like F. O. Matthiessen's *American Renaissance,* and in self-defense I could plead John Updike's wise observation that "in truth, the fragment, the sketch, the unfinished canvas, and the shattered statue are all congenial to an age of relativity, indeterminancy, and agnosticism."[19]

Yet I would be remiss if I allowed my own quest for relevant cultural analogues to stand as a feeble mimesis of Dickinson's high art. That art, I maintain, is far more than the sum of its parts. Also, though I wish to reimmerse Dickinson's texts in the nourishing context of their culture, and often attempt to read her poetry as I feel a sympathetic contemporary would have, I must recognize her art's magnetic appeal to our own age of anxiety and existential vacuity. But only by charting Dickinson's debt to her own time can we truly be sure how she may have anticipated current aesthetic and philosophical concerns. In many ways Dickinson is culturally prophetic, though more often than not I feel that her prophecy is a serendipitous accident of shifting taste, based on a misreading or misconstrual of the genres in which she was working. Holstein observes that "the best of the pieced quilts," by which he means the most visualy moving ones, possess

> a toughness in idea and execution, an often astonishing bravado in the use of design elements difficult at first to equate with the aesthetic ambiance of their times – unless it is noted that the quilts come more from the sensibilities which produced the utilitarian objects of the period than from those which made decoration. The finely realized geometry of the pieced quilt, coupled with this sophisticated sense for color and form, produced some works which mirror in a startling way contemporary painting trends. We see in many such phenomena as "op" effects, serial images, use of "color fields," a deep understanding of negative space, mannerisms of formal abstraction and the like. [*American Pieced Quilts,* 13]

Dickinson's art has been effectively related to contemporary painting, particularly to abstract expressionism, but in accomplishing this tour de force I feel that grave violence has been done to the integrity of her original motives and methods.[20] Such an attempt sacrifices the intrinsic for the extrinsic, and further diverts us from considering her work as an organic whole, with some kind of figure in the carpet that may make a kind of sense radically different from our culture-bound twentieth-century norms. To quote Emerson on his own mute, inglorious poet of the portfolio, I regard Dickinson as an artist who "was not afraid to write ill" according to the canons of her day, because she "had a great meaning too much at heart to stand for trifles, and wrote lordly for [her] peers alone" ("New Poetry," 147). Those peers belong to the past as well as to the present and the future, and if we are to measure how far Dickinson has led us toward understanding today's dissociation of sensibility, we need some *point d'appui* – like Henry Adams's stolid romanesque masonry – on which to rest our lacy arcs of speculation. Therefore I return full circle to the modest plan of restoration that I put forward at the beginning of this apologia. No full restoration of history, literary or otherwise, is possible, as Adams himself realized in his magisterial *Mont-Saint-Michel and Chartres*. But if in replacing a few of the quoins dislodged by the tremors of time, I can convince my reader that Emily Dickinson's work was of her age as well as beyond it, I will have succeeded in my own small art of critical and cultural assemblage.[21]

Chapter 1

KEEPSAKES

Mary Warner's Scrapbook

---

*In fine, in this drama, as in all great works of art, – in the Cyclo-
paean architecture of Egypt and India, in the Phidian sculpture, the
Gothic ministers, the Italian painting, the Ballads of Spain and
Scotland, – the Genius draws up the ladder after him, when the
creative age goes up to heaven, and gives way to a new age, which
sees the works and asks in vain for a history.*

Ralph Waldo Emerson

*What is important, then, is not that the critic should possess a correct
abstract definition of beauty for the intellect, but a certain kind of
temperament, the power of being deeply moved by the presence of
beautiful objects . . . The question he asks is always: – In whom did
the stir, the genius, the sentiment of the period find itself? Where
was the receptacle of its refinement, its elevation, its taste? "The
ages are all equal," says William Blake, "but genius is always
above its age."*

Walter Pater

> *A precious – mouldering pleasure – 'tis –*
> *To meet an Antique Book –*
> *In just the Dress his Century wore –*
> *A privilege – I think –*
>
> *His venerable Hand to take –*
> *And warming in our own –*
> *A passage back – or two – to make –*
> *To Times when he – was young –*
>
> *His quaint opinions – to inspect*
> *His thought to ascertain*
> *On Them[e]s concern our mutual mind –*
> *The Literature of Man –*

Emily Dickinson

A Dickinson keepsake: portrait of Louise Norcross, ca. 1848. (By permission of Mary L. Hampson.)

From the publication of the first series of *Poems* in 1890 to the appearance of *Final Harvest* in 1962, the history of Dickinson scholarship has been bent on the establishment of a canon. Emily Dickinson's poems have been so cut up, dismembered, picked over, anthologized, and selected that we are in danger of losing touch with the original sensibility that produced them. As with any scripture, especially a secular one of such range and diversity, some gospels have been declared apocryphal, some epistles spurious, and some revelations false. Yet in reshaping Dickinson on the anvil of our own expectations and desires, we do violence to her own very considerable artistic integrity. "The fundamental law of criticism," Emerson writes in "Nature," is that "every scripture is to be interpreted by the same spirit which gave it forth."[1] For example, Dickinson's "Marriage Group" has never been a favorite with her critics; still, these poems remain significant and memorable works of art. They are also moving human documents, recalling Walter Pater's plea that we must trust the humanity of art, the spirit that informs it as well as the letter that delivers it. Pater reminds us that "nothing which has ever interested living men and women can wholly lose its vitality," and that the supreme artistic products of each generation find their source not merely in some mysterious Zeitgeist "but in a stage of society remote from us."[2]

Often this remoteness is distorted into the grotesque, the lugubrious, the camp by the fun-house mirrors of a self-conscious modernism or an impudent postmodernism that fears too vivid a reflection of those enduring yet disturbing categories into which Dickinson's first editors parceled her art: "Life," "Love," "Nature," and "Time and Eternity."[3] The Christ-centered rather than God-centered Protestantism that can be found both in Dickinson's poems on spiritual marriage and in Elizabeth Stuart Phelps's popular favorite *The Gates Ajar* (see Chapter 4) might well be denigrated as a Sentimental Love Religion,[4] but perhaps we should not react too strongly against the troublesome first adjective. As C. S. Lewis reminds us, "Cruel ages are put on their guard against sentimentality."[5] And if "sentimental" means "the product of wish rather than reason," then in varying degrees and wraps all religion is sentimental. Dickinson's sentimentality, like that of Phelps, was an imaginative way of dealing with a brute reality compounded of the patriarchal nature of residual American Calvinism and the abiding fact of sudden death. Whereas the former problem has largely disappeared, the latter one is still very much with us. Some might even lament the passing of a common language and system of belief powerful enough to produce such determined yet creative responses. Is there today any similar public frame of reference within which we can communicate our deepest feelings to one another?

Starting with sentimentality, however, does not necessarily mean finishing with it. If we regard Dickinson's writings as a fact of material culture, as a supremely artistic fragment saved from the ideological wreckage of her time, then the sentimental mode is only one missing shard that we can use to further a restoration of the whole. As an archaeologist may painstakingly reassemble potsherds until the completed object attains its full and striking rondure, so does a partial reconstruction of a literary artist's milieu allow for the proper integration of some otherwise oddly shaped pieces. Such restoration may also reveal the probable outlines of those still missing. Sometimes these lost shapes can be at best only approximations, like the tracing of missing figures in a conventional battle scene where the general composition is known but the individual mosaic has been all but obliterated. I would go so far as to affirm that certain forms of art are meaningful only when seen *in situ,* that their vitality and their significance wholly depend on such a sensitive reconstruction. At the same time, since what we are trying to reconstruct is a sensibility, a consciousness conditioned by its age, we must also beware of reducing the poet to a type and the poetry to a specimen. What of the originality of the particular artist? Will not the art product itself suffer if it is regarded *only* as a product, if it is constantly compared to vulgar examples and lesser expressions?

I would answer that a comparative archaeology of the imagination is the sole way in which true genius can be tested, and then only as long as that archaeology itself is used imaginatively, and in the proper spirit. The sentimental American poet Lydia Sigourney may well suffer by comparison to Emily Dickinson, but Emily Dickinson can only gain in comparison to such typical "sweet singers" of her time. Emerson has answered all possible objections to this kind of comparative study in his essay "Shakspeare; or, The Poet" in one of Dickinson's favorite works, *Representative Men.* Relying on the shoulders of Yankee common sense that always support the heady Greek platonizing of his great middle period, Emerson declares that "a poet is no rattle-brain, saying what comes uppermost, and, because he says every thing, saying at last something good; but a heart in unison with his time and country." He adds:

> All the debts which such a man could contract to other wit would never disturb his consciousness of originality; for the ministrations of books and of other minds are a whiff of smoke to that most private reality with which he has conversed.
>
> It is easy to see that what is best written or done by genius in the world, was no man's work, but came by wide social labor, when a thousand wrought like one, sharing the same impulse . . . Every book supplies its time with one good word: every munici-

pal law, every trade, every folly of the day; and the generic
catholic genius who is not afraid or ashamed to own his originality to the originality of all, stands with the next age as the re-
corder and embodiment of his own. [*Works* 4:199–201]

Emily Dickinson's private reality can never be violated when it is
seen in relation to the larger public reality of her culture. "I marked a
line in One Verse – because I met it after I made it – and never consciously touch a paint, mixed by another person," Dickinson wrote to
T. W. Higginson in August of 1862. But her consciousness of her own
originality remained undisturbed, for she stubbornly added, "I do not
let go it, because it is mine" (*L* 2:415). She was a soul who carefully
selected her own society from her culture, just as from all other souls
she "elected" only one (J 664) in a blasphemous parody of the orthodox
doctrine of predestination. Her use of a common Calvinist rhetoric,
already reeling from the redefinitions of gradualists like Horace Bush-
nell and sentimentalists like Harriet Beecher Stowe, confirmed the tight
logic of its grammar while ironically narrowing the syntax and personalizing the meanings. Saint John's one hundred and forty-four thousand
sealed in the Book of Revelation had dwindled down to a perfectionism
of two. Moreover, Calvinism was not the only language that Dickinson
spoke with an individual accent: There were competing dialects of
Transcendentalism, Gothicism, primitivism, occultism, and Ruskinism.
Unless we have a convenient Rosetta Stone handy, these conflicting
tongues threaten to erect their own bewildering tower of Babel, sometimes sharing common roots and cognates, sometimes jarring against
each other in apparent discord and dissonance.

I

One might resolve the dilemma by claiming that all of these voices are
but varieties of the prevailing Esperanto of romanticism, yet to call
Dickinson a romantic accomplishes little more than to call an urn Grecian. Dickinson was a particular kind of romantic in a particular place
and a particular time – nineteenth-century America – and she obviously
gloried in the fact of universal indigenous expression, even to the extent
of calling attention to it through a deliberately awkward adverb:

> Because I see – New Englandly –
> The Queen, discerns like me –
> Provincially –   [J 285]

Walter Pater reminds us that the "strange web of imagery," "quaint
conceits," and "unexpected combinations" to be found in the allegori-

cal interpretation of the Renaissance are but "an element in the local colour of a great age" (*Renaissance*, 13). It is to local color that we must return if we are to comprehend both the unity and the variety of Emily Dickinson's sensibility, as well as the select yet intensely artistic response of that sensibility to its surrounding culture. But culture itself is no indivisible, monolithic thing, for we respond in various ways and degrees to different levels and kinds of culture. In an important essay entitled "Folk Art," Henry Glassie has effectively discriminated among these varieties of response by classifying their sources under three headings of public culture. "With regard to this public culture," Glassie writes, "some of the ideas in the artist's mind may be considered conservative, some normative, some progressive – or, in the usual terms of the folklorist, folk, popular, and elite (or academic)."[6]

A folk response is one sanctioned by tradition and tied to local traits and settled expectations; a popular response is conditioned by what is contemporaneous, fashionable, normative, and transient; an elite response takes account of certain classic, cosmopolitan, and supposedly transcendent values known only to a group that is self-consciously avant-garde in its expression of them. These responses tend to meld together and may even metamorphose over time, as what was popular at one moment may, through isolation or cultural lag, become the folk art of today. Reciprocally, some of the genuine folk art of yesterday is now an integral part of that appreciation of pure, minimal, and uncluttered forms so sacred to current elitist aesthetics. For the purposes of the literary archaeologist, Glassie's categories hold true really only for one artistic generation, a span long enough for the folk nature of an idea to become established over time while also allowing the historian of sensibility to measure the ephemerality of popular taste as well as the torque of avant-garde theory. Furthermore, any individual artist will register these responses in a complex, shifting, and creative manner, not always seeing the fine differences or nice discriminations that are the gifts of scholarly hindsight. As Glassie writes, these abstract distinctions "are most useful when thought of as opposing forces having simultaneous existence in the mind of every individual, though one or another of the modes of thinking may predominate in certain individuals or in the groups they combine to form" (258).

Emily Dickinson's poetry similarly contains mixed modes, and no single one can be said to have dominated her consciousness. We can find an amalgam of popular and folk responses in a particular poem, and clusters or sequences of poems that embody wholly elite ideas.[7] They are all products of Dickinson's remarkable sensibility, her "generic catholic genius," and Glassie's tripartite distinction, broad as it is, gives us a means of locating the level of her relation to the juggernaut of "public culture" without violating her originality of response. Yet what poet has seemed more hermetically sealed off from her intellectual environment than the reclusive "White Moth of Amherst"? "I do not cross my Father's ground," she replied to her mentor, T. W. Higginson (after receiving an invitation to visit Boston and attend a lecture on the Greek goddesses), "to any House or town" (*L* 2:460). Just as the legend of the "White Moth" is itself largely a myth (though a self-created one), so is Dickinson's separation from her culture an equally spurious assumption. Physical insulation does not mean cultural isolation, and it was that same father, the formidable Edward Dickinson, who bought her "many Books" but begged her "not to read them" because he feared that "they joggle the Mind" (*L* 2:404).

Read them she did, mind-joggling or not, since books were her lifeline to the world beyond the closed chamber of her soul. Moreover, the door to that chamber did not shut completely until Dickinson was well into her thirties, and as a young woman she was in the thick of discussions about such then-burning issues as the "truth" of Mrs. Browning's *Aurora Leigh* and the virtues (or vices) of the spasmodic school.[8] Later her Cambridge-based Norcross cousins and her sister-in-law, Susan Dickinson, who "stood nearer to the world" than the poet, acted as agents of elite culture, funneling new books and journals and ideas into her room in the Homestead, while her brother Austin's assiduous collecting of paintings, both European and American, confronted her directly with the world of high art. As early as 1860, the Norcross cousins were placing orders for Dickinson at the Burnham Antique Bookstore, orders for volumes so "academic" that they raised the eyebrows of Bostonians inured to the eccentric demands of local bluestockings.[9] " 'Burnham' must think Fanny a scholastic female," Dickinson haughtily replied, secure in her own private torrid zone. "I wouldn't be in her place! If she feels delicate about it, she can tell him that the books are for a friend in the East Indies" (*L* 2:368).

Dickinson's correspondence with Thomas Wentworth Higginson was itself a measure of how wide her intellectual net was cast, though as we shall see Higginson himself thought of her as an odd folk survival, writing untutored ballads that somehow belonged to the infancy of true womanhood. He saw her poems as the visions of an innocent oracle like the girl described in Elizabeth Oakes Smith's once-famous poem *The Sinless Child:* a "woman-soul, all tender, meek" who was "gifted with the power of interpreting the beautiful mysteries of our earth."[10] Yet Higginson was only one of a number of important vessels of high culture with whom Dickinson was in constant contact. As David Higgins writes:

For a shy spinster in a small town, Emily Dickinson knew a surprising number of notable contemporaries. Her regular correspondents, all but a few, were known to the public of the day. Among her closest friends were the Reverend Charles Henry Wadsworth, sometimes considered second only to Henry Ward Beecher (himself a friend of the family) as a pulpit orator; Samuel Bowles, whose *Springfield Republican* had gained a national reputation, T. W. Higginson, a leading man of letters and reformer; Helen Hunt Jackson, author of *Ramona* and (in Emerson's opinion) the best poet of her time; and Josiah Holland, editor of *Scribner's Monthly Magazine* and best-selling novelist. The one man who indisputably returned Emily's love was Judge Otis P. Lord of the Massachusetts supreme court.[11]

Higgins also observes that even "those correspondents who were not well known themselves were usually close to the New England Olympus" (*Portrait,* 13), and we might add that Edward Everett Hale, the author of *The Man without a Country,* and Washington Gladden, a leader of the Social Gospel movement, were among Dickinson's irregular correspondents (see *L* 1:282–3 and 3:731). Her brother Austin was a friend of the well-known architect Calvert Vaux and owned an inscribed copy of his *Villas and Cottages* (1864); America's most notable landscape architect, Frederick Law Olmstead (planner of New York's Central Park), advised him on the layout of the grounds of his house. That house, the Evergreens, an imposing wooden Italianate villa built next door to the Dickinson Homestead in 1856 and adapted from plans in Andrew Jackson Downing's *The Architecture of Country Houses* (1850), was the setting for a lively provincial "salon" conducted by Susan Huntington Dickinson. The "magnetic visitors" at Susan's "Noctes Ambrosiana" included at one time or other such "high-minded earnest men and women" as Ralph Waldo Emerson, Senator Thomas Hart Benton, Wendell Phillips, Bishop F. Dan Huntington, George William Curtis, Frances Hodgson Burnett, Henry Ward Beecher, and Harriet Beecher Stowe.[12] If, as Emerson himself suggests in "Shakspeare," even the world of municipal law can supply words to the poet, then the Dickinson family's multitude of political and legal acquaintances, such as Rufus Choate, must also be pooled with this impressive roster of cultural envoys.

As for the folk aspect of Emily Dickinson's sensibility, her birth in Amherst and her inheritance of the traditions of the Connecticut River Valley ensured an ongoing contact with a conservative culture as expressed in village rituals, local customs, and communal liturgical practices. The specter of Jonathan Edwards ruled her early life, for the valley had been the site of the first Great Awakening in America and had been periodically burned over since 1743 by various religious revivals that the pious called "refreshings." These served only to reaffirm the old ways and the old values; Amherst College – which Dickinson's grandfather, Samuel Fowler Dickinson, had bankrupted himself in helping to found – was a voice in the wilderness crying out against the defections of Yale and Harvard from Puritan orthodoxy. Emily Dickinson's father, Edward Dickinson, was called "a man of old type, *la vieille roche* of Puritanism,"[13] and her own choice of antique common meter, the meter of Isaac Watts's early eighteenth-century hymns, in an age of extraordinary metrical experimentation marks her as a true folk artist, in form if not always in content.

Whereas the folk nature of Dickinson's work stolidly inheres in its conservative form, the popular dimension is more elusive precisely because of its diffuseness. The poet's taste for sentimental, sensational, and Gothic narratives has been usually brushed aside as an embarrassing aberration, yet this taste pervaded her sensibility and endured until the end of her life. Only recently have Sandra M. Gilbert and Susan Gubar recognized that "the fictional shape Dickinson gave her life was a gothic and romantic one . . . because the gothic/romantic mode was so frequently employed by all the women writers whom this poet admired more than almost any other literary artists."[14] Her very last letter to the Norcross cousins appropriated the title of a best-selling occult thriller, Hugh Conway's *Called Back* (1883), which Richard B. Sewall calls "a novel in the sentimental-melodramatic mode at its worst."[15] It is obvious that this work was only one of many links in the intellectual underground railroad that operated between Cambridge and Amherst, a work so discussed in letters and pondered over in reveries that it could become a code word for the ultimate occult adventure of death itself.

Sewall contends that "Dickinson's allusions to sub-literature diminished rapidly after the mid 1860's" (*LED* 2:673), but he neglects to point out that by 1865 her poetic taste, her poetic form, and her poetic sensibility had already achieved their definitive shapes. As Martha Dickinson Bianchi writes in "The Books of Revelation" (given here as Appendix A) of the selection of volumes found on her aunt's mantel after Dickinson's death in 1886: "None of this particular group was published later than 1860; and, quite apart from the authors in her father's library, or her own frequently professed favorites, they preserve a distinct eloquence of their time and subjective influence upon her."

Using the subjective criterion of the subliterary as a guide, any critic could banish scores of Dickinson poems – poems that do not conform with strictly modernist or postmodernist academic standards – to a howling wilderness of "bad taste." Many a critic has done so, while simultaneously condemning Dickinson's "Dear Preceptor," Thomas Wentworth Higginson, for his supposed insensitivity and obtuseness. Yet who today in reading over the corner reserved for "original poetry" in nineteenth-century newspapers like the *Springfield Republican* would be able to discern the poem Johnson numbers 986 – "A narrow Fellow in the Grass" (published on February fourteenth, 1866, under the title "The Snake") – as the work of an unknown genius? "The Snake" is at first glance little different from countless other sprightly, tongue-in-cheek nature poems of the period, many of them outright parodies of more elevated productions published in new high-toned literary journals like the *Atlantic Monthly*. Consider Higginson's initial problem in discriminating among the following excerpts from two wonderful "effusions" that were sent to him by aspiring young poets after reading his essay "Letter to a Young Contributor" in the April 1862 issue of the *Atlantic:*

> My little home
> Is safe and sound
> And I'm a til-
> ler of the ground.[16]

> We play at Paste –
> Till qualified, for Pearl –
> Then, drop the Paste –
> And deem ourself a fool –   [J 320]

On April seventeenth Higginson wrote to the *Atlantic's* editor, James T. Fields: "I forsee that 'Young Contributors' will send more worse things than ever now. Two such specimens of verse as came yesterday & day before – fortunately *not* to be forwarded for publication!" (*YH* 2:55). Without its telltale Johnson number, would we be able to say much more for the second specimen, if put in the critical predicament of suddenly judging extraordinarily childlike sentiments, eccentric off-rhymes, and deliberately naive punctuation? That Higginson should have received the distinct "impression of a wholly new and original poetic genius" upon reading such verses goes to his everlasting credit, though his recognition of "the problem never yet solved, what place ought to be assigned in literature to what is so remarkable, yet so elusive of criticism" (*Carlyle's Laugh,* 252), has been only partially answered by the establishment of a sober-looking verse canon and an equally exclusive body of scholarship.

Higginson of course had the benefit of seeing the whole manuscript of "We play at Paste," accompanied by copies of "Safe in their Alabaster Chambers" (J 216), "The nearest Dream recedes – unrealized" (J 319), and "I'll tell you how the Sun rose" (J 318). That "Safe in their Alabaster Chambers" was remarkable even in its own time is proved by the adulation of a critic as astute and cosmopolitan as Susan Dickinson, whose praise of the poem goes beyond mere family flattery. Upon receiving a copy of the original manuscript she wrote that the first stanza was "complete in itself; it needs no other, and can't be coupled. I always go to the fire and get warm after thinking of it, but I never *can* again – " (J, note to 216). Susan's criticism prompted Dickinson to experiment with some even "frostier" second stanzas, and it may have been at her urging or instigation that the poem was finally published on March first, 1862, in the *Republican* as "The Sleeping."

If this same effort moved Higginson, there is nothing in Emily Dickinson's surviving correspondence to indicate, as Thomas Johnson observes, that "he singled the poem out for special comment" (J, note to 216). To Higginson the poem must have seemed similar to the plethora of morbid graveyard verse, the product of a native Mount Auburn school (called so after the famous Cambridge garden cemetery), that could be found in any gift book, annual, or popular journal of the time. He probably would have classified it with the early effort that Johnson numbers 32:

> When Roses cease to bloom, Sir,
> And Violets are done –
> When Bumblebees in solemn flight
> Have passed beyond the Sun –
> The hand that paused to gather
> Upon this Summer's day
> Will idle lie – in Auburn –
> Then take my flowers – pray!

"Morbid" is in fact one of the terms most frequently applied to Emily Dickinson's poems about death and dying, and it seems appropriate that her own verse was first collected by two of her friends as a typical poetical remains or keepsake volume bound in spectral gray, ivory, and silver. The pages of the first series of Dickinson's *Poems* are edged with gold, and the book's cover is stamped with a dainty design of Indian pipes – also popularly called "ghost" or "corpse" flowers – which were acknowledged favorites of the deceased. Recalling his first visit to Emily Dickinson in 1870, Higginson wrote more than twenty years later, "The impression made on me was that of an excess of tension, and of an abnormal life" (*YH* 2:152); as early as 1858 Joseph Lyman, who had been recently engaged to Dickinson's sister, Lavinia, described the young poet as already "rather morbid and unnatural"

(Sewall, *Lyman Letters*, 65). Modern critics have delighted in comparing Emily Dickinson with Mark Twain's lugubrious poetess, Emmeline Grangerford, as a means of laughing away her mortuary preoccupations, but the bittersweet singer of *Huckleberry Finn* is only a slight distortion of a long tradition in American popular culture. Included in this tradition are not only actual poets like Julia A. Moore, the "Sweet Singer of Michigan," and Lydia Sigourney, the "Sweet Singer of Hartford," but such imaginary elegists as Mary Wilkins Freeman's pathetic "A Poetess" (1891) and William Faulkner's indomitable Rosa Coldfield of *Absalom, Absalom!*[17]

Miss Rosa's "portfolio" of odes to the Confederate dead contained over a thousand poems when Quentin Compson's grandfather first saw it in 1885, and one can but guess at its bulk when Quentin himself pays his fatal visit to her in 1910. Only in the South and in New England would the portfolio genre be preserved in its full purity, because only in these tight enclaves would the fashions popular in Victoria's early reign escape the rapid metamorphoses of modern culture. As usual, the association of Emily Dickinson with Emmeline Grangerford is a half-truth covering up Dickinson's dependence on and creative use of a full-fledged sentimental tradition. Had *Huckleberry Finn* appeared in 1895 rather than in 1885, how many academic source studies would we now possess proving that the Emily of the first series of *Poems* was the indisputable model for Twain's vampirish Emmeline?[18]

It is odd that Dickinson's immersion in this aspect of popular culture has generally been treated with as much grim outrage as we find in Twain's own attack entitled "Fenimore Cooper's Literary Offenses." Yet truth is often more tantalizing, if not stranger, than fiction. On December ninth, 1884, Austin Dickinson's mistress and Emily Dickinson's future editor, Mabel Loomis Todd, wrote in her diary that "in the evening Mr. Dickinson came in like a brilliant north west breeze and read us a sparkling little story in the current *Century*" (*YH* 2:438). That story Jay Leyda identifies as "An Adventure of Huckleberry Finn," a composite of several chapters from the finished book that was itself published on February eighteenth, 1885. These chapters deal with Huck's visit to the Grangerford family and they detail the disastrous feud that destroys it; more important, they contain the account of Huck's fascination with Emmeline Grangerford's poetry and paintings.[19]

What Austin read so enthusiastically to his mistress he must also have brought to the attention of his invalid sister, whom he visited every day and who would have been delighted with Twain's contempt for a Sunday school ethic according to which, in her own words, "Boys that 'believe' are very lonesome – Other Boys are 'lost' – " (J 1545). But how might Dickinson have responded to Twain's sketch of Emmeline, expressed through the deliberately naive persona of Huckleberry Finn? "She warn't particular," Huck says; "she could write about anything you choose to give her to write about, just so it was sadful. Everytime a man died, or a woman died, or a child died, she would be on hand with her 'tribute' before he was cold. She called them tributes. The neighbors said it was the doctor first, then Emmeline, then the undertaker."[20] Perhaps Dickinson thought of her own youth, and those times when she became "prone to mournful reverie" (L 1:76), describing Mount Auburn Cemetery as a peaceful " 'City of the dead' " where "it seems as if Nature had formed the spot with a distinct idea in view of its being a resting place for her children, where wearied & dissappointed they might stretch themselves beneath the spreading cypress & close their eyes 'calmly as to a nights repose or flowers at set of sun' " (L 1:36).

Emmeline Grangerford "pined away" and died because "she hung fire on a rhyme for the dead person's name, which was Whistler," allowing the undertaker to usurp her privilege of deathbed consolation. Dickinson referred to this kind of privilege as her "Right of Frost" (J 640), and it seemed to be a particularly strong clause in the contract between her and Master:

> Promise This – When You be Dying –
> Some shall summon Me –
> Mine belong Your latest Sighing –
> Mine – to Belt Your Eye – [J 648]

As early as the age of fourteen, Dickinson had stood watch at the deathbed of her young friend Sophia Holland and so "gave way to a fixed melancholy" (L 1:32) that her family feared for her health, both mental and physical. They sent her to recuperate with her Aunt Lavinia, the mother of the Norcross cousins, a woman who was well known for her powers of psychological healing. Dickinson never died for lack of a rhyme, but she did know that "Looking at Death is Dying" (J 281), and her final illness seems to have been precipitated in part by a devastating series of deaths of close relatives and old friends. A large proportion of her later poems are in fact impromptu elegies. "The Dyings have been too deep for me," she wrote to Mrs. Samuel E. Mack in the autumn of 1884 (L 2:843), yet her letters to the bereaved still sought to comfort and console, and the poems she enclosed were cherished as authentic keepsakes, lasting "tributes" to virtues of the deceased. Susan Dickinson's own obituary of her sister-in-law, published three days after Emily's death, alluded to this tendency by noting that "there are many houses among all classes into which her treasures of fruit and flowers and ambrosial dishes for the sick and well were constantly sent, that will forever miss those evidences of her unselfish consideration" (*YH* 2:472–3). If Amherst, like Hartford and Michigan, had its own native sweet singer, surely it was Emily Dickinson.

II

Listening to Austin's enthusiastic reading of the Grangerford–Shepherdson chapters of *Huckleberry Finn,* Dickinson would have at least been spared such bathetic performances as Emmeline's "Ode to Stephen Dowling Bots, Dec'd," which was mercifully omitted in the magazine version of the episode. But she also must have noted the paragraph that prefaced this effusion, which the *Century's* editor retained for the sake of narrative continuity: "This young girl kept a scrap-book when she was alive, and used to paste obituaries and accidents and cases of patient suffering in it out of the *Presbyterian Observer,* and write poetry after them out of her own head. It was very good poetry" (*Huckleberry Finn,* 139).

There is ample evidence from her published letters that Emily Dickinson herself kept a scrapbook of clippings from national magazines, local newspapers, and illustrated books, which she used to ornament some of her own manuscripts, turning them into emblem letters and emblem poems.[21] Among the books she scissored were her father's copies of Dickens's *Old Curiosity Shop* and the *New England Primer;* Jay Leyda reproduces an illustration clipped from the August 1876 issue of *Scribner's Magazine,* edited by a close family friend, Josiah Holland (*YH* 2:254–5). Of Dickinson's use of a tombstone illustration cut from the *Hampshire and Franklin Express* to embellish a copy of "She laid her docile Crescent Down" (J 1396), Thomas H. Johnson writes that Dickinson "enclosed funerary scraps in messages from time to time, and thus suggested clues to the inspiration for certain verses. The disparity in the date of the clipping [1856] and the poem [1877] leads one to conjecture that she kept a scrapbook or a file of items which to her were meaningful" (J, note to 1396). We know that Dickinson actually contributed to a scrapbook prepared by the family for the delectation of her nephew Gilbert, who died in 1882,[22] and she may have had a hand in selecting or collecting illustrations for two of the children's scrapbooks made out of old business ledgers now housed in the Evergreens. Gilbert's upstairs nursery still has doors festooned with cutouts clipped from newspapers and magazines of the 1870s and 1880s. Any scrapbook made up by Dickinson for her own purposes has like most of her personal library long since disappeared. However, a reasonable facsimile exists, a facsimile that can be used as a skeleton key to unlock some of those "subliterary" cabinets of popular culture sacred to the poet in the crucial decade of the 1850s.

The literary archaeologist who wishes to relate Dickinson to this culture might just as easily use the newspapers of the time – the back files of the *Springfield Republican* or the *Hampshire and Franklin Express* or its successor, the *Amherst Record* – as a general source for her sensibility, but such an endeavor would be unselective and wholly dependent on chance analogues, educated guesses, and random correspondences.[23] Even given our present knowledge about the extent of Dickinson's reading, no attempt to emulate John Livingston Lowes and his quest to chart Coleridge's creative method will let us map out an infallible "Road to Xanadu," because books mentioned in her letters tell at best only half the story of Dickinson's intellectual pilgrimage. Those volumes that she borrowed, gave away, or discussed in lost letters remain beyond our ken, not to mention some that, like Martha Dickinson Bianchi's "Books of Revelation," have vanished entirely. In short, we have no instant vade mecum like the *Gutch Memorandum Book* reposing forgotten in the British Museum, awaiting a literary detective with the ambition to sort out its scribbled trash and treasures of miscellaneous titles, verse fragments, poetic scenarios, recipes for home brew, and extracts from current readings.[24]

The artifact that comes closest to such a guide is a mid-Victorian scrapbook of clippings from contemporary newspapers kept by one of Emily Dickinson's closest friends, Mary Warner. The daughter of a distinguished professor of rhetoric at Amherst College, Mary grew up to wed an equally remarkable scholar, Professor Edward Payson Crowell. Although Mary Warner was not one of the special group of five teenage friends that Emily Dickinson mentioned in a letter to Abiah Root in March of 1846, she became very much an intimate of the succeeding decade, when both girls were in their twenties (they had the same birth year, 1830). Mary visited Emily at Mount Holyoke Female Seminary in the company of her current boyfriend, Austin Dickinson, exchanged long letters with her, and was referred to as "Sister Mary" in a letter written by the poet on January seventeenth, 1848, telling how last Thanksgiving the whole Dickinson family "went down to Prof. Warner's, where we spent an hour delightfully" (*L* 1:59). When Dickinson sent greetings to her family, Mary was usually included in them, and in a letter to her brother written on January fifth, 1852, Emily chided Mary for not returning a copy of Longfellow's *Kavanagh* that had been promised to Austin (*L* 1:165).

Extant photographs of Mary Warner justify William G. Hammond's description of her as "a pretty, modest, pleasant girl with beautiful hair" in his diary entry for April second, 1847 (*YH* 1:117). The 1860s seem to have been in many ways a watershed of Dickinson's emotional and intellectual life, for in 1861 Mary married Professor Crowell, and the poet sent a wistful note to the new bride (who had entertained no less than five other proposals) that showed how far apart their respective spheres had by then moved (L 2:236). Yet the relationship between Emily Dickinson and Mary Warner was as intense as ten years of youthful buoyancy could allow, and Jay Leyda laments that only "tokens" of Emily Dickinson's correspondence with her survive, because "in the last illness of her daughter, Jean Crowell, a friend stoked the furnace with Mary Warner Crowell's correspondence."[25]

One "token" that did escape that conflagration is Mary Warner's scrapbook, only because it was given to Susan Dickinson's daughter, Martha Dickinson Bianchi, by one of the Crowell children as – appropriately enough – a keepsake of the enduring friendship between the two families.[26]

Mary Warner's scrapbook is a substantial volume, 12 inches in length and 9¾ inches in breadth, with a dark green embossed cloth cover and gold stamping on the spine that reads "SCRAP BOOK," demonstrating that it was expressly designed for holding clippings and cutouts and was no makeshift affair of old ledgers or superannuated copybooks. Inside the front cover is pasted Mary Warner's signature on a separate strip of paper, and the legend "Amherst, Jun. 1st, 1851," is written directly below. The thirty-three pages of this scrapbook are covered with clippings scissored from a variety of local newspapers – reprints of stories and poems from such diverse publications as the *Atlantic Monthly, Putnam's Magazine,* and *Godey's Lady's Book.* Although the scrapbook opens with "A Thrilling Sketch" of the "Death of Hamilton" lifted from *Hildreth's History of the United States* and soon followed by an account of the passing of Mrs. Mary Atwood ("The aged disciple has fallen asleep"), who had in turn watched as death "bore away most of her children to distant graves" (9), it is not, like Emmeline Grangerford's compilation, a simple catalogue of obituaries. Mary Warner's album does contain an extraordinary amount of mortuary verse, beginning with "The Little Straw Hat," a keepsake poem that laments the death of a small boy, and going on to include "Our Idol," "My Brother," "Little Charlie," "The Better World," "The Dainty Wardrobe," "Our Willie," and "The Thought of a Mourning Mother," among others. In this it is only typical of its time.

Surely part of the scrapbook's purpose was to serve as a homemade anthology of consolation literature, but it was also a repository for uplifting profiles ("Edward Everett"), jokes (mostly lifted from *Punch*), collegiate effusions ("Meeting of the Oreads and Druids upon Mt. Ida," by "Professor Shortfellow," datelined "Amherst College, June, 1852"), amusing local-color sketches ("Autobiography of a Village Chorister"), high-toned sentiment ("Night," by Henry W. Longfellow), reports of mechanical and natural curiosities ("A Multum-in-Parvo Clock" – "A clock is exhibited in the city, which not only does duty as a time piece, but boils the coffee for its owner, and awakes him in time to drink it"), literary and patriotic anecdotes ("John Quincy Adams and Ge. Jackson"), dialect parodies of Transcendentalism ("Song of Nature [Not from the Atlantic Monthly]"),[27] genre pieces ("Bobbit's Hotel" from *Trotty's Wedding Tour,* by Elizabeth Stuart Phelps), moral apologues ("Doing Good"), and a large dose of tearful tales ("Little Giddie," by Sophie May; "Little Dill," by Emily Huntington Miller; and "Little Gerty," by Anonymous).

The poets represented include Lydia Sigourney, Thomas Bailey Aldrich, Sir Philip Sidney, Charles Mackay, John G. Saxe, Henry T. Tuckerman, Thomas Hood, Walter Savage Landor, and a score of unnamed or forgotten sentimentalists. Journals cited as sources are the *New York Express, All the Year Round,* the *New York Ledger, Chamber's Journal, Frazer's Magazine,* the *Boston Poet,* the *Merchant's Ledger,* the *Berkshire Courier,* the *Boston Globe,* the *Children's Hour,* the *Boston Transcript,* the *Children's Picture Magazine,* and the *Little Corporal.* In this collection Thomas Jefferson's "Ten Rules of Life" jostle a "Cure for Erysipelas" made public by the editor of the *Salem Observer;* Annie M. Sawyer's "The Old Man's Christmas" is followed by Emerson on "Liberty of Speech"; and "Fanny Fern" appears on an equal literary footing with Washington Irving. Yet the very eclecticism of Mary Warner's choices is dictated by a sensibility which, like that of Emily Dickinson, judged on the basis of feeling alone. And as Henry James reminds us, "in the arts, feeling is always meaning" (*The Painter's Eye,* 185).

In trying to make some sense out of this apparent chaos, Glassie's categories are again useful, for we can see the pieces that focus on dialect, village life, and Yankee humor clustering together under the rubric of local color or folk culture; the mortuary poems, patriotic anecdotes, and sentimental sketches reflecting popular taste; and the smattering of "classic" authors and specimens of Victorian high seriousness demonstrating the intrusion of academic or elite culture. An article on page 21 of the scrapbook entitled "Book Making in America" and originally published in the *Boston Transcript* is an example of this last category, serving as a kind of statistical prologue to Thomas Wentworth Higginson's admonitory "Letter to a Young Contributor," which first enticed Emily Dickinson to test her poetic wings. In it is a paragraph that would have been of particular interest to Dickinson, because of both its hortatory tone and its mention of the Boston bookshop she frequented in after years through the vicarious agency of her cousin, Fanny Norcross:

About one book in one hundred only is a success. When Campbell, at a literary festival, toasted Bonaparte as a friend of literature because he once had a bookseller shot, he was a trifle too rough on this trade. It is impossible always for a publisher to decide rightly. All publishers are naturally shy of a new Mss. of poetry, for instance, for they know by experience that the deadest of all books is a dead volume of verse. The sepulchre of deceased poetry in Mr. Burnham's churchyard of old books, in Cornhill, is the largest bin in his establishment.

Perhaps Dickinson had this sardonic warning against the excesses of the letter dimly in mind when she affirmed the spirit of true literature by writing:

> A word is dead
> When it is said,
> Some say.
> I say it just
> Begins to live
> That day.   [J 1212]

One might just as well wonder if she derived her predilection for white dresses from an article called "How Balzac Did His Literary Labor," reprinted from *All the Year Round,* which described how the great French author "retired to his study," where "his costume was changed to a loose white robe, of a sort which is worn by the Dominican monks," when any serious writing was to be done (6). Does Dickinson's famous poem "A Route of Evanescence" (J 1463) owe anything to the curiosity piece entitled "Humming-Birds on Broadway" reprinted from the *New York Tribune,* which noted the "new sensation" caused by the "living specimens of these tiny members of the feathered tribe [that now] may be seen in the window of Taylor's Saloon," housed in "little crystal cages," dazzling crowds of passers-by? "Nor is this to be wondered at," the anonymous reporter informs us,

> for what with the flashing irridescence of their plumage, changing with every motion, from emerald to ruby and gold; their marvelous delicacy of form; their extreme rapidity of flight, now hovering over the honey-laden calyx, now darting from spray to spray, or perching upon a twig, coquettishly pluming themselves with their long, slender beaks, they are really objects of grace and beauty worthy of the admiration of every beholder. [21]

Another filler, headed "A Jolly Life," speculates that "insects must lead a truly jovial life. Think what it must be to lodge in a lily! Imagine a palace of ivory or pearl, with pillars of silver and capitals of gold, all inhaling such a perfume as never arose from human censer!" (1).

Thinking and imagining along these lines is precisely what Dickinson did in a host of poems about the life of butterflies and bumblebees that reproduce in verse the fanciful fairy paintings so beloved by her Victorian contemporaries.[28] Yet this life was not by any means unequivocally "jovial": In Dickinson's miniature world, butterflies sometimes bravely waltz out, only to be wrecked, drained, quenched, or whelmed "in Noon" (J 533, variant verbs noted). Gallant bumblebees are swept away by a "sudden Freight of Wind," leaving the spar of a "single Clover Plank" to vanish in a "not" that also puns on the "knot" of fate and the "nought" of nihilism (J 1343).

A keepsake like Mary Warner's scrapbook shows us in high relief both the possibilities and the limitations of a traditional source-study approach to Emily Dickinson's genius. If we can find sources for her poems in both popular filler and elite philosophy – in Fanny Fern and Ralph Waldo Emerson – these studies mean little unless we can demonstrate how Dickinson transmuted her culture as well as how she transcribed it.

III

Rather than a source hunter's game preserve, Mary Warner's scrapbook becomes a theme seeker's token or talisman, a guiding anthology of ideas, models, and patterns that furnishes us with the prototypes, stereotypes, and archetypes of Dickinson's time. It is surely no *Holinshed's Chronicles* or *Plutarch's Lives,* but is relevant to her art in the way in which Thomas Kyd's works provide us with a living, contemporary, and very material parallel to Shakespeare's plays. Like the silver plate of a daguerreotype, this scrapbook is a carefully prepared surface on which the unique wholeness of Dickinson's sensibility – both negative and positive – can be allowed to develop, and it is also a reflecting mirror that forces us to recognize the ephemerality of our own tastes, the elitism of our own judgments, the failings of our own popular prejudices. Least we fear that such development and reflection destroy that "distinct impression of a wholly new and original genius" vouchsafed to Higginson, we have Emerson's compensatory observation in "Shakspeare; or, The Poet" that "if we require the originality which consists in weaving, like a spider, their web from their own bowels; in finding clay and making bricks and building the house; no great men are original" (*Works* 4:189).

Emerson's words can be directly applied to a great woman poet who took as her emblem of the artist the image of the spider. How Dickinson developed and enriched this emblem can be seen if we compare her spider poems to a didactic use of the same trope in a poem by Lydia

Sigourney entitled "The Insect Teacher" that appears on page 4 of
Mary Warner's scrapbook. Sigourney's poem is prefaced by an epigraph from none other than "KING SOLOMON," that is, Prov.
30:29 – "The spider taketh hold with her hands, and is in king's palaces." The spider illustrates the last of "four things which are little
upon the earth, but they are exceeding wise," the other creatures being
prudent ants, tunneling "conies" (small mammals), and martial locusts.
Sigourney writes:

> See! with what untiring skill, –
> What an energy of will,
> All unaided, – all forlorn,
> Housewife's hate, and beauty's scorn, –
> How the spider builds her bower
> High in the halls of regal power. –
>
> Is the mansion of thy care
> Made by wealth and taste so fair,
> By Misfortune's fearful sway,
> Laid in dust? – or reft away? –
> – – Yield no thought to blank despair,
> Firm in faith, and strong in prayer,
> Rise! – the ruin to repair.
>
> For the Spider, homeless made,
>   Hunted from each loved retreat,
> Not dejected, not afraid,
> Toiling thro' the gloomiest shade
>   Gathereth vigor from defeat: –
> Child of Reason! – deign to see
> What an insect teacheth thee.

To Sigourney the spider is an object lesson in the virtue of perseverance, but her poem, recapitulating the moral of the famous fable about
Robert the Bruce and the spider, and anticipating a similar though more
graceful rendering of the same truth in Walt Whitman's "A Noiseless
Patient Spider," is above all addressed to a willing "Child of Reason."
Emily Dickinson, who rejected the "dry Wine" of Calvinist logic (J
728), used the industrious spider to emphasize ironically yet poignantly
the distance between life and death, domesticating King Solomon's
"palaces" and Sigourney's "halls of regal power" to a scene of humble
tragedy:

> Buzz the dull flies – on the chamber window –
> Brave – shines the sun through the freckled pane –

Fearless – the cobweb swings from the ceiling –
Indolent Housewife – in Daisies – lain!   [J 187]

The busy housewife herself, rather than her "mansions," is here a dead
"ruin" that no industry can repair, as the windows become dotted with
flyspecks and the ceiling is festooned with telltale cobwebs, all owing to
an unaccustomed but grimly enforced "Indolence." Dickinson, like
Poe, rejects the "Heresy of the Didactic" and chooses to see the spider
not as an "Insect Teacher" but as an insect artist, a metaphor of the poet
herself:

> The Spider as an Artist
> Has never been employed –
> Though his surpassing Merit
> Is freely certified
>
> By every Broom and Bridget
> Throughout a Christian Land –
> Neglected Son of Genius
> I take thee by the Hand –   [J 1275]

Dickinson's spider is a pagan artificer in an orthodox Christian
world, a primitive folk survival so in tune with the *genius loci* that even
the assiduity of new immigrants like Dickinson's own Irish maid, Maggie Maher, cannot completely eradicate its delicate craftsmanship.[29] This
artistic spider is playful and much too self-indulgent for Puritan economy to tolerate, an aesthete who juggles words for his own amusement
and who must pay the penalty of seeing both himself and his art swept
into the abyss of time:

> The Spider holds a Silver Ball
> In unperceived Hands –
> And dancing softly to Himself
> His Yarn of Pearl – unwinds –
>
> He plies from Nought to Nought –
> In unsubstantial Trade –
> Supplants our Tapestries with His –
> In half the period –
>
> An Hour to rear supreme
> His Continents of Light –
> Then dangle from the Housewife's Broom –
> His Sophistries – forgot –   [J 605][30]

The spider-poet, like Dickinson herself, walked a threadlike path
over an immense void. Both were fully conscious that the product of

this precarious capering, whether it be a minutely constructed geometric web or a finely woven tapestry of words, was subject to imminent destruction. To Puritanical eyes, a "Yarn of Pearl" can be merely clever fibbing, spinning of a tall tale, rather than the creation of an opalescent object of great rarity and beauty. "Floss," "gauze," and "gossamer" are Dickinson's recurrent images for the fragile web of words in which she dressed her thoughts, the fascicles that she herself threaded by hand and that at last became her own papery cocoon. When she is startled into acute self-consciousness by the sudden coming of mortality in "Because I could not stop for Death," the poet discovers that she is attired in only the flimsiest of raiment: "For only Gossamer, my Gown – My tippet – only Tulle" (J 712). Tested pragmatically against the concrete reality of Death's scythe or the housewife's broom, the gossamer nets spun by both spider and poet seem mere "Sophistries," an empty rhetoric whose plausibility is soon banished by the brute facts of existence. Yet Dickinson also realizes that such an art is fully as wonderful as it is perishable, an ideal "Pearl of Great Price":

> The fairest Home I ever knew
> Was founded in an Hour
> By parties also that I knew
> A spider and a Flower –
> A manse of mechlin and of Floss –   [J 1423]

Ultimately, Dickinson used the spider to test her own special notion of the rationale of verse. In doing so, she discovered that there was another and deeper kind of knowledge than the proverbial wisdom of King Solomon. Judged by conventional standards of logic – the Lockean sensationalism of Jonathan Edwards or the Scottish commonsense school realism of Sigourney or Dickinson's own father – the spider was at best a model of industry and at worst an imp of Satan. The American Puritan poet Edward Taylor had warily stigmatized the sly arachnid of his "Upon a Spider Catching a Fly" as a noxious "Venom Elfe" out to trap foolish souls, though he also cautioned that his reader should practice the cunning of the spider in trafficking with the stinging agents of a fallen world.[31] Jonathan Edwards characterized the spider as a "noisome insect" in such hellfire-and-brimstone sermons as "Sinners in the Hands of an Angry God" and "Future Punishment of the Wicked Unavoidable and Intolerable": Cast into the flames, it became "a little image of what you will be the subject of in hell, except you repent and fly to Christ."[32] Even in his lyrical disquisition on the natural history of the "Balloon, or Flying Spider" (written for an English correspondent when he was only eleven years of age), the observant Edwards began by remarking that "of all Insects no one is more wonderfull than the Spider especially with Respect to their Sagacity and admirable way of working" (*Representative Selections,* 3).

Mary Howitt, the immensely popular and prolific author of hymns, ballads, and all kinds of children's literature, with whose works Dickinson was familiar through the pages of *Parley's Magazine,* caps the long line from Proverbs to Jonathan Edwards by merging the industrious with the demonic. Her familiar nursery verse "The Spider and the Fly: An Apologue," subtitled "A New Version of an Old Story," begins with the famous question " 'Will you walk into my parlor?' said the Spider to the Fly" and closes with a melodramatic scene that would be more appropriate to a Victorian "Blood" or "Penny Dreadful":

> Alas, alas! how very soon this silly little Fly,
> Hearing his wily, flattering words came slowly flitting by;
> With buzzing wings she hung aloft, then near and nearer drew,
> Thinking only of her brilliant eyes, and green and purple hue –
> Thinking only of her crested head – poor foolish thing! At last,
> Up jumped the cunning Spider, and fiercely held her fast.
> He dragged her up his winding stair, into his dismal den,
> Within his little parlor – but she ne'er came out again![33]

Howitt's tacked-on moral, warning "dear little children, who may this story read," against the "idle, silly, flattering words" of evil counselors provides just barely enough redeeming social value to rescue her tale from the horror–pornography that is its essential feature. In her own sprightly way, Howitt exhausts and subverts the public, normative wisdom of the spider trope, both secular and religious. Her spider is a double-tongued deceiver, an oily seducer, and an avaricious Bluebeard; her fly is a foolish streetwalker, a vain exhibitionist, and a half-willing victim of her own undisciplined excess. Howitt's fly is also a fly purely in the generic sense, obviously a butterfly rather than a bluebottle, and since Dickinson often identified herself with the butterfly, as in "My Cocoon tightens – Colors tease – " (J 1099), we might well wonder at her reactions to this perverse "Apologue," where it is made quite plain that the spider's motives are culinary as well as sexual. That the poem was originally published as one of Howitt's *Sketches of Natural History* (1834) adds another turn of the philosophical screw that was to be tightened twenty-five years later by Charles Darwin's *Origin of Species.*

In considering the spiders of the house or of the field, Dickinson's only traditional choice of meaning seemed to be divided among depravity, industry, rapacity, or sophistry. Yet in "Safe in their Alabaster Chambers" she had seen from a greater height the empty results of all popular and proverbial logic: "Ah, what sagacity perished here!"[34] The wisdom of Solomon and the wisdom of the Calvinist Saints were equally subject to the corruptions of moth and rust. If she were to wrest a meaning from the spider's endeavor, it had to be one that flew in the face of ordinary reason or hypocritical religion:

> A Spider sewed at Night
> Without a Light
> Upon an Arc of White.
>
> If Ruff it was of Dame
> Or Shroud of Gnome
> Himself himself inform.
>
> Of Immortality
> His Strategy
> Was Physiognomy.   [J 1138]

Here the spider-artist is no gymnast or prima ballerina, but a determined craftsman who works by the glare of his own materials – painfully – in isolation and obscurity. The "Arc of White" can be either a bare piece of cloth or a blank piece of paper; the final result an ornamental "Ruff" of words or the winding-sheet for some fabled, chthonic creature, a guardian of great treasures hidden deep within the earth. Dickinson once signed a letter to T. W. Higginson "Your Gnome," but whether she herself was to be considered a grand dame of poetry or an impish freak of letters was part of her equivocal legacy to posterity. Like Hawthorne's Hester Prynne, Dickinson could only ply the steadfast trade of the solitary sewer, and the phenomenon of her art, no matter how beautiful or how serviceable, was designed never to reveal fully the secret passion that created it. "Her needle-work was seen on the ruff of the Governor," Hawthorne writes of Hester Prynne in *The Scarlet Letter;* "military men wore it on their scarfs, and the minister on his band; it decked the baby's little cap; it was shut up, to be mildewed and moulder away, in the coffins of the dead."[35] Perhaps it was Dickinson's Neoplatonic belief that the achievement of the art far exceeded the value of the finished product itself which caused her to direct that her poems should be destroyed, along with all of her other papers, after her death, a wish luckily circumvented by the veneration of an adoring sister.

This belief in the transcendental integrity of art conjures up Hawthorne's bright allegory of "The Artist of the Beautiful" more than the dark shadows of *The Scarlet Letter,* though the darkness remains, the "night" of the first stanza of this culminating spider poem inking the final tercet, rendering the whole in harsh chiaroscuro. Hawthornesque ambiguities are indeed relevant here, for in fixing on the ancient pseudoscience of "Physiognomy" – a word that itself encapsulates the root for "gnome" and "gnomic" – Dickinson indicates that there are other strategies, other methods, other illuminations than those given solely by the light of reason. The spider could inculcate a lesson startlingly different from that of Sigourney's "Insect Teacher," yet this sweet singer's focus on key concepts such as "skill," "faith," and "progress," on the mood words "unaided" and "forlorn," and even her description of the insect as "Not dejected, not afraid, / Toiling thro' the gloomiest shade / Gathering vigor from defeat" bracket Dickinson's exemplum. Dickinson, too, is taught by the spider, but that teaching remains a hermetic one, and her spider gives away no easy secrets about artistic or earthly salvation. Her poem tantalizes by promising the time-tested, applied wisdom of the proverb (folk), or the epigrammatic, bourgeois, obvious truth of the moral apologue (popular). At its core, however, is an exclusive, transcendent, antididactic theory of art for art's sake (elite). This workman forms himself while he also "informs" the material with the spiritual; we are the gnomons or judges forced to scan the outside features and divine the inward meanings, each according to our own peculiar "lights."

IV

Stripped bare of sentimentality and didacticism, "A Spider sewed at Night" seems to us a very contemporary, a very existential poem. But whereas here she weaves folk, popular, and elite strands of culture together so effortlessly as to make the result appear seamless, Dickinson's more exclusive and typical work in each of these categories has caused problems for her modern critics. Using Mary Warner's scrapbook as both springboard and sounding board, I now propose to explore Dickinson's varied responses to these tripartite levels of culture. My next three chapters explore her use of popular motifs, whereas Chapter 5 deals with the folk elements of her poetic forms and imagery. This folk strain has been well documented through much research into the relation of Dickinson's poems to Puritan hymnology, yet in many respects it is the most elusive and fragile of our cultural constructs, being tied to an oral tradition that is largely lost to us today. Therefore I focus on the visual dimensions of nonacademic art embedded in her work that link her to the "homely world" of the quilt, the sampler, the theorem (stenciled folk painting, usually on velvet), and naive painting.

Chapter 6, on Dickinson's interest in T. W. Higginson and Transcendental nature writing, takes us to an elite sphere of culture that is present in the Warner scrapbook, but it also takes us beyond the scrapbook itself. My last three chapters attempt a major reconstruction of the rich milieu of Victorian aesthetics, the Ruskinian culture of high art that

Dickinson absorbed largely through Susan and Austin Dickinson and their superb collection of prints and paintings, both American and European. The Warner scrapbook enters here as a kind of chorus, reaffirming the study of sublime cloudscapes and landscapes as a new book of revelation open to all. For though its presence and authority may flame or fade as our investigation continues, this antique portfolio remains a potent keepsake. Through it we can still find some of the clay and the bricks Dickinson used to build her own house of poetic "Possibility" (J 657), fairer and more enduring than the prosy models she was genius enough not to spurn entirely.

Chapter 2

DARK PARADE

Dickinson, Sigourney, and the Victorian Way of Death

═══════════════════

It was a sabbath afternoon, when a dead infant was brought into the church. The children of the small congregation, wished to sit near it, and fixed their eyes upon its placid brow, as on a fair piece of sculpture. The sermon of the clergyman, was to them. It was a paternal address, humbling itself to their simplicity . . . Earnestly and tenderly they listened, as he told them how the baby went from its mother's arms, to those of the compassionate Redeemer. When the worship closed, and the procession was formed, the children, two and two, followed the mourners, leading each other by the hand, the little girls clothed in white.

Lydia H. Sigourney

Have not ribbons, cast-off flowers, soiled bits of gauze, trivial, trashy fragments of millinery, sometimes had an awful meaning, a deadly power, when they belonged to one who should wear them no more, and whose beautiful form, frail and crushed as they, is a hidden and a vanished thing for all time?

Harriet Beecher Stowe

> *Death sets a Thing significant*
> *The Eye had hurried by*
> *Except a perished Creature*
> *Entreat us tenderly*
>
> *To ponder little Workmanships*
> *In Crayon, or in Wool,*
> *With "This was last Her fingers did"—*
> *Industrious until—*
>
> *The Thimble weighed too heavy—*
> *The stitches stopped—themselves—*
> *And then 'twas put among the Dust*
> *Upon the Closet Shelves—*

Emily Dickinson

Kellogg mourning print, lithograph, ca. 1835. (From the author's collection.)

On March seventeenth, 1896, Mary Warner Crowell sent Susan Dickinson a loving acknowledgment for "the little package of notes, scribbled so long ago," written to her by the recently deceased Austin, who
was once her beau. She added, "These bright March days bring back so
many reminiscences of sugaring parties and such pleasures in which
Austin was always the leader, and looking over these little billet-doux
makes me forget how long ago it was." Thirteen years earlier, she had
responded to the sudden death of Susan's son, Gilbert Dickinson, by
writing, "You had one thing for which always to be thankful, that you
had the dear boy so long," and she enclosed a poem of consolation,
carefully transcribed, entitled "The Alpine Shepherd."[1] The poem was
by Mrs. James Russell Lowell,[2] and in this way, Mary Crowell partially
repaid a debt to the Dickinson family that had been tendered in a
similar bereavement. For in April of 1856 Emily Dickinson had sent her
"Dear Mary" a copy of James Pierpont's popular consolation verse
entitled "My Child," which contained stanzas such as

> I know his face is hid
> Under the coffin lid,
> Closed are his eyes, cold is his forehead;
> My hand that marble felt –
> O'er it in prayer I knelt,
> Yet my heart whispers that, he is not there!   [L 2:325]

Dickinson offered her specimen of *Kinder-Totenlieder* on the third anniversary of the death of Mary Warner's sister, Anna Charlotte Warner,
writing, "I send the verses of which I spoke one day – I think them very
sweet – I'm sure that you will love them – They make me think beside,
of a Little Girl at *your* house, who stole away one morning, and tho' I
cannot find her, I'm sure she 'is there' " (L 2:326–7). Richard Sewall
notes that as late as 1881, Dickinson referred to George Parson Lathrop's
"very similar elegy," entitled "The Child's Wish Granted," as "piteously
sweet" in a letter to the beloved Norcross cousins (*LED* 2:673). It is
obvious, then, that Mary Warner and Emily Dickinson shared a sensibility, and that a portion of this sensibility remained firm and unchanging
long after they took their separate paths of private poet and public matron. Neither "The Alpine Shepherd" nor "My Child" nor "The Child's
Wish Granted" appears in Mary Warner's scrapbook, though as I have
noted there is no lack of poems on death – especially poems on the death
of children. Rather than dismiss such an interest as a low and perverse
morbidity, ascribing it to a general or particular psychopathology, we
must acknowledge that Dickinson's fascination with death was an authentic response to a popular cultural genre that had its own unique
strength and purpose. For the type of mortuary poetry that can be found

so often in Mary Warner's scrapbook had a profound effect on Emily Dickinson's sensibility. It set standards of taste, provided models of behavior, refined images of grief, and developed strategies of consolation that the poet would test in her own individual manner.

> When I have lost, you'll know by this –
> A Bonnet black – A dusk surplice –
> A little tremor in my voice
> Like this!   [J 104]

I

The image of the mourning maiden had archetypal resonances for the popular culture of Dickinson's time, though now it survives only as a quaint device carved, stitched, or etched on early Victorian gravestones, samplers, and prints. Even by Mark Twain's day this dominant icon of the American version of English graveyard poetry, the Mount Auburn school, had begun to degenerate into what today we would term "kitsch." Henry Glassie writes that "Huck Finn at the Grangerfords' provides the modern reader with a flood-lit view into the home of a mid-nineteenth century carrier of the popular culture" ("Folk Art," 260), though his very use of the noun "carrier" seems to connote an infectious disease of epidemic proportions. He joins Twain in burlesquing this "art in the neo-classical-maudlin mode" that so spooked the impressionable Huck and gave him a severe case of the "fantods." After contemplating the crayons produced by the deceased Emmeline Grangerford, Huck mused:

> They was different from any pictures I ever see before; blacker, mostly, than is common. One was a woman in a slim black dress, belted small under the arm-pits, with bulges like a cabbage in the middle of the sleeves, and a large black scoop-shovel bonnet with a black veil, and white slim ankles crossed about with black tape, and very wee black slippers, like a chisel, and she was leaning pensive on a tombstone on her right elbow, under a weeping willow, and her other hand hanging down her side holding a white handkerchief and a reticule, and underneath the picture it said "Shall I Never See Thee More Alas." [*Huckleberry Finn,* 137–8]

Although this formulaic rendering had become a grotesque stereotype by 1884, the part of Mark Twain that was still a boy back in the Hannibal, Missouri, of the 1830s responded deeply and appropriately to what was the main heraldic device of consolation. Ann Douglas notes that only a decade later, Mount Auburn Cemetery itself was thronged by "statues of what one popular graveyard guidebook calls 'weeping female figures,' "[3] and we tend to forget sometimes just how "weepy" and "girlish" and sensitive Huck is, and how often he faints or gets the fantods throughout the course of his adventures. Moreover, our laughter at his gullibility tends to obscure Huck's role as the naive representative of a holistic folk world, who gets into real trouble only when he swallows entire and with relish the fashionable modes that are presented to him by a duplicitous popular culture. Huck's resistance to bourgeois acculturation is one of the great moral strengths of Twain's book, yet his innocent acceptance of "carriers" of the normative, like Emmeline Grangerford, is also one of its enduring charms. "Poor Emmeline made poetry about all the dead people when she was alive," Huck muses, "and it didn't seem right that there warn't nobody to make some about her, now she was gone; so I tried to sweat out a verse or two myself, but I couldn't seem to make it go, somehow" (141).

Huck responds as the sentimental gospel of death dictates that he should; by sedulous imitation he hopes to produce a "tribute," just as Emmeline Grangerford's crayon is itself only an awkward copy of somebody else's sketch, silk embroidery, or tinted lithograph. And when he admits that he "liked all that family, dead ones and all," Huck is expressing another one of the main tenets of the new Sentimental Love Religion: the unbreakable bond of kinship, the family circle eventually reunited in heaven.[4] This motif can be found as early as William Wordsworth's poem "We Are Seven" (1798), in which the poet hears about the certainty of family ties between the dead and the living from the innocently trusting lips of a simple child, who stubbornly refuses to acknowledge that two of her siblings are really gone.[5]

The idea of the child as oracle was central not only to Wordsworthian romanticism but to the popular culture that it encouraged. Huckleberry Finn is an ironic capstone of this tradition, providing an unconscious commentary on its stereotypes – a different kind of spiritual truth – by the varying degrees of his reactions to external appearance and inner reality. But Emily Dickinson, too, manipulated the stance of the child for her own particular purposes, speaking with childhood's prophetic voice even as she donned (like Mark Twain in his old age) its prescribed garb of spotless white. In an 1852 letter to Susan Gilbert, Dickinson adapted the refrain of "We Are Seven" for her own personal use (L 1:215), and in poems such as "I met a King This Afternoon!" (J 166), she affirmed childhood's regal authority as much as Lydia Sigourney did in her retelling of the biblical story of Samuel, who provided American Victorians with an archetype of the child-mourner:

Instruct us, prophet-child!
Amid the watches of the night to say –
"*Speak, Lord! thy servants hear;*" and at the dawn
Rise up and light the soul-lamps, and go forth,
Our brow still beaming with the smile of heaven.[6]

Lydia Hunt Sigourney, "widely hailed as 'the sweet singer of Hartford' and the most popular poetess in America before the Civil War,"[7]
uneasily assumed the mantle of the adult seer in poems such as "Imitation of the Prophet Amos." Emily Dickinson dared to become herself
the child in the temple, lecturing its chief priests and scribes in deliberately naive accents borrowed from Isaac Watts's *Divine and Moral
Songs for Children* (1720). Dickinson also knew, however, that the soul
lamps lit by both poets and prophets had to shine forth with a "Vital
Light" (J 883) in order to attain the "Circumference" of lasting rather
than momentary meaning. She reacted selectively to the popular gospel of consolation. Sometimes she accepted its formulas without question; sometimes she subverted them through exaggeration, burlesque,
and distortion; sometimes she used them only as pretexts for outright
skepticism and satire. In doing so Dickinson was continuing a process
of transformation that had long appropriated classical means for romantic ends. We can see this process by examining in more detail the
ruling sentimental icon of mourning maiden, mute tombstone, and
melancholy weeping willow.[8]

The blank marble plinth of the tomb, for example, where the names
of the loved dead were stitched in needlework or drawn on paper or
printed on mass-produced lithographs (see the illustration at the beginning of this chapter), represented the neoclassical, stoical base of the
paradigm. In American culture this "Granitic Base" (J 789) had its
foundation in the death of George Washington on December fourteenth, 1799, for Washington epitomized classical ideals of balance,
reason, and virtue. The extraordinary outburst of public mourning for
this austere father figure, who was a national monument even before
his death, made private grief legitimate and justified a more open pos-
ture of bereavement and consolation. As Anita Schorsch writes, "To
mourn [Washington] was, in true Roman spirit, an act of patriotism,
the love of one's country and its beloved founder being equated with
the love of God" (*Mourning Becomes America,* 8). The marble tombstone
itself, usually topped by an urn, was borrowed from Greek and Etruscan art. Washington's death coincided with the high tide of European
neoclassicism, and its iconography contrasted radically with the grim
death's-heads, dancing skeletons, and winged skulls of Puritan stone
carving. Significantly enough, in "Unto like Story" (J 295) Dickinson

herself refers to death as a "Beckoning – Etruscan invitation – / Toward Light." Here was a clean, well-lighted place for the soul to dwell in, an "Alabaster Chamber" where the spirit of the deceased could be safely housed and reverenced.

Unlike the cinerary urn borne by the noble Roman matron in Benjamin West's great neoclassic history painting *Aggripina with the Ashes of Germanicus* (1769), the fanciful urn of the popular marble tombstone held memories rather than ashes, and was often itself surmounted by a finial made in the image of a petrified eternal flame. The tombstone or tomb house was set in a gardenlike environment, soon to be reproduced on a grand scale in such famous rural cemeteries as Brooklyn's Greenwood and Cambridge's Mount Auburn. In prints, samplers, and imitative crayons like those of Emmeline Grangerford, this garden was formal and severely stylized to indicate further classical control and balance. Sometimes it shrank to the compass of a single weeping willow tree. The willow in turn was a traditional emblem of Christian mourning, since it shed its leaves like tears, seemed perpetually drooped in thoughtful reverie, and had the power to regenerate itself after being cut down (thereby foretelling the resurrection of the dead). Moreover, the weeping willow's ability to thrive in wet areas and soak up excess moisture made it a natural embodiment of those sanitary concerns that prompted so much nineteenth-century cemetery reform.[9] Lydia Sigourney, who was the author of a tiny but formidable book of consolation verses entitled *The Weeping Willow* (1847), summed up the spiritual resonances of this living emblem in a poem included in her last collection, *Gleanings:*

> Pale Willow, drooping low,
>   In gentle sympathy –
> Thy flexile branches wave
>   Like broken harp-strings o'er the grave
> Where our lost treasures lie.   [37]

If the tombstone represented art, and the weeping willow nature, the mourning maiden herself, drawn from an ancient iconography of diaphonous classical nymphs revived in designs, sculptures, and paintings by such artists as John Flaxman, Antonio Canova, and Angelica Kauffman, gradually became a symbol of sublime Christian hope. This veiled figure, who finally exchanged the flimsy raiment of classical Greece or Napoleon's empire for the heavy black mourning dress of Victoria's reign, might be termed "Woman Weeping," in contrast to Emerson's galvanic and frankly masculine image of "Man Thinking" (*Works* 1:84). With her penchant for unrestrained sympathy and unending sentiment – "Shall I Never See Thee More Alas" – Woman Weeping at first

substituted stoical resignation for self-reliance, and brooding recollection for active thought. Yet as her presence came to dominate the
triptych, she also symbolized the triumph of an age of feeling over an
age of reason. Beginning as an allegory of unalloyed remorse, of incon-
solable and perpetual grief in the pagan manner, Woman Weeping was
Christianized and romanticized until she took on a Madonna-like calm.
The growing power of the Sentimental Love Religion answered Emmeline Grangerford's despairing question with an unfaltering "Yes!"
The loved dead would be seen again in a domesticated heaven, and
sometimes their angelic voices even whispered warnings in the ears of
those who were left below, or at least of those who were spiritually
attuned to such higher communications.

The new gospel of consolation preached spiritual elevation as the
cure for psychological depression, developing its own set of uplifting
responses to the fact of sudden death. Ann Douglas notes that this
changed attitude also gave birth to a new secular scripture of consolation literature, an "enormously popular genre" that "included obituary
poems and memoirs, mourners' manuals, prayer guide-books, hymns
and books about heaven." She adds that "such writings inflated the
importance of dying and the dead by every possible means; they sponsored elaborate methods of burial and commemoration, communication
with the next world, and microscopic viewings of a sentimentalized
afterlife" (*Feminization,* 201–2). Once again, the child was at the center
of this new revelation; infant salvation replaced a Calvinistic emphasis
on infant damnation, and justification by death and suffering overcame
the capriciousness of justification by grace.[10] Sigourney, who practiced
nearly every form of consolation literature, both prosaic and poetic,
reiterated these doctrines in her epistle "Loss of Children" in *Letters to
Mothers* (1838), a typical specimen of the genre. "Sometimes," she
wrote,

> grief loses itself in gratitude, that those who once called forth so
> much solicitude, are free from the hazards of this changeful life.
> Here temptations may foil the strongest, and sins overshadow
> those, whose opening course was most fair. From all such
> dangers, the early smitten, and the "lambs whom the Savior tak-
> eth untask'd, untried," have forever escaped. To be sinless, and at
> rest, is a glorious heritage.[11]

The concept of the sinless child countered orthodox ideas of natural
depravity and was gradually extended to include all Christian adults
who struggled valiantly with disease and against the brutal embraces of
"The Spoiler," Death. Since human nature was now seen as basically
angelic rather than demonic, the doctrine of eventual reunion in heaven

became a logical corollary of the gospel of consolation. Speaking of the death of twin infants, Sigourney remarked for example that "a family broken up on earth, [is] re-assembled in Heaven. Those who dwelt for a little time in the same tent of clay, are gathered together, around the altar of immortality (*Letters to Mothers,* 220–1). Because the family circle was never really broken, even by death, there was no reason to suppose that the loved dead were not still with us, in the form of invisible presences and guardian angels who attempted to guide our steps along the weary pilgrimage that remained.

In contemplating the death of a child, Emily Dickinson accepted and practiced this popular gospel of consolation, and she seems to have believed fully in its allied doctrines of infant salvation and the guardian presence of the angel-child. Sigourney had written that "the glorified spirit of the infant, is as a star to guide the mother to her own blissful clime," so that as a result "the thoughts and affections are drawn upward" (*Letters to Mothers,* 206). In attempting to console Susan upon the sudden death of eight-year-old Gilbert in October 1883, Dickinson declared, "I see him in the Star, and meet his sweet velocity in everything that flies," while she affirmed, "now my ascended Playmate must instruct *me.*" And she prayerfully added: "Show us, prattling Preceptor, but the way to thee!" (*L* 3:799). To Dickinson as to Sigourney, the loved dead were astral guides and spiritual mediums to a better world. The asterisk traditionally added to a roster of names in order to denote the deceased became a concrete emblem of their starry destiny,[12] as in the consolation poem Emily sent to the son of her close friend Samuel Bowles:

> Who abdicated Ambush
> And went the way of Dusk,
> And now against his subtle Name
> There stands an Asterisk
> As confident of him as we –
> Impregnable we are –
> The whole of Immortality
> Secreted in a Star.   [J 1616]

Like the ultimate Protestant that she was, however, Dickinson modified other tenets of the popular gospel of consolation to suit her own wavering belief. She had always been uncertain about the concept of immortality, which even in the poem just quoted remains enigmatic, "Secreted" in the physical reality of the star. "Is immortality true?" she anxiously inquired of Washington Gladden as late as 1882, when disturbed by the death of Charles Wadsworth and the illness of Otis P. Lord, but even this famous Christian soldier's resoundingly positive answer could not have satisfied all her nagging doubts (*L* 3:731). Dickinson was raised with a respect for facts, and as the one rebel against orthodoxy in a family all of whom eventually became church members, affirming some kind of "operation of the spirit" on their immortal souls, she could not entirely swallow the candied placebo of a family reunion in heaven or the idea that afflictions were an inevitable means to sanctifying grace. Caught between the stern rock of her Calvinist upbringing and the hard place created by her own uncompromising conscience, Dickinson was forced to wonder if her childlike impudence would be any more welcome in heaven than it was in Amherst:

> On such a night, or such a night,
> Would anybody care
> If such a little figure
> Slipped quiet from it's chair –   [J 146]

As we shall see, Dickinson solved this problem by imagining a purely conjugal heaven built not for the restoration of old family ties but for the fulfillment of new personal relationships that had been thwarted on earth. Dickinson's heaven was not static but progressive, and it remained her only hope of abandoning a self-imposed state of spiritual infancy for complete sexual and psychic maturation. Similarly, in "Safe in their Alabaster Chambers" (J 216) she questioned whether death was in fact the terrible call to judgment preached by the religious heirs of Jonathan Edwards. Yet neither could she accept it as the expectant slumber exalted by sentimentalists who fondly quoted Christ's words to the ruler of the synagogue whose daughter had suddenly died: "Weep not; she is not dead, but sleepeth" (Luke 8:52). Rather, to Dickinson, death was

> A long – long Sleep – a famous – Sleep –
> That makes no show for Morn –
> By stretch of Limb – or stir of Lid –
> An independant One –
>
> Was ever idleness like This?
> Upon a Bank of Stone
> To bask the Centuries away –
> Nor once look up – for Noon?   [J 654]

Death might be a sleeping so profound that no Christ or last trump or pearly gate could tempt an awakening. In spite of her early admiration for Mount Auburn, Sigourney's "most sacred city of the dead," Dickinson invariably set her graveyard poetry not amid a landscaped garden cemetery but in neglected country burying grounds. She re-

mained skeptical that storied urn and animated bust could truly preserve the memory of the beloved:

> After a hundred years
> Nobody knows the Place
> Agony that enacted there
> Motionless as Peace
>
> Weeds triumphant ranged
> Strangers strolled and spelled
> At the lone Orthography
> Of the Elder Dead   [J 1147]

Rather than lasting memorials to human grief, tombstones themselves
became pathetic testaments to the inconstancy of affection, mute
emblems[13] without expression:

> She laid her docile Crescent down
> And this confiding Stone
> Still states to Dates that have forgot
> The News that she is gone —
>
> So Constant to it's stolid trust,
> The Shaft that never knew —
> It shames the Constancy that fled
> Before it's emblem flew —   [J 1396]

If we compare Dickinson's focus on the shameful flight of human
constancy from its hollow mortuary token to the concluding passage of
Sigourney's "Tomb of a Young Friend at Mount Auburn," we can
begin to see just how Dickinson went about transforming the popular
paradigm of Woman Weeping. Sigourney writes:

> The granite obelisk and the pale flower
> Reveal thy couch. Fit emblems of the frail
> and the immortal.
>   But that bitter grief
> Which holds stern vigil o'er the mouldering clay,
> Keeping long night-watch with its sullen lamp
> Had fled thy tomb, and faith did lift its eye
> Full of sweet tears; for when warm tear-drops gush
> From the pure memories of a love that wrought
> For others happiness, and rose to take
> Its own full share of happiness above,
> Are they not sweet?[14]

Dickinson's rendering of the motif is terse and ironic; the constancy of remorse decamps precisely because it is human and does not possess the obdurate quality of stone. The "bitter grief" of Sigourney's ode demonstrates the failure of old-fashioned pagan stoicism; classical attitudes and the "sullen lamp" of commemoration are replaced by a trustful Christian faith, as the tearful waters of feeling literally gush forth from the stern rock of resignation, melting all doubts. Unsure of what "happiness" may lie "above," Dickinson cannot follow Sigourney in the elevating flight of love up the ladder of belief while the cold facts of mortality continue to stare her in the face, paralyzing faith with a Medusa's glower. Whether death was memorialized by neoclassic columns and urns or by the exotic obelisks and cenotaphs popular in the new garden cemeteries, its "livid Surprise" still had the power to "Cool us to Shafts of Granite— / With just an Age—and Name— / And perhaps a phrase in Egyptian" to signify its own ultimate enigma (J 531).

Moreover, Dickinson's concept of herself as a perpetual child who would gain maturity and socialization in a private Eden rather than stay as she was, a second- or third-class spiritually retarded citizen, caused her to modify another one of the ideas sacred to the sentimentalists: the democratization of death. Death was the great leveler, the Jacksonian demogogue who equalized all estates with the sweep of his great scythe. In an early letter to Mrs. J. G. Holland, Dickinson appropriated this stance in a rather manic and affected fashion, seeing death everywhere and exclaiming, "Ah! dainty—dainty Death! Ah! democratic Death! Grasping the proudest zinnia from my purple garden,—then deep to his bosom calling the serf's child!" (L 2:341). Since the "serf" in question was one of her father's handymen, the letter is more revealing of Dickinson's aristocratic conception of her own status than of the mortuary open-door policy expressed in an appropriate passage from Sigourney's "Greenwood":

> A ceaseless tide of immigration flows
>   Through thy still gate, for thou forbiddest none
> On thy close-curtain'd couches to repose
>   Or lease thy narrow tenements of stone;
> It matters not, where first the sunbeam shone
>   Upon their cradle,—'neath the foliage free
> Where dark palmettos fleck the torrid zone,
>   Or mid the icebergs of the Arctic Sea,
> Thou dost no passport claim,—all are at home with thee.
>
> [*Gleanings*, 11]

Sigourney was merely updating the eighteenth-century egalitarianism that found its most prominent model in William Cullen Bryant's "Thanatopsis," where the earth itself becomes "one mighty sepulchre"

She could trust only fact, the microscopic or clinical evidence of her own close observation. Though what the dying eye saw could not be seen by the living eye of the watcher, that watcher might still record as minutely and objectively as possible the behavior of the dying eye, that is, how things were rather than how they seemed to be. Yet as often as Dickinson could write, "She died – *this* was the way she died" (J 150), she knew that the private mythology she based on the public *ars moriendi*[17] of the sentimental gospel of consolation required her own preparation for death. This was the chief "trial" of her initiation into the princely order composed solely of herself and her lover, that lone aristocracy of two:

> The Test of Love – is Death –
> Our Lord – "so loved" – it saith –
> What Largest Lover – hath –
> Another – doth –   [J 573]

Like Christ, Dickinson thought it "no / Extravagance / to pay – a Cross –" (J 571) for the privilege of eventual coronation in heaven. Grounded in a Calvinist scrupulousness and in a sentimental preparationism, Dickinson's poems on death became dress rehearsals for her own beatific vision of her lover's face, in which pain mixed with pleasure and anxiety jostled anticipation. Dickinson learned that "Looking at Death, is Dying" (J 281), whether she acted only as watcher ("As by the dead we love to sit" [J 88]) or as the chief actor in this drama of departure:

> Dying! Dying in the night!
> Wont somebody bring the light
> So I can see which way to go
> Into the everlasting snow?
>
> And "Jesus"! Where is *Jesus* gone?
> They said that Jesus – always came –
> Perhaps he does'nt know the House –
> This way, Jesus, Let him pass!   [J 158]

In this relatively early dress rehearsal for death, the Calvinist elements are more marked, as the dying soul has only two "ways" to trudge into the blankness of eternity, and the longed-for vision is that of Jesus, who will escort Dickinson along the dark road of death to a homelike heaven rather than to a prisonlike hell. The last verse of the poem is a plea that Susan, whose nickname was "Dollie," would preside over the deathbed ritual either in body or (if she has herself already passed through the "great gate" of heaven) in spirit, and help to bring Dickinson safely through the final agony:

in which the high and the humble assume an equal rank.[15] Dickinson's own version of this idea can be found in a poem written about 1864:

> Color – Caste – Denomination –
> These – are Time's Affair –
> Death's diviner Classifying
> Does not know they are –
>
> As in sleep – All Hue forgotten –
> Tenets – put behind –
> Death's large – Democratic fingers
> Rub away the Brand –   [J 970]

Since in Christian thought heaven was a "perfect – pauseless Monarchy" (J 721), death became a means of promotion as well as a mere bureaucratic reclassification. Thanatos conferred a regal degree that raised a commoner to the status of the titled nobility. "Courtiers quaint, in Kingdoms / Our departed are," Dickinson wrote of the loved dead (J 53), though gradually she trimmed her honors list of new aristocrats to only two candidates: herself and her lover. A poem written about 1860 emphasizes the exclusivity of her private mythology while it also may pun on the name of the man who was eventually to become the acknowledged Master of her later emotional life, Judge Otis P. Lord:

> Wait till the Majesty of Death
> Invests so mean a brow!
> Almost a powdered Footman
> Might dare to touch it now!
>
> Wait till in Everlasting Robes
> This Democrat is dressed,
> Then prate about "Preferment" –
> And "Station", and the rest!
>
> Around this quiet Courtier
> Obsequious Angels wait!
> Full royal is his Retinue!
> Full purple is his state!
>
> A Lord, might dare to lift the Hat
> To such a Modest Clay,
> Since that My Lord, "the Lord of Lords"
> Receives unblushingly!   [J 171]

While her lover became successively a lord, an earl, and a king, Dickinson herself was promoted to duke, czar, and empress. She became "Queen of Calvary," a royal infanta who lifted her "childish plumes" of mourning in "bereaved acknowledgement" of Nature's regimentals: the "unthinking Drums" of an all-too-punctual spring (J 348). Since both compensation and consummation could be attained only through death, dying was a way of being "born to the purple," a coronation as much as a crucifixion. Dickinson eagerly appropriated the Arminian heresy of justification through suffering that allowed sentimentalists to counter the Calvinist dogma of predestination, but in doing so she also was forced to confront the new gospel's emphasis on deathbed rituals and their weighty significance.

II

Emily Dickinson had been early schooled in this "science of the grave" (J 519) by her upbringing in a Calvinist community where deathbed behavior was taken as one of the barometers by which one could measure the rise or fall of the individual soul. If such behavior was characterized by calm acceptance and Christian composure, the chances were good that the soul could be sure of its election and that it was destined to join the Saints; if the dying person railed against death and abjured a hope of heaven, eternal hellfire and brimstone seemed equally imminent. Some orthodox ministers kept "Death Books" in which the circumstances attending a death and any special last words or actions were noted down as a basis for the funeral sermon, which often made an explicit comment on whether the deceased had died in the hope of the resurrection. For this reason one of the leitmotifs of Emily Dickinson's letters concerning death is her formulaic query, "Was he (or she) willing to die?" since willingness to die was a certain sign of one's confidence in a heavenly destiny.[16]

As early as 1854 Dickinson was asking for such details from the pastor of her father's late law clerk, Benjamin F. Newton, to whom she had been particularly close. This pastor, Edward Everett Hale, was not yet famous as the author of "The Man without a Country," and Dickinson's letter is unusual in its formality if not in its urgency. As if believing that an answer to the physical formula would give her the certainty of spiritual truth, Dickinson reiterated her request in her closing paragraph: "He often talked of God, but I do not know certainly if he was his Father in Heaven – Please Sir, to tell me if he was willing to die, and if you think him at Home, I should love so much to know certainly, that he was today in Heaven" (L 1:283). As late as 1878, Dickinson informed T. W. Higginson that "Mr. Bowles was not willing to die" (L 2:611), referring to another recently deceased friend, and in an early poem she had puckishly applied both the formula and the deathbed conventions it symbolized to the passing away of Summer:

> We trust that she was willing –
> We ask that we may be.
> Summer – Sister – Seraph!
> Let us go with thee!   [J 18]

By preaching justification through suffering, the popular gospel of consolation gradually drained the Calvinist tradition of its insistence on a deathbed conversion, but the pull toward Christian spiritualism still allowed for the possibility of ecstatic revelations and significant last words:

> These – saw Visions –
> Latch them softly –
> These – held Dimples –
> Smooth them slow –   [J 758]

As high priestess of the Mount Auburn school, Sigourney herself chose her own last words – "I love everybody" – with a craftsman's care, lifting them from one of her own works of fiction. In her *Letters to Mothers* she recorded a typically melodramatic closing scene. Describing a particularly pious man who in his last illness daily read and explained the Scriptures to his family, she wrote:

> Once, while remarking upon a chapter, he suddenly exclaimed, "What brightness do I see? Have you lighted any candles?" They replied that they had not, for it was a summer's afternoon, and the twilight had not come. Then, in a clear, glad voice, he said, "now, farewell world! and welcome heaven! for the day-star on high, hath visited me. Oh, speak it when I am gone, and tell it at my funeral, that God dealeth familiarly with man. I feel his mercy, I see his majesty, whether in the body or out of the body. I cannot tell: God knoweth. But I behold things unutterable." And filled with joy, he expired. [238–9]

Many times Dickinson witnessed deathbed behavior, but she could never be sure exactly what "Visions" were vouchsafed the dying person:

> I've see a Dying Eye
> Run round and round a Room –
> In search of Something – as it seemed –
> Then Cloudier become –
> And then – obscure with Fog –
> And then – be soldered down
> Without disclosing what it be
> 'Twere blessed to have seen –   [J 547]

> Somebody run to the great gate
> And see if Dollie's coming! Wait!
> I hear her feet upon the stair!
> Death wont hurt—now Dollie's here!

Yet as Dickinson became more and more an outcast in her own family, she could not depend on "saved" individuals like Susan to plead her case with higher powers, and her fashioning of a private cult out of the elements of the Sentimental Love Religion and the popular gospel of consolation made dying a much more ominous eventuality. While her identification of herself or her lover as a Christ figure was but a logical extension of the new doctrine of justification by suffering, the exclusivity of Dickinson's concept of the afterlife bordered on blasphemy. Death became literally an all-or-nothing proposition. Rather than a vision of light, of Jesus, or her lover, deathbed throes might bring only a trivial deliverence from pain; rather than a grand test of her philosophy of heavenly compensation, dying might be the ultimate indignity; rather than opening the door to Hades or paradise, "The Spoiler" might simply conduct her toward an oblivion that invalidated all faith as well as all reason:

> I heard a Fly buzz—when I died—
> The Stillness in the Room
> Was like the Stillness in the Air—
> Between the Heaves of Storm—
>
> The Eyes around—had wrung them dry—
> And Breaths were gathering firm
> For that last Onset—when the King
> Be witnessed—in the Room—
>
> I willed my Keepsakes—Signed away
> What portion of me be
> Assignable—and then it was
> There interposed a Fly—
>
> With Blue—uncertain stumbling Buzz—
> Between the light—and me—
> And then the Windows failed—and then
> I could not see to see—   [J 465]

Is the "light" obscured by the fly in the final stanza a "divine and supernatural light," the brightness of the day-star as seen by the pious Christian in Sigourney's anecdote, or is it merely the "light of common day" that illuminates the fallacy of hope? Compare Dickinson's insider's view of deathbed experience with Sigourney's own last moments, as "witnessed" by a pious, obedient, and supposedly trusting daughter:

> The struggle for breath ended, and she lay for about ten minutes in apparent unconsciousness. Then her eye lighted up with unearthly brightness, as if a glimpse had been given her into the world beyond. Something unseen by our mortal eyes was doubtless revealed to her. It was but for an instant, and then, just at ten o'clock, without a struggle, the glad spirit was released. "Thanks be unto God, who giveth the victory through our Lord Jesus Christ."[18]

Dickinson has taken the clichés of nineteenth-century popular culture and turned them in upon themselves: "I heard a Fly buzz – when I died" is similar to hundreds of mortuary effusions that dwell on the details of deathbed scenes, from Thomas Hood's use of the imagery of tempestuous struggle in "The Death-Bed":

> We watched her breathing thro' the night,
>   Her breathing soft and low,
> As in her heart the wave of life
>   Kept heaving to and fro,[19]

to the standard description of the clouding of earthly vision in Sigourney's "The Passing Bell":

> To Beauty's shaded room
> The Spoiler's step of gloom,
>   Hath darkly stole,
> Her lips are ghastly white
> A film is o'er her sight
>   Pray for the soul.[20]

The telling difference is that Dickinson makes a shorthand of conventional imagery while also questioning the whole meaning of the spiritual significance of material things. While she boldly appropriates the fancy coffin furniture of her times, she uses it to construct her own streamlined poetics. Such images as the "violet-tinted eye" of Sigourney's poem on her dead son (*Gleanings,* 260) are repeated with vivid concreteness in

> She bore it till the simple veins
> Traced azure on her hand –
> Till pleading, round her quiet eyes
> The Purple Crayons stand.   [J 144]

The eyes increasingly became the focus of sentimental scrutiny, both the eye of the witness to deathbed torments and the eye of the dying person himself.[21] As a "window of the soul," the eye absorbed all the attention that before had been directed at the entire passion drama of death:

> Fight sternly in a Dying eye
> Two Armies, Love and Certainty
> And Love and the Reverse.   [J 831]

Now the spiritual was wholly merged in the material, and the very fact of physical deterioration became a rite of passage ensuring divine forgiveness. Atonement came through a personal crucifixion by fever or lingering disease: One's last days or hours were purgatory or hell enough to guarantee an instantaneous translation to heaven. Or at least one could hope so:

> The Eyes glaze once – and that is Death –
> Impossible to feign
> The Beads upon the Forehead
> By homely Anguish strung.   [J 241]

This doctrine of justification by death and suffering allows us to understand the great paradox of the popular gospel of consolation: the mingled emphasis on both the corporeal and the marmoreal – the fascination with a clinical report of excruciating pain, and an equal obsession with the calm, marble-like features of the corpse itself, petrified by rigor mortis:

> 'Twas warm – at first – like Us –
> Until there crept upon
> A Chill – like frost upon a Glass –
> Till all the scene – be gone.
>
> The Forehead copied Stone –
> The Fingers grew too cold
> To ache – and like a Skater's Brook –
> The busy eyes – congealed –   [J 519]

The corporeal emphasis in popular mortuary poetry of the time recognized suffering as a necessary prelude to the transformation of the sanctified corpse into an icon. In turn, this icon and any "keepsakes" associated with its marmoreal permanence took the place of the Catholic crucifix that was denied to most American Protestants of Puritan heritage. The sculptural metaphors of these poems – death as spoiler, destroyer, reaper; death throes as spearpoints, shafts, and darts; brows made of marble or ice or covered with the damp "dews" of fever; the grave as a house and heaven as a home – seem incomprehensible today unless we realize that they were a means of personalizing and universalizing Christ's own New Testament passion. As late as March of 1884 Emily Dickinson could write to one of her closest friends, "I hope your own are with you, and may not be taken – I hope there is no Dart advancing or in store" (L 3:816). While the dead become beautifully composed statues, serene icons of the resurrection, the dying by contrast are perspiring, writhing, and tortured creatures, nailed to a private rugged cross and subjected to an individualized scourging, mocking, and crowning with thorns. Hence Lydia Sigourney's poem "The Lost Sister," with its typical morbid anatomy of the closing eye as well as its insistence on immediate postmortem sanctification:

> It's gather'd film
> Kindled one moment with a sudden glow
> Of tearless agony, – and fearful pangs,
> Racking the rigid features, told how strong
> A mother's love doth root itself. One cry
> Of bitter anguish, blent with fervent prayer,
> Went up the Heaven, – and, as its cadence sank
> Her spirit enter'd there.   [*Poems*, 59]

Even those seemingly closest to God do not escape. Witness "Death of a Clergyman":

> Death smote thee sore,
> And plung'd his keen shaft in the quivering nerve,
> Making the breath that stirr'd life's broken valve
> A torturing gasp, but with thy martyrdom
> Were smiles and songs of praise.   [Sigourney, *Poems*, 83]

It is all too easy to dismiss such scenes as exercises in latent necrophilia or some kind of genteel Victorian pornography. Ann Douglas, in her discussion of the American "Domestication of Death," writes that "barred by external taboos and internal anxieties from elaboration on the overtly sexual acts of impregnation and childbirth," the sentimentalists instead "concentrated on illness and death: they were more interested in the moments at which crude energy failed than in those at which it accelerated" (*Feminization*, 202). In a post-Freudian world, this is a compelling argument, yet we must also acknowledge that these excruciating descriptions were based on a long tradition of meditation on "the last things" that eventually crystallized into a specific interest in "making a good ending," in learning how to die.

III

Nancy Lee Beaty has traced this tradition of the *ars moriendi* or "craft of dying" from an anonymous tractatus of the fifteenth century to Jeremy Taylor's *Holy Dying* of 1651. Calling the form of this craft a "liturgical drama," Beaty reminds us that Victorian deathbed scenes were equally ritualistic and formalized. As Dickinson herself writes, this frank theatricality had both internal and external associations:

> What harm? Men die – externally –
> It is a truth – of Blood –
> But we – are dying in Drama –
> And Drama – is never dead –   [J 531]

The ritualistic drama of the *ars moriendi* remained remarkably coherent in form up to the time of the Reformation, and in the three parts of Thomas Becon's *The Sicke Mannes Salve* (1561), which Beaty takes as an excellent example of a Calvinistic craft, we can see the basic three-act structure of expected deathbed drama that was transmitted to America through the Puritans. This structure later became firmly embedded in such sentimental versions of the craft as Sigourney's *Letters to Mothers*. The first act of the traditional paradigm stresses the uncertainty of life and proper Christian acceptance of afflictions; the second act celebrates triumph over the world through a forsaking of its material tokens, culminating in the making of a will and the recitation of a creed; the third act details the actual death agony itself, the fear of dissolution and pain, and an examination of as many as "seven signs which fully certify that one is predestinate to eternal salvation" (Beaty, *Craft,* 120). What might be called the supernatural denouement of the drama, an emphasis on visions and apparitions in the midst of the final struggle, then takes place:

> As the final "extreme agony and conflicte" with the "infernal army" draws nearer . . . the dying man prays to Christ, gazes on his Lord with eyes of faith, and is assured of the presence of angels in his chamber to strengthen and defend him. The friends' commendations and intercessions alternate with their "comfortable exhortations" to faith and courage and with his own (weakening) signs of continued faith. In the coda following his death, an unexpected eulogy of the deceased precedes the usual prayers of thanksgiving and petition; and the treatise proceeds as far as the first preparations for the funeral. [Beaty, *Craft,* 120]

The final emphasis on the physical horrors of death is an exhortation to the living that they, too, will have to pass in pain and suffering through the Valley of the Shadow. It also strengthens the relationship between the dying layman, Moriens, and the divine Christ, since both share a passion and a crucifixion. As we have seen, the popular gospel of consolation takes this relationship to its ultimate synthesis: The dying person becomes Christ, whether this person be man, woman, or child. All of the elements of the traditional *arts moriendi* are preserved, but sentimentalists like Sigourney at the same time strip away the heavy Calvinist emphasis on damnation, replacing it with the new and radical doctrines of justification by suffering, atonement through pain, and sanctification by death. They also elaborate the epilogue, coda, or denouement into a new fourth act complete in itself, as visions, eulogies, and funeral rites become extraordinarily concrete and self-validating. "No Cross, No Crown!" is one of the popular poems that Mary Warner clipped out for inclusion in her scrapbook, and Dickinson too was fully aware that she would have to play her part as "Empress of Calvary" in order to attain the desired consummation of a heavenly reunion.

But it is the new fourth act that sentimentalists added to this ancient tradition that accounts for the odd mixture of the "sculptural" adjectives we have noted, alternating with vivid descriptions of the dissolution of the flesh. John Morley reminds us that "Victorian beliefs, and especially Victorian religious beliefs, were corporeal; religion had little of the abstract quality of modern religious thought,"[22] but this last act of the Victorian *ars moriendi* goes beyond the corporeal to what I have called the marmoreal. The marmoreal was in some sense only an extension of the faith of an intensely materialistic age, and the overwhelming Victorian desire to possess, preserve, and embalm things *as things* seems in marked contrast to our own contemporary emphasis on making them easily disposable, deliberately obsolescent, and annoyingly self-disintegrating. Yet we can understand the dark brilliance of Emily Dickinson's death poetry only by realizing that in the popular tradition from which she drew her imagery, the dead themselves were considered frozen emblems of the resurrection, actual tokens of the longed-for afterlife:

> Too cold is this
> To warm with Sun –
> Too stiff to bended be,
> To joint this Agate were a work –
> Outstaring Masonry –   [J 1135]

This realization returns us once more to the concept of the keepsake, the memorial token that, owned, touched or bequeathed by the loved dead, took on the connotations of a sacred relic. In "I heard a Fly buzz – when I died," Dickinson as a latter-day Moriens follows both the traditional craft of dying and its Victorian sentimental variations by abjuring the world and willing away her "Keepsakes," as well as signing away "What portion of me be / Assignable." But the expected vision of a delivering Christ and the "commendations and intercessions" of friends are frustrated, even ironically undercut, by the loud buzzing of the fly, and a final confession of faith is never achieved. A perfect and holy dying is spoiled by awkwardness, confusion, and doubt.

Wedding rings, Bibles, locks of hair, and other mementos of the dying weigh down the mortuary verses of the time as well as the sentimental novels that sprang from the same love religion. These objects were to be preserved and cherished as emblems of the new-made Saints as well as tokens of the covenant between the living and the dead. Harriet Beecher Stowe's Little Eva distributes portions of her golden curls on her deathbed in *Uncle Tom's Cabin,* and Huck Finn reports of the Grangerfords that "they kept Emmeline's room trim and nice and all the things fixed in it just the way she liked to have them when she was alive, and nobody ever slept there" (*Huckleberry Finn,* 141). The disuse of a perfectly good bedroom constitutes a true revelation of the sacred to the homeless Huck, but it is also an indication of the conspicuous consumption encouraged by a rising new bourgeois society. The dictates of popular culture soon overcame the down-to-earth practicality of the folk world, whose main motto had been "Use it up, wear it out, make it do." On the very first page of Mary Warner's scrapbook is a poem entitled "The Little Straw Hat," which begins:

> The dear little hat, and it hangs there still –
> And its voice of the past bids our heart-strings thrill,
> For it seems like a shadow of days passed o'er,
> Of the bright one gone who that hat once wore.

This poem goes on in seven more stanzas to contemplate the poignant meanings of this keepsake, whose child-owner now wears a "glittering crown" while his voice "blends . . . mid the cherub choir." "The Dainty Wardrobe" on page 32 expresses the same veneration for material relics of the deceased, in this case an infant who "died without a name":

> There's a little drawer in my chamber
> Guarded with tender care,
> Where the dainty clothes are lying,
> That my darling shall never wear;

And there, while the hours are waning
   Till the house is all at rest,
I sit and fancy a baby
   Close to my aching breast.

In "Little Charlie," on page 13, Thomas Bailey Aldrich writes:

O rare pale lips! O clouded eyes!
O violet eyes grown dim!
Ah well! this little lock of hair
Is all of him!
Is all of him that we can keep
For living kisses, and the thought
Of him and Death may teach us more
Than all our life hath taught!

As in her attitude toward tombstones, Dickinson was of her time in sharing a reverence for such tokens ("I keep your lock of hair as precious as gold and a great deal more so" (*L* 1:9), yet she remained suspicious of their ability to escape the dilapidations of time and memory:

In Ebon Box, when years have flown
To reverently peer,
Wiping away the velvet dust
Summers have sprinkled there!

To hold a letter to the light –
Grown Tawny now, with time –
To con the faded syllables
That quickened us like Wine!

Perhaps a Flower's shrivelled cheek
Among it's stores to find –
Plucked far away, some morning –
By gallant – mouldering hand!

A Curl, perhaps, from foreheads
Our Constancy forgot –
Perhaps, an Antique trinket –
In vanished fashions set!

And then to lay them quiet back –
And go about it's care
As if the little Ebon Box
Were none of our affair!   [J 169]

In the popular gospel of consolation, the preciousness of the objects left by the deceased was elevated to include their earthly remains as

well, and as Ann Douglas observes, "It seems no accident that corpses
were increasingly made to resemble dolls" (*Feminization*, 209). The
loved dead themselves became keepsakes, as advances in embalming
and the invention of waterproof tombs and airtight burial cases actually
allowed sentimentalists to treat the corpse as the metaphorical gem,
treasure, or idol it so often is in the lofty lamentations of mortuary
verse.[23] Again Dickinson was skeptical about this extraordinarily concrete manifestation of the sentimental *ars moriendi*, even as she appropriated some of its most marmoreal aspects for her own cultic purposes:

> I've dropped my Brain – My Soul is numb –
> The veins that used to run
> Stop palsied – 'tis Paralysis
> Done Perfecter on stone.
>
> Vitality is Carved and cool.
> My nerve in Marble lies –
> A Breathing Woman
> Yesterday – Endowed with Paradise.
>
> Not dumb – I had a sort that moved –
> A Sense that smote and stirred –
> Instincts for Dance – a caper part –
> An Aptitude for Bird –
>
> Who wrought Carrara in me
> And chiselled all my tune
> Were it a Witchcraft – were it Death –
> I've still a chance to strain
>
> To Being, somewhere – Motion – Breath –
> Though Centuries beyond,
> And every limit a Decade –
> I'll shiver, satisfied.   [J 1046]

In her *Letters to Mothers*, Lydia Sigourney had asked, in the tradition
of Moriens's abjuration of the world, "May not a christian be able to
yield without repining, the dearest idols to Him who loved him and
gave himself for him?" (210). A poem pasted on page 4 of Mary
Warner's scrapbook answered this formulaic question with an equally
formulaic "Yes," while also acknowledging Sigourney's truth that "to
have their most precious treasures swept utterly away, and find that
home desolate, which was wont to resound with the voice of young
affection, and the tones of innocent mirth, is a sorrow which none can
realize, save those who bear it" (*Letters to Mothers*, 210). The poem is
entitled "Our Idol":

Close the door lightly,
  Bridle the breath,
Our little earth-angel
  Is talking with death.
Gently he woos her,
  She wishes to stay,
His arms about her –
  He bears her away.

Music comes floating
  Down from the dome;
Angels are chanting
  The sweet welcome home.
Come, stricken weeper,
  Come to the bed,
Gaze on the sleeper –
  Our idol is dead!

Smooth out the ringlets,
  Close the blue eye –
No wonder such beauty
  Was claimed in the sky;
Cross the hands gently
  O'er the white breast
So like a wild spirit
  Strayed from the blest;
Bear her out softly,
  This idol of ours,
Let her grave slumbers
  Be 'mid the sweet flowers.

In a particularly plaintive letter to Susan written in 1854, Dickinson sighed that her friend need not fear for her loneliness, for "I often part with things I fancy I have loved, – sometimes to the grave, and sometimes to an oblivion rather bitterer than death," adding, "Few have been given me, and if love them so, that for *idolatry*, they are removed from me – I simply murmur *gone*, and the billow dies away into the boundless blue, and no one knows but me, that one went down today" (*L* 1:305–6). The reference to the corpse as an "idol" gradually became, as did all the nineteenth-century sentimental euphemisms, a cliché, yet once again it connotes the conflict between paganism and Christianity that was at the heart of the popular gospel of consolation. In "A Clock Stopped" (J 287), the human body becomes for Dickinson a "trinket," since her true treasure – transformation from human carbon to deific diamond – lies in a heaven of her own imagining. And finally, in a poem written about 1872, Dickinson applied these popular conventions to the death of friendship itself:

> Now I knew I lost her –
> Not that she was gone –
> But Remoteness travelled
> On her Face and Tongue.
>
> Alien, though adjoining
> As a Foreign Race –
> Traversed she though pausing
> Latitudeless Place.
>
> Elements Unaltered –
> Universe the same
> But Love's transmigration –
> Somehow this had come –
>
> Henceforth to remember
> Nature took the Day
> I had paid so much for –
> His is Penury
> Not who toils for Freedom
> Or for Family
> But the Restitution
> Of Idolatry.   [J 1219]

The materiality represented by the mortuary poems of Sigourney and those that can be found in Mary Warner's scrapbook gives to Dickinson's art its feel for the rich stuffs and ebony surfaces of what Dickinson herself called the "eclat of Death" (J 1307). Such was the tone of the popular culture of her times, but paradoxically that culture was only following the lead of an elite personage who set the style for the mid-nineteenth-century's fascination with keepsakes, souvenirs, and memorial relics of all kinds. It is this climactic conjunction of high and low, as represented by the ritual imagery of the Victorian funeral, that I now attempt to explore.

IV

Queen Victoria kept marble replicas of the feet and hands of her children on her desk at Osborne on the Isle of Wight, and after the death of her beloved Prince Albert in 1861 her retreat into the soberest of widowhoods set a regal seal on the rituals of the Sentimental Love Religion. For years things were preserved just as Albert had left them, and every night his valet had orders to set out his evening clothes as if he were still going to descend to dinner. As John Morley observes, "Victoria, in her grand grief for the Prince Consort, assembled an array of mourning objects almost Egyptian in their comprehensiveness" (*Death,* 14). The bell-jar protection of loved objects from moth and rust merged with the concept of bodily remains as a precious cameo carved by the great sculptor, Death. As we have seen, the corpse became a gem to be cherished, preserved, and placed in an appropriate setting. Robert W. Habenstein and William M. Lamers write in their *History of American Funeral Directing* that

> throughout the 19th-century in America, by means of experimentation carried out by a considerable number of people, the old fashioned coffin slowly became transformed into the modern casket. Coffin and casket makers sensed goals which at one time or other they tried especially to reach in their improvements: their product should have increased utility; it should better indicate the importance of the dead person and his family: it should provide more protection against grave robbers, and the forces of dissolution, and finally it should be more artistic, more beautiful, the better to harmonize with the aesthetic movement in burials. [259]

As the new Victorian tomb houses and garden cemeteries became more and more elaborate, approaching the status of small palaces, so did the actual receptacles in which the loved dead were placed reflect a growing material reverence for their "priceless" remains. The plain, utilitarian, wedge-shaped coffin of the Puritans, meant to return man to the dust from which he came and so emblemize his mortal corruptibility, was replaced by the shapely, luxurious casket, meant to frame, enhance, and show off its contents. This development was "distinctly American" and ran the gamut from improved wrought-iron coffins to patented airtight mummy cases inspired by the Egyptian revival that informed Queen Victoria's grand mourning and sprinkled obelisks and cenotaphs throughout Greenwood and Mount Auburn. Dickinson herself mentions in an 1850 letter to Jane Humphrey that the Brewster family had hopes of seeing a young relative who had died "away at a mission" because her body had been "preserved in spirit" (*L* 1:96), perhaps in an airtight "Fisk Metallic Burial Case," with a porthole-like cover, similar to the one in which Henry Clay's remains were preserved. One of Clay's mourner's noted the aesthetic beauties of this device, first patented in 1848, for "the sarcophagus, in which the remains were inurned, resembles the outlines of the human body."[24] Americans of the 1850s seemed so concerned with the material preservation of their political idols that they neglected the irony implicit in the last name of this ponderously "inurned" statesman, or the fact that the original Latin and Greek meaning of the term "sarcophagus" was that of a flesh-eating stone coffin.

As Habenstein and Lamers point out, such innovations in the design of coffins recall, besides the Egyptian sarcophagus, both "the iron torpedo, and the strong box" (*American Funeral Directing,* 263). If, to the sentimentalists, death was a sleep, then the coffin naturally became a bed; if the corpse was a gem, a coffin could be a showcase (some actually were made of plate glass); and if the loved dead were precious stones, a casket was the appropriate castle keep in which to secrete them. Anna L. Angier writes, "Sacred treasures sleep within / Our pleasant hill of graves," and Mrs. C. W. Hunt says of the deceased "Georgiana":

> She lay within her coffin-cell
>   Like a priceless pearl in costly shell,
> Enshrined in light, so pure – so rare,
> A breath would leave a shadow there.

This "costly shell" is even more graphically described by the anonymous author of "The Little Coffin":

> 'Twas a tiny, rose-wood thing,
> Ebon bound, and glittering
> With its stars of silver-white
> Silver tablet, blank and bright
> Downy pillowed, satin lined,
> That I loitering, chanced to find
> 'Mid the dust and scent and gloom
> Of the undertaker's room,
> Waiting, empty – oh! for whom?[25]

Dickinson's "Ebon Box" of keepsakes was really no different from this kind of fancy burial case, upholstered in rich materials, where, as the author of *Agnes and the Key of Her Little Coffin* (1857) explained, an actual "lock and key" had been substituted for the "remorseless screws and screwdrivers" of old-fashioned pine packing cases (Douglas, *Feminization,* 204):

> Ample make this Bed –
> Make this Bed with Awe –
> In it wait till Judgment break
> Excellent and Fair.

> Be it's Mattress straight –
> Be it's Pillow round –
> Let no Sunrise' yellow noise
> Interrupt this Ground –   [J 829]

While the terrors of death could not be lessened, its emblems and accoutrements were at least made palatable to a new genteel popular culture. The strategies of consolation developed by the Sentimental Love Religion stressed peaceful rest, aesthetic pleasure, and pious preservation over stern judgment, harsh utilitarianism, and physical decay. As Washington Irving admitted in "Rural Funerals" in *The Sketch Book:* "There is a dismal process going on in the grave, ere dust can return to its kindred dust, which the imagination sinks from contemplating." Airtight caskets, marble mausoleums and garden cemeteries were surely one way to "soften the horrors of the tomb, to beguile the mind from brooding over the disgraces of perishing mortality, and to associate the memory of the deceased with the most delicate and beautiful objects in nature."[26]

In late January of 1875, referring to the death of her father six months before, Dickinson wrote to Mrs. Holland, "Mother is asleep in the Library – Vinnie in the Dining Room – Father – in the Masked Bed – in the Marl House" (*L* 2:537), and enclosed a poem that underlined the equivocal pleasures of new, "comfortable" burials:[27]

> How soft this Prison is
> How sweet these sullen bars
> No Despot but the King of Down
> Invented this repose   [J 1334]

Much earlier she had abstracted the cold comforts of this new gentility into a brittle imagism and mocked its transformation of the grave into a well-furnished stronghold in one of her most famous stanzas:

> Safe in their Alabaster Chambers –
> Untouched by Morning
> And untouched by Noon –
> Sleep the meek members of the Resurrection –
> Rafter of satin,
> And Roof of stone.   [J 216]

Perhaps the sentimentalists, like the Calvinist Saints, could so exaggerate the "last things" that they cut themselves off from an enjoyment of living reality, building too many alabaster chambers of doctrine and dogma. Time and nature would destroy them all, as they had the mighty monuments of Egypt; what use, then, was such safety or sagacity? Yet as a constant mourner who carried a "coffin in [her] heart" (J 39), Dickinson also was guilty of that "possessive idolatry" so dear to the Mount Auburn school:

> If I may have it, when it's dead,
> I'll be contented – so –
> If just as soon as Breath is out
> It shall belong to me –
>
> Until they lock it in the Grave,
> 'Tis Bliss I cannot weigh –
> For tho' they lock Thee in the Grave,
> Myself – can own the key – [J 577]

Gradually the grave became for Dickinson not a permanent residence but a stopping-off place, a "small Domain" (J 943), a beacon whose "little Panels" were glowing with a welcoming light (J 611), a boardinghouse or wayside "Inn" that entertained "Peculiar Travelers" (J 115), or finally a "little cottage" where one could play at being husband and wife – literally, a subterranean honeymoon hotel (J 1743). The funeral in turn became a regal procession, a royal progress. Here Dickinson could draw both upon her own private mythology of death as a grand "Imperator" (J 455) who conferred a distinguished rank upon his followers and upon the typical panoply of Victorian funeral customs themselves. In his *Death, Heaven and the Victorians,* John Morley quotes an illuminating passage from the *Supplementary Report – into the Practice of Interment in Towns* of 1843, which establishes the chivalric origins of nineteenth-century burial rituals. "Are you aware," the learned author, Edwin Chadwick writes,

> that the array of funerals, commonly made by undertakers, is strictly the heraldic array of a baronial funeral, the two men who stand at the doors being supposed to be the two porters of the castle, with their staves, in black; the man who heads the procession, wearing a scarf, being a representative of a herald-at-arms; the man who carries a plume of feathers on his head being an esquire, who bears the shield and casque, with its plume of feathers; the pall-bearers, with batons, being representatives of knights-companions-at-arms; the men walking with wands being supposed to represent gentlemen-ushers with their wands: – are you aware that this is said to be the origin and type of the common array usually provided by those who undertake to perform funerals? [19]

If Dickinson was not entirely aware of the antiquarian origins of this "array," she surely was conscious of its aristocratic pomp and circumstance, even as carried on in a country town like Amherst rather than in a great metropolis like London. A dispossessed Calvinist, she hungered for what was the nearest thing to High Church ritual:

> One dignity delays for all –
> One mitred Afternoon –
> None can avoid this purple –
> None evade this Crown!
>
> Coach, it insures, and footmen –
> Chamber, and state, and throng –
> Bells, also, in the village
> As we ride grand along!
>
> What dignified Attendants!
> What service when we pause!
> How loyally at parting
> Their hundred hats they raise!
>
> How pomp surpassing ermine
> When simple You, and I,
> Present our meek escutscheon
> And claim the rank to die!   [J 98]

Before her family moved back to the brick Homestead originally built by her grandfather on Amherst's Main Street, from her upstairs bedroom window of their wooden house on Pleasant Street Dickinson could almost daily watch funeral processions winding into the village cemetery (L 1:31). She well knew that the "numb look" of houses in which a death had occurred was a "Sign" that "There'll be that Dark Parade – / Of Tassels – and of Coaches – soon – " (J 389). It was a wholly fitting spectacle to accompany the deposit of the loved dead in their treasure-house beneath the earth, yet if Dickinson had been interested only in depicting sentimental burial customs, she would have produced poems little more interesting than Lydia Sigourney's "Journey with the Dead":

> Weary and sad, their course is bent
>   To seek an ancient dome,
> Where hospitality hath made
>   A long-remembered home;
> And one with mournful care they bring
>   Whose footstep erst was gay
> Amid these halls; why comes she now
>   In sorrow's dark array?   [Poems, 71]

While Dickinson abandons Sigourney's flowery style and deliberately "poetic" diction for the heft and weight and imagistic compression of Watts's hymns, the individual apocryphal books she adds to the main canon of the popular gospel of consolation turn its heterodoxy inside out. Death becomes not merely a porter or a herald or an esquire (J 608), but a sinister "Gentleman-usher" who is also a best man, a groom or proxy who stands in for the true lover delayed in a remote paradise. This knight errant might even try to exercise a macabre *droit de seigneur:*

> Death is the supple Suitor
> That wins at last—
> It is a stealthy Wooing—
> Conducted first
> By pallid innuendoes
> And dim approach
> But brave at last with Bugles
> And a bisected Coach
> It bears away in triumph
> To Troth unknown
> And Kindred as responsive
> As Porcelain   [J 1445]

The gentle wooing of the "little-earth angel" in the anonymous "Our Idol" from Mary Warner's scrapbook has become dangerously insistent, even rapacious. What emerges is what we might call an "anticonsolation poem," turning the pieties of sentimentalism into a grim Victorian dance of death—though the dance may be more a new-fashioned Viennese waltz than an old-fashioned country jig. Just as Dickinson assumed the role of Moriens in "I heard a Fly buzz—when I died," taking an egocentric liberty that Sigourney would allow only for the ethereal stage of Christian spiritualism that followed actual deathbed scenes (as in her "Voice from the Grave of a Sunday-School Teacher" [*Poems,* 178]), so did Dickinson continue to take an insider's view of her own grand funeral procession:

> Because I could not stop for Death—
> He kindly stopped for me—
> The Carriage held but just Ourselves—
> And Immortality.
>
> We slowly drove—He knew no haste
> And I had put away
> My labor and my leisure too,
> For His Civility—

We passed the School, where Children strove
At Recess – in the Ring –
We passed the Fields of Gazing Grain –
We passed the Setting Sun –

Or rather – He passed Us –
The Dews drew quivering and chill –
For only Gossamer, my Gown –
My Tippet – only Tulle –

We paused before a House that seemed
A Swelling of the Ground –
The Roof was scarcely visible –
The Cornice – in the Ground –

Since then – 'tis Centuries – and yet
Feels shorter than the Day
I first surmised the Horses Heads
Were toward Eternity –   [J 712]

In this poem all the clichés of the sentimental gospel are emptied of their well-intended meanings and become props by which Dickinson constructs a surreal "tribute" to her own special brand of spiritual materialism. Death is a gentleman caller, part suitor and part "usher," observing all the genteel conventions and customary civilities. Yet he is also like the sinister undertaker at the Wilks funeral in *Huckleberry Finn,* who

> slid around in his black gloves with his softy soothering ways, putting on the last touches, and getting people and thing all ship-shape and comfortable, and making no more sound than a cat. He never spoke; he moved people around, he squeezed in late ones, he opened up passage-ways, and done it all with nods and signs with his hands . . . He was the softiest, glidingest, stealthiest man I ever see. [232]

The hearse is euphemistically described as a carriage, and the "dews" that traditionally bead the forehead of the dead become an unhealthy draft of frosty air, like the wind from out of the cloud in Poe's poem "Annabel Lee" that chills and kills his beloved.[28] Consciousness again turns to marble, as the tomb house with its classical cornice is finally reached and Dickinson begins her long wait for reunion with her lover, like the trusting but forsaken heiress of Henry James's *Washington Square.* The poet leaves hanging the question whether her long discipline of a life of willful renunciation, "sumptuous Destitution" (J 1382), and childlike anticipation will be rewarded by the beatific vision of her Master's unveiled face.

The pause before the house in the ground begins to last for centuries, and we do not know if Dickinson is looking back on the road not taken, the road of earthly fulfillment and ordinary marriage, with a despairing sigh of eternal regret or a blissful sigh of heavenly satisfaction. Celestial marriage would be the ultimate validation of her justification through death, the reward of a totally successful *ars moriendi,* but the poem is itself only another dress rehearsal, where the poet is clothed in the scanty cerements of the grave. The light tulle and gossamer of poetry can provide little protection against the frigid assaults of the Spoiler.

"Because I could not stop for Death" ends appropriately enough with a dash, since, as Dickinson wrote in a late lyric (J 1454), death was a hyphen, a mark that could leave the syllables of a word broken and unfinished or connect them to a new meaningful "Compound Vision" (J 906). Materiality can go only so far, and though in many poems Dickinson expressed a confidence about the facts of celestial marriage and a certainty about the life of maturation and passionate domesticity that lay beyond the grave, her deliberate ambiguity here indicates the same shakiness of faith that surrounds the light seen at the end of "I heard a Fly buzz – when I died." Both poems end with a cinemalike fade-out, but whether it is to be followed by a "Hollywood ending" remains moot. Ultimately, "Because I could not stop for Death" presents a devastating triumph of the marmoreal over the corporeal, where the lack of overt fleshly suffering ironically underlines the blunt prophecy of Mary Warner's favorite Christian slogan, "No Cross, no Crown!"

V

Dickinson's appropriation of the props of the Sentimental Love Religion and the popular gospel of consolation involve a process of personalization, internalization, exaggeration, and inversion that can be seen in her responses to other aspects of her contemporary culture. Quite literally, she could not stop with a sentimental punctuation that made the grave a period and the afterlife an apostrophe. Death became an ambiguous hyphen, and paradise, if it existed, could be depicted only by a passionate exclamation point. Yet to use another typographical metaphor current with Dickinson, she "italicizes" images that have been given to her by the roman orthodoxies of her time, taking what is common and ordinary and setting it off in a bold, startling, and structurally independent way. Even her actual funeral was an example of this kind of Emersonian originality, one that selected, transformed, and inverted motifs rather than inventing new ones out of thin air. As Jay Leyda writes:

> The instructions left by Emily Dickinson for her funeral sound like the directions for a pageant of her allegiances. Following her father she was also to avoid the hearse, with its mock solemnity; he had been borne to the graveyard by the professors and successes of Amherst; she asked to be carried by the six Irishmen she had known. Led by Thomas Kelley of the single strong arm, Dennis Scannel, Stephen Sullivan, Patrick Ward, Daniel Moynihan and Dennis Cashman carried Emily Dickinson to the place she still occupies. When Edward Dickinson was buried, the town had closed in his honor, but his daughter's plan was quieter: she asked to be carried out the back door, around through the garden, through the opened barn from front to back, and then through the grassy fields to the family plot, always in sight of the house.[29]

Dickinson was not alone in planning her own obsequies, for the sentimental emphasis on the Victorian panoply of death encouraged such speculations in both high and low. Ann Douglas tells us that the Unitarian minister and novelist Sylvester Judd "left directions for his own laying out: he was arranged for viewing in apparent comfort on his couch, as if in quiet natural slumber" (*Feminization*, 200). Queen Victoria also closely instructed her heirs on the manner of her interment. Interestingly enough, this "Crape Deity," as John Morley calls her, insisted on an all white funeral.[30] Dickinson, who abjured the "Dark Parade" of ebony hearse, tasseled horses, and muffled undertaker – "the Man / Of the Apalling Trade" (J 389) – anticipated royalty by commanding her own dazzling "White Exploit" (J 922). It was certainly no accident that one of the two landscapes that hung in the bedroom of the Amherst recluse was a Currier and Ives engraving of a view of Windsor Castle and Deerpark.[31] Dickinson's funeral was no vulgar spectacle but, as Leyda notes, a "pageant," the mourning procession of a Yankee princess done in early Pre-Raphaelite style. Every detail of the ritual had as many allegorical resonances as did the emblems in a Rossetti painting. In effect it was not only an innovative late Victorian "happening" but Dickinson's last poem, a living witness to her symbolic intent to go "White Unto the White Creator" (J 709), as well as to approach her heavenly lover in the spotless draperies of a spiritual virgin.

Her little white casket was unusually "dainty" (*YH* 2:474), a receptacle ordinarily reserved for young children. This was matched by the

pliant flannel robe especially designed for her by her sister-in-law, Susan, who commented, "When we come into the world we are wrapped
in soft, white flannel, and I think it fitting that we leave it that way,"[32]
making explicit the Victorian resemblance between grave clothes and
baby clothes (Morley, *Death,* 255). T. W. Higginson was permitted to
view the remains and saw their sculptural perfection surmounted by the
marmoreal smile that Sigourney had described in what became her
most famous poem, "Death of an Infant":

> But there beam'd a smile,
> So fix'd, so holy from that Cherub brow,
> Death gazed, and left it there. He dar'd not steal
> The signet-ring of heaven.[33]

Higginson noted in his diary that Dickinson's face showed "a wondrous restoration of youth – she is 54 [55] & looked 30, not a gray hair
or wrinkle, & perfect peace on the beautiful brow. There was a little
bunch of violets at the neck & one pink cypripedium; the sister Vinnie
put in two heliotropes by her hand 'to take to Judge Lord' " (*YH*
2:475). In the language of flowers popular in the ritual of early Victorian courtship, where each flower had a specifically coded meaning,
violets stood for "Faithfulness, Watchfulness, Modesty and Rural Happiness." The cypripedium, a native American wild orchid known more
familiarly as the Lady's Slipper, connoted "Capricious Beauty" and
bore the tantalizing motto, "Win me and wear me." Whereas these two
floral emblems defined the opposite poles of Dickinson's outward personality, shy retirement and jocose playfulness, the two heliotropes
were keys to her inner life. They symbolized Dickinson's "Devotion"
unto death and beyond,[34] making material her private solar myth and
the imagery of the phototropic sunflower turning constantly to follow
the path of its "Lord," the sun, that dominates her poems about spiritual marriage.

The majority of the mourners, like Helen Jameson, found the funeral
to be "poetical" and "unlike any other I ever attended and very beautiful," but a few noted the irregularity of the poet's being carried out of
the rear hall and through the open barn. Eudocia Flynt, reporting on
the gossip attendant on Dickinson's obsequies, two weeks later entered
in her diary these startling facts: "Emily Dickinson's funeral observed,
private, no flowers, taken to the Cemetery – by Irishmen, out of the
back door, across the Fields!! her request – " (*YH* 2:475). Not only was
Dickinson as elusive in death as she had been in life, but she slipped out
the back way of the family homestead, an exit traditionally reserved
only for murderers, reprobates, and outcasts.

In passing out the rear hall through the garden and open barn, Dickenson said a last, symbolic farewell to the flowers and animals she loved, while she simultaneously defied public opinion and renounced the patriarchal house in which she had immured herself for over twenty years, exchanging it for the heavenly house "not made with hands." In her own account of the funeral, Dickinson's niece, Martha Dickinson Bianchi, wrote with seeming extravagance: "On an improvised bier of pine boughs, entirely covered by a pall of blue sand-violets which fell so low they swept the grass on either side as they passed, she was borne in a soft white coffin by laborers, who had all worked upon her father's land and reverenced her almost as the Madonna."[35] Yet in many respects Dickinson's last rites were simply a refinement of the Protestant idol worship encouraged by the popular gospel of consolation, and in essence they were even more feudal than the baronial pomp of the typical Victorian funeral cortege.

Like "A Spider sewed at Night," Dickinson's funeral mixed elite, popular, and folk responses to her culture. Her procession was a "Walking Funeral," favored by the English ecclesiologists with their love of medieval ceremony (Morley, *Death,* 30), but it also had its roots in nonconformist American Puritan traditions (Stannard, *Puritan Way,* 104). Its theatricality was paralleled by the funeral arrangements of the wealthy English eccentric Charles Scarisbeck, who had commissioned the famous Gothic revival architect A. W. Pugin to reconstruct his country house in that style in 1837. As Mark Girouard comments, "In 1860 the corpse of Charles Scarisbeck was carried, as he had directed in his will, in a straight line from the house to the church, across three ditches, a meadow, a wheat field, and a field of cabbages, and through a gap in the presbytery wall which he had ordered to be left open, to the mystification of the workmen, when the wall was built twelve years earlier."[36] Although no walls were left open or knocked down to allow Dickinson to make her unconventional backdoor exit, her obsequies were just as symbolic, courtly, and "sentimental."

Appropriately enough they ended in a mixture of paganism and Christianity, with prayers and recitations of orthodox biblical passages by the clergy balanced against T. W. Higginson's reading of Emily Brontë's poem "Immortality." Beginning with the declaration "No coward soul is mine," this romantic manifesto brashly addresses the "God within the breast" and pantheistically concludes:

> There is not room for Death,
> Nor atom that his might could render void
> Since thou art Being and Breath,
> And what thou art may never be destroyed.[37]

Little did Emily Dickinson's mourners know that in attending these unique services on May nineteenth, 1886, they were "witnessing" the fourth, final, and transfiguring act of a remarkable American *ars moriendi*.

Frazar Stearns. (From William Augustus Stearns, *Adjutant Stearns*, 1862.)

Chapter 3

KINDRED SPIRITS

Dickinson, Stowe, and the Wars of Romance

═══════════

*How, in fact, can we help feeling a vivid sentiment of admiration in
the presence of that high love which neither time nor fortune can
overcome; of that ardor of passion which neither blood nor tears can
extinguish, which survives hope, and which, as a last testimony,
breaks the very portals of the tomb; passion so exalted and superhu-
man, that tradition has been able to express it only with the aid of
the marvellous?*

Orlando Williams Wight

There never was a war that was not inward.

Marianne Moore

*No Romance sold unto
Could so enthrall a Man
As the persual of
His Individual One—
'Tis Fiction's—to dilute to Plausibility
Our Novel—When 'tis small enough
To credit—'Tis'nt true!*

Emily Dickinson

Emily Dickinson subtly personalized her century's conception of the
dead as astral guides and ushers when she wrote, in an undated prose
fragment, "We do not think enough of the Dead as exhilirants—they
are not dissuaders but Lures—Keepers of that great Romance still to us
foreclosed" (*L* 3:919). If in our own time the sweet singer of Amherst
has become a romantic figure, we should not blame early biographers
or modern playwrights. Dickinson was already a living legend when
Mabel Loomis Todd arrived in town in 1881, for a year later she wrote
in her journal that Austin Dickinson's sister was commonly referred to
as "the Myth." She continued:

She has not been out of her house for fifteen years. One inevitably
thinks of Miss Haversham [*sic*] in speaking of her . . . No one *has*

79

seen her in all those years except her own family. She is very brilliant and strong, but became disgusted with society & declared she would leave it when she was quite young. It is hinted that Dr. Holland loved her very much & she him, but that her father who was a stern old New England lawyer & politician saw nothing particularly promising or remarkable in the shy, half-educated boy, & would not listen to her marrying him. [YH 2:377]

As wrong (or as right) as Todd was about the facts in the case of Emily Dickinson, we find here an outline of the public myth of the "White Moth of Amherst" that in turn was based on the poet's own private mythologizing of her self. And if we are interested in an artist's inner sensibility as well as his outer history, in his culture as well as his psychology, the relation of popular conventions to public and private mythmaking may be more important to our total understanding than determining whether during her time at Mount Holyoke Female Seminary Emily Dickinson protested against becoming a Christian or only against fasting on Christmas (see LED 2:360. 18). That she felt she was "standing alone in rebellion," as she wrote to Jane Humphrey in April of 1850 (L 1:94), is enough, even if the conflicting accounts of this incident agree that Dickinson carried out her protest by sitting still rather than dramatically springing to her feet. She struggled in her own way with the vestigial Calvinism that was represented by Mount Holyoke, her father, and, more generally, Connecticut Valley traditions. But her methods of coping – whether they were acceptance, compromise, or defiance – were drawn from the culture of Victorian America, a culture that was itself engaged in coping strategies. Chiefly she had recourse to a Sentimental Love Religion that represented the most popular level of that culture. At this level, death, love, the afterlife, nature, and art were all bound in fealty to the great idea of romance, whether it was found in theology, history, fiction, or real life. It is this concept of romance as a fundamental element of Dickinson's popular culture that I survey in this chapter, as a means of determining the shape and texture of that private mythology[1] which so vitalizes her poetry.

If Mabel Todd inevitably thought of Dickens's fabulous and slightly lunatic Miss Havisham in pondering the mysteries of Dickinson's later life, it is because Dickinson herself thought of George Lewes's *Ranthorpe; or, a Poet's First Struggles* (1847), George Eliot's *The Mill on the Floss* (1860), and Orlando Williams Wight's *Romance of Abelard and Heloise* (1853) as defining certain aspects of her early life:

> Unto my Books – so good to turn –
> Far ends of tired Days –

It half endears the Abstinence –
And Pain – is missed – in Praise –   [J 604)

Of all these "Books of Revelation" (see Appendix A) Wight's florid but
deeply felt retelling of the tale of the famous French lovers would seem
to be the most revealing for an understanding of Dickinson's own
conception of her emotional destiny. In a first chapter significantly
entitled "Genesis," Wight outlines the archetypal nature of this relationship. "Real romance is real history," he declares, since "most of us have
lived a romance more beautiful and pathetic than ever yet has been
described by the pen of man." He continues:

> Experience is the light whereby one is able to read all romantic
> history. We know when the historian writes fiction instead of
> truth, for within us is a test. Truth to life, we demand. The
> romancer must faithfully give us the experience of his own heart,
> or faithfully report the experience of others. Nothing less than the
> history of real life will satisfy us. Truth is stranger than fiction,
> and truth we must have.[2]

The truth of Emily Dickinson's private mythology may seem to us
today to be "stranger than fiction" – indeed, so much so that it is cur-
rently fashionable to dismiss it as either a conscious fable or a psychotic
projection. Yet it is also founded on the truth of inner experience, the
touchstone by which Dickinson as well as Wight tested "the history of
real life," real life in this case being the life of the soul.

I

Dickinson's private myth is easily abstracted from her poetry and her
letters. There is no doubt it was precipitated by that legendary love
affair, occurring sometime in the late 1850s and early 1860s, about
which there has been so much critical speculation yet so little of real and
abiding fact. Certainly, Emily Dickinson found and lost some Master
who was already married and unavailable, whether it was the gruff,
controversial Otis Lord, the dashing and magnetic Samuel Bowles, or
the brooding, scholarly Charles Wadsworth.[3] To this Master Emily
Dickinson was the most devoted of disciples: When he was Christ, she
was a self-sacrificing John or Mary (J 497); when he was king, she was
the servile page or courtier (J 151); when he was the strong and genial
sun, she was the phototropic sunflower, the adoring Daisy who followed lovingly in his steps (J 106). Significantly, in the Victorian language of flowers the daisy was an emblem of innocence. For want of a
more definite attribution and because of the conjunction of "Lord" and

"Sun" imagery that characterizes her love poems as well as that scant but anguished correspondence which centers around this mysterious relationship, the so-called Master letters, I will refer to Dickinson's unknown lover simply as "Phoebus."

The solar myth founded on this relationship, no matter how tenuous or one-sided it may have been in reality, was the most powerful inner fact in the evolution of Dickinson's sensibility. It could justly be called "The Romance of Daisy and Phoebus." I summarize it as follows: An outcast in her own family, unable to share in their crisis conversions to orthodoxy, Daisy becomes a self-proclaimed picaro of the spirit – an orphan, a gypsy, a soul-wanderer. Outwardly submissive but inwardly rebellious, she lives only for her secret art of poetry. Like a peasant girl wooed by a prince in disguise, she falls joyfully in love with Phoebus, a mysterious figure whom she calls "Master," "Savior" (J 217), "Lord," or "Saxon"[4] and around whom she builds a private love religion. On him she centers all the praise and adoration she has withheld from the Puritan God. Phoebus is, however, already committed to a high-born lady as well as to the church, and so their love is necessarily Platonic, never to be consummated on earth. Both Daisy and Phoebus bind themselves to a spiritual marriage that can find fulfillment only in heaven, while Nature itself witnesses and seals their troth. This "natural-law" rather than "common-law" arrangement brings Daisy as much agony as it does ecstasy; she remains faithful to her bond while Phoebus wavers in his attention and then dies, withdraws, or disappears. In a late coda where the masks of "Daisy" and "Phoebus" are dropped, Master is reincarnated in the person of Judge Otis Phillips Lord after he is freed by the death of his wife and Dickinson is freed by the death of her father. Lord proposes marriage, but by this point Dickinson has become so accustomed to her life of "sumptuous Destitution" that she refuses to wed. Lord himself dies, and Dickinson yearns for ultimate satisfaction beyond the grave, though to her dying day she harbors doubts about the validity of her personal version of the Sentimental Love Religion, since its wishful compensations can only be tested by the *peine forte et dure* of death itself.

The first three acts of this admittedly simplistic summary sound like the plot of countless nineteenth-century ballets and operas, with Verdi's *Luisa Miller,* based on Schiller's play, or Adam's *Giselle* seeming the closest parallels. Dickinson admitted that her poems were as "full as Opera" (J 326), but the fourth and final segment, that involving Judge Lord, is subdued and less melodramatic and is more in the style of Mary Wilkins Freeman, especially her famous local-color tale "A New England Nun" (1891) – a title often applied to Dickinson by her early critics. They could see more clearly than we, perhaps, that whether the romance of Dickinson's life – her dream life, her sensibility – was large or small, "high" or "humble," it was still romance:

> Only a Shrine, but Mine –
> I made the Taper shine –
> Madonna dim, to whom all Feet may come,
> Regard a Nun – [J 918]

As noted before, Sandra Gilbert and Susan Gubar have characterized Dickinson's self-shaped myth as a deliberate fiction, identifying it specifically as a Gothic novel (594), and William Shurr has given the myth both detail and cogency in his impressive study of the fascicles. All the Dickinson children engaged in this romantic kind of mythmaking, Lavinia telling dire stories of their father's tyrannical behavior and Austin addressing his mistress, Mabel Loomis Todd, as "my Christ." She replied "Oh! my love, my king! My star and guide and heaven-sent light – Do you not know that my soul is knit to yours by an Almighty hand? Through you I see God" (*LED* 1: 181–2). The rhetoric employed by Austin and Mabel to sanctify their illicit affair may well have been drawn itself from Emily Dickinson's letters, for it was Austin who preserved the drafts of the epistles to Master that are still extant, rescuing them from the general holocaust the poet ordained for all her private correspondence.[5]

This rhetoric of passion, part of the long tradition surveyed by C. S. Lewis in his *Allegory of Love,* was endemic to a romantic age; one could as well find sources for it in the novels of the Brontë sisters so beloved by the poet. The love-sick Jane Eyre, too, calls Mr. Rochester "Master," and confesses that

> My future husband was becoming to me my whole world, and more than the world: almost my hope of heaven. He stood between me and every thought of religion, as an eclipse intervenes between man and the broad sun. I could not, in those days, see God for his creature; of whom I had made an idol. [297]

Shurr has suggested Browning's *Sonnets from the Portuguese,* Longfellow's *Kavanagh,* Thoreau's *A Week on the Concord and Merrimack Rivers,* Coventry Patmore's *Angel in the House,* and Emily Brontë's *Wuthering Heights* as possible analogues for this "central story of nineteenth-century literature, of the marriage made in heaven, prevented on earth, but to be celebrated eternally in heaven" (*Marriage,* 125). No doubt Dickinson saw her impossible situation mirrored in just about any work that moved her deeply, but as the relevance of Longfellow and Thoreau attests, the fact of local color cannot be excluded from Dickinson's reformulation of this archetypal romance of star-crossed lovers. The fact of her New England nurture gave her paradigmatic myth a particularly tart, frostbitten flavor. Moreover, as she matured she was bound to discover that she did not stand entirely alone in her rebellion against the black marble forces of orthodoxy, for certain native and kindred spirits shared her experience, romanticizing in it remarkably similar ways.

Dickinson's personal romance was a unique version of a general cultural conflict between Lockean rationality and the Neoplatonic sensibility that had been raging long before her birth in 1830. Jonathan Edward's use of reason to justify the fundamental irrationality of Calvinist thought in such works as his *Treatise on the Freedom of the Will* (1754) made him the Napoleon of this battle in America, and especially in New England, where the stereotype of "stern old lawyers," politicians, ministers, and deacons became so fixed a convention by 1858 that Oliver Wendell Holmes could openly parody it in his "Logical Story" of the downfall of Calvinist logic, "The Deacon's Masterpiece; or, The Wonderful 'One-Hoss Shay.' "[6] The attenuated rationalism of American Calvinism eventually succumbed to that perfervid renewal of Christian Platonism that I have called a Sentimental Love Religion, but not without a battle – a battle royal, if we include the culminating Armageddon of the Civil War.

Jonathan Edwards in his latter-day role as bogeyman-deacon shaped the inner lives of all those who were forced to endure an orthodox upbringing: Austin Dickinson, for example, speaking of Deacon David Mack, a pillar of the First Congregational Church and a "Puritan of the Puritans," said that after his first sight of him at the age of four, "I thought I had seen God." (*LED* 1:121). Susan Dickinson, remembering Deacon Luke Sweetser's Bible class, recalled that "he weighed down our youthful spirits every Sunday morning with his pictures of ourselves as rebellious sinners in the hands of an avenging God, with possible death before another dawn staring us in the face" (*FF,* 155). With such memories, it is little wonder that Susan Dickinson turned more and more to High Church ritual, thinking at one time late in her life of actually becoming a Roman Catholic and being dissuaded by no less than Bishop F. Dan Huntington, who himself had abandoned Harvard Unitarianism to don the sacerdotal robes of American Anglicanism. Austin Dickinson tried his best to liberalize a First Congregational Church that its own minister claimed was fifty years behind him in thought, eventually turning to the secret cult of passion whose mythic terms had first been formulated by his sister. In borrowing both from Calvinism and from Catholicism, Emily Dickinson disestablished both churches but constructed a dissenting chapel that was as open as all nature. Yet this sanctuary was also so private that it could hold but a single Elect couple within its narrow confines:

> The Sweetest Heresy recieved
> That Man and Woman know –
> Each Other's Convert –
> Though the Faith accommodate but Two –   [J 387]

What was the true nature of Emily Dickinson's "heresy" in founding a Sentimental Love Religion – the First Church of Christ, Naturalist – that was at one and the same time more exclusive than Congregationalism, more Arminian than Unitarianism, more accommodating than Universalism, and more hierarchical than Catholicism? This heresy inevitably returns us to a consideration of the character of the New England deacon, personified in Emily Dickinson's father, Squire Edward Dickinson. Doubtless this lion was not as fierce as he was later painted by his children, yet after one glimpse of his "thin, dry & speechless" figure during a visit with the poet in August of 1870, T. W. Higginson could write his wife, "I saw what her life had been" (*YH* 2:153).

What must Edward Dickinson himself have thought when he read the profile of "Deacon Solomon Jones" in Dr. Josiah Gilbert Holland's *Letter to the Joneses* (first published in Samuel Bowles's *Springfield Republican* in 1863), castigating the effects of a rigid system of family government on his unfortunate children? Josiah Holland knew the Dickinson family well because of his involvement with the *Springfield Republican,* and while there seems to be little basis to Mrs. Todd's suggestion that he was Emily Dickinson's lover, he and his wife remained two of her most intimate correspondents. Surely Emily would have appreciated Holland's sketch of the redoubtable deacon, who tried to dominate the civic and religious life of "Jonesville" as if it were a pocket borough, for Edward Dickinson was himself accused in print of being a "bigot" and a "partisan" (*YH* 2:35). In turn, Holland condemns Jones for browbeating the populace, managing the church, and imposing his opinions on his neighbors until "there was not a man, woman, or child in the village who did not feel your presence as that of an independent, arbitrary power, that permitted no liberty of will around it."[7] And as for the Jones children:

> They did not fear God half so much as they did you, though, if I remember correctly, you represented Him to be a sort of infinite Deacon Solomon Jones . . . They became hypocrites through their fear of you, and they learned to hate you because you persisted in treating them as servile dependents. You put yourself before them and thrust yourself into their life in the place of God.

You bent them to your will with those strong hands of yours and you had "an orderly family." [18]

Edward Dickinson was no such ogre, but he did blight his children's lives, keeping Austin by him in Amherst, prevailing on him not to go West and seek his fortune in a new country by offering the bribes of a share in his law practice, a partnership in his business dealings, and the use of a palatial dwelling built to order on a lot next door to the Homestead (see Appendix B, "Austin Dickinson as connoisseur"). And while single blessedness is no curse, both Emily and her sister Lavinia remained unmarried, one in retreat from the world and one in continual combat with it. Through peer pressure and family "order," all the children joined the church but Emily, Austin being finally persuaded by his fiancée Susan's insistent orthodoxy.

Emily Dickinson did not go the way of Deacon Jones's daughter, who ran off "with one who was not worthy of her," and Austin did not go the way of Jones's son, who "madly became a debauchee, and disgraced your home, and tortured your heart" (24). But to his father's dismay Austin did devote himself to the acquisition of expensive paintings, fast horses, and – eventually – fast women, while Emily Dickinson certainly eloped in spirit, if not in fact, from Squire Dickinson's paternal roof. Holland writes of Miss Jones's defection:

> She did it simply because she found a man who loved her, and gave her the consideration due her as a woman – a love and a consideration which she had never found at home, where she was regarded by you as the dependent servant of your will. She was nothing at home; and badly as she married, she is a better and a freer and a happier woman than she would have been had she continued with you. [25]

Dickinson did choose "to continue," but she also told T. W. Higginson that her father was "too busy with his Briefs – to notice what we do" (L 2:404). In covert defense Emily played the part of the orphan, the gypsy, the little match girl shut out in the cold, or a Jane Eyre threatened by an unfeeling aunt and stupid cousins. Mount Holyoke Female Seminary became Charlotte Brontë's dismal Lowood Academy, and Emily expressed her deep sense of alienation and her inner rebellion in such poems as "They shut me up in Prose" (J 613), "I was the slightest in the House" (J 486), and the cooly defiant

> I'm ceded – I've stopped being Their's –
> The name they dropped upon my face
> With water, in the country church
> Is finished using, now,

And They can put it with my Dolls,
My childhood, and the string of spools,
I've finished threading – too –   [J 508]

In the New England theology, God was a stern father; in New England romance, the father was a stern God. Both paternal figures locked those who dared to stray from their homes, meetinghouses as well as family mansions, outside in the bitter cold of earthly unregeneracy and eternal damnation. I need not rehearse here the well-known story of Dickinson's growing separation from her Puritan faith that began at Mount Holyoke and ended with her withdrawal from Amherst's First Congregational Church. Her apostasy was a gradual one, marked by the growing frequency with which she absented herself from the Communion service. In May of 1874 she wrote to Mrs. Holland, "When a Child and fleeing from Sacrament I could hear the Clergyman saying 'All those who loved the Lord Jesus Christ – were asked to remain' – My flight kept time to the Words" (L 2:524–5). Dickinson's reason for this flight was not that she felt herself to be a bold, incorrigible infidel, but that she believed herself to be unworthy, and so was actually *more* Puritanical than the latter-day Puritans around her. Sure knowledge of the unregeneracy of her own heart was, like the Jansenists' Port Royal, the stronghold of her resistance to false conversions and all-too-easy gracious affections. In 1846 she came as close as she ever was to come toward a true "change of heart"; she wrote Abiah Root, "The few short moments in which I loved my Saviour I would not now exchange for a thousand worlds like this." "But," Dickinson continued,

the world allured me & and in an unguarded moment I listened to her syren voice. From that moment I seemed to lose my interest in heavenly things by degrees . . . I felt my danger & was alarmed in view of it, but I had rambled too far to return & ever since my heart has been growing harder & more distant from the truth & now I have bitterly to lament my folly – & also my own indifferent state at the present time. [L 1:30–1)

In an era of pressure-cooker revivalists like Charles Grandison Finney, Emily Dickinson was a throwback to what Cotton Mather called the "Golden Age," "the First Age" of New England Puritanism. If she were to become a Christian, she would be a primitive rather than a progressive one, and she knew her Jonathan Edwards too well to consider a few fluttering feelings to be the "Divine and Supernatural Light" of true Pauline conversion. From the so-called New Divinity of the New England theology, refined by disciples of Edwards such as Nathaniel Emmons, Samuel Hopkins, and Edwards Park, Dickinson knew that the outstanding characteristic of a genuine crisis conversion was its thoroughly permanent nature.[8] It imparted a sixth, supernatural sense, an amazing grace that signaled that the regenerate had somehow become God-like, and so one of the Elect. Had Dickinson been born into a pre-Edwardsian Puritanism, the very doubt that was so much a part of the manic-depressive syndrome that ruled her emotional life would have been a more acceptable spiritual symptom. No true Saint was ever perfectly sure of his ultimate destiny nor absolutely secure in his election. But Edwards made it painfully clear that the divine and supernatural light of conversion "does not consist of any impression made upon the imagination," since "natural men may have lively impressions on their imaginations; and we cannot determine but the Devil, who transforms himself into an angel of light, may cause imaginations of outward beauty, or visible glory, and of sounds and speeches, and other such things; but these are things of a vastly inferior nature to the spiritual light."[9]

As early as 1846 Dickinson had come to an honest recognition that the feelings in her breast were "lively impressions" rather than "gracious affections," and she decided, like Emerson, to be a true child of the Devil rather than a false daughter of Christ.[10] In March of that year she prefaced her description of an all-too-brief season with the Savior by remarking, "I think of the perfect happiness I experienced while I felt I was an heir of heaven as of a delightful dream, out of which the Evil one bid me wake & again return to the world and its pleasures" (L 1:30). Having been burned once, throughout the 1850s she resisted the series of great "refreshings" that swept Amherst and its environs, leaving her terribly isolated from her classmates, her friends, and her own family:

> But I, grown shrewder – scan the Skies
> With a suspicious Air –
> As Children – swindled for the first
> All Swindlers – be – infer –   [J 476]

Because Dickinson had so scrupulously judged herself, she also remained skeptical of all others in their fashionable rush to climb aboard the glory wagon; in April of 1850 she wryly contrasted her own stubborn stand with that of her social set.

Abby, Mary, Jane, and the farthest of all my Vinnie have been seeking, and they all believe they have found; I can't tell you *what* they have found, but *they* think it is something precious. I wonder if it *is?* How strange is this sanctification, that works such a marvellous change, that sows in such corruption, and rises in golden glory, that brings Christ down, and shews him, and lets him select his friends! [*L* 1:94]

The arch tone is that of a girl who has not been invited to the senior prom, but it also shows the wry satire that would be compressed in the single word "meek" that Dickinson applied to the sleeping Saints, those confident, lamblike "members of the Resurrection" (as if the resurrection were a private club) who in "Safe in their Alabaster Chambers" are not even sure of inheriting the earth. Yet such satire masked a genuine anguish so deep that it can be gauged only by examining Dickinson's poetry against the background of New England romance as it was floridly exemplified in the works of Harriet Beecher Stowe, particularly *The Minister's Wooing* of 1859 and *Oldtown Folks* of 1869. There seems little doubt that Dickinson was familiar with both of these novels, yet in terms of her sensibility it is important to realize that she lived them as well as merely read them.[11]

II

The Minister's Wooing and *Oldtown Folks* tell essentially the same story or relate the same myth, a myth once again based on the facts of life in Puritan New England. A young man dies or is thought to have died without experiencing sanctifying grace. This traumatic event shakes the very basis of orthodox belief in the mind of a "scrupulous soul" who loves him, his mother or his betrothed, and leads her to reject the strict constructions of Puritan doctrine. The Father-God of Calvinism is supplanted by the Brother-Christ of a new Sentimental Love Religion that substitutes incremental goodness (gradualism) for instantaneous perfection (Pauline crisis conversion). Woman becomes a means to salvation, a living gospel, and the purity of romantic love provides a Platonic stairway to heaven replacing what Stowe called the "rungless ladder" of harsh Calvinist dogma. As Gail Parker shrewdly observes, "Sentimentalism restructured the Calvinist mode of salvation, making the capacity to feel, and above all to weep, in itself evidence of redemption."[12]

The actual biographical background of these novels can be traced to the death of Stowe's son in 1857 and that of her sister Catharine Beecher's fiancé, the promising mathematician Alexander Metcalf Fisher, in 1822. Both young men died by drowning, both without publicly professing their faith in God; hence there was no certainty that they had attained salvation. After Catharine Beecher's bereavement, neither her father, Lyman, nor Nathaniel Emmons, who preached the funeral sermon, could assure her that her betrothed was saved. Rather than believe that Fisher had gone to hell, or consider his dire fate God's perverse instrument of her own reclamation, Catharine Beecher rejected the entire theological framework that dictated such harsh alternatives. After an initial "outburst of indignation and abhorrence" in 1836 – the year that Emerson's *Nature* was published – she produced her *Letters on the Difficulties of Religion,* using logic itself to demolish the frightful pseudorationality of Edwards on the will.[13] Dickinson did the same thing in her own deliberately childlike refutation of Calvinism's double-entry bookkeeping:

> You're right – "the way *is* narrow" –
> And "difficult the Gate" –
> And "few there be" – Correct again –
> That "enter in – thereat" –
>
> '*Tis* Costly – So are *purples!*
> 'Tis just the price of *Breath* –
> With but the "Discount" of the *Grave* –
> Termed by the *Brokers* – "*Death*"!
>
> And after *that* – there's Heaven –
> The *Good* Man's "*Dividend*" –
> And *Bad* Men – "go to Jail" –
> I guess –   [J 234]

Harriet Beecher Stowe's reaction to the sudden death of her son was less outwardly dramatic but for precisely that reason more inwardly painful, as her novels amply attest. In *Oldtown Folks,* the theological system preached by old Dr. Stern "was calculated, like a skillful engine of torture, to produce all the mental anguish of the most perfect sense of helplessness with the most torturing sense of responsibility" (403). Yet as Stowe also notes, "it cannot be denied that Nature in her teaching is a more tremendous and inexorable Calvinist that the Cambridge Platform or any other platform that ever was invented" (71). If nature was an "inexorable Calvinist," the horror of its inexorability was the "dry, thin & speechless" calculation of a New England deacon magnified to Michelangelesque proportions:

> It's easy to invent a Life –
> God does it – every Day –
> Creation – but the Gambol
> Of His Authority –
>
> It's easy to efface it –
> The thrifty Diety

Could scarce afford Eternity
To Spontaneity –

The Perished Patterns murmur –
But His Perturbless Plan
Proceed – inserting Here – a Sun –
There – leaving out a Man –   [J 724]

The capricious economy of scarcity that willed the allotment of grace
in the New England theology implied that if God was not a miser he
had to be a monster. Although Stowe's novels are set in a New England fifty to sixty years before Emily Dickinson's religious struggle,
we must remember that they reflect widespread contemporary concerns
that deeply touched all who had been raised in the shadow of Calvinism. Indeed, Stowe refused to publish *Oldtown Folks* in the *Atlantic
Monthly* because of the negative reactions she expected from its conservative and orthodox readers. The Esther Avery of that work is very
like Dickinson in being a daughter of the Puritans, who illustrates that
"moral traits, like physical ones, often intensify themselves in course of
descent, so that the child of a long line of pious ancestry may sometimes suffer from too fine a moral fiber, and become a victim to a
species of morbid *spiritual ideality*" (455). In *The Minister's Wooing*
(1859), the victim of the New England theology's juggernaut is the
morbidly introspective Mrs. Marvyn, who "while her husband was a
deacon of the Church," still

for years, had sat in her pew while the sacramental elements were
distributed, a mournful spectator. Punctilious in every duty, exact, reverential, she still regarded herself as a child of wrath, an
enemy to God, and an heir of perdition; nor could she see any
hope of remedy, except in the sovereign, mysterious decree of an
Infinite and Unknown Power, a mercy for which she waited with
the sickness of hope deferred. [105]

Again we recall Dickinson's flight from the sacrament and such
statements as her lament to Abiah Root, "You are learning control
and firmness. Christ Jesus will love you more. I'm afraid he don't
love me *any!*" (*L* 1:104). Stowe's answer to the catch-22 of Calvinism
was to replace Locke with Plato, the Father-God of Jehovah with the
Brother-God of Christ, New England theology with New England
romance. God himself – the merciful God of the New Testament
rather than the jealous deity of the Decalogue – became the great
maker of romance, and the divine and supernatural flame of Pauline
conversion was softened into the steady glow of gradualism, a "radi-

ance, as when one places a light behind some alabaster screen sculptured with mysterious and holy emblems" (*MW*, 362).

Eventually Esther, who had "passed through two or three periods of revivals of religion, and seen others far less consistent gathered into the folds of the Church," is saved from complete despair by the "conversion" that so altered Emily Dickinson. "Esther's deliverance," writes Mrs. Stowe, "came through that greatest and holiest of all the natural sacraments and means of grace, – LOVE" (*Oldtown Folks*, 481). She finds her salvation in the affection of a "poetic soul, – one of those rare order to whom the love of woman is a religion! – a baptism! – a consecration!" (482). Mrs. Marvyn, too, triumphs over her season in hell, precipitated by the supposed death of her supposedly unregenerated son, James, but she does so only by abandoning rational Calvinism for the Christ-centered gospel of suffering and consolation offered by her black servant, Candace. Even so, her "paroxysms of opposition" (*MW*, 338) against the New England theology chasten her son's fiancée, the stainless Mary Scudder, into a new realization of the shortcomings of orthodoxy. James returns alive, hopeful, and assured of Christ's friendship; Mary's innocence is tempered by experience; the romantic heart triumphs over the rationalistic head.

It was Dickinson's unique fate to play all the victims' roles in Stowe's archetypal New England romance, and play them tragically. She was at one and the same time the suffering Mrs. Marvyn, the lost James, the redeemed Esther, the troubled Mary. Yet the great irony of her private version of this Sentimental Love Religion was that the manic-depressive syndrome that afflicted her before her heterodox conversion to passion was intensified, not pacified, by this new "consecration." Stowe had argued that any romance was better than none at all, for even

> if you awoke bitterly betrayed and deceived, still give thanks to God that you have had one glimpse of heaven. The door now shut will open again. Rejoice that the noblest capability of your eternal inheritance has been made known to you; treasure it, as the highest honor of your being, that ever you could so feel, – that so divine a guest ever possessed your soul. [*MW*, 122]

Dickinson could sometimes agree with this utter self-abnegation, and use the rhetoric of popular revivalism to justify it to her remote Master as well as to herself:

> If I'm lost – now –
> That I was found –
> Shall still my transport be –

That once – on me – those Jasper Gates
Blazed open – suddenly –

That in my awkward – gazing – face –
The Angels – softly peered –
And touched me with their fleeces,
Almost as if they cared –
I'm banished – now – you know it –
How foreign that can be –
You'll know – Sir – When the Savior's face
Turns so – away from you –   [J 256]

Having rid herself of Calvinism's Father-God, Dickinson perversely chose a soul-hero who was in many ways even more tyrannical and remote, more demanding and imperious. The Master of her private mythology offers a love pathetically incapable of fulfillment, inverting the whole morphology of Stowe's Sentimental Love Religion by centering perfection on a male rather than a female figure. Dickinson's conversion was, in her own mind, no doubt a genuine one, yet as we shall see, it promised no deliverance but a continuing captivity narrative of savage intensity. Like Stowe, Dickinson turned to Marianism as a means of solving the spiritual dilemma outlined in *The Minister's Wooing*, for in New England Calvinism, "no rite, no form, no paternal relation, no faith or prayer of church, earthly or heavenly, interposed the slightest shield between the trembling spirit and Eternal Justice," and so the individual "entered eternity alone, as if he had no interceding relation in the universe" (*MW*, 341). The tendency toward Roman Catholic or High Church ritual as a cure for the cold vacancy of the New England theology Marianized the New England girl, elevating her from a Puritan maiden, complete with antique spinning wheel, into a Protestant image of the suffering Virgin.

Thus Mary Scudder cherishes "an old engraved head of one of the Madonnas of Leonardo da Vinci" and feels "the seaworn picture as a constant vague inspiration" (*MW*, 250). "We, that have seen pictures," Stowe writes, "think, as we look on her girlish face, with the lines of statuesque beauty, on the tremulous, half-infantine expression of her lovely mouth, and the general air of simplicity and purity, of some old pictures of the girlhood of the Virgin" (19). After James's supposed death transforms Mary into "a sanctified priestess of the great worship of sorrow," her Catholic friend, Madame de Frontingnac, sees "something so sacred in the expression of Mary's face that [she] crossed herself, as she had been wont before a shrine" (385). James confesses that her "image had stood between me and low, gross vice" (70), and it is Mary's "creative presence" as a "soul-artist" that leads him gradually but surely to an operable Christian faith. While Stowe's Sentimental Love Religion parodies the patriarchal nature of Calvinism by caricaturing its God as a dessicated New England deacon, it affirms the matriarchal amplitude of the New Testament by extending the dogma of the immaculate conception to *all* women. To be born female is to be born a sinless evangelist. Even the cynical Miles Coverdale of Nathaniel Hawthorne's *Blithedale Romance* admits that

> I have always envied the Catholics their faith in that sweet, sacred Virgin Mother, who stands between them and the Deity, intercepting somewhat of His awful splendor, but permitting His love to stream upon the worshipper, more intelligibly to human comprehension, through the medium of a woman's tenderness.[14]

It was Dickinson's fate in her special inversion of this hagiolatry not only to be the innocent victim of a wrathful Calvinist Jehovah but to be caught, as a suffering Mater Dolorosa, between her lover and his God. Dickinson becomes in her poems not the sweet Virgin protector of the Holy Family, but the bereaved, anguished Mother of the crucified Christ. Her lot was to pass directly from an angelic annunication of romantic love to the sorrowful mysteries of Golgotha and the deposition from the cross. She endured like the Mary of the Gospels a pietà, an inward crucifixion:

> That I did always love
> I bring thee Proof
> That till I loved
> I never lived – Enough –
>
> That I shall love alway –
> I argue thee
> That love is life –
> And life hath Immortality –
>
> This – dost thou doubt – Sweet –
> Then have I
> Nothing to show
> But Calvary –   [J 549]

Hawthorne's attraction toward Marianism (best expressed through the figure of Hilda in *The Marble Faun*) led his daughters eventually to become nuns, one Catholic and one Episcopalian. Dickinson, cloistered within her father's house, took instead the white veil of a spiritual Carmelite:

> A solemn thing – it was – I said –
> A Woman – white – to be –

And wear – if God should count me fit –
Her blameless mystery – [J 271]

Orlando Wight's *Romance of Abelard and Heloise* provides a historical
frame for this leaning toward monasticism; if earthly marriage is impossible, spiritual marriage in heaven is seen as the natural alternative.
Wight observes of his medieval lovers that

> separation having become necessary, the convent was an asylum,
> sure and sacred, where each of them might carry a thought with
> which could never be associated any other image than that of
> God. In pronouncing the same religious vows, they renounced,
> for heaven, their conjugal tie, which seemed broken upon earth.
> [234]

The "conjugal tie" between Dickinson and Phoebus was a marriage in
name only, a vow or a "troth" rather than a true nuptial. Even so,
Dickinson was ready to sacrifice her sexual identity itself in order to
fulfill the terms of this rigid contract. Like Abelard, who suffered the
ignominy of castration at the hands of his enemies, she found that her
love transcended the body:

> Rearrange a "Wife's" affection!
> When they dislocate my Brain!
> Amputate my freckled Bosom!
> Make me bearded like a man!
>
> Blush, my spirit, in thy Fastness –
> Blush, my unacknowledged clay –
> Seven years of troth have taught thee
> More than Wifehood ever may!
>
> Love that never leaped its socket –
> Trust entrenched in narrow pain –
> Constancy thro' fire – awarded –
> Anguish – bare of anodyne!
>
> Burden – borne so far triumphant –
> None suspect me of the crown,
> For I wear the "Thorns" till *Sunset* –
> Then – my Diadem put on.
>
> Big my Secret but it's *bandaged* –
> It will never get away
> Till the Day its Weary Keeper
> Leads it through the Grave to Thee. [J 1737]

Dickinson's use of the language of courtly love in her poems about this kind of spiritual marriage is justified by Wight's affirmation that "woman asks no more in this world than to be sincerely loved. When she is queen of one devoted heart, then she has a kingdom that sufficeth for her ambition" (*Abelard and Heloise,* 13). Given our own century's increasing attention to the spiritual and legal liberation of women, such a sentiment today may seem anathema. Yet we must accept it as a fact of nineteenth-century sensibility, accelerated by Victorian materialism and its marmoreal possessiveness. If we *do* entertain the romantic idea that love, passionate love, is the sole province of woman, two puzzles about Emily Dickinson's private mythology find a general answer. First of all, her philosophy of renunciation can be understood not as an exercise in masochism but as an extraordinary act of faith. Wight helps us to see this when he inquires into the source of Heloise's power as an artist, which derives from deprivation rather than fulfillment. Had she been allowed to live an ordinary domestic existence,

> the love of Heloise would have occupied her whole life; she would have remained enveloped in the mysterious joys of the connubial state and in the tranquil sweets of maternity. Like so many other females, she would have borne to the tomb the secret of that divine force which was given her, and of that admirable sentiment which *believes all, hopes all, suffers all.* A misfortune has revealed to us that secret, and that misfortune has made us admire all the treasures concealed in her soul. She has been made a queen by a crown of thorns. [242]

This crown of thorns would be exchanged for a queenly "Diadem" in the heaven to come, but in the meantime, as "Rearrange a 'Wife's' affection" shows, it entailed a "sad and bitter royalty!" (Wight, *Abelard and Heloise,* 242). The idea that it is only through suffering that we achieve transcendence is again consummately romantic. But what role did Phoebus play in Dickinson's adaptation of this central romantic myth? No critic or biographer has been able to identify with certainty the Master who so engaged Dickinson's heart in the late 1850s and early 1860s; save for the revelation of her late love for Otis Phillips Lord, she has managed to keep her secret "bandaged" to this day. Still the character of Phoebus, at least as it was understood by Dickinson, is to some extent glossed by Wight's portrait of Abelard the lover:

> This complete forgetfulness of self, the generous abdication of her own personality, which places Heloise in turn in the rank of superior souls, is also a kind of valuable index for understanding Abelard. What kind of a man must he have been who, with one word,

irrevocably fixed the destiny of the first woman of her century?
He shows himself, he calls her: Here I am, Heloise responds; and
from her virginal sphere she descends toward him, as upon an
inclined plane. If any thing can give us a just idea of his merit, it is
surely the violent and enduring love with which he inspired Heloise. She would not have made an ordinary man her God. [231–2]

Phoebus was no ordinary man; neither was Charles Wadsworth, nor
Samuel Bowles, nor Otis Lord. All were "superior souls," and the doctrine of Platonic love bound Dickinson to each of them. She consciously
chose the genre that exalted this Sentimental Love Religion over a mundane, drab reality. Dickinson preferred romance to novel, heart to head,
the inner to the outer (J 451). That this romance also had its dark side was
a fact she was willing to accept as long as she could express such darkness
in the extravagant terms of Gothicism. Even so, she internalized the
haunted abbeys and frowning châteaus of Poe and Radcliffe in such
poems as

> One need not be a Chamber – to be Haunted –
> One need not be a House –
> The Brain has Corridors – surpassing
> Material Place – [J 670]

As we shall see, Dickinson remained a romantic in an age that surely
and steadily tended toward economy of plot and realism of description.
It was for this reason that she wrote to T. W. Higginson in December
of 1879, commenting on his recently published *Short Studies of American
Authors,* that while "Hawthorne appalls, entices," one "hesitate[s]" in
considering the worth of Howells and James (*L* 2:649). There is no
doubt that in spite of her own bent toward playfulness and parody, she
would have been horrified at Mark Twain's savage retelling of the
"Story of Abelard" and his dismissal of its "nauseous sentimentality" in
his 1869 *The Innocents Abroad.* Yet much of Twain's bitterness flowed
from the fact that he himself had once been seduced by the tale's high
romance. Dickinson's sensibility, her mythology, and her literary preferences were formed long before the Civil War; although she continued
to read current fiction and poetry after it, unlike Twain she remained in
essence an Old Believer.

III

Her literary conservatism explains why Emily Dickinson cannot be
classed with the practitioners of what Nina Baym has called "women's
fiction": female writers who countered the sentimental insistence on

woman's "bondage to sex" by urging them on to independence, strength of mind, and a new freedom of the will.[15] Dickinson was suspicious of women reformers, and her excessive gentility was offended by militant feminism; as for "freedom of the will," she had long ago, like Catharine Beecher, slain that theological dragon and substituted for it a romantic submission to the divine will of Phoebus. It was on the will especially that New England romance focused, simply because "Edwards on the Will" had become the cornerstone of New England theology.

Stowe set *The Minister's Wooing* in colonial Newport and chose to revolve its anguished plot around the figure of the Reverend Samuel Hopkins, a keen disciple of Edwards. Hopkins developed the scrupulosity of New England Calvinism to an undreamed-of excess, summed up in the phrase "Willingness to be Damned." He maintained that damned natural men should praise God for his infinite mercy in saving even a small portion of the human race from the hellfire deserved by all, and that even a regenerate Saint should be willing to be condemned to hell if such sacrifice would satisfy the needs of "Being in General."

There is certainly a hint of this kind of ultimate submission in Dickinson's use of the mortuary formula, "Was he (or she) willing to die?" for here in one paradoxical dogma were embodied both the cruelty and the idealism of the New England theology. Yet the same impossible double bind was transferred piecemeal to Dickinson's private mythology, since when it did not eventuate in marriage, Stowe's New England romance became of necessity a drama of self-sacrificial martyrdom. As she writes of such upward-seeking benevolence in *The Minister's Wooing,* "Every impulse of beauty, of heroism, and every craving for purer love, fairer perfection, nobler type and style of being than that which closes like a prison-house around us, in the dim, daily walk of life, is God's breath, God's impulse, God's reminder to the soul that there is something higher, sweeter, purer, yet to be attained" (121). In like Platonic moods, Dickinson could agree:

> Through the strait pass of suffering –
> The Martyrs – even – trod.
> Their feet – upon Temptation –
> Their faces – upon God –
>
> A stately – shriven – Company –
> Convulsion – playing round –
> Harmless – as streaks of Meteor –
> Upon a Planet's Bond –
>
> Their faith – the everlasting troth –
> Their Expectation – fair –

> The Needle – to the North Degree –
> Wades – so – thro' polar Air!   [J 792]

Yet when her Master himself became a doubting Thomas (*L* 2:373), no
scanning of "martyrs albums" (J 38) could alleviate the bitterness of a
dream destroyed:

> I took one Draught of Life –
> I'll tell you what I paid –
> Precisely an existence –
> The market price, they said –
>
> They weighed me, Dust by Dust –
> They balanced Film with Film,
> Then handed me my Being's worth –
> A single Dram of Heaven!   [J 1725]

Such is the terrible irony of Emily Dickinson's private myth of romance. For though it appropriated the outward emblems of the new
Sentimental Love Religion, it did not free her from the internal conflict
of the New England theology: its manic-depressive syndrome of bitter
self-recrimination on one hand and what Stowe described as "mysterious elevations of faith and reactions of confiding love" (*MW*, 338) on
the other. This fever of belief was bound to have its crisis, and that
crisis coincided with the general trauma of the American Civil War.
Although Dickinson wrote T. W. Higginson, newly enlisted in the
Union army, "War feels to me an oblique place" (*L* 2:423), the bloody
angle of national discord touched her most deeply on her own home
grounds – those of the interior life:

> To fight aloud, is very brave –
> But *gallanter,* I know
> Who charge within the bosom
> The Cavalry of Wo –   [J 126]

The War between the States was another outward and visible sign of
Dickinson's own silent and inner torment, which had begun long before
the firing on Fort Sumter. It brought all the opposites of her consciousness
together in a fierce conjunction that could truly be called "metaphysical."
As Daniel Aaron has written, "Far from drawing her from her seclusion, it
drove her farther into herself. Yet isolation did not signify indifference.
The War inflamed her imagination, illuminated old enigmas, touched her
deeper sympathies."[16] Elizabeth Stuart Phelps, who was to merge New
England romance with the popular gospel of consolation in her best-
selling secularized version of heaven, *The Gates Ajar,* asked: "Is there not
an actual, occult force in the existence of a general grief? It swells to a tide

whose invisible flow covers all the little resistance of common, human joyousness. It is like a material miasma. The gayest man breathes it, if he breathes at all; and the most superficial cannot escape it."[17] Dickinson was far from superficial, and about 1864 she noted in a letter to her Norcross cousins that "sorrow seems more general than it did, and not the estate of a few persons, since the war began; and if the anguish of others helped one with one's own, now would be many medicines" (L 2:436). Again the irony was that while romance swept the field of her surrounding culture, and the Sentimental Love Religion eventually triumphed, Dickinson suffered a devastating defeat and had to endure a painful "Reconstruction" of her singular private mythology.

The American call to arms gave the sentimental gospel of love and consolation a strident urgency, imparting to it the flavor of a holy war. Dickinson had always been fond of martial imagery, and her early poetry is full of the pomp and circumstance of military glory:

> How many *Bullets* bearest?
> Hast Thou the Royal scar?
> Angels! Write "Promoted"
> On this Soldier's brow!   [J 73]

In this preference, Dickinson was little different from her orthodox contemporaries who also applauded the patriotic hero, whether celebrated or unsung. One of the most famous and popular of Victorian hymns was Sabine Baring-Gould's "Onward, Christian Soldiers" of 1865, in which Christ becomes "the royal Master," but it was only the culmination of a long tradition linking Christianity with both martyrdom and militarism. The theme of battle is a popular one in Mary Warner's scrapbook; it contains on page 21 a poem "by an American" entitled "Balaklava," which an unknown editor assures us is "greatly superior to Tennyson's 'Charge of the Light Brigade,' and equal, in our opinion, to Halleck's 'Marco Bozzaris' " (another Dickinson favorite). There is also a poem titled "On the Death of Napoleon" (16), a humorous sketch of a "Battle Incident" (8), and a poem called "After the Battle" excerpted from *Chamber's Journal*. The anonymous poem entitled "No Cross, no Crown!" on page 17 begins with a melancholy student who in a dream vision sees

> Prophets, Martyrs crucified:
> Stern Patriots, who for Freedom died;
> And Poets, who died desolate,
> Scanning the wondrous scroll of Fate;
> While glory round their foreheads shone,
> He read upon their lips of stone –
> No Cross, no Crown!

and concludes:

> This be the motto of the brave
> And this the watchword of the slave;
> The Patriot's, with the people's scorn;
> The Martyr's with his garland's thorn.
> Whoever seeks to win a name,
> Whoever toils for Freedom's fame,
> Whoever human tears would dry,
> Let this forever be his cry –
> No Cross, no Crown!

In contrast, Dickinson's curiosity about the nature of the regminental promotion conferred by the mandated slaughter of brother by brother took on a violent, obsessive quality. The loss or defection of Master led to a breakdown that John Cody has labeled psychotic,[18] as the New England theology and her own private passion wound the strings of her soul to the snapping point. To appropriate the words that Elizabeth Stuart Phelps wrote about her own mother, whose work was known to Dickinson, "She lived one of those rich and piteous lives such as only gifted women know; torn by the civil war of the dual nature which can be given to women only" (*Chapters*, 12). Dickinson loved and lost, and in doing so she almost lost the very mind that had given Master such vibrant significance. Her own dual nature learned that there also could be two kinds of death, inner and outer, and two kinds of graves to contain them:

> The Color of the Grave is white –
> The outer Grave – I mean –
>
> . . . .
>
> The Color of the Grave within –
> The Duplicate – I mean –
> Not all the Snows c'd make it white –
> Not all the Summers – Green –   [J 411]

As the South withdrew from the Union, so did Master leave for parts unknown, probably not without a sense of relief that he was escaping such an all-devouring passion. But Dickinson was still a slave to her religion of romance; only death could emancipate her. Sometime she thought of herself as a dungeoned captive, similar to Byron's "Prisoner of Chillon" (*L* 2:374). Like Emerson's genius-poet, she could take the word "Abolition" from the civil debate whirling around the fact of slavery and turn it into a private and resonant symbol (J 306). More often, however, she played the role of martyr-poet. She was the spartan heroine of a Children's Crusade, a shrinking Daisy who "never flinched thro' that awful parting, but held her life so tight [Master] should not see the wound" (L 2:391). Or posing both as the consumptive maiden of consolation verse and as the innocent victim of an unprovoked gue-rilla attack, she complained, "I've got a cough as big as a thimble – but I don't care for that – I've got a Tomahawk in my side but that don't hurt me much. Her master stabs her more – " (L 2:392).

Long before the end of the war Dickinson had listed herself as miss-ing in action, for psychically she did experience a temporary death:

> 'Twas fighting for his Life he was –
> That sort accomplish well –
> The Ordnance of Vitality
> Is frugal of it's Ball.
>
> It aims once – kills once – conquers once –
> There is no second War
> In that Campaign inscrutable
> Of the Interior.   [J 1188]

In an undated prose fragment she wrote: "Tis a dangerous moment for any one when the meaning goes out of things and Life stands straight – and punctual – yet no signal comes. Yet such moments are. If we sur-vive them they expand us, if we do not, but that is Death, whose if is everlasting" (L 3:919). For the duration of the Great Rebellion, Dickin-son stood rigidly at attention, giving only the most objective reports of her psychological and spiritual status – her name, rank, and serial num-ber – in such remarkable poems as "After great pain, a formal feeling comes" (J 341). Yet even in collapse Dickinson clung, like the Confed-eracy, to her tattered aristocratic code, taking as her heroes those doomed and noble knights whose names and deeds would echo through Southern fiction down to the time of William Faulkner. Ro-land at Roncesvalles and the Chevalier Bayard had firm niches in her private pantheon of anguish:

> Success is counted sweetest
> By those who ne'er succeed.
> To comprehend a nectar
> Requires sorest need.
>
> Not one of all the purple Host
> Who took the Flag today
> Can tell the definition
> So clear of Victory
>
> As he defeated – dying –
> On whose forbidden ear

The distant strains of triumph
Burst agonized and clear!   [J 67]

If the Civil War forced Dickinson to confront her complex relationship
to a Christ-like Master, it also pitted the last vestiges of patriarchal Calvinism against the new legions that preached matriarchal romance, the sentimental gospel of love. The nation had to choose between the two Christs
of Julia Ward Howe's "Battle Hymn of the Republic." One was "born
among the lilies" with a transfiguring, almost feminine beauty; the other
"tramp[led] out the vintage" of divine wrath on a treasonous conspiracy,
like the Christ of Jonathan Edwards's hellfire-and-brimstone sermons,
who crushed sinners under his feet without mercy, sprinkling his pure
garments with their blood. If "Our God" was indeed "marching on,"
what kind of a God was he, and where was he marching to?[19]

Like the Wars of the Roses in Shakespeare's history plays, the
American Civil War provided an epic background for the acting out of
these intense wars of romance, both public and private. The conflict
between the deacon and the Madonna was as irrepressible as that between Free Soil and the cotton kingdom, and its outcome was just as
predictable. The New England theology could withstand a few isolated
cases of scrupulous rebellion, but how could it face the loss of an entire
generation of young men who in sacrificing their lives on the altar of
their country, simultaneously condemned themselves to eternal hellfire
and damnation, all for the lack of a public profession of religion? Such a
slaughter made even the antique liberalism of the Half Way Covenant
seem tyrannicial; the stakes of salvation were now an all-or-nothing,
eternal life or eternal death proposition. As Elizabeth Stuart Phelps
remembered, "Our country was dark with sorrowing women . . . Our
gayest scenes were black with crape" (*Chapters,* 96). Assuming the
pensive pose of a New England Virgin Mary, she continued:

> It came to seem to me, as I pondered these things in my own
> heart that even the best and kindest forms of our prevailing beliefs
> had nothing to say to an afflicted woman that could help her
> much. Creeds and commentaries and sermons were made by
> men. What tenderest of men knows how to comfort his own
> daughter when her heart is broken? What can the doctrines do for
> those desolated by death? They were chains of rusty iron, eating
> into raw hearts. The prayer of the preacher was not much better;
> it sounded like the language of an unknown race to a despairing
> girl. Listen to the hymn. It falls like icicles on snow. Or, if it
> happen to be one of the old genuine outcries of the church, sprung
> from real human anguish or hope, it maddens the listener, and she
> flees from it, too sore a thing to bear the touch of holy music. [98]

The needs were manifest, and urgent: to know with as much surety
as was humanly possible the destiny of these murdered souls, and to
console with equal compassion those women left to mourn them. Such
needs – the passions to know, to be sure, to remember – pushed the
corporeality of the Victorian gospel of death to new heights of materialism. In this bloodiest, most mechanized of modern wars, where as
Melville observed, "all went on by crank, / Pivot, and screw, / And
calculations of caloric,"[20] it is no accident that the technology of embalming gained wide acceptance. Thomas H. Holmes, who invented a
fluid that would preserve bodies "forever, or at least as long as stone,"
first gained fame as the embalmer of several eminent war officers,
whose funerals were national events.[21] Preservation of the flesh as a
means of ascertaining the "physiognomy" of one's spiritual state was
matched by the widespread use of photography. A host of Daguerrean
"operatives" captured the features of enlisted men on sensitized tablets,
which themselves became treasured keepsakes, locked away in little
caskets of velvet, gilt, leather, or ebonized gutta-percha.

For much of the war, Emily Dickinson was technically *hors de
combat,* her spiritual wounding having culminated in the actual physical failure of her eyesight. This problem necessitated an unusual stay
with her Norcross cousins for most of 1864 and 1865, in order to
consult a well-known Cambridge physician who specialized in diseases
of the eye. Whether or not we believe her condition to have been
psychosomatic, Dickinson knew who was responsible for her traumatic loss of vision. Master had put out her eye with his blinding
image of romantic love (J 327), and so, in a characteristic reversal of
male–female roles, she had to play Samson at the mill wheel. Again
she was forced to justify her martyrdom, to sift herself and all kindred
spirits for some clue about the meaning and magnitude of their sacrifice. The task was all the more terrifying because she had to do it in
the dark. Yet Stowe had written significantly that once sanctified by
personal romantic experience, no matter how pathetic, "if we use
them wisely, our eyes will ever after be anointed to see what poems,
what romances, what sublime tragedies lie around us in the daily walk
of life; 'written not with ink but in fleshy tablets of the heart' " (*MW,*
122–3).

IV

For Dickinson, all of these concerns were epitomized by the early death
of the son of the president of Amherst College. Frazar Stearns was
killed at the battle of Newbern, March fourteenth, 1862, but Dickinson
seems to have marked him out as doomed in the equivocal New Year's

greeting she sent to her Norcross cousins on December thirty-first, 1861. Reporting in florid terms another local tragedy, she wrote:

> Mrs. Adams had news of the death of her boy, to-day, from a wound at Annapolis. Telegram signed by Frazer Stearns. You remember him. Another one died in October – from fever caught in the camp. Mrs. Adams herself has not risen from bed since then. "Happy New Year" step softly over such doors as these! "Dead! Both her boys! One of them shot by the sea in the East, and one of them shot in the West by the sea" . . . Christ be merciful! Frazer Stearns is just leaving Annapolis. His father has gone to see him to-day. I hope that ruddy face won't be brought home frozen. Poor little widow's boy, riding to-night in the mad wind, back to the village burying-ground where he never dreamed of sleeping! Ah! the dreamless sleep! [L 2:386]

Dickinson's sentimental language here follows the conventions of the Victorian *ars moriendi,* while at the same time it betrays a bizarre kind of death wish in relation to Stearns himself. The Gothic melodrama of her lament for the "Poor little widow's boy," with whom as a spiritual orphan she identified herself, is eclipsed by her chill vision of the "frozen" face of Frazar Stearns, converting him into one of those marble figurines of the early dead that we have seen were a staple of popular consolation verse. Dickinson's premonition was to prove only too true, and in late March of 1862 she sent an unusually detailed letter to her inquisitive cousins summarizing in her own unique way the gossip and newspaper accounts that described the death and burial of this young Amherst hero. Her words preserve the iconic significance of Frazar Stearns's life and death as effectively as Thomas Holmes's patent embalming fluid, "Inominata," turned the corpses of Civil War heroes into everlasting stone. Not only does this curious document show Dickinson's vicarious participation in the great conflict between North and South, but its calculated idol worship demonstrates that Stearns had somehow become a symbol of her own assassinated selfhood. I take the liberty of quoting this remarkable letter at length:

> Dear Children,
>   You have done more for me – 'tis the least I can do, to tell you of brave Frazer – "killed at Newbern," darlings. His big heart shot away by a "minie ball."
>   I had read of those – I didn't think that Frazer would carry one to Eden with him. Just as he fell, in his soldier's cap, with his sword at his side, Frazer rode through Amherst. Classmates to the right of him, and classmates to the left of him, to guard his

narrow face! He fell by the side of Professor Clark, his superior officer – lived ten minutes in a soldier's arms, asked twice for water – murmured just, "My God!" and passed! Sanderson, his classmate, made a box of boards in the night, put the brave boy in, covered with a blanket, rowed six miles to reach the boat, – so poor Frazer came. They tell that Colonel Clark cried like a child when he missed his pet, and could hardly resume his post. They loved each other very much. Nobody here could look on Frazer – not even his father. The doctors would not allow it.

The bed on which he came was enclosed in a large casket shut entirely, and covered from head to foot with the sweetest flowers. He went to sleep from the village church. Crowds came to tell him good-night, choirs sang to him, pastors told him how brave he was – early-soldier heart. And the family bowed their heads, as the reeds the wind shakes.

So our part in Frazer is done, but you must come next summer, and we will mind ourselves of this young crusader – too brave that he could fear to die. We will play his tunes – maybe he can hear them; we will try to comfort his broken-hearted Ella, who, as the clergyman said, "gave him peculiar confidence" . . . Austin is stunned completely. Let us love better, children, it's most that's left to do. [L 2:397–8]

The details of young Stearns's death, including his portentous last words, are related as clinically and as mordantly as any sentimental eulogist could wish, yet this spiritual autopsy fails to answer the paramount question posed by the orthodox Calvinist: "Was he willing to die"? Dickinson's elaborate report on Stearns's last hours and his elaborate funeral rites indicates an unquenchable desire to unlock the secrets of his very soul, to pry open that "large casket shut entirely, and covered from head to foot with the sweetest flowers," to stare directly upon the marmoreal face of death. Stearns becomes in Dickinson's transmutation a white knight, a Galahad or Parsifal who is now the object of a private cult of reverie:

> Bless God, he went as soldiers,
> His musket on his breast –
> Grant God, he charge the bravest
> Of all the martial blest!
>
> Please God, might I behold him
> In epauletted white –
> I should not fear the foe then –
> I should not fear the fight!   [J 147]

Her brother Austin seemed to take the blow as personally as she did, for in a letter written about the same time to Samuel Bowles, Dickinson confessed that "Austin is chilled – by Frazer's murder – He says – his Brain keeps saying over 'Frazer is killed' – 'Frazer is killed,' just as Father told it – to him. Two or three words of lead – that dropped so deep, they keep weighing – "(L 2:399). Whether or not her plea to Bowles that he tell Austin "how to get over" the trauma of these words was a cryptic request for consolation, using (as Thomas Johnson suggests), her brother's name as a "cover," Frazar Stearns's death epitomized the crisis of failure in Dickinson's private inversion of New England romance. His "murder" paralleled hers, for about 1861 she wrote to Master: "If you saw a bullet hit a bird – and he told you he was'nt shot – you might weep at his courtesy, but you would certainly doubt his word. One drop more from the gash that stains your Daisy's bosom – then would you *believe?*" (L 2:373). Dickinson's assurance that Stearns had achieved some kind of spiritual victory, symbolized by her image of the young man being received into Eden with the fatal minie ball still inside his breast, like a shining and interior red badge of courage, was tied to her own hope that she would somehow achieve fulfillment, decoration, and distinction in heaven. Yet in imaginatively resolving Stearns's destiny by identifying with his fate, she was forced to share his entombment as well as his resurrection. Just as she had deified herself as a New England madonna, so did she secularize Frazar Stearns as a latter-day Christ. The account of his passing sent to the Norcross cousins is her terse retelling of the passion according to Saint Matthew, as Frazar cries out for water, questions his god, suffers on the cross of war, and becomes the rigid centerpiece of a military pietà.

Following Stearns's funeral procession not only in her heart but in her soul and in her mind, Dickinson became one with what Oliver Wendell Holmes called "This martyr generation" (*Works,* 266). In a poem that repeated the deadening effect of the news of Stearns's death on her brother's startled consciousness, she tried to "school" herself to the surprise, set in mental block type, of the first grim dispatch – "Killed at Newbern":

> It dont sound so terrible – quite – as it did –
> I run it over – "Dead", Brain, "Dead."
> Put it in Latin – left of my school –
> Seems it dont shriek so – under rule.   [J 426]

A full dress rehearsal of Stearns's obsequies entailed her own descent into the Valley of the Shadow, which now included psychological as well as physical death:

I felt a Funeral, in my Brain,
And Mourners to and fro
Kept treading – treading – till it seemed
That Sense was breaking through –

And when they all were seated,
A Service, like a Drum –
Kept beating – beating – till I thought
My Mind was going numb –

And then I heard them lift a Box
And creak across my Soul
With those same Boots of Lead, again,
Then Space – began to toll,

As all the Heavens were a Bell,
And Being, but an Ear,
And I, and Silence, some strange Race
Wrecked, solitary, here –

And then a Plank in Reason, broke,
And I dropped down, and down –
And hit a World, at every plunge,
And Finished knowing – then –   [J 280]

The drums of a wartime funeral service merge with the tolling bells of simple village rites to produce a surreal cacophony, a Dead March that grates upon the very soul. External and internal death are merged, and though Dickinson "finishes knowing," we are left with the same ambiguity that obscures meaning at the end of "I head a Fly buzz – when I died." Whether an ultimate knowledge of an individual's destiny is gained or lost, what swallows up all exegesis is the very terror of the question itself. Once again, Harriet Beecher Stowe provides us with a key to the psychic power of this poem, when in *The Minister's Wooing* she describes Mrs. Marvyn's Calvinist sense of the abyss while pondering the fate of her lost son:

> Thus it happened, that, while strong spirits walked, palm-crowned, with victorious hymns, along these sublime paths, feebler and more sensitive ones lay along the track, bleeding away in lifelong despair . . .
>
> This, then, was the awful dread which was constantly underlying life. This it was which caused the tolling bell in green hollows and lonely dells to be a sound which shook the soul and searched the heart with fearful questions. And this it was that was lying with a mountain weight on the soul of the mother, too keenly

agonized to feel that doubt in such a case was any less a torture than the most dreadful certainty. [*MW*, 340–1)

In the excruciating largo that is "I felt a Funeral, in my Brain," Dickinson like Stowe's bewildered individual soul enters eternity alone, with "no interceding relation in this universe" save the sepulchral figure of Silence, veiled and with its fingers to its lips.[22] What made Frazar Stearns's obsequies so important to the poet was that he, too, was a manic-depressive of the spirit, a victim of the New England theology. Her longing to rehearse his sacrifice, embalm his memory, and envision him in paradise was an attempt to create a ritual that would ameliorate the terrible migraine of Calvinist doctrine that had tormented them both. Again, this compensatory ritual is very material and very High Church; it combines the clanging militancy of Tennyson's "Charge of the Light Brigade" with the rolling organ tones of his elegaic "In Memoriam," and through it Stearns becomes more than a kindred spirit.[23] Like a Catholic saint who has suffered martyrdom, Stearns in turn intercedes for Dickinson with the remote God who has both blessed and blasted her with the divine and supernatural light of romance. In an inversion of traditional biblical typology, Frazar Stearns and Jesus Christ are now shadows, types of which the poet herself is an antitype: the queen of Calvary.

V

The sources for Dickinson's apotheosis of Frazar Stearns are once again popular and public; they can all be found in their orthodox forms in a memorial volume published by President Stearns in the year of his son's death. This small keepsake, entitled *Adjutant Stearns* and adorned with a frontispiece engraved from a daguerreotype of the dead hero in his uniform, records such praises as Professor Tyler's encomium that "few persons of his age have ever won a better title to the description of the chevalier, who was known as the knight without fear and without reproach."[24] Here too we confirm that the news of Stearns's death, even when "prudently and tenderly announced by Professor Tyler, broke upon the townspeople of Amherst like a thunderbolt" (102). We can also find excerpted the very newspaper accounts that Emily Dickinson followed so eagerly and that she incorporated in her detailed letter to the Norcross cousins:

> The body was inclosed in a black casket, which was draped with the American flag, and his sword rested against it. Beautiful evergreens and flowers nearly covered the coffin, – the tribute of classmates and distant friends. The exercises were listened to with

breathless silence by the large congregation: and each one seemed to feel that they had an interest in the sad bereavement. [106]

Dickinson's morbid personal interest in this "sad bereavement" was made even keener by her knowledge of Stearns's unquiet religious spirit, expressed in the troubled eyes that crease the face of the frontispiece to his father's memorial volume (reproduced at the beginning of this chapter). Like Dickinson, Frazar Stearns had a "nervous, excitable temperament" that made him into a "scrupulous soul" whose dealings with evangelical Calvinism were a refined poetry of torture. Prompted to make a public confession of faith at the age of twelve, he was received into the church, yet three years later we find him in the throes of severe spiritual depression. At this time he wrote:

> I cannot live any longer in such a condition. I must do something – I know not what. O what would not I give, if I only had a Christian's hope! but I am afraid all is lost. I have strayed and wandered far from God, and I fear. How can I be saved after what I have done? [13]

Stearns especially regretted the unfulfilled covenant of his too-hasty conversion, but during the strong revival of religion in 1858, "as the result of which more than ninety-six thousand hopeful conversions to Christ were enumerated," he was again deeply moved. Only a generation ahead of Dickinson in age, Stearns began to share her burnedchild's response to transforming religious fires: "The suspicion that he might have deceived himself, and have been living in a delusion, excited and grieved him, and awakened in him some terrible doubts respecting the genuineness of revivals and even of Christianity itself" (22) This spiritual anguish, like the nervousness that prompted Dickinson's father to withdraw her from Mount Holyoke, led in Stearns's case to an attack of typhoid fever and a recuperative sea voyage. Interestingly enough, there also appear to have been some attendant psychological trauma and a marked infantilism:

> This protracted sickness not only prostrated his physical nature, but after a while enfeebled his mind. He became in some respects almost a child again, and could best be entertained with hearing the books which he had read in his childhood, and in listening to childish tales which had long since ceased to interest him. [29]

There are affinities here both to Emily Dickinson's determined childlike stance and to her experience of, as she wrote to her dear fellow children the Norcross cousins in late May of 1863, a "snarl in the brain which don't unravel yet" (L 2:424). For a considerable time Stearns

could interest himself in nothing, suffering a complete loss of will
similar to that described in "After great pain, a formal feeling comes."
The letters that he wrote while in this condition are excruciating to
read: Like Dickinson at the Communion service he "felt as an outcast –
as one who had no right to be there" (54); to his father he says, "You
tell me to 'rejoice evermore,' and 'pray without ceasing.' I can do
neither, for I seem to believe nothing. O! the misery – the agony I
endure you cannot imagine; and sometimes I wish I had died when I
thought I believed, rather than live to become (as I fear I shall) an
infidel" (32–3).

There is little need to narrate the rest of Frazar Stearns's spiritual
history, for it consists of the hard emotional facts of the New England
theology largely unmitigated by the extravagant fancy of New England
romance, save in one particular. Unlike the fictional Esther Avery and
James Marvyn, Stearns found release in the form of a conversion to the
self-destructive romance of war, not to the personal romance of love. In
him, Stowe's Platonic alternative became all-consuming, anticipating
the chief dictum of the American-Victorian Idealism of the Harvard
philosopher Josiah Royce: "Be loyal to Loyalty!" Just as Emily Dickinson committed herself wholly to a dominant Master figure, so did
Frazar Stearns merge his religious yearnings with self-sacrificial fanati-
cism: His "Master" became the Union cause, and he too courted death
as both a test and a justification of his faith. When he heard that another
young patriot had been killed he said, "It is a glorious death. I should
be willing to have stood in his place, if I could save the country" (63–
4). Before the war he had expressed his death wish in an unfocused
fashion, thinking, "If I get to heaven, it will be because God is merciful, and I am to be taken away when I 'have a fit' of serving Him" (59).
Civil strife had the decisive effect of sharpening and formalizing this
goal. Now to die in battle for the greater glory of the Union cause
assured an escape from the prison-house world of the New England
theology while it promised salvation through suffering and justification
through death. It was a way in which this "poor, stray sheep" could
finally touch the remote Calvinist God, a way in which this God might
speak to him or perhaps even through him.

Stearns's patriotic fervor was extraordinary; it is no wonder that
Austin Dickinson felt stunned by the news of his death, and perhaps
chagrined as well, for while Austin had exercised his privilege of paying
the five-hundred-dollar fee to arrange for a substitute when he was
drafted (*LED* 2:536), Stearns, fired by a "sacred enthusiasm," called
"loudly for everybody, particularly the best portion of our community,
to enlist" (*Adjutant Stearns,* 74). "Our cities are menaced, and our very
homes threatened, merely because we are willing to *pay money* but not

enlist ourselves," he thundered (71). Even his father was exhorted to drop his academic duties and join up "as chaplain of some regiment," because "thousands would follow you into the field, and whether you live or die, your name would ascend on the lips of the nation, and your soul would go up to God filled with his Holy Spirit" (75). More extraordinary still was the public testimony of the volume entitled *Adjutant Stearns*. Here the president of an academic institution that was one of the citadels of orthodoxy at last enlisted in the ranks of a Sentimental Love Religion that automatically admitted heroes like his son to the Eden of the saved.

There was nothing in the New England theology and very little in Frazar Stearns's own manic-depressive religious history to confirm that he was the recipient of truly gracious affections. Yet on the basis of "something like 'an assurance of hope,' " which Frazar had received when communing with the sublime expanse of ocean during his voyage to Bombay to regain his health, William Augustus Stearns allowed active patriotism and outward martyrdom to cancel any continuing doubts about his son's tormented inner life. It may have been wishful thinking that led him to his final sketch of the boy's character, but wishful thinking was the very basis of the new sentimental gospel of consolation. Such affective thought demonstrated the ultimate triumph of romanticism over rationalism. President Stearns wrote:

> He fell doing his duty as a Christian soldier, and I am satisfied. It is said, that after the battle of Newbern, as soon as the smoke had cleared away, and the roar of the cannon had ceased, and silence had taken the place of excitement and confusion, a beautiful bird rose and hovered over camp, and sang in a strain of the sweetest melody. Thus calmly rise the spirits of Christian soldiers from the awful din of the battle-field, singing with a clearer, more joyous, and more entrancing note, as they ascend to heaven. And why should not friends be satisfied, when their fallen sons and brothers have died trusting in God and doing their duty? [158]

Thus did Frazar Stearns's sacrifice confirm Emily Dickinson's personal martyrology:

> The Martyr Poets – did not tell –
> But wrought their Pang in syllable –
> That when their mortal name be numb –
> Their mortal fate – encourage Some –   [J 544]

Not only would she continue to "play his tunes" when joined in commemorative observance with the Norcross cousins (for William Stearns reveals that Frazar, like Dickinson herself, was a gifted musician who "picked out the notes of simple tunes, on the piano, with delight" when he was not yet four years old, and who "generally preferred, whether in social circles or in private, to improvise his music" [*Adjutant Stearns*, 149–50]). She totally internalized Frazar Stearns's death,[25] and dwelt on his marmoreal apotheosis in order to compensate for her own obscure Antietams of the spirit:

> My portion is Defeat – today –
> A paler luck than Victory –
> Less Paeans – fewer Bells –
> The Drums don't follow Me – with tunes –
> Defeat – a somewhat slower – means –
> More Arduous than Balls –
>
> Tis populous with Bone and stain –
> And Men too straight to stoop again,
> And Piles of solid Moan –
> And Chips of Blank – in Boyish Eyes –
> And scraps of Prayer –
> And Death's surprise,
> Stamped visible – in Stone –   [J 639]

Moreover, Dickinson had the satisfaction of seeing the gospel of suffering and consolation embraced by no less a personage than the head of Amherst College himself:

> While prayer for the preservation of the child could not be heard, since God, in his wisdom, had better purposes, prayer for inward strength was signally answered; for, "when suffering abounded, consolations did much more abound" . . . Christ himself said to his followers: "In the world ye shall have tribulation, but be of good cheer; I have overcome the World." If men were wise they would pray less for preservation from trouble, and more for cheerful submission and power to endure it. A German poet has said: "The way to Heaven lies over Golgotha." We must take the way if we would reach the city. By higher authority we learn of the white-robed ones above, – that "these are they who came out of great tribulation." [*Adjutant Stearns*, 103–4]

Friends like Samuel Bowles might parody Dickinson's personal martyrology by calling her "a Queen Recluse" who had "overcome the world," and jokingly inquire of her brother: "Is it really true that they ring 'Old Hundred' & 'Aleluia' perpetually, in heaven – ask her; and are dandelions, asphodels, and Maiden's [vows?] the standard flowers of the ethereal?" (*YH* 2:76) Those who "doubt[ed] her snow" (*L* 2:394), however, also had to doubt the sacrifice of a Frazar Stearns as well as the compensatory heaven it earned him:

> Of Tribulation – these are They,
> Denoted by the White.
> The Spangled Gowns, a lesser Rank
> Of Victors, designate –
>
> All these – did conquer –
> But the Ones who overcame most times –
> Wear nothing commoner than Snow –
> No Ornament – but Palms –
>
> "Surrender" – is a sort unknown
> On this Superior soil –
> "Defeat", an Outgrown Anguish,
> Remembered – as the Mile
>
> Our panting Ancle barely passed,
> When Night devoured the road –
> But we – stood – whispering in the House –
> And all we said – was
> *SAVED!*   [J 325]

No one who witnessed the impressive solemnities of Frazar Stearns's funeral thought of asking Emily Dickinson's favorite post-mortem question – "Was he willing to die?" – because the answer was such an obvious one. Who was more eager, more precipitate in choosing death than the twenty-one-year-old first lieutenant? "I am very sure I am quite ready to die an *ignominious* death, as a private or officer, or do anything for our beloved country," he wrote his father. A more pragmatic Irish private corresponding with a friend in Amherst expressed the darker side of this truth when he said of Frazar Stearns that although he was "the noblest soldier that the world ever afforded," he was also "too brave for his own good" (*Adjutant Stearns,* 140).

As the national slaughter continued, the heroic or ignominious deaths of thousands of unprofessed young men like Frazar Stearns made answers about the nature of their life in the world beyond more important than queries about the past state of their souls. In silent company with such kindred spirits as Harriet Beecher Stowe and Elizabeth Stuart Phelps, Emily Dickinson turned her attention from material torments of internal and external death to the corporeal rewards of the paradise such martyrdom ensured. For while it was Stowe who preached the holy war of the Sentimental Love Religion, it was Phelps who perfected the vision of the heavenly house that crowned it. This house was (to appropriate some of Dickinson's favorite biblical quotations) "not made by hands," yet it had as many "Mansions," Platonic and otherwise, as its future occupants could ever have hoped or demanded.[26] It is that house that we next attempt to enter.

Bergonzoli, *Angelic Love,* 1876. (By permission of the Free Library of Philadelphia.)

Chapter 4

PARADISE DEFERRED

Dickinson, Phelps, and the Image of Heaven

And all those descriptions and word-paintings of heaven with which ambitious poetry and oratory so often strive to interest and astonish us are as pitiful caricatures of the ineffable reality as a child's notion of the universe—a flat, earthly plane a score of miles in circumference, and a firmament above it a little greater in altitude. The heaven they describe is but the poor, flitting phantasms of man's childish fancy. But heaven, as it is, is the perfect realization of the infinite and transcendent imagination of God.

Charles Wadsworth

To create a Paradise with "Thou Shalt Not" written over the door would be to deny Paradise, making it into a material negation.

William Blake

In Heaven they neither woo nor are given in wooing—what an imperfect place!

Emily Dickinson

After struggling with love and death, the popular culture of Emily Dickinson's day went on to construct its own Valhalla for the fallen heroes of the great war between Calvinist rigor and Platonic romance. These heroes included the infant dead as well as unconverted soldiers and martyr-poets, but whereas the marmoreal dimension of sentimentality froze such victims into "ceremonious" tomb sculptures (J 341), its corporeal or fleshly aspect allowed for growth, comfort, and even marriage in the New Jerusalem of the afterlife. The radical picture of this heaven that Elizabeth Stuart Phelps sketched in her 1868 American best-seller, *The Gates Ajar,*[1] was simultaneously the climax of the Sentimental Love Religion, a major challenge to orthodox Protestant piety, and the herald of a new materialism that was to characterize what Mark Twain and Charles Dudley Warner aptly called the Gilded Age. This quiet revolution in sensibility was accomplished by one who had been raised in the very

Geneva of American Calvinism, Andover Seminary. Phelps was the granddaughter of Mose Stuart, Andover's renowned professor of sacred literature and champion of rigorous Germanic methods of linguistic inquiry; her father, Austin Phelps, became professor of rhetoric and homiletics, finally assuming the presidency of the seminary in 1870.

There are many striking biographical similarities between the upbringing of Elizabeth Phelps and that of Emily Dickinson: the presence of a stern, domineering father figure; the later sense of repression and frustration; the defiance of the doctrines of orthodox theology; the early wish to achieve fame through writing; the stimulus of Mrs. Browning's *Aurora Leigh* as a catalyst of that ambition. Like Emily Dickinson, Elizabeth Phelps showed a mixture of great reverence, great affection, great fear, and great resentment toward her father. Unlike Edward Dickinson, however, Austin Phelps was not a human steam engine of unbounded political and economic energy. After attaining the height of his profession, he suffered a nervous collapse that made him a slave to insomnia and mental enervation for more than twenty years; ironically, he seems to have become the victim of the stern New England theology he had sworn to preach, preserve, and promulgate. Obsessed with the horror of sin yet staunchly defending the "wisdom and justice and necessity" of God's future punishment of it, his tortured soul gave vent to the remarkable prayers suing for worldly increase and otherworldly profit – the American Protestant ethic at its most neurasthenic – that his daughter reprints in her pious memoir of his life:

> I also thank Thee, O God, for Thy condescending to watch over my pecuniary interests. I commit them anew to Thee. Do Thou continue to save me from losses! . . . Protect my estate at Bar Harbor and save me from discomfort and misfortune there! Deliver my summer home from flames! Thy will, not mine, be done in these things. Yet *Thou* knowest that I need them without my asking. Do Thou grant them as Thou dost care for the falling sparrow! Amen, O Lord Amen![2]

With equal fervor, Emily Dickinson had pleaded at the bar of justice, though with less tangible results, for Phoebus was only loaned to her, not given in fee simple:

> Of Course – I Prayed –
> And did God Care?
> He cared as much as on the Air
> A Bird – had stamped her foot –
> And cried "Give me" –
> My Reason – Life –
> I had not had – but for Yourself –

'Twere better Charity
To leave me in the Atoms's Tomb
Merry, and Nought, and gay, and numb –
Than this smart Misery.   [J 376]

In his moments of darkest despair, even Austin Phelps himself would
say "with a low, weary cry 'Oh, daughter . . . I wish it were the end of
the world' " (*Memoir*, 116). Yet it was his wife and that daughter who
had to bear the brunt of the grim theology that caused him so much
spiritual anguish. Speaking of life at Andover, his daughter admitted
that "there have been times when the inevitable limitations of [its]
horizon have seemed as familiar as the coffin-lid to the dead" (*Chapters*,
25) and Elizabeth Stuart Phelps the elder gave up her life in the struggle
to be both a best-selling author and the busy wife of a distinguished
professor and preacher. Mrs. Phelps was the author of such popular
favorites as *The Angel on the Right Shoulder*, *The Tell-Tale*, and *A Peep
at Number Five;* her genteel picture of the trials and tribulations of a
young clerical couple entitled *The Sunnyside* sold more than one hundred thousand copies. Emily Dickinson herself owned a copy of a work
that became her posthumous tribute, *The Last Leaf from Sunnyside*, published in 1854. The cynical Austin Phelps had remarked, after reading
"overdrawn memoirs indited by devout children," that "everybody's
mother is a remarkable woman," but it is obvious that he and his severe
faith were largely to blame for his wife's own steady demise, since Mrs.
Phelps "lived before women had careers and public sympathy for
them." She soon became exhausted by too much work and too much
childbearing, the "conflict between genius and domestic life"; "the
struggle killed her, but she fought till she fell" (*Chapters*, 15).
    Austin Phelps, out of desperation, perversity, or pity, almost immedi-
ately married her doomed tubercular sister, who quickly was supplanted
by yet a third spouse. In an extraordinary public ritual, the elder Elizabeth Stuart Phelps's baby was baptized beside his mother's coffin, as a
shaft of sunlight illuminated her draped portrait. In a private rechristen-
ing and inner consecration just as extraordinary, her daughter, born
"Mary Gray," became an avenging Elizabeth Stuart Phelps the second.
    Of her mother, Phelps remarked, "It was impossible to be her
daughter and not to write." Her reading of Elizabeth Barrett Browning's *Aurora Leigh* at the age of sixteen confirmed this ambition, as it
did Emily Dickinson's, to "do some honest, hard work of my own in
the World Beautiful, and for it" (*Chapters*, 66). Dickinson was to find
her work out of the world, but Browning's verse narrative dramatizing
a talented woman's choice between the artistic life and bourgeois domesticity strengthened Phelps's aspiration to avoid her mother's dilemma by practicing a single-minded, celibate Platonism rather than a

schizophrenic, connubial Calvinism. The influence of *Aurora Leigh* on
Emily Dickinson's sensibility has led one critic to charge her with outright plagiarism,[3] but once again the power of such romances was more
in freeing the New England mind from the New England theology
than in enchaining it to a sedulous imitation. As Phelps remarks:

> There may be greater poems in our language than "Aurora
> Leigh," but it was many years before it was possible for me to
> suppose it; and none that ever saw the hospitality of fame could
> have done for that girl what that poem did at that time. I had
> never had a good memory – but I think I could have repeated a
> large portion of it; and know that I often stood the test of haphaz-
> ard examinations on the poem from half-scoffing friends, some-
> times of the masculine persuasion. Each to his own; and what
> Shakespeare or the Latin Fathers might have done for some other
> impressionable girl, Mrs. Browning – forever bless her strong and
> gentle name! – did for me. [*Chapters, 65*]

Hence Emily Dickinson's awesome reverence for Mrs. Browning, for
whom she composed three elegies (J 363, J 593, J 312), and for the whole
saga of the Browning courtship with its handsome, dashing lover; retiring, intellectual heroine; and stern, possessive father. The real-life story
of Elizabeth Barrett Browning's elopement to Italy was the very type of
high romance, with a denouement denied to the humbler one of Daisy
and Phoebus. Romance in all forms was a safety valve for Dickinson's
generation, those rebellious souls who had to endure the rigors of Calvinist discipline, and this factor accounts for their attraction to such
seemingly vapid and now largely forgotten works as Ik Marvell's *Reveries of a Bachelor* and James O. Bailey's *Festus*. Though the younger Elizabeth Stuart Phelps was born fourteen years after Dickinson, the two
women shared a Puritanical religious climate little different from, and
perhaps even more exacting than, that endured by Anne Bradstreet. It
was only natural that their sensibility would be shaped by the continuing
dialectic between Calvinism and Platonism. The presence of a reprint of
Phelps's children's story entitled "Bobbit's Hotel," first published in
1870, on the last pages of Mary Warner's scrapbook demonstrates not
only her lasting popular appeal as a writer but the fact that this popularity
itself reflects a general concern with "the unseen and the unsaid realities"
that governed the inner lives of nineteenth-century American women.

I

In Phelps's private mythology, the bogeyman-deacon of the New England theology was embodied not so much in the figure of her father,

who softened all of the Five Points of Calvinism save "Unlimited Repro-
bation," suffering many of the torments of the unregenerate as a consequence, as in the Reverend Edwards A. Park, whose first name signaled
that he was a worthy heir of the ideals of the old-time religion. Although
Park in fact worked toward a certain liberalizing of Calvinist dogma, his
doctrines were harsh when judged by the new gospels of sentimental
love and consolation, and it is no accident that he spent the last years of
his life laboring on a biography of his namesake, Jonathan Edwards, that
was never completed. As it was, he became the memorialist of two of
Edwards's sternest disciples, Nathaniel Emmons and Stephen Hopkins,
and in the pulpit he (like Edwards) laced the dry wine of the New
England theology with a fiery cordial of heart-wringing revivalism. In
this capacity, his oratorical powers directly touched even Emily Dickinson, who reported to her brother on November twenty-first, 1853:

> Oh Austin, you dont know how we all wished for you yesterday.
> We had such a splendid sermon from that Prof Park – I never
> heard anything like it, and dont expect to again, till we stand at
> the great white throne, and "he reads from the book, the Lamb's
> book." The students and chapel people all came, to our church,
> and it was very full, and still – so still, the buzzing of a fly would
> have boomed like a cannon. And when it was all over, and that
> wonderful man sat down, people stared at each other, and looked
> as wan and wild, as if they had seen a spirit, and wondered they
> had not died. [L 1:272]

The sermon that Park gave was his standard and time-tested one on
Judas, and so effective was it that twenty years later Dickinson remembered that "the loveliest sermon I ever heard was the disappointment of
Jesus in Judas. It was told like a mortal story of intimate young men. I
suppose no surprise we can ever have will be so sick as that. The last 'I
never knew you' may resemble it" (L 2:502–3). Yet Elizabeth Stuart
Phelps, who both studied under Park and socialized with him, was
equivocal in her praise of his ability to turn emotion on or off as if it
were a water tap. "A skeptical critic," she wrote archly, "might have
wondered whether the tears welled, or the face broke, or the voice
trembled, always just at the right moment, from pure spontaneity"
(Chapters, 41). The prepackaged nature of "The Peter Sermon" and
"The Judas Sermon" offended her romantic love of the true and the
genuine, and in 1896 she seemed to regard the aged minister as the relic
of a cause well and rightly lost, for though "in his youth he was the
progressive of evangelical theology," she saw that "in his age he stands
the proud and reticent conservative, the now silent representative of a
departed glory, a departed severity – and, we must admit, of a departed

strength – from which the theology of our times has melted away" (38).

No matter how strong the snowy Matterhorn of New England theology might look from the perspective of a sentimentalized Christianity that had by 1896 become as soft as vanilla ice cream, Elizabeth Stuart Phelps must be acknowledged as one of the chief contributors to its deliquescence. In *The Gates Ajar,* Edwards Park is parodied as the abstract, overly rational orthodox minister Dr. Bland, and in her memoirs she tells in a dramatic and symbolic fashion how the rumblings of Civil War first shook the foundations of Calvinism's seemingly immutable sovereignty. Recreating one of Park's regular Tuesday evening lectures to the assembled daughters of Andover in the summer of 1861, she writes that as "depravity, election, predestination, and justification are filing sternly" by,

> sharp upon the doctrines there falls across the silence and the sweetness of the moonlit Hill a strange and sudden sound. It is louder than theology. It is more solemn than the professor's system. Insistent, urging everything before it, – the toil of strenuous study, the fret of little trouble, and the dreams of dawning love, – the call stirs on. It is the beat of a drum.
>
> The boys of old Phillips, with the down on their faces, and that eternal fire in their hearts which has burned upon the youths of all the ages when their country has commanded: "Die for me!" are drilling by moonlight . . .
>
> "An infinite wrong deserves an infinite punishment" – The theologian's voice falls solemnly. The girls turn their grave faces to the open windows. Silence helps the drum-beat, which lifts its cry to Heaven unimpeded; and the awful questions which it asks, what system of theology can answer? [*Chapters,* 70–2]

We hear again those drums that resound in the background of so many of Emily Dickinson's poems of the 1860s, drums that marshaled a fifth column of female Christian soldiers, facing like the poet the awful questions posed by an equally awful theology. The only possible answers were already contained in the Sentimental Love Religion that had been preached in many consolation verses dealing with the plight of the "early dead": justification through love and salvation through suffering. Those heresies that before had been almost solely the province of the Mount Auburn school and its *Kinder-Totenlieder* were now of necessity applied to the beardless boys, like Frazar Stearns, who had sacrificed their last full measure of devotion on the altar of patriotism. The unimaginable horror was no longer simply infant damnation, but damnation itself, and the reasons of the heart swept away all the clever

syllogisms that orthodoxy could contrive. The tragic results of the
New England theology were no longer the private property of Catharine Beecher, Harriet Beecher Stowe, or Emily Dickinson but multi-
plied a thousandfold on the nation's battlefields. Elizabeth Stuart Phelps
herself joined the ranks of the bereaved when her fiancé, Samuel Hopkins Thompson, was killed at the battle of Antietam on October
twenty-second, 1862, less than six months after graduating from
Andover.[4] The result of her brooding over this young man's death was
The Gates Ajar, in which Lieutenant Thompson (who died shouting,
"Form on me, boys, form on me!") is metamorphosed into the figure
of Royal Cabot, the martyred brother of the sorrowing heroine.
Phelps's book was in turn addressed to a country "dark with sorrowing
women" and oppressed with unanswerable questions.

   The Gates Ajar became a literary phenomenon because it answered
those questions and provided a popular alternative to a cultural crisis; as
we have seen, the urgency of the Civil War accelerated an irrepressible
conflict between masculine Calvinism and feminized sentimentalism,
between the New England theology and New England romance, that
had been building for years. This crisis of belief finally took the form
of – to use George Fredrickson's suggestive title – an "Inner Civil
War,"[5] yet Phelps's appeal would hardly have been so successful had
she not, like Emily Dickinson, shared personally in a tragedy that had
suddenly become public and even commonplace:

> No man can understand
> But He that hath endured
> The Dissolution – in Himself –
> That Man – be qualified
>
> To qualify Despair
> To Those who failing new –
> Mistake Defeat for Death – Each time –
> Till acclimated – to –   [J 539]

   In forging her private mythology, Emily Dickinson had already, by
the time *The Gates Ajar* was first published in November of 1868,
explored most of the ideas about a domestic heaven and a spiritual love
beyond the grave that were embodied in the book.[6] Phelps's autobiography indicates that her popular novel was begun as early as 1864, so
that, if we follow Thomas Johnson's dating of Dickinson's poems,
there is even some direct overlay with the composition of a few of the
poet's relevant verses. More important, *The Gates Ajar* puts into some
kind of meaningful order the sentiments, symbolism, and philosophy
that make up Dickinson's "marriage group," while rescuing her love
poetry from repeated charges of extreme idosyncrasy and aberration.[7]

When we read *The Gates Ajar* today – more than one hundred years
after James T. Fields sent its astonished author an initial royalty check for
six hundred dollars with a note that informed her, "Your book is moving grandly. It has already a sale of four thousand copies" (*Chapters*,
109) – what strikes us is how closely the unreconciled, bereaved Mary
Cabot of the opening pages resembles the Emily Dickinson who so often
rebelled against the "Perturbless Plan" (J 724) of an unrelenting Calvinist
God. Mary's brother, Royal, has been killed in the war, and according to
the conventions of New England romance she can find no comfort in the
strict doctrines of an overly scrupulous Calvinism that put the question
of the state of the young man's soul above the fact of his brave self-sacrifice. Especially bitter are the visits of Job's comforters like Deacon
Quirk, who counsel submission to the almighty will, while they remind
the bereaved girl:

> "I believe he never made a profession of religion, but there is no
> limit to the mercy of God. It is very unsafe for the young to think
> that they can rely on a death-bed repentance, but our God is a
> convenant-keeping God, and Royal's mother was a pious woman.
> If you cannot say with certainty that he is numbered among the
> redeemed, you are justified, perhaps, in hoping so." [*Gates*, 15]

Mary Cabot's psychic pain is composed of a double bereavement,
since the death of her brother in turn precipitates the loss of her faith.
"Has everything stopped just here?" she asks, remembering "our talks
together in the twilight, our planning and hoping and dreaming together; our walks and rides and laughing; our reading and singing and
loving, – these, then, are all gone out forever?" (18). Mary's first reaction is a complete denial or rejection of any abstract conception of the
New Jerusalem. As she writes of her brother in a secret journal of her
grief:

> He was a good boy. Roy was a good boy. He must have gone to
> Heaven. But I know nothing about Heaven. It is very far off. In
> my best and happiest days, I never liked to think of it. If I were to
> go there, it could do me no good, for I should not see Roy. Of if
> by chance I should see him standing up among the grand, white
> angels, he would not be the old dear Roy. I should grow so tired
> of singing! Should long and fret for one little talk, – for I never
> said goodby, and –
> I will stop this. [10]

Mary Cabot realizes that she is bringing herself to the brink of madness (a "bare, blank sense" that recalls the catatonia of "After great
pain") by meditating on such "infidel" and futile ideas, but Emily

Dickinson started her inquiry from exactly the same point of desperate skepticism:

> We Pray – to Heaven –
> We prate – of Heaven –
> Relate – when Neighbors die –
> At what o'clock to Heaven – they fled –
> Who saw them – Wherefore fly?
>
> Is Heaven a Place – a Sky – a Tree?
> Location's narrow way is for Ourselves –
> Unto the Dead
> There's no Geography –
>
> But State – Endowal – Focus –
> Where – Omnipresence – fly?   [J 489]

"Heaven is so cold!" she exclaimed in a letter to her Norcross cousins dated "Spring, 1861" (*L* 2:376), and the poet could not conceive of a paradise that did not include the private and the personal. A few years before, she had written to Mrs. Josiah Holland:

> My only sketch, profile, of Heaven is a large, blue sky, bluer and larger than the *biggest* I have seen in June, and in it are my friends – all of them – every one of them – those who are with me now, and those who were "parted" as we walked, and "snatched up to Heaven."
>   If roses had not faded, and frost had never come, and one had not fallen here and there whom I could not waken, there were no need of other Heaven than the one below – and if God had been here this summer, and seen the things that *I* have seen – I guess that He would think His Paradise superfluous. [*L* 2:329]

But the loss of the loved one can temporarily turn even the earthly paradise into an engine of exquisite torture, for as Emerson had long before noted in "Nature": "There is a kind of contempt of the landscape felt by him who has just lost by death a dear friend. The sky is less grand as it shuts down over less worth in the population" (*Works* 1:11). With no hope of an orthodox paradise and no Transcendental capacity to appreciate the earthly one, Mary Cabot finds in nature another version of the rack, a false and thoughtless comforter like the unfeeling Deacon Quirk or the too chatty Miss Meta Tripp. "The lazy winds are choking me," Mary writes of the first stillness of the May days, which bring only a "bitter Peace" and a renewed sense of emptiness:

> Their faint sweetness makes me sick. The moist, rich loam is ploughed in the garden; the grass more golden than green, springs

in the warm hollow by the front gate; the great maple, just reaching up to tap at the window, blazes and bows under its weight of
scarlet blossoms. I cannot bear their perfume; it comes up in great
breaths, when the window is opened. I wish that little cricket just
waked from his winter's nap, would not sit there on the sill and
chirp at me. I hate the bluebirds flashing in and out of the carmine
cloud that the maple makes, and singing, singing, everywhere.
[*Gates*, 24]

Emily Dickinson recorded exactly the same reaction to a paradoxically bountiful nature blooming in the face of deep internal scars in a
number of poems, most notably, "I dreaded that first Robin, so" (J
348). Here what Phelps calls the "creeping" approach of spring becames
a veritable water torture to the bereaved sensibility. In the following
shorter descant on the same theme, Dickinson writes:

> The Morning after Wo –
> 'Tis frequently the Way –
> Surpasses all that rose before –
> For utter Jubilee –
>
> As Nature did not care –
> And piled her Blossoms on –
> And further to parade a Joy –
> Her Victim stared upon –
>
> The Birds declaim their Tunes –
> Pronouncing every word
> Like Hammers – Did they know they fell
> Like Litanies of Lead –
>
> On here and there – a creature –
> They'd modify the Glee
> To fit some Crucifixal Clef –
> Some Key of Calvary –   [J 364]

Again, such analogues of sensibility might be found in any number
of contemporaneous romantic works that deal with the agonies inflicted
by the New England theology. In *The Minister's Wooing,* for example,
Harriet Beecher Stowe begins her chapter entitled "The Bruised Flax-
Flower," detailing the aftermath of the report of James Marvyn's death
and its effect on Mary Scudder, with the following description:

> The next day broke calm and fair. The robins sang remorselessly
> in the apple-tree, and were answered by bobolink, oriole, and a
> whole tribe of ignorant little bits of feathered happiness that

danced among the leaves. Golden and glorious unclosed those
purple eyelids of the East, and regally came up the sun; and the
treacherous sea broke into ten thousand smiles, laughing and
dancing with every ripple, as unconsciously as if no form dear to
human hearts had gone down beneath it. Oh! treacherous, deceiv-
ing beauty of outward things! beauty, wherein throbs not one
answering nerve to human pain! [320]

New England romances like *The Minister's Wooing* might allow
Dickinson to share her earthly torment, but they did not assuage her
grief or teach her about its ultimate compensations:

> They say that "Time assuages" –
> Time never did assuage –
> An actual suffering strengthens
> As Sinews do, with age –
>
> Time is a Test of Trouble –
> But not a Remedy –
> If such it prove, it prove too
> There was no Malady –   [J 686]

It is not earthly remedy or nostrum but rather the searching exploration
of the very nature of the heaven to come and the substitution of a warm
domestic paradise for the cold orthodox stereoptye of a city of pearl and
jasper that make *The Gates Ajar* increasingly relevant to the parallel
development of Dickinson's poetry.

II

All her life, Emily Dickinson sought spiritual brothers and sisters.
These liberal voices countered the harsher accents stressing election and
damnation that had jarred her orthodox upbringing. In February of
1859 she wrote to Mrs. Joseph Haven, "Mr. S[eelye] preached in our
church last Sabbath upon 'predestination,' but I do not respect 'doctrines,' and did not listen to him" (L 2:346). As we have noted, Edward
Everett Hale, Thomas Wentworth Higginson, Charles Wadsworth, and
Washington Gladden were all called upon at one time or other to act as
spiritual comforters who could provide some concrete answers to the
question "Is immortality true?" (L 3:731).

Just such a role is assumed in *The Gates Ajar* by Mary Cabot's devout
but heretical aunt, Winifred Forceythe. Winifred is the logical development of the sentimental stereotype of that salvific woman we find in the
works of both Hawthorne and Harriet Beecher Stowe. She even has, like
Hester Prynne of *The Scarlet Letter,* a wayward, unpredictable child

whom she names not "Pearl" but, appropriately, "Faith." Yet Mrs. Forceythe differs from earlier fictional angel-evangels (Hawthorne's Hilda, Stowe's Little Eva) in that she reflects the more limited, "reconstructive" concerns of postwar America. Her guides are reason, the Bible, and common sense, and her strategy is to induce a gradual rather than an immediate conversion experience. She dies at last, not in a melodramatic crowd of weeping relatives and descending cherubim, swooning from a painless "decline," but agonizingly and realistically of an inoperable cancer of the breast. Winifred Forceythe is, in fact, a type of the new no-nonsense Christian woman, a believable idealization of Elizabeth Stuart Phelps herself and her own long-suffering mother, "whose heart has not enfeebled her head, but whose head could never freeze her heart!" (*Chapters,* 14). In discussions with the pedantic, ultra-orthodox Dr. Bland, she emerges as a worthy lay opponent, for

> a woman who knows something about fate, freewill, and foreknowledge absolute, who is not ignorant of politics, and talks intelligently of Agassiz's latest fossil, who can understand a German quotation, and has heard of Strauss and Neander, who can dash her sprightliness ably against his old dry bones of metaphysics and theology, yet never speak an accent above that essentially womanly voice of hers, is, I imagine, a phenomenon in his social experience. [*Gates,* 74]

Winifred Forceythe's own special faith has been bequeathed to her by her dead husband, a practical, hardworking missionary, and what she brings to her bereaved niece is the comfort of a Christ-centered rather than a God-centered Protestantism. Even the Son is recognized as once having denied the Father, and it is possible to forgive the "wickedness" of hating great Jehovah himself. Once more the loved one, whether man, woman, or child, is transfigured by this militant Sentimental Love Religion into a corporeal avatar of the suffering Christ, just as Christ is, in turn, transformed into a loving personal guardian. As Charlotte Brontë told Harriet Beecher Stowe in a conversation from the World Beyond, conducted through a spiritualist medium who recorded her words by means of a sensitive pencil, or planchette, "Never think of [Christ] as afar off, but as with you, close to you, hand to hand, and heart to heart – the elder Brother, the tender, everlasting Friend."[8] This image is fulfilled in *The Gates Ajar* by the figure of Royal Cabot. Heaven becomes not simply a home but a very private kind of paradise, furnished with very concrete and material wish fulfillments. The first barrier to go is the old orthodox conception of the impossibly remote New Jerusalem, because as Mary Cabot reports of one of Dr. Bland's most abstract sermons, "He gave me glittering generalities, cold com-

monplace, vagueness, unreality, a God and a future at which I sat and
shivered" (51). It is the impersonality of this future at which she rebels,
for

> There was something about adoration, and the harpers harping
> with their harps, and the sea of glass, and crying, Worthy the
> Lamb! and a great deal more that bewildered and disheartened me
> so that I could scarcely listen to it. I do not doubt that we shall
> glorify God primarily and happily, but can we not do it in some
> other way than by harping and praying? [49]

Rather than Mary Cabot's anger, what Emily Dickinson displays in
her reaction to the orthodox heaven is most often parody and satire, a
kind of reductio ad absurdum that eventuates in the ephemeral paradise
depicted in poems such as

> I went to Heaven –
> 'Twas a small Town –
> Lit – with a Ruby –
> Lathed – with Down –
>
> Stiller – than the fields
> At the full Dew –
> Beautiful – as Pictures –
> No Man drew.
> People – like the Moth –
> Of Mechlin – frames –
> Duties – of Gossamer –
> And Eider – names –
> Almost – contented –
> I – could be –
> 'Mong such unique
> Society –   [J 374]

In this mocking, attenuated dream vision and in a butterfly poem that
her first editors entitled "From the Chrysalis" (J 1099), Dickinson
seems both to confirm and to deny the injunction of her beloved
Charles Wadsworth, in his sermon entitled "The Ceasing of the
Manna," that

> for us while in the flesh to conceive of [heaven] is as impossible as
> for the chrysalis, shut up in its little pendulous shell, to conceive
> of the bright and boundless sphere into which it is presently to
> burst and soar on its new pinions. Hence I say the futility, nay,
> the very falsity of all our attempts to describe heavenly things. We
> gather together in thought some of the fairest and grandest things

we have known on earth – "trees of life," and "rivers of pleasure," and "thrones of power," and "crowns of glory," and fashion according to our childish taste a little, pitiful, tinsel, mimic Paradise, and call the place Heaven. Alas! alas! for our folly.[9]

About 1866, Dickinson puckishly inquired of Catherine Scott Turner (Anthon), "*Will* folks get rested, Katie? You spoke of 'Heaven' you know. 'I' will take *so many beds*. Theres you & me & Vinnie & the 'other house.' & the *Israelites* & those *Hittite* folks, it *does* appear confused to me!" (L 2:451–2). But the question that Dr. Bland's sermon attempted to answer but never did – "What is Heaven?" – remained a nagging one, even though Dickinson could mischieviously toy and juggle with its terms as she does in "Where bells no more affright the morn" (J 112) or in

> What is – "Paradise" –
> Who live there –
> Are they "Farmers" –
> Do they "hoe" –
> Do they know that this is "Amherst" –
> And that I – am coming – too –
>
> Do they wear "new shoes" – in "Eden" –
> Is it always pleasant – there –
> Wont they scold us – when we're homesick –
> Or tell God – how cross we are –
>
> You are sure there's such a person
> As "a Father" – in the sky –
> So if I get lost – there – ever –
> Or do what the Nurse calls "die" –
> I shant walk the "Jasper" – barefoot –
> Ransomed folks – wont laugh at me –
> Maybe – "Eden" a'nt so lonesome
> As New England used to be!   [J 215]

This poem was probably sent to someone like her sister-in-law, Susan, who as a devout church member was presumably "saved" or "ransomed" and so could stand as an advocate for Emily in that Eden from which she had been shut out by her stubborn unregeneracy. New England was "lonesome" precisely because Dickinson remained, religiously, outside the believing community and an alien in her own family circle. In her second letter to T. W. Higginson, of April fifteenth, 1862, she wrote, for example, "They are religious – except me – and address an Eclipse, every morning – whom they call their 'Father' "

(*L* 2:404). The concept of heaven as "Our Home" that Aunt Winifred stressed as part of her "sweet heresy" of salvation through suffering could not entirely appeal to a poet who confesses:

> I never felt at Home – Below –
> And in the Handsome Skies
> I shall not feel at Home – I know –
> I dont like Paradise –
>
> Because it's Sunday – all the time –
> And Recess – never comes –
> And Eden'll be so lonesome
> Bright Wednesday Afternoons –   [J 413]

Dickinson rejected the Sunday school heaven, like Mary Cabot and Winifred Forceythe, because it was all too silly when subjected to a pragmatic commonsense scrutiny.[10] "I believe the love of God may be taught not to seem like bears," she wrote her cousins in early March of 1861 (*L* 2:372), relying on their shared childhood knowledge of Watts and the Bible,[11] and in view of Dickinson's mention of celestial farmers, it is interesting to note that Aunt Winifred employs exactly the same example to overcome Deacon Quirk's fundamentalism in *The Gates Ajar*. Replying to this yeoman's stubborn contention, hoe in hand, that in heaven he will be clothed in a white robe and be "engaged in such employments as befit sinless creatures in a spiritooal state of existence" (103), Mrs. Forceythe displays both her common sense and her subdued satirical vein:

> "Now, Deacon Quirk," replied Aunt Winifred, looking him over from head to foot, – old straw hat, calico shirt, blue overalls, and cowhide boots, coarse, work-worn hands, and "narrow forehead braided tight," – "just imagine yourself, will you? taken out of this life this minute, as you stand here in your potato-field (the Deacon changed his position with evident uneasiness), and put into another life, – not anybody else, but yourself, just as you left this spot, – and do you honestly think that you should be happy to go and put on a white dress and stand still in a choir with a green branch in one hand and a singing-book in the other, and sing and pray and never do anything but sing and pray, this year, next year, and every year forever?" [103]

Although Mrs. Forceythe attempts to undermine the stereotype of paradise as depicted in Revelation, she is yet no real iconoclast, for she wishes only to replace it with a more modern and sensible heaven. Since Aunt Winifred is also a committed gradualist, however, her first step is to achieve a purely symbolic interpretation of the Scriptures and not reject them altogether. As she explains to her niece,

"Can't people tell picture from substance, a metaphor from its meaning? That book of Revelation is precisely what it professes to be, – a vision, a symbol. A symbol of something, to be sure, and rich with pleasant hopes, but still a symbol. Now, I really believe that a large proportion of Christian church-members, who have studied their Bible, attended Sabbath schools, listened to sermons all their lives, if you could fairly come at their most definite idea of the place where they expect to spend eternity, would own it to be the golden city, with pearl gates, and jewels in the wall. It never occurs to them, that, if we are to walk golden streets, how can we stand on a sea of glass? How can we 'sit on thrones'? How can untold millions of us 'lie in Abraham's bosom'?" [54]

In her poems on spiritual martyrdom, such as "Of Tribulation these are They," Emily Dickinson had already followed out to its extremest limit Mrs. Forceythe's suggestion that the images of the Book of Revelation could be used purely as metaphor. But she went one step further in also appropriating the language of Calvinist dogma to describe her crisis conversion to love. Jehovah had nothing to do with this kind of Platonic predestination; it was a wholly self-determined, self-reliant sainthood:

> Of all the Souls that stand create –
> I have elected – One –
> When Sense from Spirit – files away –
> And Subterfuge – is done –
> When that which is – and that which was –
> Apart – intrinsic – stand –
> And this brief *Drama in the flesh* –
> Is shifted – like a Sand –
> When Figures show their royal Front –
> And Mists – are carved away,
> Behold the Atom – I preferred –
> To all the lists of Clay!   [J 664]

This love was, at the same time, a baptism ("I'm ceded – I've stopped being Their's" [J 508]), a communion ("There Came a Day at Summer's Full" [J 322]), and a confirmation ("He touched me, so I live to know [J 506]). Dickinson's sacramental passion conferred both an immediate sanctifying grace, the privilege of the lover's presence in this world, and a long-term justifying grace, the assurance of his company in the world beyond. Her "conversation" was a very special kind of divine and supernatural light that totally isolated her from those who

had not experienced such an intense illumination, and a shy blush was
the only outward sign of her truly gracious affections:

> Mine – by the Right of the White Election!
> Mine – by the Royal Seal!
> Mine – by the Sign in the Scarlet prison –
> Bars – cannot conceal!
>
> Mine – here – in Vision – and in Veto!
> Mine – by the Grave's Repeal –
> Titled – Confirmed –
> Delirious Charter!
> Mine – long as Ages steal!   [J 528]

Here is where more of the discussion about the future state in *The
Gates Ajar* helps us to understand Dickinson's very personal but by no
means unique approach to the problem of immortality. Two of the
points brought out in this discussion are directly relevant to Dickinson's concept of her white election as a short-term deprivation and a
long-term fulfillment. The first is that immortality and life in the
heaven to come are not purely spiritual but of a definite physical or
"embodied" character. Elaborating on this idea, originally advanced
by Saint Thomas Aquinas,[12] Aunt Winifred affirms:

> "All the *tendency* of Revelation is to show that an embodied state
> is superior to a disembodied one. Yet certainly we who love God
> are promised that death will lead us into a condition which shall
> have the advantage of this: for the good apostle to die 'was gain.' I
> don't believe, for instance, that Adam and Eve have been wander-
> ing about in a misty condition all these thousands of years. I
> suspect that we have some sort of body immediately after passing
> out of this, but there is to come a mysterious change, equivalent,
> perhaps, to a re-embodiment, when our capacities for action will
> be greatly improved, and that in some manner this new form will
> be connected with this 'garment by the soul laid by.' " [77]

The kind of differentiation that Aunt Winifred makes between immediate posthumous embodment and then a celestial reembodiment
after "a mysterious change" may have led Dickinson to compose such
postmortem fantasies as

> I died for Beauty – but was scarce
> Adjusted in the Tomb
> When One who died for Truth, was lain
> In an adjoining Room –

He questioned softly "Why I failed"?
"For Beauty", I replied –
"And I – for Truth – Themself are One –
We Bretheren, are", He said –

And so, as Kinsmen, met a Night –
We talked between the Rooms –
Until the Moss had reached our lips –
And covered up – our names –   [J 449]

The very materialism that informed the Victorian way of death was
founded on the Lockean sensationalism that had allowed Jonathan Edwards to justify Calvinist dogma by claiming that conversion imparted
a new sixth sense over and above the five senses granted to natural
men. "Here is," he wrote in his treatise "Religious Affections,"

> a new spiritual sense that the mind has, or a principle of a new
> kind of perception or spiritual sensation, which is in its whole
> nature different from any former kinds of sensations of the mind,
> as tasting is diverse from any of the other senses; and something is
> perceived by a true saint, in the exercise of this new sense of
> mind, in spiritual and divine things, as entirely diverse from any
> thing that is perceived in them, by natural men, as the sweet taste
> of honey is diverse from the ideas men have of honey by only
> looking on it, and feeling of it. [*Representative Selections*, 236]

In the popular gospel of consolation, the marmoreal transformation of
the loved dead sometimes converted them into talking statues, vaguely
reminiscent of the commandant in the last act of Mozart's *Don Giovanni*.
Since one was now justified by death as much as by faith, it was only
logical that the sixth, supernatural sense reserved by Edwards for the
Elect should be democratized to include all the deceased, an idea that led
inevitably to the development of Christian spiritualism. Even such an
infidel as Edgar Allan Poe imaginatively explored the possibilities of this
trope in tales like his shocking "The Facts in the Case of M. Valdemar"
(1845) or in his more general dialogues of disembodied angelic beings. In
"The Colloquy of Monos and Una," written in 1841, the first-named
spirit describes in detail his earthly postmortem experience:

> It was midnight; and you still sat by my side. All others had de-
> parted from the chamber of Death. They had deposited me in the
> coffin. The lamps burned flickeringly; for this I knew by the
> tremulousness of the monotonous strains. But, suddenly these
> strains diminished in distinctness and in volume. Finally they
> ceased. The perfume in my nostrils died away. Forms affected my

vision no longer. The oppression of the Darkness uplifted itself
from my bosom. A dull shock like that of electricity pervaded my
frame, and was followed by the total loss of the idea of contact. All
of what man has termed sense was merged in the sole consciousness
of entity, and in the one abiding sentiment of duration. The mortal
body had been stricken with the hand of deadly *Decay*.[13]

Poe's statement "They had deposited me in the coffin" matches perfectly the awful passivity conveyed by Dickinson's single word "Adjusted" in "I died for Beauty," and his whole sketch is another gloss on
poems such as "I felt a Funeral, in my Brain," "I heard a Fly buzz –
when I died," and "Because I could not stop for Death," all of which
relate sensations up to and beyond the moment of dying. As late as July
of 1880, Dickinson wrote to Mrs. Holland, "Austin and I were talking
the other Night about the Extension of Consciousness, after Death and
Mother told Vinnie, afterward, she thought it was 'very improper' " (*L*
3:667). Perhaps Mrs. Dickinson would not have felt such speculation to
be improper had she realized that it sprang ultimately from the Scottish
commonsense school sensationalism that had been a mainstay of her
late husband's Calvinist and Whiggish philosophy. Her daughter Emily, as in all her dealings with her surrounding culture, condensed and
privatized this sensationalism, outdoing even Poe in her description of
the middle state between death and resurrection:

> I'll tell Thee All – how Bald it grew –
> How Midnight felt, at first – to me –
> How all the Clocks stopped in the World –
> And Sunshine pinched me – 'Twas so cold –
>
> Then how the Grief got sleepy – some –
> As if my Soul were deaf and dumb –
> Just making signs – across – to Thee –
> That this way – thou could'st notice me –
>
> I'll tell you how I tried to keep
> A smile, to show you, when this Deep
> All Waded – We look back for Play,
> At those Old Times – in Calvary.
>
> Forgive me, if the Grave come slow –
> For Coveting to look at Thee –
> Forgive me, if to stroke thy frost
> Outvisions Paradise!   [J 577]

After one had passed through the middle state of slow "conversion"
to an angelic form, "reembodiment" could take place. Dickinson wrote

to John Long Graves in late April of 1856, "To live, and die, and mount again in triumphant body, and *next* time, try the upper air – is no schoolboy's theme!" adding facetiously, "It is a jolly thought to think we can be Eternal – when air and earth are *full* of lives that are gone – and done – and a conceited thing indeed, this promised Resurrection!" (*L* 2:328). In *The Minister's Wooing,* Harriet Beecher Stowe affirms, "Could a mysterious fore-sight unveil to us this resurrection form of the friends with whom we daily walk, compassed about with mortal infirmity, we should follow them with faith and reverence through all the disguises of human faults and weaknesses, 'waiting for the manifestation of the sons of God'" (130). If such was the destiny of casual friends and acquaintances, how much more glorious would be the "triumphant body" of the earthly beloved? This kind of speculation about the nature of death and the afterlife gave Dickinson a new faith in a believable, comprehensible resurrection ("I think just how my shape will rise" [J 237]). Although she turned over and over in her mind the mystery of the exact nature of the resurrection body ("The Bone that has no Marrow," [J 1274]), no longer did she fear the gathering together of all souls on the Day of Judgment:

> Afraid! Of whom am I afraid?
> Not Death – for who is He?
> The Porter of my Father's Lodge
> As much abasheth me!
>
> Of Life? 'Twere odd I fear [a] thing
> That comprehendeth me
> In one or two existences –
> As Deity decree –
>
> Of Resurrection? Is the East
> Afraid to trust the Morn
> With her fastidious forehead?
> As soon impeach my Crown!   [J 608]

It was precisely because Dickinson now believed that she had a "Crown" reserved for her in heaven and was guaranteed a new resurrection body that death no longer seemed to have dominion over her. As late as 1884 she wrote to Mrs. Joseph A. Sweetser, referring to the recent passing of Otis Lord, "I thought the Churchyard Tarrytown, when I was a Child, but now I trust 'tis Trans" (*L* 3:818). The fact that death became a "Porter" at the gate of this new "transitory" life indicates that Dickinson also managed to adopt the ideas of heaven as a home. This home was not so much the forbidding house of her father as it was the new honeymoon cottage of the bride-to-be.

III

Elizabeth Stuart Phelps articulates just such a possibility through the voice of Winifred Forceythe in *The Gates Ajar*. She improves on the stock sentimental idea of heaven as a restitution of the family circle and provides us with a key to exactly what the idea of a "Sealed Church" of two meant to Emily Dickinson in poems such as "There came a Day at Summer's full" (J 322). Reflecting the social engineering that began to affect mass American society after the Civil War, Aunt Winifred asks herself "what could be done with the millions, who, from the time of Adam, have been gathering in Paradise, unless they lived under the conditions of organized society," and logically concludes that "organized society involves homes, not unlike the homes of this world."

> "What other arrangement could be as pleasant, or could be pleasant to all? Robertson's definition of a church exactly fits. 'More united in each other, because more united in God.' A happy home is the happiest thing in the world. I do not see why it should not be in any world . . . Eternity cannot be – it cannot be the great blank ocean which most of us have somehow or other been brought up to feel that it is, which will swallow up, in a pitiless, glorified way, all the little brooks of our delight. So I expect to have my beautiful home, and my husband, and Faith, as I had them here; with many differences and great ones, but *mine* just the same. Unless Faith goes into a home of her own, – the little creature! I suppose she can't always be a baby." [94–5]

In this way Emily Dickinson reconciled herself to joining her Phoebus in a life beyond the grave, spirited there by Death, who could be either the porter of its gates or the driver of the coach that brought her to her final and glorious destination ("Because I could not stop for Death" [J 712]). Dickinson and Phoebus were the sole members of a sealed church – "more united in each other, because more united in God," as the eloquent British preacher Frederick William Robertson had put it – a church that was to rejoice and regather in its own special heaven. Unlike the one hundred and forty-four thousand sealed of the Book of Revelation (each of whom, as Saint John tells us, bore the name of God emblazoned on his forehead [Rev. 22:4]), Dickinson's mystic seal was a totally private emblem conferred by her deified lover:

> He found my Being – set it up –
> Adjusted it to place –
> Then carved his name – upon it –
> And bade it to the East

> Be faithful – in his absence –
> And he would come again –
> With Equipage of Amber –
> That time – to take it Home –   [J 603]

Sometimes the concept of the life beyond as a domestic reunion
became almost lugubrious in its concreteness:

> The grave my little cottage is,
> Where "Keeping house" for thee
> I make my parlor orderly
> And lay the marble tea.
>
> For two divided, briefly,
> A cycle, it may be,
> Till everlasting life unite
> In strong society.   [J 1743]

Yet, as we have seen, the ideas of the grave as a cottage, a room, or a
chamber was not peculiar to Dickinson. Emma Alice Brown's eulogy
entitled "My Brother," which can be found on page 5 of Mary
Warner's scrapbook, provides a striking example of the claustrophobic
housing enjoyed by all nineteenth-century Saints who slept peacefully
in sentiment's alabaster chambers:

> Oh, briar-rose clamber,
> And cover the chamber –
> The chamber so dreary and lone –
> Where with meekly closed lips,
> And eyes in eclipse,
> My brother lies under the stone.
>
> Oh, violets cover,
> The narrow roof over,
> Oh, cover the windows and door!
> For never the lights,
> Through the long days and nights,
> Make shadows across the floor!
> . . . .
>
> Oh, dear little brother;
> My sweet little brother
> In the palace above the sun,
> Oh, pray the good angels,
> The glorious evangels,
> To take me – when life is done.

This concreteness was the one element that made *The Gates Ajar* a radical, sensational, and, in some respects, equally grotesque work. After reading *Gates*, Mark Twain wrote a satirical burlesque of it that his beloved wife, Livy, persuaded him to keep from publication until 1907–8, when it appeared (somewhat modernized) in *Harper's Magazine* as *Extract from Captain Stormfield's Visit to Heaven*. Twain could hardly have surpassed Phelps in conjuring up a Gilded Age heaven if he had tried. As it was, his parody dealt more with the bureaucratic New Jerusalem of the Saints than with Phelps's Biedermeier paradise, for who could have surpassed a vision where one expects to find "glorified lilies of the valley, heavenly tea-rose buds, and spiritual harebells" (*Gates*, 93); "whole planets turned into galleries of art" (110); little children playing with pink blocks cut from clouds and devouring heavenly gingersnaps and strawberries (121); and frustrated musicians practicing away at pianos made of celestial rosewood and steel, for "there will be machinery and pianos in the same sense in which there will be pearl gates and harps. Whatever enjoyment any or all of them represent now, something will represent them" (123).

Mark Twain chose to direct some of his most telling satire against the notion that prompted Phelps to rhapsodize about the possibility of spiritual pianos and gingersnaps, the idea that what was denied the individual in life would be given to him a hundredfold when he entered upon his existence beyond the gates. "The man who don't get his reward on earth, needn't bother," Twain writes, "he will get it here, sure."[14] His Captain Stormfield discovers that a humble tailor and failed poet named Billings has, in the afterlife, Homer and Shakespeare to attend him, Shakespeare walking backwards and scattering flowers in front of him and Homer waiting on his table at the celestial banquet. Similarly, a charitable sausage maker from Hoboken named Duffer is astonished to find himself hailed as a baronet – "Sir Richard Duffer!" – as he steps on the heavenly shore, especially since "he thought he had reasons to believe he was pointed for a warmer climate than this one" (*Extract*, 97).

Here we have a burlesque also of Emily Dickinson's philosophy of "sumptuous Destitution" and her firmly held belief that what she refrained from in this world would be given to her in the next.[15] In Dickinson's case, it was the forbidden consummation of her love for Phoebus that was the chief prize reserved in her personal paradise. Once again, Phelps provides us with a rationale for this logically impossible denouement. For if Phoebus is married, how can he enjoy the bigamous company of two wives in heaven, if *both* are to be justified through love or suffering or faith? Dickinson's situation and its anguish were almost exactly reproduced in the example of Little Clo Bentley, the girl to whom Mrs. Forceythe confidently promised a piano in heaven because her bluenosed, orthodox parents had forbidden her one on earth. As Aunt Winifred tells her niece Mary, Clo has been in a hell of doubt and despair for two years, after being abandoned by a flirtatious summer boarder. "O Mrs. Forceythe," the young girl exclaims about heaven, "what is going to become of me up there? . . . he will have some beautiful, good wife of his own, and I won't have *any*-body! For I can't love anybody else" (*Gates*, 138).

Dickinson differed from Clo in having the assurance of Phoebus's love, which lent a certain strength and solidity to their secret covenant, to the high fellowship of their sealed church of two. Yet the consummation of this love must have seemed just as futile as Clo's in a Victorian America ruled by the highest ideals of honor, duty, and genteel convention. Phoebus was no dashing, blessedly single Robert Browning who might invade the mansion on Amherst's Main Street and steal the timid Emily from the grip of Squire Dickinson himself, for Phoebus was married and a man of position and social standing. Thus, when Clo rails, "I don't see how God can *make* me happy. I wish I could be buried up and go to sleep, and never have any heaven!" she learns from Aunt Winifred

> "that she should have him there. That is, if not himself, something, – somebody who would so much more than fill his place, and that she would never have a lonely or unloved minute. Her eyes brightened, and shaded, and pondered, doubting. She 'did n't see how it could ever be.' I told her not to try and see how, but to leave it to Christ. He knew all about this little trouble of hers, and he would make it right." [*Gates,* 138]

Christ himself became the guarantor not only of celestial joy but of connubial bliss. If Dickinson was denied the possibility of becoming the wife of Phoebus on earth, she was assured of enjoying all of the privileges and intimacies of marriage in the cottage-style heaven imagined by Elizabeth Stuart Phelps:

> The Tenant of the Narrow Cottage, wert Thou –
> Permit to be
> The Housewife in thy low attendance
> Contenteth Me –   [J 961]

Her patience was indefatigable:

> Say I may wait for you – say I need go with no stranger to the to me – untried country – I waited a long time – Master – but I can wait more – wait till my hazel hair is dappled – and you carry the

cane – then I can look at my watch – and if the Day is too far
declined – we can take the chances for Heaven. [L 2:374–5]

In her poetry, the experience of death entails the loss of physical virgin-
ity as well as of spiritual naiveté, and the hour of Emily Dickinson's
resurrection is also the dawn of her celestial wedding day:

> A Wife – at Daybreak I shall be –
> Sunrise – Hast thou a Flag for me?
> At Midnight, I am but a Maid,
> How short it takes to make it Bride –
> Then – Midnight, I have passed from thee
> Unto the East, and Victory –
>
> Midnight – Good Night! I hear them call,
> The Angels bustle in the Hall –
> Softly my Future climbs the Stair,
> I fumble at my Childhood's prayer
> So soon to be a Child no more –
> Eternity, I'm coming – Sir,
> Savior – I've seen the face – before!   [J 461]

Love and Death are one, for the "Childhood's prayer" fumbled at by
the speaker is obviously *The New England Primer's* "Now I Lay Me
Down to Sleep," with its Puritanical stress on the "Lord" both keeping
and taking the trusting soul of those young Elect who are "willing to
die." The confusion of the face of the Savior with the face of the
beloved at the conclusion of this poem is a deliberate one, for Dickinson's passion has struck such deep roots that her earthly "Lord," Phoebus, could not possibly differ from her heavenly "Lord," Jesus. Paradise was "fictitious" unless she could enter it through the "Realm" of
her lover, and

> The "Life that is to be," to me,
> A Residence too plain
> Unless in my Redeemer's Face
> I recognize your own –   [J 1260]

In a letter to her Master that Thomas Johnson dates about 1861, she
wrote, "I heard of a thing called 'Redemption' – which rested men and
women. You remember I asked you for it – you gave me something
else. I forgot the Redemption in the Redeemed" (L 2:374). Once again
Dickinson was only personalizing the movement toward a more material, intimate relationship with the Lord of the New Testament that was
an integral part of the sentimental gospel of love and its revolt against
the tyrannical Father-God of the Old Testament. In a work in Mary

Warner's scrapbook that dates from about 1857, a Massachusetts poet
with the initials A. P. M. similarly focuses on the beatific vision of the
Savior's corporeal presence in a poem called "Christ in the Bliss of
Heaven":

> I think not of the starry crown,
> Or robes the saints in glory wear;
> 'Twas heaven enough to bow me down,
> Before my Saviour, Jesus there.
>
> I think not of those harps whose notes
> Swell sweetly o'er the heavenly plains;
> The Saviour's voice in music floats,
> In richer, sweeter, dearer strains.
>
> I think not of those golden streets
> Where arches rise o'er pearly gates;
> Or mansions in whose blissful seats,
> Rest for the weary pilgrim waits.
>
> But O, the Saviour's face to see,
> The blest Redeemer's voice to hear;
> To be from sin for ever free,
> The tempter's wiles no more to fear:
>
> To feel immortal vigor fill
> My soul, and quicken every power;
> On angel's wing to do His will,
> And with a seraph's love adore.

This kind of ecstatic effusion could date from just about any age in
the history of Christianity, but what made Emily Dickinson's heresy so
blasphemous was her merger of Christ with Phoebus, the earthly lover
with the heavenly Redeemer.[16] In her poems on celestial marriage,
"Bliss" or "Glory" becomes a euphemism for sexual fulfillment, because it combines the divine and supernatural light of Calvinistic crisis
conversion with Stowe's "greatest and holiest of all the natural sacraments and means of grace – LOVE." Such bliss becomes permanent in
heaven, for the revelation of Christ's face also lifts the veil from the
forbidden mysteries of the flesh. Dickinson's passion for Phoebus sub-
sumes the affection of mother, father, sister, and brother in one white
heat of devotion, its sole object being to scan the complete physiognomy of the beloved:

> The Stimulus, beyond the Grave
> His Countenance to see

> Supports me like imperial Drams
> Afforded Day by Day.   [J 1001]

In the same way, we strongly suspect that Mary Cabot shall find that
Christ's face assumes the features of her lost brother, Royal, and Wini-
fred Forceythe must discover (after her painful death at the conclusion of
The Gates Ajar) that the gentle Jesus meek and mild whose teachings she
has put into action is in fact none other than her transfigured husband,
John. For, as Aunt Winifred makes plain in the following dialogue with
Mary, the greatest joy of heaven is in its personal recognitions:

> "Two things that He has taught us," she said after a silence, "give
> me beautiful assurance that none of these dreams with which I
> help myself can be beyond His intention to fulfil. One is, that eye
> hath not seen it, nor ear heard it, nor the heart conceived it – this
> lavishness of reward which He is keeping for us. Another is, that
> 'I shall be *satisfied* when I awake.' "
> "With his likeness." [*Gates,* 111]

Once again, we have the confusion of "His" and "his," of the Christ
who gives and the beloved who is given, implying that the face of one
will be the face of the other. To Emily Dickinson, the human likeness
was the final passport to complete celestial ecstasy:

> The face I carry with me – last –
> When I go out of Time –
> To take my Rank – by – in the West –
> That face – will just be thine –
>
> I'll hand it to the Angel –
> That – Sir – was my Degree –
> In Kingdoms – you have heard the Raised –
> Refer to – possibly.
>
> He'll take it – scan it – step aside –
> Return – with such a crown
> As Gabriel – never capered at –
> And beg me put it on –
>
> And then – he'll turn me round and round –
> To an admiring sky –
> As one that bore her Master's name –
> Sufficient Royalty!   [J 336]

It was precisely because Dickinson bore her Master's name, or "seal,"
engraved on her soul that she assumed the role of a provincial vestal virgin,
a New England lady in waiting. Like Parson Cyrus Field in a short tale of

New England romance that Mary Warner clipped from *Putnam's Monthly Magazine* in 1856, Dickinson thought of her departed lover whenever she thought of heaven, and imagined him as one who had found "his native country, and will show me the streets thereof if I possess my soul in patience till the good time draweth nigh."[17] The name of this story, set in the Connecticut Valley against "the sturdy outline of Mt. Tom and Mount Holyoke, now green and purple in the level rays of a cloudless sunset," is "Parson Field's Experience," the experience being a crisis conversion induced by totally unselfish love. Dickinson's "experience" was more hermetic, marked by the ceremony of secret bethrothal on that day which had come at summer's full. This consecration of both self and nature entailed the immediate pain of a personal crucifixion, while it promised the eventual reward of a celestial wedding. As Dickinson declared in a poem that she sent to two of her closest spiritual counselors, Samuel Bowles and Susan Dickinson, she enjoyed the equivocal privilege of a white election, combining an earthly crown of thorns with a heavenly crown of the redeemed:

> Title divine – is mine!
> The Wife – without the Sign!
> Acute Degree – conferred on me –
> Empress of Calvary!
> Royal – all but the Crown!
> Betrothed – without the swoon
> God send us Women –
> When you – hold – Garnet to Garnet –
> Gold – to Gold –
> Born – Bridalled – Shrouded –
> In a Day –
> "My Husband" – women say –
> Stroking the Melody –
> Is *this* – the way?   [J 1072]

Again, the regal and courtly character of Dickinson's imagery finds an echo in the very name of Mary Cabot's lost "Master," her brother Royal. Since Dickinson considered her Phoebus also to be a Christ-like figure, she became the bride or bethrothed of Christ, an "Empress of Calvary." Her blasphemous private mythology dilated on the full implications of that "enrapturing figure" that Charles Wadsworth, in a sermon entitled "Citizens of Heaven," claimed was "so often repeated in the Bible," the figure of

the saved Church or the saved Christian rescued, as a princess from captivity, and united in Love's everlasting bonds with the con-

queror as the Lamb's wife! And what a home-bringing, such as
bride never knew, that will be, when in the flaming chariot of fire,
in the blessed eventide of time, upward, onward, upon the crystalline arches, along Heaven's azure and starry pathway, homeward-
bound! Homeward-bound! – through the uplifted door, through
the golden streets, through the opening ranks of angel and archangel, to the place prepared in that house of many mansions! (*Sermons*, 144)

Such was the "Home" and "Equipage of Amber" about which Dickinson so often dreamed.[18] Again those early commentators who
thought of Emily Dickinson as a New England nun were closer to the
deepest truths of her soul than most modern critics have realized. Indeed, just as a professing nun might wear the golden wedding ring of
Christ, so does there seem to have been some actual exchange of tokens
between Dickinson and her kingly Phoebus. Jay Leyda notes, for example, that "Martha Dickinson Bianchi often showed later visitors a
ring (now at Harvard) that belonged to her aunt, enjoying their mystification when they read the name 'Phillip' engraved inside." He then
adds about Otis Phillips Lord, whose later love for Dickinson was
established in 1954 by the publication of Millicent Todd Bingham's
Emily Dickinson: A Revelation that " 'Little Phil' Lord may have solved
that mystery" (*YH* 1:lix). It was to this kind of keepsake that Dickinson
referred when she wrote:

> Given in Marriage unto Thee
> Oh Thou Celestial Host –
> Bride of the Father and the Son
> Bride of the Holy Ghost.
>
> Other Betrothal shall dissolve –
> Wedlock of Will, decay –
> Only the Keeper of this Ring
> Conquer Mortality –   [J 817]

But like the dark side of "Circumference," such a ring could also be
a type of Emerson's constricting ring of fate, for the nature of Dickinson's early love caused her to be "Born – Bridalled – Shrouded – / In a
Day," baptized into a new life of the spirit, both confirmed and married
in a love incapable of earthly fulfillment, and dressed in a winding-sheet
of constant attendance on that death which would bring a heavenly
consummation of her passion. There was bound to be bitterness about
the rigidity of her earthly deprivation and the "way" she had taken
when the poet compared her lot to that of those women who could
unashamedly delight in their present marital fulfillment, a bitterness

that just barely breaks through the surface of her ecstatic (one might almost say fanatical) language in these poems. Her love may signal a triple spiritual triumph, but in the word "Shrouded" we get some indication of the long discipline of painful self-sacrifice that was to be hers, dressed always in that spotless gown symbolizing her shroudlike white election. Dickinson was not alone in thus symbolizing her covenant with eternity. Emerson's remarkable aunt, Mary Moody, rode the streets of Concord garbed in her winding-sheet and slept in a bed fashioned in the form of a coffin. As her nephew wrote of this eccentricity in his memorial sketch of her:

> Saladin caused his shroud to be made, and carried it to battle as his standard. She made up her shroud, and death still refusing to come, and she thinking it a pity to let it lie idle, wore it as a night-gown or a day-gown, nay, went out to ride in it, on horseback, in her mountain roads, until it was worn out. Then she had another made up, and as she never travelled without being provided for this dear and indispensable contingency, I believe she wore out a great many. [*Works,* 10:428–9)

Dickinson's white dress, too, became her battle standard against an uncomprehending world that called her an infidel and a pagan, while she herself was fully conscious that her mystic marriage with Phoebus had caused her to be "bridled" as well as "Bridalled," harshly strapped up, harnessed, reined in.[19] In "Title divine–is mine!" (to push the sense of this word one step further), the poet rightfully "bridles," or scornfully rebels, against her fate. For, as she had written in an earlier poem about her single-minded devotion to this peremptory and elusive Master:

> He put the Belt around my life –
> I heard the Buckle snap –
> And turned away, imperial,
> My Lifetime folding up –
> Deliberate, as a Duke would do
> A Kingdom's Title Deed –
> Henceforth, a Dedicated sort –
> A Member of the Cloud.   [J 273]

IV

Dickinson resolved her dilemma, as Winifred Forceythe partially soothed the anguish of the unfortunate Clo Bentley, by viewing her lot from the perspective of the personal heaven to come, rather than the

private hell that was and had to be as long as she lived. One can say of
her, as Emerson said of Mary Moody, that "Destitution is the Muse of
her genius – Destitution and Death." Using her tremendous powers of
reverie and imagination, Dickinson sustained herself just as Elizabeth
Stuart Phelps's fictional Aunt Winifred and Mary Cabot banished their
immediate sorrow, by endless speculations on the nature and pleasures of
the life to come ("Fitter to see Him, I may be" [J 968]). As Mrs. Forceythe explains, "It seems to me that we shall learn to see in God the
centre of all possibilities of joy." And if we remember that for her,
"God" is the loving and forgiving Christ of the New Testament rather
than the fiery and vengeful Jehovah of the Old Testament, then "the
greatest of these lesser delights is but the greater measure of His friendship. They will not mean less of pleasure, but more of Him. They will
not 'pale,' as Dr. Bland would say. Human dearness will wax, not wane,
in heaven; but human friends will be loved for love of him" (*Gates*, 131).

It was natural, once one had accepted Mrs. Forceythe's materialist
interpretation of a Christian heaven (almost as carnal in many respects
as that of Mohammed), that the believer should concentrate on the
exact details of its private joys and pleasures, even if they included
celestial pianos and heavenly gingersnaps. The materialism that had
always been a major part of the Sentimental Love Religion would,
aided by Christian spiritualism, develop such visions to an even grosser
degree, until by 1880 Eugene Crowell could assure the readers of *The
Spirit World: Its Inhabitants, Nature and Philosophy* that in the sixth
heaven (reserved for upper-middle-class whites) "the furniture is gilded
and burnished. The floors of these homes are covered with rich and
velvety carpets, wrought in beautiful patterns and colors. These homes
are also furnished with clocks, and watches are in common use among
them, and are frequently carried on their persons."[20] Dickinson was as
certain of this bourgeois heaven "As if the Checks were given" (J 1052),
and surely the poet must have derived some of her greatest earthly
satisfaction from imagining the consummation of her long troth and the
day that she and the Christ-like Phoebus would be reborn and reunited
in their spiritual bodies:

> 'Twas a long Parting – but the time
> For Interview – had Come –
> Before the Judgment Seat of God –
> The last – and second time
>
> These Fleshless Lovers met –
> A Heaven in a Gaze –
> A Heaven of Heavens – the Privilege
> Of one another's Eyes –

> No Lifetime set – on Them –
> Appareled as the new
> Unborn – except They had beheld –
> Born infiniter – now –
>
> Was Bridal – e'er like This?
> A Paradise – the Host –
> And Cherubim – and Seraphim –
> The unobtrusive Guest –   [J 625]

Such a vision, when applied to the social organization of paradise, could again become strained, grotesque, and even ludicrous. The idea that the redeemed soul would meet in this private heaven not only its lost lovers, friends, and family but also the great men and women of Scripture and history leads Mary Cabot to "wonder if Roy has seen the President. Aunt Winifred says she does not doubt it. She thinks that all the soldiers must have crowded up to meet him, and 'O,' she says, 'what a sight to see!' " (Gates, 57). Aunt Winifred herself expects to join some rather high-toned circles. "Be that as it may," she says to Mary, referring to the fact that the first of those to be met in heaven would most probably be our closet acquaintances, who would accustom us to its glories lovingly and gradually,

> "and be heaven where it may, I am not afraid. With all my guessing and my studying and my dreaming over these things, I am only a child in the dark. 'Nevertheless, I am not afraid of the dark.' God bless Mr. Robertson for saying that! I'm going to bless him when I see him. How pleasant it will be to see him, and some other friends whose faces I never saw in this world! David, for instance, or Paul, or Cowper, or President Lincoln, or Mrs. Browning. The only trouble is that I am nobody to them! However, I fancy that they will let me shake hands with them." [156]

Dickinson, too, dreamed of being ushered into an august company beyond the gates:

> Me – come! My dazzled face
> In such a shining place!
> Me – hear! My foreign Ear
> The sounds of Welcome – there!
>
> The Saints forget
> Our bashful feet –
>
> My Holiday, shall be
> That They – remember me –

My Paradise – the fame
That They – pronounce my name –   [J 431]

Such speculation led Mark Twain to fling some of his sharpest barbs
of parody in *Extract from Captain Stormfield's Visit to Heaven*. As the
captain learns, while paradise is indeed made up of many individual
private heavens, it is not a republic or a democracy but rather a strict
monarchy that has its own rigid hierarchy and social class structure.
Consequently, "there are a lot of such things that people expect and
don't get," Captain Stormfield's friend Sandy explains to him:

> For instance, there's a Brooklyn preacher by the name of Talmage,[21]
> who is laying up a considerable disappointment for himself. He says,
> every now and then in his sermons, that the first thing he does when
> he gets to heaven will be to fling his arms around Abraham, Isaac,
> and Jacob, and kiss them and weep on them. There's millions of
> people down here on earth that are promising themselves the same
> thing. As many as sixty thousand people arrive here every single
> day, that want to run straight to Abraham, Isaac and Jacob, and hug
> them and weep on them. Now mind you, sixty thousand a day is a
> pretty heavy contract for those old people. If they were a mind to
> allow it, they wouldn't ever have anything to do, year in and year
> out, but stand up and be hugged and wept on thirty-two hours in the
> twenty-four. They would be tired out and wet as muskrats all the
> time. What would heaven be, to them? It would be a mighty good
> place to get out of – you know that yourself. Those are kind and
> gentle old Jews, but they ain't any fonder of kissing the emotional
> high-lights of Brooklyn than you be. You mark my words. Mr. T.'s
> endearments are going to be declined, with thanks. There are limits
> to the privileges of the elect, even in heaven. [72 – 3]

Twain pointed only once more to the logical, or illogical, consequences of the Sentimental Love Religion in which Phelps and Dickinson firmly believed.[22] His satire does not undermine either the genuineness of that belief or its fervor any more than his famous realist attack,
"Fenimore Cooper's Literary Offenses" (1894), destroys the total worth
of a major American romancer. I would simply suggest that it was
some such counsel as that articulated through the character of Aunt
Winifred in *The Gates Ajar* which helped to convert Emily Dickinson
from the bleak "White Sustenance" (J 640) of her early Calvinist despair
to the joyful, if painful, white election of her marriage poems. It was
not *The Gates Ajar* itself that served as her vade mecum to the possibilities of what Phelps, quoting Thomas Chalmers, called "spiritual materialism," for most of her love poems were composed in or before the

year 1862. But, as the poet herself revealed, there was some definite guide, some "Primer" to which she turned in order to learn the ABCs of the paradise deferred:

> Not in this World to see his face —
> Sounds long — until I read the place
> Where this — is said to be
> But just the Primer — to a life —
> Unopened — rare — Upon the Shelf —
> Clasped yet — to Him — and me —
>
> And yet — My Primer suits me so
> I would not choose — a Book to know
> Than that — be sweeter wise —
> Might someone else — so learned — be —
> And leave me — just my A — B — C —
> Himself — could have the Skies —   [J 418]

Her primer may have been any of the many authorities cited by Elizabeth Stuart Phelps in *The Gates Ajar:* from Plato and Luther to Frederick William Robertson, the Comtesse de Gasparin, and Elizabeth Barrett Browning; one of the books of revelation, like Wight's *Romance of Abelard and Heloise;* or Dickinson's own latitudinarian interpretation of the sacred Scriptures themselves, confirmed by such ecstatic sermons as Charles Wadsworth's "Citizens of Heaven." Ultimately, her philosophy of renunciation and of wish fulfillment in heaven was a response to the liberalizing forces that left the startled deacon of Oliver Wendell Holmes's famous poem sitting amid the broken axles and rusty springs of the "One-Hoss Shay" of old-line Calvinism.

Yet the type was everywhere in her time and place. In *The Ring and the Book* (1868), Robert Browning's doomed child bride, Pompilia, dreams of celestial reunion with her priest-lover, Caponsacchi,[23] and throngs of admiring visitors to Philadelphia's Centennial Exhibition of 1876 were charmed by Bergonzoli's sublimely erotic sculpture *Angelic Love* (see the illustration at the opening of this chapter).[24] A similar study, Canova's *Cupid and Psyche,* graced the parlor of Emily Dickinson's sister-in-law, Susan Huntington Gilbert, and Charles Kingsley, that most muscular of nineteenth-century Christians, resolved his long struggle with sexuality by convincing himself that the heaven of the New Testament had to be a refined and endless orgasm. As one consequence he produced drawings of copulating seraphs that a horrified Nathaniel Hawthorne recorded, "no pure man could have made or allowed himself to look at."[25] It is against this Victorian background that Dickinson's love poetry must be read, and her playful criticism of

Scripture (Matt. 22:30) in a late letter (*L* 3:728) to Otis Phillips Lord ("in Heaven they neither woo nor are given in wooing – what an imperfect place!") be fully understood.

Still, the wildest heresies can harden into dogma. When Judge Lord finally offered Dickinson the mundane diadem of an actual earthly betrothal about the year 1878, she spurned his proposal in favor of the celestial crown she had so long promised to herself. "Dont you know you are happiest while I withhold and not confer," she wrote. "Dont you know that 'No' is the wildest word we consign to Language? . . . It is Anguish I long conceal from you to let you leave me, hungry, but you ask the divine Crust and that would doom the Bread." Only when it was right would she lift the bars of the stile that divided an earthly life of waiting from a heavenly life of loving, enter the secret garden of her dreams, "and lay you in the Moss" (*L* 2:617).

The intimacy of Dickinson's imagery, however much it may have shocked the judge, would have on the contrary seemed natural and forthright to liberated readers familiar with *The Gates Ajar* and its paradise of personal fulfillment.

The Cat, artist unknown, ca. 1840. (By permission of the National Gallery of Art, Washington, D.C.)

Chapter 5

AMERICAN GROTESQUE

Dickinson, God, and Folk Forms

The idea that any personal deity could find pleasure or profit in torturing a poor woman, by accident, with a fiendish cruelty known to man only in perverted and insane temperaments, could not be held for a moment. For pure blasphemy, it made pure atheism a comfort. God might be, as the church said, a Substance, but He could not be a Person.

Henry Adams

Well, then, I hate Thee, unrighteous picture
Wicked image, I hate thee.

Stephen Crane

Doubtless we are "fearfully and wonderfully made," and occasionally grotesquely.

Emily Dickinson

Having charted Emily Dickinson's response to a Victorian popular culture as expressed in sentimental attitudes toward love, death, and the afterlife, we must now confront a problem that is paradoxically both formal and metaphysical: her relationship to God. The problem is formal in that Dickinson's response to the Deity is intimately bound up in her use of a folk form. According to Henry Glassie's definition of "folk" as a craftsman's rigid adherence to traditional models and patterns, Dickinson cannot escape being labeled a folk artist, since she uses the plain-style hymns of Isaac Watts (1674–1748) as a consistent paradigm for her verse.[1] With the elaborate metrical intricacies of Longfellow, the Brownings, and Tennyson in vogue everywhere about her, her art remains in a deliberately archaic mode, a limner tradition far removed from courtly, high-style, or painterly technique.

Although her idiosyncratic internal variations on the iambics of common meter, long meter, and short meter were radical by eighteenth-century standards, her choice of the form itself was decidedly *retardataire* given nineteenth-century norms. Rather than imitating a plastic architectural space, her art possesses the abstraction of an emblem, stencil, or patchwork quilt. Like her spiritual ancestor, the American Puritan poet Edward Taylor, who avoided the contemporary fashions of Restoration and neoclassic verse to write in a rough-hewn, outmoded metaphysical style made popular long before his birth, Dickinson took her rubric from the past and not the present. Expressing pride in her provinciality, she once wrote to unidentified recipients, "I cannot tint in Carbon nor embroider Brass, but send you a homespun rustic picture I certainly saw in the terrific storm. Please excuse my needlework" (L 3:915–16).

It is interesting that Dickinson should also think of her poetry as an art that was considered to be at one and the same time "woman's work" and "handiwork," a skill almost exclusively the province of the female sex and a folk product that existed in its own homespun sphere apart from the sophisticated realm of charcoal drawing, tinted lithograph, or finely detailed etching. As Sandra Gilbert and Susan Gubar have demonstrated in their discussion of the relationship of Dickinson's poetry to the act of sewing (*Madwoman,* 638–42), needlework in all its modes, from the spinning of wool and flax (giving us the original meaning of the term "spinster") to the final delicacy of crewel embroidery, was an act of the female imagination as well as a domestic necessity. In 1845, at the age of fifteen, Dickinson herself embroidered a sampler with a verse whose final quaint conceit would have been applauded by her Puritan forbears:

> Jesus Permit Thy Gracious Name to stand
> As the First efforts of an infants hand
> And while her fingers oer this canvas move
> Engage her tender heart to seek thy love
> With thy dear children let her share a Part
> And write thy name thyself upon her heart   [*YH* 1:99]

Whereas the art of needlework was her inheritance as a nineteenth-century woman bound to the domestic sphere, Dickinson's art of poetry belonged, as I have noted, to an equally homely tradition in its strict adherence to hymn forms. Her experience of the power of this folk mode was shared by New Englanders of both genders who had had to endure the rigors of a Calvinist upbringing. As with the manic-depressive symptoms of the New England theology itself, the effect of hymns on the hearer had its dark and its bright sides, its agonies and its ecstasies. The ecstasies are well delineated by Lucy Larcom, the well-known poet who, as an artistically inclined factory worker, contributed to much of the success of the famous *Lowell Offering* (1840–5). Speaking in her *A*

New England Girlhood of her life as a child on the Massachusetts coast
before her family was forced to relocate to Lowell, Larcom recalled:

> Almost the first decided taste in my life was the love of hymns.
> Committing them to memory was as natural to me as breathing. I
> followed my mother about with the hymn-book ("Watts' and
> Select"), reading or repeating them to her, while she was busy
> with her baking or ironing, and she was always a devoted
> listener . . .
>
> Some of the old hymns did seem to lend us wings, so full were
> they of aspiration and hope and courage. To a little child, reading
> them or hearing them sung was like being caught up in a strong
> man's arms, to gaze upon some wonderful landscape. These
> climbing and flying hymns, – how well I remember them, al-
> though they were among the first I learned! They are of the kind
> that can never wear out. We all know them by their first lines, –
> > "Awake, our souls! away, our fears!"
> > "Up to the hills I lift mine eyes."
> > "There is a land of pure delight."
> > "Rise, my soul, and stretch thy wings,
> >   Thy better portion trace!"[2]

To Lucy Larcom, it seemed that in her childhood "the air was full of
hymns," and even in maturity "their melody penetrates deep into my
life, assuring me that I have not left the green pastures and the still
waters of my childhood very far behind me" (*Girlhood,* 73). Because of
the rigidity of Emily Dickinson's private mythology, which postponed
maturity and fulfillment to a life after death ("The power and the glory
are the post mortuary gifts" [*L* 3:920]), she never left those green
pastures and still waters, and the singsong lines of common meter, long
meter, and short meter reverberated in her mind and in her art almost
until the day of her death. Favorite snatches and cadences came not only
from Watts's *Hymns* but from his *Divine Songs for Children,* with the
Protestant ethic embedded obdurately in such rhymes as "Against Idleness and Mischief":

> How doth the little busy bee,
>   Improve each shining hour,
> And gather honey all the day
>   From every opening flower!
>
> In works of labour or of skill,
>   I would be busy too;
> For Satan finds some mischief still
>   For idle hands to do.   [*Works,* 224]

Such verses were ripe for parody. Where Lewis Carroll replaced Watts's honeybee with a "little crocodile," and had him concentrate on improving his "shining tail" rather than the industrious hours,[3] Dickinson converted him into a buccaneering bumblebee whose "Religion" was to preach free thought and

> To a delusive Lilac
> The vanity divulge
> Of Industry and Morals
> And every righteous thing
> For the divine Perdition
> Of Idleness and Spring –   [J 1522]

She parodied "Against Idleness" again in an 1878 letter to Mrs. Holland (*L* 2:604), and continued to satirize Watts's *Hymns* in other poems (J 916, for example) and letters. But at the same time the joyous hymns that appealed to Lucy Larcom also elated her; both shared a love for the Pisgah vision expressed in Watts's "There is a land of pure delight," bodily incorporated in "Where bells no more affright the morn" (J 112). William Cowper's majestic line "God moves in a mysterious way," quoted by Dickinson in an early letter (*L* 1:217), gave Larcom "an idea of the presence of One Infinite Being, that filled me with reverent awe" (*Girlhood, 63*).

Besides the standard collections like *Church Psalmody* (1831), Asahel Nettleton's supplement to Watts, *Village Hymns for Social Worship* (1824), provided food for thought, yet this food was digested in various ways.[4] On March twenty-seventh, 1853, Dickinson wrote Austin that she would send him "Village Hymns by earliest opportunity," and added, "I was just this moment thinking of a favorite stanza of your's, 'where congregations n'er break up, and Sabbaths have no end' " (*L* 1:235). She also teased her brother about a poem he had included with his last letter to her, writing with mock seriousness, "Austin is a Poet, Austin writes a psalm," and confessing to "Brother Pegasus," "I've been in the habit *myself* of writing some few things, and it rather appears to me that you're getting away my patent, so you'd better be somewhat careful, or I'll call the police!"

In her own protesting psalms, such as "I never felt at home – Below – ," Dickinson rejected a Calvinist paradise where "it's Sunday – all the time" in a way remarkably similar to that of Lucy Larcom, who confessed that she took exception to specific verses in many of her most loved hymns, including Austin's "favorite." Of it she comments:

I always wanted to skip one half of the third stanza, as it stood in our Hymn-Book: –

"Where congregations ne'er break up,
     And Sabbaths have no end."
I did not want it to be Sabbath-day always. I was conscious of a
pleasure in the thought of games and frolics and coming week-day
delights that would flit across my mind even when I was studying
my hymns, or trying to listen to the minister. And I did want the
congregation to break up some time. Indeed, in those bright
spring days, the last hymn in the afternoon always sounded best,
because with it came the opening of doors into the outside air, and
the pouring in of a mingled scent of sea winds and apple blossoms, like an invitation out into the freedom of the beach, the
hillsides, the fields and gardens and orchards. In all this I felt as if I
were very wicked. I was afraid that I loved earth better than I did
heaven. [*Girlhood,* 71–2]

Following out this same reasoning, Dickinson decided that

> The Fact that Earth is heaven –
> Whether Heaven is Heaven or not
> If not an Affidavit
> Of that specific Spot
> Not only must confirm us
> That it is not for us
> But that it would affront us
> To dwell in such a place –   [J 1408]

Lucy Larcom loved to learn the scores of "*glad* hymns" that expressed her childlike sense of the natural paradise and its overflowing
ebullience of youth, yet she could not escape the preponderance of
"sorrowful ones" that were given to her to memorize "as a task"
(*Girlhood,* 69). In the more grimly orthodox Amherst and its environs,
these sorrowful dirges overpowered the religious consciousness of those
who had both to learn and to hear them, almost eclipsing the bright
vision of the "climbing and flying" tunes. Austin Dickinson himself
recalled the introduction of a double bass viol as an aid to Congregational worship in 1839. He wrote in 1889 in an official memoir entitled
"Representative Men of the Parish":

Josiah Ayres managed it, and the tones he drew from its lower
chords in his accompaniment to the singing of some of Watts'
Favorite Hymns, haunt me even now.
     Such lines as
          "That awful day will surely come."
          "That last great day of woe and doom,"
and

"Broad is the road that leads to death," etc.,
seemed to me sufficiently depressing in plain print; sung with the
accompaniment, they were appalling – to a boy.[5]

Austin's memory was probably jogged by an extraordinary Sunday
when, sick in bed, he heard part of a lively amateur theatrical enacted at
the dinner table by Judge Otis Phillips Lord. In her "Magnetic Visitors," Susan Dickinson writes that

> perhaps because it was Sunday we naturally got upon the subject
> of hymnology in New England. The Judge, remarking that he
> was brought up on "Watts and Select" unabridged, asked if any of
> us were familiar with the hymn beginning:
>
> > "My thoughts on awful subjects roll
> > Damnation and the dead."
>
> In astonishment we answered, "No!" – whereupon he laid down
> his fork, made himself a little more stiff and erect behind his old-
> fashioned silk stock than usual, if that were possible, and recited
> with an energy worthy of himself, and the subject, the whole
> hymn. There was really a horrible grandeur about it, although our
> nervous laughter might have misled one in the next room as to
> our real emotions. [13]

Judge Lord's performance prompted Lavinia Dickinson "to give us
one of her famous representations of one early choir, with bass viol
accompaniment." After singing "stoutly and with real minor threat and
pathos" the beginning of "Broad is the road which leads to death," she
masterfully imitated the part of "the superannuated Village soprano"
whose voice cracked in reaching for the high notes, as well as the
"harrowing discord" of the bass viol as it "moaned along without her."
The applause of the dinner guests was so tumultuous that it induced the
sick Austin to ring his bell, "requesting us to remember that it was
Sunday" (14).

Emily Dickinson was nine years old when Josiah Ayres's bass viol
was acquired, and if performances of these kinds of Calvinistic *Dies Irae*
seemed "appalling" to boys like Austin, and caused, as Martha Dickinson Bianchi remembered, even a modern, more freethinking generation
to listen with "teeth chattering" (*Life and Letters,* 70), there is no need to
calculate the extent of their effect on an impressionable and increasingly
unregenerate young female sinner in the later 1840s. Much of Dickinson's poetry was a continuing dialectic that used the imagery, premises,
and metrics of Puritan hymnology as a basis for a personal psalmody of
questioning and protest. When we read the abstracts of Calvinist doctrine in *Watts and Select* or *Village Hymns,* we are inevitably reminded

that many of Dickinson's poems are in turn heretical paraphrases of or replies to these same orthodox sentiments. "Safe in their Alabaster Chambers" mocks the piety of

> The saints who now in Jesus sleep,
> His own almighty power shall keep,
> Till dawns the bright illustrious day,
> When death itself shall die away,

whereas "I heard a Fly buzz – when I died" makes an ironic inside narrative of

> In vain our fancy strives to paint
>   The moment after death,
> The glories that surround the saint,
>   While yielding up his breath,

and "I cannot live with you" secularizes the Christ-centered fervor of

> I cannot live contented here,
>   Without some glimpses of thy face;
> And heaven, without thy presence there,
>   Will be a dark and tiresome place.[6]

Although Emily Dickinson's use of a folk form was consistent, the content enframed within that form was drawn variously from elite, popular, or corresponding folk levels of culture. This consistency of form allowed Dickinson to condense and abstract complex motifs as she fitted them to the purposely limited requirements of her art, as rigid as the geometric patterns dictated for patchwork quilts. In this process she was similar to any folk artist who adapts innovative ideas to pre-scribed conventions. We have already studied such a melding and blending of styles in "A Spider sewed at Night" and in the unwritten poem that was her funeral, but it is especially in Dickinson's poems about the "strong arms" of the Calvinist God that we confront a characteristic synthesis of the contemporary and the archaic.

I

Once again, Henry Glassie defines for us the integral process of folk art. Speaking of Pennsylvania German artisans, he notes that a synthesis of new material and old forms "not only enables variation within a tradition," but also "facilitates creativity," for

> when a new idea is presented to the artist he does not have to reject or accept it completely. Through the process called *bricolage*

by Claude Lévi-Strauss, the new idea is broken down and compared with old ones and a composite idea is developed to suit the artist's psychobiological nature and his social and physical environment. The novel synthetic idea may be a compromise of fashionable and unfashionable ideas; its result may be seen by the folklorist as partially folk and by the art historian as an incomplete expresssion of a "style" or as a mixture of "styles" . . . the mental dynamics of *bricolage* allowed for very complicated syntheses of old and new ideas. ["Folk Art," 260]

The dynamics of *bricolage* can be charted in Emily Dickinson's whole response to the idea of the folk as both a style and a refuge. In a romantic age that was consciously devoted to a revival of primitive ideas, the folk song, ballad, and hymn became the expression of an imaginary realm of emotional power associated with the childhood of the race and the untutored voice of nature itself. Mary Warner's scrapbook contains a "Ballad" by Thomas Hood, representative of the continuing conversion of folk materials into popular and elite imitations that resulted in such forms as the art ballad and the art fairy tale.[7] Dickinson in turn wrote what might be called art hymns, and she was quite conscious of participating in a ballad revival that was more than a simple matter of scansion. In her private mythology, the ballad, like the hymn, was a heart song that reflected the full devotion of Daisy to Phoebus, the pitiful last lament of the dying swan:

> Sang from the Heart, Sire,
> Dipped my Beak in it,
> If the Tune drip too much
> Have a tint too Red
>
> Pardon the Cochineal —
> Suffer the Vermillion —
> Death is the Wealth
> Of the Poorest Bird.
>
> Bear with the Ballad —
> Awkward — faltering —
> Death twists the strings —
> 'Twas'nt my blame —
>
> Pause in your Liturgies —
> Wait your Chorals —
> While I repeat your
> Hallowed name —   [J 1059]

If the distance between Dickinson and her deific Master is so great that it provokes an aria that verges on the pathetic, what follows from the tremendous distance between Dickinson and the Calvinist God who was the focus of New England hymnology? Dickinson was not as silent a rebel as Lucy Larcom, but in trying to defend her orthodoxy, her niece opened up a way by which we can gauge the distorting perspective of this distance. Martha Dickinson Bianchi called upon her mother as a witness to Emily Dickinson's fundamental spirituality. Susan Huntington Gilbert had joined the First Congregational Church in 1851 at the age of twenty, and her lifelong religious quest was deepened, not diminished, by the tragic death of her youngest son, Gilbert, in 1883. Bianchi writes that

> spurning all canting phrases, Emily remained a docile child of God and a rebellious heir of His kingdom. Susan realized that, although Emily took liberties with the Puritan vernacular and dogma when venting her baffled impatience with the Inscrutable, these impish flashes were no more to the underlying God-consciousness of the real Emily than the gargoyle on the roof is to the heart of the Cathedral within. [FF, ss]

Bianchi has been much criticized for her romantic and apologetic attitude toward the poet. Although she often posed as that most yielding of Victorian heroines, the bride of Christ,[8] Dickinson was hardly a "docile child of God." Yet if we examine this statement from the perspective that accepts the validity of the visual in apprehending the structure of life as well as the structure of poetry, Bianchi's reporting of her mother's observation becomes both cogent and insightful. Exploring her analogy, we realize that the real cathedral is not so much Emily Dickinson's God-consciousness as it is that vernacular New England Calvinism which shaped and buttressed it, and the gargoyle seems a near-perfect figure to represent her fanciful, sometimes capricious sense of the grotesque.

The only problem with the metaphor is that it is not an indigenous one. Although in one early poem Dickinson claims to have "heard an Organ talk, sometimes – / In a Cathedral Aisle" (J 183), and she experiences "the Heft / Of Cathedral Tunes" in her chilling "There's a certain Slant of Light" (J 258), she had never seen a cathedral save in her own Gothic imagination. Dickinson had never even been inside a Catholic church, for the first mass ever celebrated in Amherst was in the house of John Slater, an Irish Catholic, in 1840 and the first Catholic church was not built until 1871, when her retreat from the world was well established. Chartres and Rheims were light-years away from the stern meetinghouse upbringing that she actually knew. Emily Dickinson consistently saw "New Englandly," and the glories of medieval architecture were far more available to her well-traveled niece, whose second volume of poems was in fact entitled *The Cathedral* (1901). Tinged by the mellow glow of a Gothic revival fostered by John Ruskin and soon to be eulogized by Henry Adams in his *Mont-Saint-Michel and Chartres,* Bianchi's "The Gargoyles" expresses a fin-de-siècle aestheticism quite different from Emily Dickinson's sparer Puritan complaints:

> O beasts from out the forest of the soul,
>   What sport of human frailty makes ye grin?
> Did cunning hands, grown weary of the throng
>   Of angel hordes, yield for the nonce to sin –
> Give sacrilege her way and fashion ye?
>   Flaunting your jest at holiness abroad,
> What mediaeval imps of man's revenge
>   Are ye? Exórcised in the name of God![9]

If Emily Dickinson's art is Gothic, it is a home-grown variety that skews and distorts externals in order to probe internals, the secret haunted chamber of the mind itself. Vestigial Calvinism, amplified through the fearsome images and sonorous tunes of Watts's *Hymns,* gave a definite structure to her building of this private Headlong Hall, while it also provided a ghostly portrait of the absentee landlord who administered, tyrannized over, and entailed it: God himself. As Lucy Larcom explains, one of the reasons for the impressiveness of Watts's hymns for a child "is that they are either addressed to a Person, to the Divine Person, – or they bring Him before the mind in some distinct way, instead of being written upon a subject, like a sermon" (*Girlhood,* 65–6). A general answer concerning the true nature of this person had already been given by Harriet Beecher Stowe, who in *The Minister's Wooing* has Mrs. Marvyn admit that "any father, who should make use of such power over his children as they say the Deity does with regard to us, would be looked upon as a monster by our very imperfect moral sense" (355). In a letter to her own daughter Hattie, who had accepted the arguments of German skepticism and was in danger of rejecting Christianity altogether, Stowe was forced to rehearse this debate on an even more personal level:

> As long as we are in mortal bodies the view of things spiritual must be subject to cloud and eclipse and when we put up our telescope to see the heavenly bodies some crawling thing or other will come between us and them and appear a magnified monster shutting out their beauty . . . No poor suffering child, you do *not* hate your Father in Heaven any more than you do me and the

horrible image that rises before your mind and which you think you hate is the fly that has crept between the glasses of the telescope and is magnified as a monster. [Wagenknecht, *Harriet Beecher Stowe*, 216]

For a poet who often thought of herself as a bird – an unassuming wren, robin, or phoebe, as well as a regal swan – it was not the image of the magnified fly that shaped Dickinson's full-length portrait of the threatening heavenly Father. The beast that roamed the forests of her soul was more like Henry James's tigerish "Beast in the Jungle" of 1903, though in turn it was both mentally real and rurally domestic.

Dickinson's situation as a vernacular poet caused her to develop a *bricolage* that was her eclectic version of carpenter Gothic. When this mixture of folk and popular motifs crystallized in a distinct personal vision of Calvinism's monster-god, the result was the epitome of the American grotesque. Just as carpenter Gothic revels in the fanciful and the piquant and just as the grotesque encompasses a ludicrous or comic element, so is the full picture of Dickinson's religious consciousness not without its quality of what her sister-in-law, according to Bianchi, identified as "the impish" and what the poet herself called (in reference to a rare display of her father's humor) "a little excess of *Monkey!*" (*L* 1:121). These same qualities of the vernacular, the grotesque, and the comic can be found in a remarkable American primitive painting of about the year 1840 (see the illustration at the beginning of this chapter). Now part of the collection of Edgar William and Bernice Chrysler Garbisch at the National Gallery of Art, it can serve, I believe, as an appropriate analogue of the unique God-consciousness manifested in Dickinson's poetry.[10]

This anonymous work, entitled by its owners *The Cat,* presents the viewer with the terrifying, enormous head of a striped and bewhiskered feline – enormous, that is, in proportion to the two dwarfish trees that stand on either side of it. The head of the cat emerges, as do the trunks of the trees, from a green field of tall, flatly rendered grass that (if we follow the logic of perspective, rather than the imagistic logic of the painting) could not possibly conceal the remainder of the cat's monolithic anatomy. The subject of the painting remains a disembodied and slightly ridiculous figure with a self-satisfied grin that, as William Carlos Williams observed,[11] foreshadows that of Lewis Carroll's Cheshire variety in *Alice in Wonderland*. Moreover, the landscape into which this monster intrudes was once patently one of idyllic serenity, a stylized folk paradise like the later Edens of the French primitivist and proto-surrealist Henri Rousseau. Two bright birds of plumage still lodge in the miniature trees, a scarlet cardinal on the left and an improbable blue and gold finch on the right. The universe of *The Cat* contains an un-bearably precise sense of balance while suffering its own kind of primal fall. For the great round mass of the cat's head holds firmly clenched in its teeth the dead mate of the startled finch. There is a serpent in paradise, a predator who is allowed to roam at will by the unseen keeper of the garden.

The Cat is a powerful folk image of terror and the grotesque. Its meticulous style reminds us, as Donald B. Kuspit has written, that "it is as a direct result of his practical desire to fix detail" that the folk artist "achieves the visionary quality of his art – the sense of an eternalized image with a kind of enforced memorableness." Kuspit concludes that "it is because he so urgently wants to know exactly what he has before him that he seems to become what the Shakers called a 'first witness' of the subject matter, envisioning it rather than simply seeing it."[12] In *The Cat,* we are first witnesses to a vision of fear rather than one of love. The colorful beauty of the birds is irrelevant to the gargantuan hunger at the center of the painting. The cat's greed is made even more ludi-crous by the distortion of his features and the obvious fact that he is considering whether it is worth his while to drop his dead prey and try for one of its live companions who perch so tantalizingly within his grasp. The question that the cat most assuredly ponders is one that Dickinson herself asked in a poem comparing the available natural para-dise to the pie-in-the-sky heaven of optimistic Christian belief:

> Which is best? Heaven –
> Or only Heaven to come
> With that old Codicil of Doubt?
> I cannot help esteem
>
> The "Bird within the Hand"
> Superior to the one
> The "Bush" may yield me
> Or may not
> Too late to choose again.   [J 1012]

"The Charms of the Heaven in the bush," Dickinson wrote to Sam-uel Bowles about 1858, "are superceded I fear, by the Heaven in the hand, occasionally" (*L* 2:338). The unwritten caption of *The Cat,* too, is the ancient proverb "A bird in the hand is worth two in the bush," but here the question is posed by the very being who has become master of the garden, and not by one of its humble and terrified occu-pants. This totem-like animal, set in a nightmare landscape of delicacy overawed by power, conveys the mystery of a Blakean Song of Inno-cence transformed into a topsy-turvy Song of Experience. He is a

purely American version of that "Tyger, tyger burning bright" whose
brutal universe of absolute law has about it a compelling awkwardness
of vision as well as a fearful symmetry of form. Most hypnotic and yet
most grotesque of all the elements of the composition are the cat's
baleful, deep-set yellow eyes. This predatory monster, more akin to the
chimera, basilisk, and gryphon than to the ordinary *Felis domesticus,*
ogles the birds in the bush while he unconcernedly mangles the bird
clamped firmly in mouth. Serenely malefic, he is the soul of the empty,
dreamlike quality of the painting. He triumphs as this garden's commanding presence, its archon or demiurge, self-contained in his sinister
playfulness: a pure, terrible, and grotesque cat-god.

It is just such a god that Dickinson fashioned in her attempt to
transfer the cruel and paradoxical images of New England Calvinism
to the canvas of her own archly playful imagination. Not the medieval
gargoyle but an archetypal folk image such as *The Cat* provides the
best analogue for a study of the dramatic qualities of her God-consciousness. Even so, we must again acknowledge that Dickinson, like
Blake, was in many respects a deliberate naif. Her early valentine
verses (J1, J3) show a mastery of standard Augustan verse forms,[13] and
her creative use of hymn meters allies her to romantics like Coleridge
who consciously chose the lyric challenges of the ballad stanza over
the sure felicity of the heroic couplet. Whereas Blake later adopted the
sonorous cadences of Macpherson's *Ossian* to match the sublimity of
conception that inspired his late *Prophetic Books,* Dickinson remained
content to plane her private mythology to the starker requirements of
long meter, common meter, and short meter. As Henry Glassie reminds us, "While the elite artist may be willing to risk his standing to
appear ahead of his times, it is only a rare folk artist who strives for
innovation; his replication is an affirmation of a tradition" ("Folk
Art," 259). Yet both these poets turned orthodoxy's weapons against
itself. Blake pointed to Jehovah as the fearful maker of the Tyger;
Dickinson saw the same problem reduced to an ordinary household
event. In Dickinson's backyard metaphysic, the question who framed
the sinister lineaments of the family cat was answered by her invoca-
tion "Burglar! Banker – Father!" (J 49):[14] the God of Jonathan Edwards, the "Eclipse" her own family addressed each day at morning
prayer (*L* 2:404):

> Papa above!
> Regard a Mouse
> O'erpowered by the Cat!
> Reserve within thy kingdom
> A "Mansion" for the Rat!

Snug in seraphic Cupboards
To nibble all the day,
While unsuspecting Cycles
Wheel solemnly away!   [J 61]

In trying to make her peace with that engine of contrived torture
that was the New England theology strictly applied, Dickinson constructed a closed imagistic world in which she first assumed the role
of victim, toyed with by an aloof cat-god who possessed the power of
imparting or withholding sanctifying grace. As Albert Gelpi writes,
"She pleaded as a helpless mouse, knowing well that to Him she
might seem a 'Rat.' "[15] Even if condemned to hellfire, the poet still
prayed for some kind of ultimate Arminian justification, some altera-
tion of the cosmic plan in which the damned, the outsider, the natural
man could earn through earthly suffering a small nook in that heavenly house which, as Jesus assures us in John 14:2, has "many mansions." Yet she made such a cold compensation appear grotesque by
following out the image to its ultimate absurdity. The picture of a
snug and secure celestial mouse, nibbling away at eternity in the wain-
scot of heaven, could hardly be called a pious commentary on the
orthodox idea of paradise. That plain style of thought and metaphor
which induced Edward Taylor to choose the kitchen spinning wheel
as a vehicle of doctrine in his poem "Huswifery" is here turned upside
down and inside out.

Dickinson was only exaggerating those aspects of native American
Puritanism that were themselves obviously strained and absurd when
removed from the sheltering sacred canopy of faith. Michael Wigglesworth in his 1662 versification of Calvinist dogma, *The Day of Doom*,
had deliberated on the fate of infants who died unconverted and unregenerate. Here Christ (who is not the advocate and fellow sufferer
extolled in the Sentimental Love Religion but an avatar of the strong-
armed Calvinist Father) is silent as "the Judge most dread" firmly up-
holds the doctrine of infant damnation and announces, with relevant
scriptural glosses, that

You sinners are, and such a share
      as sinners may expect,
Such you shall have; for I do save
      none but mine own Elect.

Yet to compare your sin with their,
      who liv'd a longer time,
I do confess yours is much less,
      though every sin's a crime.

> A crime it is, therefore in bliss
>   you may not hope to dwell;
> But unto you I shall allow
>   the easiest room in Hell.[16]

The doomed infants immediately cease their plea for mercy, since "Their Consciences must needs confess / [God's] Reasons are the stronger." Urizen ruled in New England as firmly as he did in Albion, though his reign was less secure in Emily Dickinson's day, as Oliver Wendell Holmes's "Logical Story" of the downfall of "The Deacon's Masterpiece" proved. If pious church members could conceive of a heavenly landlord whose close calculations allotted the easiest room in hell to such humble tenants, was she much amiss in speculating that his eternal mansions might harbor some unsuspected angelic vermin? The desperate yet sprightly "Papa Above" is Dickinson's grotesque parody of "Our Father," the Lord's Prayer; and Jean McClure Mudge goes so far as to suggest that the cat in this poem is "quite possibly her father, whom she once called an excellent 'Mouser' " (*Image of Home,* 174).

Besides thinking of herself as a songbird, Dickinson identified with the other species of the cat's natural prey, for in a letter to T. W. Higginson written in June of 1862 she pleaded, "I have a little shape – it would not crowd your Desk – nor make much Racket as the Mouse, that dents your Galleries – " (*L* 2:409). Yet the drolly ironic ending of "Papa Above," with the secure, even "Elect," rodents calmly gnawing at the larder of salvation as "Unsuspecting Cycles / Wheel solemnly away," foreshadows the more famous burlesque of Calvinist piety in "Safe in their Alabaster Chambers" (J 216). It was of this latter poem that Susan Dickinson had written, "I always go to the fire and get warm after thinking of it, but I never *can* again" (J, note to 216).

The remote solidity of God's "perturbless plan" did not bother Dickinson so much as his seeming playfulness in enacting it from day to day. Both the sleeping saints and the celestial mice were beyond the carrot of hope and the whiplash of despair. It was the living who had to deal with Chinese tortures of the spirit:

> He fumbles at your Soul
> As Players at the Keys
> Before they drop full Music on –
> He stuns you by degrees –
> Prepares your brittle Nature
> For the Etherial Blow
> By fainter Hammers – further heard –
> Then nearer – Then so slow
> Your Breath has time to straighten –

Your Brain – to bubble Cool –
Deals – One – imperial – Thunderbolt –
That scalps your naked Soul –

When Winds take Forests in their Paws –
The Universe – is still –   [J 315]

This intriguing mesh of imagery makes the unnamed "He" of the poem at one and the same time a virtuoso artist, a fearsome savage, and a Jovian hurler of thunderbolts. Yet its final picture of bestial winds taking up whole tracts of forests "in their Paws" alerts us that what is being recorded is a salon version of the cat-and-mouse game that the Calvinist "Nobodaddy" constantly plays with Dickinson's soul. The same trope appears in the "fond Ambush" of "I know that He exists" (J 338), where the gaming proves "piercing earnest" as God plays his final trump card, the black ace of death. Dickinson uses the imagery in its full force when she writes:

The Whole of it came not at once –
'Twas Murder by degrees –
A Thrust – and then for Life a chance –
The Bliss to cauterize –

The Cat reprieves the Mouse
She eases from her teeth
Just long enough for Hope to teaze –
Then mashes it to death –

'Tis Life's award – to die –
Contenteder if once –
Than dying half – then rallying
For consciouser Eclipse –   [J 762]

II

In the menagerie of animals that parades through Dickinson's poetry, the cat (along with the snake) emerges as one of her few natural villains. Even the tiger of "A Dying tiger – moaned for Drink" (J 566) and the leopard of "Civilization – spurns – the Leopard!" (J 492) are recognized as having their place in the general order of things. In the former poem, the tiger becomes an uncomprehending victim of it. Somehow it is the ordinary house cat that is singled out for extraordinary censure:

She sights a Bird – she chuckles –
She flattens – then she crawls –
She runs without the look of feet –
Her eyes increase to Balls –

Her Jaws stir – twitching – hungry –
Her Teeth can hardly stand –
She leaps, but Robin leaped the first –
Ah, Pussy, of the Sand,

The Hopes so juicy ripening –
You almost bathed your Tongue –
When Bliss disclosed a hundred Toes –
And fled with every one –   [J 507]

Surely Dickinson would have agreed with Edith Wharton's definition of a cat as nothing more than "a snake in furs." Here the fortunate
Robin, another type of the poet ("The Robin's my Criterion for Tune"
[J 285]), escapes from the ophidian Pussy because its natural habitat is a
higher realm. This is that house not built on sand but founded in the
cliffs of heaven (Matt. 7:26–7). The gift of feathers is compared
obliquely to the sanctifying grace of an orthodox crisis conversion, the
precious "Bliss" of a divine and supernatural light. Yet escape, like
election, is a rare event in a world so red in tooth and claw. What
particularly upset Dickinson was the cold calculation of the cat, its
seeming malice aforethought.

Birds remained her Little Nells, her babes in the wood, her holy
innocents. In "His Bill is clasped – his Eye forsook" (J 1102), Dickinson went to extravagant lengths to eulogize a songbird that had been
"assassinated" by some thoughtless hunter, a crime that to her out-
raged mind resembled nothing less than "The firing in Heaven, / On
Angels – squandering for you / Their Miracles of Tune – ." Here she
was one not only with Blake, who in his "Auguries of Innocence"
warned that "A Skylark wounded on the wing / A Cherubim does
cease to sing," but with her mentor, T. W. Higginson, who had
urged in "April Days" that the lover of nature go armed only "with
that best of fowling-pieces, a small spy-glass: the best, – since how
valueless for purposes of observation is the bleeding, gasping, dying
body, compared with the fresh and living creature, as it tilts,
trembles, and warbles on the bough before you!" (ODP, 241). In "If I
can stop one Heart from breaking" (J 919), Dickinson affirmed that
the act of helping "one fainting Robin / Unto his Nest again" could
justify an entire life. Her older nephew, away on a visit, was addressed as "Dear Ned-Bird," and Sue's younger son, the beloved
Gilbert, figures in a dialogue sent to his mother about 1880, entitled
"Memoirs of Little Boys that live – ":

"Were'nt you chasing Pussy," said Vinnie to Gilbert?
"No – she was chasing herself" –

"But wasn't she running pretty fast"? "Well, some slow and some fast" said the beguiling Villain – Pussy's Nemesis quailed – Talk of "hoary Reprobates"!

Your urchin is more antique in wiles than the Egyptian Sphinx – [*L* 3:673]

Obviously, Dickinson, always a dog lover and owner of the redoubtable Newfoundland Carlo, was on the side of "Pussy's Nemesis." Indeed, she had played that role herself many times, for Emily Dickinson's unswerving distaste for cats was paralleled by her sister Lavinia's extravagant devotion to them. As early as the 1840 portrait of the Dickinson children by O. A. Bullard (now at Harvard), we can clearly see that Lavinia is holding a tablet on which the outline of a black cat has been traced.[17] As John Cody writes, Lavinia

> had always been fond of cats, and by the time she reached her late forties and early fifties the mansion crawled with them. As many lonely, childless women do, she babied them and talked to them. She hovered over her feline retinue with a fierce maternal possessiveness and reacted like a lioness when anyone attempted to harm or disturb her "pussies." [*After Great Pain*, 469]

When Vinnie's Tabby, Drummy-doodles, Buffy, and Tootsie escaped the grounds, extravagant rewards were offered if they strayed too far or too long. In an 1873 letter to her Norcross cousins, Dickinson remarked of her sister's obsession, with a dry reference to a famous Arctic explorer lost in 1847,[18] "The 'pussum' is found. 'Two Dollars reward' would return John Franklin" (*L* 2:510). In a poem written about 1871, she even seemed to caricature the intolerant Vinnie – or at least the old-maidish intolerance that Vinnie exemplified – as a self-satisfied feline, while contrasting this cat-in-the-manger attitude to the free spirits represented by the traditional image of the boy and his dog:

> A little Dog that wags his tail
> And knows no other joy
> Of such a little Dog am I
> Reminded by a Boy
>
> Who gambols all the living Day
> Without an earthly cause
> Because he is a little Boy
> I honestly suppose –
>
> The Cat that in the Corner dwells
> Her martial Day forgot

The Mouse but a Tradition now
Of her desireless Lot

Another class remind me
Who neither please nor play
But not to make a "bit of noise"
Beseech each little Boy –   [J 1185]

Dickinson was not above small acts of sabotage and reprisal in this comic war of the cats that divided the otherwise devoted sisters. In September of 1871 she asked the absent Susan to "tell Mattie that 'Tim's['] Dog Calls Vinnie's Pussy names and I don't discourage him" (L 2:489–90), and in early January 1881 she wrote to the Josiah Hollands that "Vinnie had four Pussies for Christmas Gifts – and two from her Maker, previous, making six, in toto, and finding Assassins for them, is my stealthy Aim" (L 3:687). One of Dickinson's cousins remembered that Lavinia's "large yellow pet cat lost its long fluffy tail by some accident, which [Emily] sent in playful humor to the present scribe. There was a pink ribbon tied round this disconnected appendage, with a verse accompanying it that unfortunately is lost." As Jay Leyda notes, "Lavinia saw a reprint of this article, in the Boston *Transcript* (Sept. 28, 1894), and denied the incident angrily; Ellen Dickinson wrote . . . 'I can, if necessary prove the story of the Cat's tail being sent to me by Emily' " (YH 2:482).

By 1897, Lavinia was buying an average of thirty-one quarts of milk a month to sustain her "feline retinue," each of whom was privileged to drink from a separate saucer placed on the kitchen floor by her faithful maidservant, Maggie Maher.[19] Years earlier in August of 1876, Emily had written to her Norcross cousins informing them, "Vinnie has a new pussie the color of Branwell Brontë's hair. She thinks it a little 'lower than the angels,' and I concur with her. You remember my ideal cat has always a huge rat in its mouth, just going out of sight – though going out of sight in itself has a peculiar charm" (L 2:559). To Dickinson, Vinnie's pets always had the smell of brimstone about them. Once, when particularly exasperated by their abundance at the Homestead, her niece remembered that she

> put four superfluous kittens on the fire-shovel and softly dropped them into the first convenient jar the cellar offered, her family being in church – her chosen time for iniquity. This especial jar happened to be full of pickle brine. The sequel was very awful; occurring when the austere judge Otis P. Lord of Salem was visiting my Grandfather, and as in all such emergencies of detection she fled to her own room and turned the key; holding reproach at bay until she chose to come out and ignore it.[20]

Martha Dickinson Bianchi summed up the situation after recalling a particular Sunday when her aunt nearly sent her home with a whole litter of Lavinia's favorites. "No," Bianchi wrote, "Aunt Emily never appreciated cats. They were always getting under her feet as she carried precious tea-cups in or out, or delicate concoctions of her own, often causing a slip, a smash, a day of reckoning. She was sated with them from their kittenhood up" (*FF,* 6–7).

In a more tolerant mood, Dickinson wrote to Mrs. Holland of Vinnie's "new pussy," "We call her the 'minute hand,' " because she "catches a mouse an hour" (*L* 2:561). But in the letter to Fanny and Louise Norcross in which she coupled Vinnie's cat with the most disreputable member of the Brontë clan, the poet also remarked: "I dream about father every night, always a different dream, and forget what I am doing daytimes, wondering where he is. Without any body, I keep thinking. What kind can that be?" (*L* 2:559). Her father had died suddenly in 1874, and his loss was emblematic of the kind of swift disappearance peculiar to a world ruled by the Calvinist cat-god, a world in which not only rats and mice and robins but solid men and women were subject to an unexpected, traumatic "going out of sight." If Dickinson had firmly rejected Jonathan Edwards's picture of a fiery pit opening up beneath the feet of backsliding sinners, she still had to reconcile herself to that undiscovered country that swallowed up her friends and family one by one:

> I noticed People disappeared
> When but a little child –
> Supposed they visited remote
> Or settled Regions wild –
>
> Now Know I – They both visited
> And settled Regions wild
> But did because they died
> A Fact withheld the little child –   [J 1149]

That such a design was built into the scheme of existence, as the cat's easy voracity is built into the perversely pretty world of the folk painting in the Garbisch collection, became for Dickinson the one equation that her most brilliant poetic algebra could not solve. Her natural theology had to take account of a God who did what he did out of, as Robert Browning's Caliban expressed it, "envy, listlessness or sport."[21] The terror of the situation was no doubt increased by a literary work that we know had a great impact on her. Here again Lévi-Strauss's idea of *bricolage* comes into full play, for Dickinson merged her folk image of the cat-god with one belonging to the popular realm of high Gothic romance.

III

Just as many folk artists used popular prints as sources for their own special renderings of landscape or genre scenes, skewing their perspective while accommodating them to a wholly private vision, and skilled needleworkers availed themselves of the fashionable patterns that helped to make *Godey's Lady's Book* so successful, so did Dickinson have available to her a well-known model of feline perversity. This was Harriet Prescott Spofford's sensational tale "Circumstance," first published in the *Atlantic Monthly* for May of 1860. Susan Dickinson sent her copy of the *Monthly* over to Emily with the story marked in the table of contents by a heavily inked "X." In January of 1903, Susan reminisced, in a piece printed in the *Springfield Republican,* about the poet's reaction. This essay, entitled "Harriet Prescott's Early Work," contained the transcript of an important letter that once again confirms the poet's interest in popular literature. Susan wrote:

> I missed in your citation of her [Spofford's] early work to find no mention of "Circumstance," the most highly imaginative and thrilling tale I have ever read. I cannot understand the ignorance I find of it everywhere. Read in sympathetic tone to folk of eager mind, it has never failed me in dramatic effect. After first reading it, I sent it at once to my sister-in-law, Emily Dickinson. Immediately she wrote me: –
> > Dear S.: This is the only thing I ever saw in my life I did not think I could have written myself. You stand nearer the world than I do. Send me everything she writes. [22]

Dickinson's mind was a little too eager to sustain the power of the tale, for later, in answering some inquiry about her reading posed by her "Dear Preceptor," T. W. Higginson, who was also Prescott's teacher and mentor, [23] she replied, "I read Miss Prescott's 'Circumstance,' but it followed me, in the Dark – so I avoided her" (*L* 2:404). The language used by the poet in the letters to her sister-in-law and to Higginson is interesting for its visual emphasis: She *sees* Spofford's fictional image so vividly that it haunts her both day and night. [*]

"Circumstance" (as Susan Dickinson indicates) is a wild, Gothic thriller of the *Blackwood* variety, based on an incident in Cotton Mather's *Magnalia Christi Americana.* The plot concerns an unfortunate pioneer woman who is stalked by an "Indian Devil," or native American panther, and who saves herself from death and mutilation by pacifying the beast with the singing of old hymn tunes. The story may seem melodramatic when read today, yet William Dean Howells included it in his volume *The Great Modern American Stories* as late as

1920. He remembered when it was first published that twenty thousand "friends" of Columbus, Ohio (the "sum of the little city's population . . . all people my own age say of twenty or twenty-one"), were his partners in "the awful joy of Miss Prescott's (not yet Mrs. Spofford's) tremendous story of *Circumstance,* still unsurpassed of its kind. We thrilled over it severally and collectively (the whole 20,000 of us), and are still ready to swear it unsurpassed, though we are now over seventy or eighty years old and 200,000 in number."[24] Howells confirms Susan Dickinson's report of the lasting effect of the tale on the *Atlantic's* captivated audience, and well might its sensationalism have followed Dickinson in the dark. Here, for example, is Spofford's description of the legendary Indian Devil himself:

> Suddenly, a swift shadow, like the fabulous flying-dragon, writhed through the air before her, and she felt herself instantly seized and borne aloft. It was that wild beast – the most savage and serpentine and subtle and fearless of our latitudes – known by hunters as the Indian Devil, and he held her in his clutches on the board floor of a swinging fir-bough. His long sharp claws were caught in her clothing, he worried them sagaciously a little, then, finding that ineffectual to free them, he commenced licking her bare arm with his rasping tongue and pouring over her the wide streams of his hot, foetid breath. So quick had this flashing action been that the woman had had no time for alarm; moreover, she was not of the screaming kind: but now, as she felt him endeavoring to disentangle his claws, and the horrid sense of her fate smote her, and she saw instinctively the fierce plunge of those weapons, the long strips of living flesh torn from her bones, the agony, the quivering disgust, itself a worse agony, – while by her side, and holding her in his great lithe embrace, the monster crouched, his white tusks whetting and gnashing, his eyes glaring though all the darkness like balls of red fire, – a shriek, that rang in every forest hollow, that startled every winter-housed thing, that stirred and woke the least needle of the tasselled pines, tore through her lips. A moment afterward, the beast left the arm, once white, now crimson, and looked up alertly.[25]

If anything crystallized Emily Dickinson's attitude toward a capricious, feline, and predatory fate, it was the vividness of Spofford's Indian Devil. This was the cat-god full-fledged and full-blown, a human being his prey and not a mere wayside robin. The very title of the story defined for the poet an attribute, almost another person, of the God who ruled the darkness as well as the light:

All Circumstances are the Frame
In which His Face is set –
All Latitudes exist for His
Sufficient Continent –

The Light His Action, and the Dark
The Leisure of His Will –
In Him Existence serve or set
A Force illegible.   [J 820]

It is the Indian Devil of the eastern wilds of Maine and not the medieval gargoyle that springs out from the forest of Dickinson's soul to prowl through the *hortus conclusus* of her poetry. The name "Indian Devil" itself reflects the old Puritanical fear of the savage and the demonic, as reported in many an early Indian captivity narrative. But the grotesquerie of the woman's situation itself, her extraordinary "circumstance," surely impressed the poet as much as the repulsive figure of her fierce captor. The idea of singing to keep death at bay, of singing, as Dickinson wrote T. W. Higginson on April twenty-fifth, 1862, because "I had a terror – since September – I could tell to none – and so I sing, as the Boy does by the Burying Ground – because I am afraid" (*L* 2:404), found its natural literary analogue in Prescott's nameless victim. And in the terrifying habits of the Indian Devil – in its bloodthirstiness, its quick and active seizure of its prey while concealed in ambush, its mangling of the flesh of its victim by powerful teeth and claws, its propensity for killing more than it really needed for subsistance, its leisurely playing with its catch – the poet recognized the God of her own personal experience, the God whom C. S. Lewis was to call "the Cosmic Sadist and Eternal Vivisector."[26] "Let Emily sing for you because she cannot pray," she wrote to her Norcross cousins in late January of 1863, after the girls were suddenly orphaned by the death of their father (*L* 2:421). A poignant letter to the Hollands of about the same time hints at Dickinson's own trials as an isolated, "unsung" poet:

Perhaps you laugh at me! Perhaps the whole United States are laughing at me too! *I* can't stop for that! *My* business is to love. I found a bird, this morning, down – down – on a little bush at the foot of the garden, and wherefore sing, I said, since nobody *hears?*
One sob in the throat, one flutter of bosom – "*My* business is to *sing*" – and away she rose! How do I know but cherubim, once themselves, as patient, listened, and applauded her unnoticed hymn? [*L* 2:413]

But a major difference remains between the attitude of Spofford's victim, locked in the deadly embrace of the Indian Devil, and that of

Emily Dickinson, enduring a private captivity and tormented by the game of hide-and-seek played by a Calvinist cat-god. Spofford's heroine does not taunt her cruel master with "A too presumptuous Psalm" (J 513) but rather sings hymns of "the Great Deliverance":[27] "Not once did she say, 'Lord, how long wilt thou look on; rescue my soul from their destructions, my darling from the lions,' – for she knew that the young lions roar after their prey and seek their meat from God. 'O Lord, thou preservest man and beast!' she said" (167). Such perfect faith was denied the poet, and the hymns Dickinson sang were more often bitter and mocking protests at the pain exacted by such overwhelming circumstances, detailing "the agony, the quivering disgust, itself a worse agony." Like the Nathaniel Hawthorne praised by Herman Melville in his review of *Mosses from an Old Manse,* Dickinson persevered in shouting "No! in thunder!" in the face of the Deity Himself:

> "Heavenly Father" – take to thee
> The supreme iniquity
> Fashioned by thy candid Hand
> In a moment contraband –
> Though to trust us – seem to us
> More respectful – "We are Dust" –
> We apologize to thee
> For thine own Duplicity –   [J 1461]

In her hunger and thirst after justice Dickinson sympathized with others toyed with by the Old Testament God. The "Moral" of the near sacrifice of Isaac by Abraham as recorded in Genesis was "with a Mastiff / Manners may prevail" (J 1317). Of the "Romance" of Moses' Pisgah vision of the land flowing with milk and honey and Jehovah's denial of the prophet's entrance into it (Deut. 3:25–7), she wrote that his martyrdom

> Surpasses sharper stated –
> Of Stephen – or of Paul –
> For these – were only put to death –
> While God's adroiter will
>
> On Moses – seemed to fasten
> With tantalizing Play
> As Boy – should deal with lesser Boy –
> To prove ability.   [J 597]

"Moses was'nt fairly used," she reiterated in a late poem, "Ananias was'nt" (J 1201).

In the age of D. F. Strauss, Christian Bauer, and Ernest Renan,

Dickinson applied her own kind of higher criticism to that Scripture which (as she wrote to her nephew Ned in a "Diagnosis of the Bible, by a Boy") was "an antique Volume – / Written by faded Men / At the suggestion of Holy Spectres –" (J 1545). As with Renan, it was not merely textual criticism or philological quibbles that swept away the enforced belief of Dickinson's childhood; it was a fundamental revulsion at the cruel and inhuman paradoxes of an entire theological system. Paralleling Renan's quest in his *Life of Jesus* (1863), she sought for a more human, knowable form of divinity, a somber if still gigantic Christ whom she could actually touch through her relationship to the majestic Phoebus. Dickinson had been warned that the liberal Christian thinking of Theodore Parker was "poison" (L 2:358), but she found support for private heresy in his statement that "there has never been an age when man did not crucify the Son of God afresh."[28] Until the end of her life, she sang her psalms of protest out of a need to express her abiding sense of outrage at the cosmic scheme of things, but more and more she had the sense of a spiritual helpmate, a companion in her suffering:

> I sing to use the Waiting
> My Bonnet but to tie
> And Shut the Door unto my House
> No more to do have I
>
> Till His best step approaching
> We journey to the Day
> And tell each other how We sung
> To Keep the Dark away.   [J 850]

Dickinson sings most of all "To keep the Dark away," to fend off whatever private Indian Devil lurks in the shadows of her fear. Similarly, it was impossible for the pioneer woman of Spofford's "Circumstance" to contemplate fully the awful nature of the fiend who held her in his grip. A complete realization of her fate, of the abominable circumstance in which she found herself, would have driven her to madness or paralyzed the very voice that kept the monster pacified. Spofford's trusting heroine finds a final deliverance in the steady hand of the husband she believed had deserted her. Her perfect faith is rewarded, as he shoots the monster, and they return home only to find that their remote settlement has been reduced to ashes. "Desolation and death were indeed there," Spofford writes, "and beneficence and life in the forest. Tomahawk and scalping-knife, descending during that night, had left behind them only this work of their accomplished hatred and one subtle foot-print in the snow" (172).

For Dickinson, who complained to Phoebus, "I've got a Tomahawk in my side" (*L* 2:392), there was to be no such deliverance. Although on a folk level the romance of Daisy and Phoebus often reads like a typical Puritan spiritual autobiography, in which conversion to the lover replaces conversion to the deity, it significantly lacks this genre's archetypal final escape from captivity – whether of the Indian or of the Devil. The poet would have been more impressed with Spofford's description of the ultimate agonies of the trapped woman as she realizes that her husband and child are nearby and only waiting for the right moment to destroy the beast than with that salvific denouement which to Susan Dickinson "seemed always to me like an anti-climax" ("Prescott's Early Work"), sending her back to "the gray opening note of the tragic symphony":

> Now, as she sang on in the slow, endless, infinite moments, the fervent vision of God's peace was gone. Just as the grave had lost its sting, she was snatched back again into the arms of earthly hope. In vain she tried to sing, "There remaineth a rest for the people of God," – her eyes trembled on her husband's, and she could only think of him, and of the child, and of happiness that yet might be, but with what a dreadful gulf of doubt between! She shuddered now in the suspense; all calm forsook her; she was tortured with dissolving heats or frozen with icy blasts; her face contracted, growing small and pinched; her voice was hoarse and sharp – every tone cut like a knife, the notes became heavy to lift, – withheld by some hostile pressure, – impossible. One gasp, a convulsive effort, and there was silence, – she had lost her voice. ["Circumstance," 170–1]

Was deliverance worth the terrible price of living in a world ruled by such circumstance? This is a question that Dickinson continually asked herself, though Spofford did not. Spofford preferred to end her tale on a note of Miltonic optimism: In spite of the destruction of house and home, life itself was a gift enough and "for the rest, – the world was all before them, where to choose." There was little choice, however, in a block universe[29] that to Emily Dickinson seemed

> As if a Goblin with a Guage –
> Kept measuring the Hours –
> Until you felt your Second
> Weigh, helpless, in his Paws –
>
> And not a Sinew – stirred – could help,
> And sense was setting numb –

When God – remembered – and the Fiend
Let go, then, Overcome –

As if your Sentence stood – pronounced – ₁
And you were frozen led
From Dungeon's luxury of Doubt
To Gibbets, and the Dead –

And when the Film had stitched your eyes
A Creature gasped "Repreive"!
Which Anguish was the utterest – then –
To Perish, or to live?   [J 414]

"The instant holding in it's claw / The privilege to live" (J 948) became an emblem of the dark Gothic side of Dickinson's entire emotional, psychic, and poetic experience. As in the case of the anonymous artist who painted *The Cat,* the magnitude of this instant distorted the picture of the poet's God-consciousness to grotesque proportions; the exact form of the specter that haunted her verse, the image of the cat-god, came from sources as diverse as the comic battle with her sister over the ways of household pets, the wrathful Jehovah pictured in Watts's *Hymns,* and the power of a popular tale of sensation like "Circumstance." As Georges Poulet writes of Dickinson's preoccupation with "a moment of absolute surprise which lifts her out of her life," what is impressive about her poetry is "the persistence of regret, the constant rawness of the wound. It seems that time is composed of a repeated pain and that in each of its moments one is stricken as if for the first time."[30] For Dickinson there is no exit from this circumstance, since the wilderness is an interior one and the fierce Indian Devil lurks in the recesses of the mind itself:

It is easy to work when the soul is at play –
But when the soul is in pain –
The hearing him put his playthings up
Makes work difficult – then –

It is simple, to ache in the Bone, or the Rind –
But Gimblets – among the nerve –
Mangle daintier – terribler –
Like a Panther in the Glove –   [J 244]

It all depends on who does the playing, the soul or whatever force holds the soul in its grasp:

God is indeed a jealous God –
He cannot bear to see

> That we had rather not with Him
> But with each other play.   [J 1719]

Long after Emily Dickinson's death, a family friend remembered that "one day Vinnie's cat brought in a Wilson thrush, and when I expostulated, she said, 'You must blame the Creator.' "[31] In the grimly playful poetry of Vinnie's sister, we can see that blame assume the grotesque proportions of an original, because uniquely felt, series of American folk masterpieces.

Chapter 6

THE EARTHLY PARADISE

Dickinson, Higginson, and the Society of Nature

========

The best thoughts and purposes seemed ordained to come to human
beings beneath the open sky, as the ancients fabled that Pan found
the goddess Ceres when he was engaged in the chase, whom no other
of the gods could find when seeking seriously. The little I have
gained from colleges and libraries has certainly not worn so well as
the little I learned in childhood of the habits of plant, bird, and
insect. That "weight and sanity of thought," which Coleridge so
finely makes the crowning attribute of Wordsworth, is in no way so
well matured and cultivated as in the society of Nature.

T. W. Higginson

And so, perchance, in Adam's race,
Of Eden's bower some dream-like trace
Survived the Flight and swam the Flood
And wakes the wish in youngest blood
To tread the forfeit Paradise
And feed once more the exile's eyes . . .

Ralph Waldo Emerson

I am glad you are in the open Air – that is nearest Heaven –

Emily Dickinson

Claude Lévi-Strauss's concept of *bricolage* dictates that it would be difficult to find a poem by Emily Dickinson that does not incorporate some
elements from a level of culture other than the folk, the mode from
which those very poems take both their form and their frame. It is in
Dickinson's domestication of Calvinist images and ideas that we most
surely see the conjunction of folk form and folk content, especially
when she is dealing with the patriarchal God, whether he appears in
sentimental guise as "Our Old Neighbor" (J 623) or in his more terrible
and usual manifestation as a teasing "Mighty Merchant" (J 621). This
cosmic village bully is, as we have seen, also an untrustworthy Indian
giver who takes back what he has conferred as cavalierly as he holds

181

Arthur Parton, *Woodland Scene,* ca. 1876. (By permission of Mary L. Hampson.)

back what is most desired. Yet just as Dickinson domesticated both the New England theology and the canons of sentimental love, so did she privatize the elite speculations about nature and art that were so much a staple of her mid-Victorian milieu. While her physical concept of the deity was bound up with her folk response to the metaphysics of Calvinism, her reaction to romantic philosophies of nature and art involved equally concrete tutorials in these elitist mysteries.

In the case of art, philosophical awareness came to Dickinson through her sister-in-law Susan's devotion to the works of John Ruskin; experiential knowledge derived from direct contact with the paintings, both American and foreign, collected mainly by her brother, Austin. Austin too, with his intense interest in civic beautification, his botanical expertise, and his personal acquaintance with famous landscape architects like Frederick Law Olmstead, contributed to her love of the sublime and the picturesque. Characteristically, Dickinson domesticated fine views and prospects to the nature's half-acre that was her father's backyard. Some of her appreciation for nature was assuredly popular as well as elite, and her sentimental conception of it as "the Gentlest Mother" (J 790) is even parodied in the burlesque Emersonian "Song of Nature [Not from the Atlantic Monthly]" that can be found on page 20 of Mary Warner's scrapbook. But it was Thomas Wentworth Higginson who introduced Emily to a Transcendental appreciation for wild as opposed to cultivated nature, and in this chapter I explore the symbiotic relationship through which Emerson's elite message that "Nature is the symbol of spirit" (*Works* 1:22) found its fulfillment in the elective affinities between a remote Boston Brahmin and an obscure Amherst poet.

I

Of all Emily Dickinson's select society, the intimate companions of her interior life, none has been more maligned than T. W. Higginson. Yet it was Higginson, most frequent contributor to the prestigious *Atlantic Monthly* in its formative years, who saved Dickinson's psychic life by acting as the chief apostle of Transcendental culture in its most highminded Victorian incarnation: the worship of natural beauty. He also made her a silent partner in that wider circle of largely female writers who followed upon the outburst of creative thought that F. O. Matthiessen has called the "American Renaissance." These authors of the late 1850s and early 1860s succeeded Emerson and Melville as Brahms and Mahler succeeded Schubert and Beethoven in music, and they included such figures as Harriet Beecher Stowe, Elizabeth Stuart Phelps, and Higginson's other remarkable young protégée, Harriet Prescott Spofford.[1]

In "The Decline of the Sentimental," written in 1887, a year after Emily Dickinson's death, Higginson marveled at "the diminished hold" of sentimentality, defining it as "a certain rather melodramatic self-consciousness, a tender introspection in the region of the heart, a kind of studious cosseting of one's finer feelings." He added, "Perhaps it is not generally recognized how much more abundant was this sort of thing forty years ago than now, and how it molded the very temperaments of those who were born into it, and grew up under it."[2] Producing art that was by turn lyrical, rhapsodic, melancholic, and mawkish, Stowe, Phelps, and Spofford were fervent evangelists of the Sentimental Love Religion, and all were practitioners of an inflated, lavish, and mannered style that Henry James, in a review of Spofford's 1864 novel *Azarian,* castigated as "a succession of forced assaults upon the impregnable stronghold of painting; a wearisome series of word-pictures, linked by a slight thread of narrative, strung together, to use one of Miss Prescott's own expressions, like 'beads on a leash.' "[3] This "gemmy" style was the natural outgrowth and overgrowth of Stowe's Platonic romanticism once it was divorced from the chastening demands of the known and the familiar. Yet whether such romance was transplanted, like Spofford's *Sir Rohan's Ghost* of 1860, to Old England, or forced, like her *Azarian,* upon New England, Higginson continued to welcome it. He was a firm disciple of "The Newness" in whatever form it chose to manifest itself, and his October 1864 review of *Azarian* in the *Atlantic* itself began with an apt and colorful description of this flagrantly exotic art that firmly related it to the portfolio tradition:

> If one opened the costly album of some rare colorist, and became bewildered amid successive wreaths of pictured flowers, with hues that seemed to burn, and freshness that seemed fragrant, one could hardly quarrel with a few stray splashes of purple or carmine spilt heedlessly on the pages. Such a book is "Azarian"; and if few are so lavish and reckless with their pigments as Harriet Prescott, it is because few have access to such wealth. If one proceeds from the theory that all life in New England is to be pictured as bare and pallid, it must seem very wrong in her to use tints so daring; but if one believes that life here, as elsewhere, may be passionate as Petrarch and deep as Beethoven, there appears no reason why all descriptive art should be Quaker-colored.[4]

It is no wonder, then, that Higginson asked Emily Dickinson if she had read Spofford's work, for Spofford was the main exponent and Dickinson the secret disciple of this florid style and its tumultuous word-painting. Had not Dickinson lived through her private mythology a high

romance that was indeed as "passionate as Petrarch and deep as Beethoven," and did she not in her poetry strive for tints even more extravagant
than purple and carmine to describe the redemptive "Blaze" of her crisis
conversion to Love?

> I found the words to every thought
> I ever had – but One –
> And that – defies me –
> As a Hand did try to chalk the Sun
>
> To Races – nurtured in the Dark –
> How would your own – begin?
> Can Blaze be shown in Cochineal –
> Or Noon – in Mazarin?   [J 581]

As Rebecca Patterson has demonstrated in her chapter "Emily Dickinson's Palette," each of the poet's hues has a specific emotional and
symbolic value attached to it, for as a "belated Romantic" she "knew
that a poet handled color words as a painter handled colors, and when
she decided to become a poet she set about acquiring a serviceable
selection of color words as one more element in the vocabulary appropriate to her craft."[5] The source of this vocabulary was not only the
biblical Book of Revelation but contemporary literature: the poetry of
the Brownings, Alexander Smith, and other spasmodics[6] and American
novels like Stowe's *Agnes of Sorrento* and Spofford's *Azarian*. Higginson
noted that this style derived ultimately from Keats, who partially inspired a school of painting similarly infatuated with color – the Pre-
Raphaelites. The chief defender of these painters, John Ruskin, in turn
made the art of word-painting and the art of criticism synonymous.

Now perhaps we can see the full significance of Dickinson's reply to
Higginson about her reading: "You inquire my Books – For Poets – I
have Keats – and Mr and Mrs Browning. For Prose – Mr Ruskin – Sir
Thomas Browne – and the Revelations" (L 2:404). The name of Sir
Thomas Browne, with his studied pomp of language, completes a pedi-
gree of the sources of the florid style. Since we know that Dickinson
was also an early devotee of Tennyson, "feasting" on *The Princess* as
early as 1848 (L 2:66), avidly following his literary progress thereafter,
Henry James's truncated literary history of what he contemptuously
calls "the Azarian school" is also relevant. "What manner of writing is
it," he asks with magisterial disgust, "which lends itself so frankly to
aberrations of taste?"

> It is that literary fashion which, so to speak historically, was
> brought into our literature by Tennyson's poetry. The best name
> for it, as a literary style, is the ideal descriptive style. Like all

founders of schools, Tennyson has been far exceeded by his disciples. The style in question reposes not so much upon the observation of the objects of external nature as the projection of one's
fancy upon them. It may be seen exemplified in its youthful vigor
in Tennyson's "Dream of Fair Women"; it is exemplified in its
effete old age in Mr. Alexander Smith and Miss Prescott, *passim*.
[Review of *Azarian*, 269]

We have sampled some of Harriet Prescott Spofford's style in her
Gothic thriller "Circumstance," and once again there is no need to
build a macadamized road to Xanadu from her work to that of Dickinson's. It was the poet's genius to condense and crystallize, to distill
and domesticate this spasmodic exuberance through the folk form of
her verse, tempering the lush sensuousness and exotic word-painting
of the Azarian school with the stern angularity and stark abstraction of
"homespun" Puritan discipline. From Spofford Dickinson learned a
vocabulary of passion associated with tropical flowers, rich stuffs,
fabulous jewels, and fantastic colors, but she also managed to contain
such a vocabulary within a unique artistic medium that was purely her
own, anticipating the celebrated "telegraphic" style of post–Civil War
American letters. Even a sentimental description in Spofford's *Sir Rohan's Ghost* of a "little brown thief, with his wide, sherry-colored
eyes, his mouth and hands full of gray stolen fruits,"[7] could be transmuted into the prose self-portrait that Dickinson sent to Higginson in
July of 1862: "I . . . am small, like the Wren, and my Hair is bold,
like the Chestnut Bur – and my eyes, like the Sherry in the Glass, that
the Guest leaves – " (*L* 2:411).
    It is one of the great ironies of American literary history that Spof-
ford would long outlive Dickinson, and come to praise her "wondrous
verse" in an article published in *Harper's Bazaar* in 1892, never suspecting that her own earlier work had been one of its chief inspirations.[8]
But by the end of the Civil War, the romance of Daisy and Phoebus
was over, as was the heyday of the "ideal descriptive style." Just as
Dickinson withdrew from the world at this time, after some kind of
cure of both her eyesight and her mindsight had been effected, so was
her sensibility fixed and her taste permanently molded by the high
romantic art that had flourished in the antebellum period.
    The Civil War was a crisis not only for Dickinson's private mythol-
ogy but for the nature of American elite culture itself, for while the
Sentimental Love Religion went on to dominate popular taste, the
florid style that had been its hallmark crumbled before the imperative
demands of a new realism. In later years, when the aged Spofford was
asked why she had not continued in the vein of her earlier romantic

extravaganzas, she replied that it was because "the public taste changed. With the coming of Mr. Howells as editor of the *Atlantic,* and his influence, the realistic arrived." She added sadly, "I doubt if anything I wrote in those days would be accepted by any magazine now."[9] Eventually, Spofford joined the New England local colorists and herself produced more sober, "Quaker-colored" fictions, but the death knell of her earlier manner had been sounded by Henry James in his devastating 1865 *North American Review* attack on *Azarian.*

James chose Balzac's *Eugénie Grandet* (1833) as a model of realism in spite of its descriptive qualities, because "Balzac does not *paint,* does not copy, objects; his chosen instrument being a pen, he is content to *write* them." While all outward aspects of the characters were "reproduced with the fidelity of a photograph," still "these things are all described *only in so far as they bear upon the action,* and not in the least for themselves" (272–3). Emily Dickinson firmly shut the door on such newfangled theorizing. The painter and not the photographer or the scientist remained her ideal artist, and just as the form of her poetry remained faithful to the common meter of Isaac Watts's hymns, so did its vibrant color adhere to the lush word-painting of the 1850s and early 1860s. It was the *Atlantic Monthly* under the editorship of James Russell Lowell and James T. Fields that shaped her preferences and tempted her ambition, not the later disciples and promoters of the so-called realistic school. Writing five years after Edward Dickinson's passing, she confessed to Higginson, "I . . . have known little of literature since my Father died" (*L* 2:635). Her later literary interests were centered in memorial volumes and biographies of earlier greats, like the Brontës and George Eliot. Responding to a laudatory critical assessment contained in Higginson's *Short Studies of American Authors* published later this same year, 1879, she affirmed her unswerving loyalties. "Mrs. [Helen Hunt] Jackson soars to your estimate lawfully as a Bird" she wrote, "but of Howells and James, one hesitates" (*L* 2:649).

As Sewall notes (*LED* 2: 567), there is little doubt that Higginson himself was the most enduring of Dickinson's literary loyalties. In the letter in which she admitted not having kept up with current literary developments, she also added, "Your Pages and Shakespeare's, like Ophir – remain – " (*L* 2:635). It was because of the skillful nature essays published in the *Atlantic* in the years immediately preceding the Civil War, and later collected in the volume entitled *Out-Door Papers* (1863), that Dickinson thought of Higginson as her artistic master. Although most commentators have lingered long on the fact that Dickinson first responded to Higginson because of his "Letter to a Young Contributor," published in the April 1862 *Atlantic,* it was in fact his early nature essays to which she reacted most intensely.[10] In her second letter to him she

revealed, "My size felt small – to me – I read your Chapters in the Atlantic – and experienced honor for you – I was sure you would not reject a
confiding question" (L 2:405) – which is simply to say that she had long
been a reader of his literary essays as well as his critical articles.

It is difficult for us to think of the hermetic, housebound woman of
later years as the vigorous "out-door girl" admired and encouraged by
Higginson, yet it appears that until the death of her dog Carlo in the
winter of 1866 (an event that paralleled the death of something in
herself), Dickinson was an active amateur naturalist, roaming the Amherst hills in search of the rare, the hidden, or the precious botanical
specimen. "I explore but little since my mute Confederate [died]," she
wrote to Higginson in June of 1866, "Yet the 'infinite Beauty' – of
which you speak comes too near to seek" (L 2:454). Her "Father's
ground," which she now never crossed to "any House or town" (L
2:460), became a microcosm of nature's general laws and processes.
Like James Russell Lowell peering at his "Garden Acquaintance" from
his study window in Cambridge, Dickinson had not locked herself out
of the earthly paradise; she had only contained and intensified it.[11]

After her withdrawal to an almost exclusively interior existence,
Dickinson read and reread Higginson's nature essays, along with those
of Thoreau and Lowell, just as many nineteenth-century naturalists read
botanical and natural history catalogues – as a means of inducing reverie
or a mood of Transcendental meditation. These nature essays were for
Dickinson a variety of Taylorean "Sacramental" or "Preparatory"
meditations before she experienced the actual high communion of June
and July; they were winter daydreams of a summer reality. In all of the
naturalists whose writings she cherished, and in Dickinson herself, we
find mention of the deep psychic meaning of such reveries for the
Victorian mind. Lowell writes, for example:

> One of the most delightful books in my father's library was
> White's Natural History of Selbourne. For me it has rather gained
> in charm with years. I used to read it without knowing the secret
> of the pleasure I found in it, but as I grow older I begin to detect
> some of the simple expedients of this natural magic. Open the
> book where you will, it takes you out of doors. In our broiling
> July weather one can walk out with this genially garrulous Fellow
> of Oriel and find refreshment instead of fatigue . . . The book has
> also the delightfulness of absolute leisure. Mr. White seems never
> to have had any harder work to do than to study the habits of his
> feathered fellow-townsfolk, or to watch the ripening of his
> peaches on the wall. His volumes are the journal of Adam in
> Paradise. [*Study Windows*, 1]

Thoreau had long anticipated Lowell, however. In the "Natural History of Massachusetts," first published in the third number of the *Dial* in July of 1842, he had begun his essay by declaring:

> Books of natural history make the most cheerful winter reading. I read in Audubon with a thrill of delight, when the snow covers the ground, of the magnolia, and the Florida keys, and their warm sea-breezes; of the fence-rail, and the cotton-tree, and the migrations of the rice-bird; of the breaking up of winter in Labrador, and the melting of the snow on the forks of the Missouri; and own an accession of health to these reminiscences of luxuriant nature.[12]

The lines that Emerson quotes from an unnamed "Arabian poet" in "Man the Reformer" come to mind when we consider how much the romantic sensibility depended upon such lexicons for renewal and refreshment in all seasons of the soul:

> Sunshine was he
> In the winter day;
> and in the midsummer
> Coolness and shade.   [*Works* 1:255]

Similarly, Higginson writes in the essay entitled "My Out-Door Study" that "even the driest and barest book of Natural History is good and nutritious, so far as it goes, if it represents genuine acquaintance; one can find summer in January by poring over the Latin catalogues of Massachusetts plants and animals in Hitchcock's Report (*ODP*, 258). This is the very report that Thoreau reviewed in the *Dial,* and of which Dickinson wrote to Higginson in 1877: "When Flowers annually died and I was a child, I used to read Dr. Hitchcock's Book on the Flowers of North America. This comforted their Absence – assuring me they lived" (*L* 2:573). For the young Dickinson, forbidden the new Transcendental scriptures, Hitchcock's book functioned as a bible, a travelogue, and a manual of consolation. In the burst of creative writing and thinking that followed hard upon the liberalizing spirit of American Transcendentalism, old, dry, and barren books of natural history whose precise and factual pages had given uncommon joy to many diverse readers were transformed into a new genre, of which Thoreau's *Walden* became the epitome. This genre might be called "poetic natural history," taking its cue from William Ellery Channing's suggestive subtitle to his 1873 biography of Thoreau: *The Poet-Naturalist.*[13] Poetic natural history was dedicated not to dry lists or bare facts but, as Lowell had intimated, to recreating the journal of Adam in paradise.

The essays of T. W. Higginson were suffused with the genial fellowship that Lowell had detected in White, and Thoreau in his more solitary musings made White's "delightfulness of absolute leisure" a whole philosophy of life. It prompted Thoreau to remark in the essay "Walking," "I think that I cannot preserve my health and spirits, unless I spend four hours a day at least—and it is commonly more than that—sauntering through the woods and over the hills and fields, absolutely free from all worldly engagements" (*Major Essays,* 196). Strange to say, Emerson himself, although he was its spiritual father, existed only on the fringes of this genre, for, as Higginson observed in his "Out-Door Study," "One is tempted to charge even Emerson, as he sometimes charges Wordsworth, with not being of a temperament quite liquid and musical enough to admit the full vibration of the great harmonies" (*ODP,* 259). The chief desideratum of this new and motley group of poetic naturalists was a strict attention to exact and pertinent detail, combined with the "liquid and musical" response that seemed to be missing in Emerson's too-hasty transcendence from the minute particular to the abstract Over-soul. Emerson was not interested primarily in fact but in spirit, since "Spirit is the Creator. Spirit hath life in itself" (*Works* 1.27); in "Blight" (1847) he even warned against unsympathetic "young scholars" who

> . . . invade our hills,
> Bold as the engineer who fells the wood,
> And travelling often in the cut he makes,
> Love not the flower they pluck, and know it not,
> And all their botany is Latin names.   [*Works* 9:140]

Indeed, the heyday of American nature writing belonged not to the seed time of the Transcendental revolt but rather to its harvest, to the ripe and mellow numbers of the *Atlantic Monthly* of the late 1850s and early 1860s, far from the cerebral, Germanic pages of the *Dial.* It coincided with the flush times of the Azarian school and its florid descriptive style. Higginson particularly praised Spofford for her sensuous apprehension of nature; writing of *Azarian* itself he claimed that

> there is not, perhaps, another individual among us who could have written the delicious descriptions of external Nature which this book contains, — not one of the multitude of young artists, now devoting their happy hours to flower-painting, who can depict color by color as she depicts it by words. We hold in our hands an illuminated missal, some Gospel of Nature according to June or October, as the case may be. [Review of *Azarian,* 516]

In Dickinson's private mythology, too, the gospel of the Sentimental Love Religion was intimately bound up with the illuminated gospel of nature:

There came a Day at Summer's full,
Entirely for me –
I thought that such were for the Saints,
Where Resurrections – be –

The Sun, as common, went abroad,
The Flowers, accustomed, blew,
As if no soul the solstice passed
That maketh all things new –

The time was scarce profaned, by speech –
The symbol of a word
Was needless, as at Sacrament,
The Wardrobe – of our Lord –

Each was to each The Sealed Church,
Permitted to commune this – time –
Lest we too awkward show
At supper of the Lamb. [J 322]

The phrase "communion with nature" has become a camp cliché in
modern times, but it had profound meaning for Emily Dickinson's
rhapsodic second generation of high romantics. It had an even pro-
founder meaning for Dickinson herself, since nature, in the form of the
summer's day, was the supreme witness to Daisy's mystic marriage
with Phoebus. Here was a communion service from which she did not
have to flee in scrupulous terror of profaning both the sacrament and
her conscience, because nature was a communion table on which the
sacred offerings were always spread, free for the asking:

Oh Sacrament of summer days,
Oh Last Communion in the Haze –
Permit a child to join.

Thy sacred emblems to partake –
Thy consecrated bread to take
And thine immortal wine! [J 130]

Just because such a communion was free, however, it was the communicant and not the celebrant who now had to exercise due restraint.
"It is necessary to use these pleasures with great temperance," Emerson had warned, and it was just such a temperance that Dickinson
began to practice in the late 1860s and that culminated in her ascetic
role of New England nun and in her philosophy of deprivation and
"sumptuous Destitution." Lest the distribution of the sacrament become common and cheap, and the communicant lax and unworthy, it

was better to leave the sacred elements untouched or learn to do
without them entirely:

> Art thou the thing I wanted?
> Begone – my Tooth has grown –
> Supply the minor Palate
> That has not starved so long –
> I tell thee while I waited
> The mystery of Food
> Increased till I abjured it
> And dine without Like God –   [J 1282]

The last line of the second version of this poem, composed around
1873 – "Subsisting now like God" – was even more blasphemous in its
import, for it implied not only a simile of manner but a true consanguinity of substance. As "Empress of Calvary," Dickinson had earned a
place next to the exclusive Trinity itself. God's table was no longer
"spread too high for Us" (J 690), since Dickinson had finally husbanded
the power to spurn even the invitation of divine fiat, and the rude table
itself, always heavy with abundant gifts of the earthly paradise, sufficed
more as ornament than as foundation. She might go so far as to "touch
the Curious Wine," or handle the consecrated wafers, but imaginative
attainment had banished the gnawing ache, as if by massive and major
surgery. With a gesture of quiet skeptical triumph, rather than one of
joyful thanksgiving or servile gratefulness, she discovered

> That Hunger – was a way
> Of Persons outside Windows –
> The Entering – takes away –   [J 579]

II

By 1873 Dickinson had inverted Plato's ladder of love, the figure with
which sentimentalists like Stowe had replaced the perverse "rungless
ladder" of New England Calvinism. Now her soul worked not upward
from the material to the spiritual, but rather downward and outward
from the gross to the purity of a tasteless but self-sustaining absolute
negation. In this way Dickinson obviated the necessity of remaining
divinity's humble pensioner, subject to the Calvinist God who "gave a
Loaf to every Bird – / But just a Crumb – to Me –" (J 791). By fully
assuming control of the amazing graces of natural communion, she put
herself on an equal footing with the parsimonious deity himself. But in
the late 1850s and early 1860s, infinite beauty, as she wrote T. W.
Higginson, came too near for her to have to seek it out. In words that
must have seemed cryptic to Higginson, she wrote on June ninth, 1866:

Paradise is of the option, Whosoever will Own in Eden notwith-standing Adam and Repeal. [*L* 2:454][14]

Dickinson's poetic paraphrase of a common romantic sentiment, per-haps best expressed by Hawthorne in his "Buds and Bird Voices," where he writes that "each human soul is the first-created inhabitant of its own Eden,"[15] demonstrates undeniably that she was (in nicety of language, at least) her father's daughter – the daughter of a shrewd and clever country lawyer. This sentiment was so common that even a gloomy poem on page 7 of Mary Warner's scrapbook, entitled "The River of Death," pauses to observe that earth is still "A goodly heri-tage" and that with the "summer landscape" at hand, "scarce brighter, sure, were heaven, / Had Love its dwelling in this world of ours." Dickinson went beyond popular feeling, however, in affirming that nature was both unfallen and resanctified by the redeeming love of Phoebus. The earthly paradise was a freehold open to every individual who dared to stake a claim; Eden was still accessible, and the Garden could still be entered, even though Adam had supposedly been expelled from it by an angel with a flaming sword, and all his titles repealed and abrogated:

> Who has not found the Heaven – below –
> Will fail of it above –
> For Angels rent the House next our's,
> Wherever we remove –   [J 1544]

Because Dickinson fused the Transcendental gospel of nature with the new gospel of sentimental love, the unfallen earthly paradise also became a constant reminder of her separation from Phoebus, as well as a confirmation of her ecstatic, momentary union with him. Perhaps punning on Hawthorne's paradisal image of "an old moss-covered mansion" in "The Old Manse" and "Buds and Bird Voices," Dickin-son in an unfinished poem written about 1868 characteristically asso-ciated the bliss of heaven on earth with the transient ecstasy of Puritan crisis conversion:

> Paradise is that old mansion
> Many owned before –
> Occupied by each an instant
> Then reversed the Door –
> Bliss is frugal of her Leases
> Adam taught her Thrift
> Bankrupt once through his excesses –   [J 1119]

Just as her private theology was a *discordia concors* uniting Calvinism (ultimate limitation) with Universalism (ultimate openness), so did her

passion for nature merge with the passion of the Crucifixion. For Dickinson had not roamed the Amherst hills only with Carlo. As a poem
written about 1862 reveals, Phoebus himself had sometimes joined her
in these rambles:

> We *walk*–I leave my Dog–at home–
> A *tender–thoughtful* Moon
> Goes with us–just a little way–
> And–then–we are *alone*–   [J 663]

The full consecration of their love had come not on a midsummer
night's eve but at the high noon of the season, as Dickinson revealed in
"There came a Day at Summer's Full," which she sent to Higginson
with her second letter, dated April twenty-fifth, 1862. Whereas the first
four stanzas of this poem record the joyful mysteries of her private
mythology–conversion, communion, marriage–the last three emphasize the sorrowful ones–crucifixion, separation, entombment:

> The Hours slid fast–as Hours will,
> Clutched tight, by greedy hands–
> So faces on two Decks, look back,
> Bound to opposing lands–
>
> And so when all the time had leaked,
> Without external sound
> Each bound the Other's Crucifix–
> We gave no other Bond–
>
> Sufficient troth, that we shall rise–
> Deposed–at length, the Grave–
> To that new Marriage,
> Justified–through Calvaries of Love–   [J 322]

Such was Dickinson's agony in the Garden. But that the earthly paradise remained a paradise and not a wasteland was due largely to such
aids to reflection as Higginson's nature essays. They confirmed Dickinson's extravagant response to an open-air heaven; as late as the spring of
1876 she wrote her "Dear friend":

> Your thought is so serious and captivating, that it leaves one
> stronger and weaker too, the Fine of Delight.
>   Of it's Bliss to yourself, we are ignorant, though you first teach
> us "that which is born of the Spirit is Spirit"–
> It is still as distinct as Paradise–the opening your first book–
> It was Mansions–Nations–Kinsmen–too–to me–
>   I sued the News–yet feared–the News
>   That such a Realm could be–

"The House not made with Hands" it was –
Thrown open wide to me –
I had long heard of an Orchis before I found one, when a child,
but the first clutch of the stem is as vivid now, as the Bog that
bore it – so truthful is transport – Though inaudible to you, I have
long thanked you. [L 2:552–3]

The first quotation in this short but fervent testimonial significantly
deals with Christ's secret disciple, Nicodemus, a "man of the Phari-
sees" and "a ruler of the Jews" who comes to Jesus by night and
addresses him as "Rabbi" just as Dickinson addressed Higginson as
"Master." Christ tells Nicodemus about the kingdom of God, stating
that a personal regeneration is necessary to obtain it and answering his
querulous follower with the words, "That which is born of the flesh is
flesh; and that which is born of the Spirit is Spirit. Marvel not that I
said unto thee, Ye must be born again" (John 3:6, 7). The second
quotation comes from another favorite Dickinson Scripture passage
whose resonances we have already explored, 2 Cor. 5:1. Here Saint
Paul, describing his earthly labors and anticipating his heavenly rewards, informs his brothers in Christ, "For we know that if our earthly
house of this tabernacle were dissolved, we have a building of God, an
house not made with hands, eternal in the heavens." These words are a
talisman that frees Dickinson from the rigors of Calvinist orthodoxy,
while they stress the corporeal, architectonic dimension of her private
mythology.

In the letter preceding this one she joyously exclaims, as if Higginson
had drawn a secret Christian emblem in the sand, "But two had mentioned the 'Spring' to me – yourself and the Revelations. 'I – Jesus – have
sent mine Angel' " (L 2:551). The quotation comes this time from Rev.
22:16, following soon after the description of the new heavenly Jerusalem, and it is Saint John's assurance that his testimony is a true one, that
his vision is authentic. What Dickinson has done is to transfer this
heavenly tabernacle to an earthly one, for her nature is the real and
immediate temple of the spirit, like Keats's many-chambered mansion
of life, where she may commune in holy fellowship with her true kin
and countrymen, "the Butterfly – and the Lizard – and the Orchis" (L
2:412). Besides being a Christ-like rabbi or teacher, announcing a new
gospel or "good news" of salvation through nature, Higginson is identified in Dickinson's eclectic typology as a Gabriel who has called her
back to this lost Eden, as well as a Paul whose own conversion experience in the midst of natural beauty confirms her romantic one.

Higginson began his inquiry into the relations of the soul with nature
in his *Out-Door Papers,* though Dickinson had already read most of

these pieces when they first appeared in the *Atlantic Monthly*. What were the characteristics of Higginson's nature writing that endeared him to Dickinson even more than Lowell or Emerson or Thoreau? If we examine just one of his essays – for example, "My Out-Door Study" – we can see that it was a style, a tone, and an approach that were shared by another major American school of art flowering at exactly the same time, the so-called Hudson River school of painting. First of all, the very title of Higginson's essay and of his whole collection itself indicates a desire to break away from a conventional "studio" approach to landscape and experience it directly, bareheaded and at first hand. "Art may either rest upon other Art," Higginson writes, "or it may rest directly upon the original foundation; the one is easier, the other more valuable. Direct dependence on Nature leads to deeper thought, and affords the promise of far fresher results. Why should I wish to fix my study in Heidelberg Castle, when I possess the unexhausted treasures of this out-door study here?" (*ODP*, 261)

Higginson's impulse is unashamedly romantic and Transcendental; Emerson called for an "original relation to the universe," and Walt Whitman wrote that "we have had man indoors and under artificial relations . . . but never before have we had *man in the open air,* his attitude adjusted to the seasons and as one might describe it, adjusted to the sun by day and the stars by night."[16] Significantly, Higginson was not of the first generation of American romantics. Like Dickinson, he was attached to the baroque, post–American Renaissance lushness of Spofford and the Azarian school as well as to the spartan late essays of Henry David Thoreau, which appeared along with his own in the *Atlantic Monthly* of the late 1850s and early 1860s. It was from Thoreau that Higginson got his very idea of an open-air approach to nature, basing it on an anecdote related in "Walking": "When a traveller asked Wordsworth's servant to show him her master's study, she answered, 'Here is his library, but his study is out of doors' " (*Major Essays,* 198). If Higginson was Dickinson's literary master and preceptor, Thoreau was Higginson's. In "My Out-Door Study" Higginson writes:

> Leslie says of "the most original landscape-painter he knew," meaning Constable, that, whenever he sat down in the fields to sketch, he endeavored to forget that he had ever seen a picture. In literature this is easy, the descriptions are so few and so faint. When Wordsworth was fourteen, he stopped one day by the way-side to observe the dark outline of an oak against the western sky; and he says he was at the moment struck with "the infinite variety of natural appearances which had been unnoticed by the poets of any age or country," so far as he was acquainted with them, and

"made a resolution to supply in some degree the deficiency." He spent a long life in studying and telling these beautiful wonders; and yet, so vast is the sum of them, they seem almost as undescribed as before, and men to be still as content with vague or conventional representations. On this continent, especially, people fancied that all must be tame and second-hand, everything long since duly analyzed and distributed and put up in appropriate quotations, and nothing left for us poor American children but a preoccupied universe. And yet Thoreau camps down by Walden Pond, and shows us that absolutely nothing in Nature has ever yet been described, – not a bird nor a berry of the woods, nor a drop of water, nor a spicula of ice, nor summer, nor winter, nor sun, nor star. [257–8]

In "Nature" Emerson had declared that "our age is retrospective" and asked why revelations should be taken at second hand. Thoreau took up that challenge, and Higginson followed in Thoreau's footsteps. Yet in spite of Emerson's admonition in "Self-Reliance" that "man is timid and apologetic . . . he does not say 'I think,' 'I am,' but quotes some saint or sage" (*Works* 2:67) we can see from the passage just quoted from Higginson that Higginson is far more "studious" a stylist than Thoreau, fonder of quotation, more conscious of tradition, and far less egotistically terse and aphoristic. The more relaxed nature of Higginson's style stems from his closer association with the liquid subtleties of the Azarian school. His prose is in fact a masculine version of Spofford's mellifluous word-painting, which Henry James had rather condescendingly characterized as an exclusively feminine mode. In his *North American Review* blast, James wrote that Spofford "uses far too many words, synonymous and meaningless words. Like the majority of female writers, – Mrs. Browning, George Sand, Gail Hamilton, Mrs. Stowe, – she possesses in excess the fatal gift of fluency" (275). It was because of an excess of this same fluency that Higginson, his own best critic, yearned for a more robust cast of expression:

I have fineness and fire, but some want of copiousness and fertility which may give a tinge of thinness to what I write . . . What an abundance, freshness and go there is about the Beechers, for instance. They are egoistic, crotchety and personally disagreeable, and often "make fritters of English" but I wish I could, without sacrificing polish, write with that exuberant and hearty zeal . . . Shakespeare may have written as the birds sing, though I doubt it – but minor writers at least have to labor for *form* as the painter labors – the mere inspiration of thought is not enough . . . There must be a golden moment but also much labor within that mo-

ment. At least it is so with me, and I cannot help suspecting that it
is even so with the Shakespeares. [*TWH*, 274–5]

Higginson's comparison of his exacting poetic style with the struggle
of an artist to bring forth form on canvas again allies him to the word-
painting of the Azarian school, and the "polish" of his nature writing
matches the silver or golden sheen that suffuses the work of Hudson
River school artists like Asher B. Durand. The dean of this school,
Durand specialized in woodland scenes radiant with shafts of mellow
light and the golden glow of declining suns. It is significant that when
Higginson published a small collection of his own verse in 1889, he
entitled it *The Afternoon Landscape,* a phrase taken from an opening
"prelude" that celebrated the "spread" of old age's "glow / O'er the
changed landscape of time's afternoon."[17] Durand was one of the first
American artists to exhibit oil sketches painted directly from nature, in
the open air, and he was famed for his botanical realism, since a
knowledgeable viewer could always tell the exact species of trees depicted in his compositions by the shape of their individual leaves. Even
random flowers and plants were similarly faithful to horticultural canons of truth.[18]

Just as Mary Warner's scrapbook provides a reasonable facsimile for
her forays into popular culture, so does there exist in Dickinson's immediate environment a material parallel to the kind of elite and Transcendental painting practiced by Durand. Among the collection of canvases amassed by Austin and Susan Dickinson, there is a very large (46″
× 38″) *Woodland Scene* by Arthur Parton that carries on the Durand
tradition of blissful tranquillity and botanical exactness (see the illustration at the opening of this chapter). Although of relatively late date (ca.
1876), this landscape and other Hudson River school studies in the
Evergreens collection demonstrate that T. W. Higginson's worship of
luminous American natural beauty was shared by the more advanced
members of the Dickinson family, among whom we must number the
then-obscure Emily.[19]

It was precisely Higginson's nearness to nature and his high exaltation that prompted Dickinson to choose him as a confidant. She was
not alone, for Higginson was rightly regarded in his own times as one
of the masters of the new genre of the nature sketch. Thoreau himself
praised Higginson's essay "Snow," and the delighted author wrote to
the editor of the *Atlantic,* James T. Fields, that he was "the only critic
whom I should regard as really formidable on such a subject" (*Letters
and Journals,* 114). Higginson told Spofford: "I have more [letters] about
'April Days' than about anything I have written – sick women, young
farmers, etc. One odd anonymous person, signing *Su Su,* sent me a

root of double bloodroot postmarked 'Snow's store, Vt.'. It seemed pretty that bloodroot should come out of Snow's Store – though I suppose the donor never thought of it" (*TWH*, 157). Others, too, were reading Higginson's "Chapters" in the *Atlantic,* and experiencing "honor" for him, but none was more enthusiastic or reverent than Emily Dickinson. To her, Higginson's essays were not simply a new form of Transcendental art, they were gospel itself, the continuing "Revelations of the Book / Whose genesis was June" (J 1115). Like a faithful disciple renewing her vows Dickinson wrote to Higginson in January 1876: "That it is true, Master, is the Power of all you write" (*L* 2:546).

III

At his best Higginson certainly deserved all the praise that his admirers, including Dickinson, could lavish on him. By his own account he spent "days and weeks on single sentences," and in his nature essays he set the highest possible standards for the craft of writing, standards that he was to refine in his famous "Letter to a Young Contributor." Dickinson quoted from this piece in a letter she sent fifteen years after its initial publication in 1862. "Often, when troubled by entreaty," she wrote, "that paragraph of your's has saved me – 'Such being the majesty of the Art you presume to practice, you can at least take some time before dishonoring it' " (*L* 2:573). In "My Out-Door Study," Higginson's ideal was no less than an absolute fidelity to the form as well as the spirit of nature itself:

And for literary training, especially, the influence of natural beauty is simply priceless. Under the present educational systems, we need grammars and languages far less than a more thorough out-door experience. On this flowery bank, on this ripple-marked shore, are the true literary models. How many living authors have ever attained to writing a single page which could be for one moment compared, for the simplicity and grace of its structure, with this green spray of wild woodbine or yonder white wreath of blossoming clematis? A finely organized sentence should throb and palpitate like the most delicate vibrations of the summer air. We talk of literature as if it were a mere matter of rule and measurement, a series of processes long since brought to mechanical perfection; but it would be less incorrect to say that it all lies in the future; tried by the out-door standard, there is as yet no literature, but only glimpses and guideboards; no writer has yet succeeded in sustaining, through more than some single occasional sentence, that fresh and perfect charm. If by the training of a lifetime one

could succeed in producing one continuous page of perfect ca-
dence, it would be a life well spent, and such a literary artist
would fall short of Nature's standard in quantity only, not in
quality. [*ODP, 254*]

Here we have some justification for the many nature poems of Emily
Dickinson. Each individual work was a spontaneous sketch attempting
to capture the simplicity and grace not only of a spray of wild woodbine, or a white wreath of blossoming clematis, but of bees, butterflies,
and all manner of woodland creatures as seen in the open-air heaven of
the earthly paradise. As she wrote to Higginson in August of 1862:

When much in the Woods, as a little Girl, I was told that the
Snake would bite me, that I might pick a poisonous flower, or
Goblins kidnap me, but I went along and met no one but Angels,
who were far shyer of me, than I could be of them, so I hav'nt
that confidence in fraud which many exercise. [*L 2:415*]

Because Dickinson's celebration of nature was intimately connected
with her own private mythology and the consecration of her love for
Phoebus, natural facts were not merely symbols of spiritual facts in the
Emersonian sense, but also emblems and tokens of an individual passion. Even the clematis, which Higginson presented as an ultimate
challenge for the skill of the aspiring poet-naturalist, took on a deep
personal resonance, becoming an organic keepsake of her consuming
Platonic love:

> 'Tis customary as we part
> A trinket – to confer –
> It helps to stimulate the faith
> When Lovers be afar –
>
> 'Tis various – as the various taste –
> Clematis – journeying far –
> Presents me with a single Curl
> Of her Electric Hair –   [J 440]

Not every nature poem by Emily Dickinson, of course, carries such
symbolic weight. Many of her poems are exercises, pure and simple, in
capturing those subjects of natural beauty that Higginson proposed as
problems for the budding literary artist. In writing these poems she
accepted the contention of the Azarian school that the writer's true
model was the painter, a concept underlined by Higginson through his
references to such landscapists as Constable and his own practice of the
literary equivalent of Asher B. Durand's painterly technique. Yet Dickinson's compression of language through the discipline of a folk form

and the force of her own genius allowed her to practice in poetry that saving simplicity which Henry James had deemed so lacking in the novels of Harriet Prescott. "Her paragraphs," James wrote in his review of *Azarian,*

> read as if in composition she completely ignored the expedient of erasure. What painter ever painted a picture without rubbing out and transposing, displacing, effacing, replacing? There is no essential difference of system between the painting of a picture and the writing of a novel. Why should the novelist expect to do what his fellow-worker never even hopes to acquire the faculty of doing, – execute his work at a stroke? It is plain that Miss Prescott adds, tacks on, interpolates, piles up, if we may use the expression; but it seems very doubtful if she often takes counsel of the old Horatian precept, – in plain English, to scratch out. A true artist should be as sternly just as a Roman father. A moderate exercise of this Roman justice would have reduced "Azarian" to half its actual length. The various descriptive passages would have been wonderfully simplified, and we might have possessed a few good pictures. [273]

A glance at the work sheets of Emily Dickinson's poetry, with their alternative choices of words scribbled on top, bottom, and margin, each choice indicating a subtle change in compressed meaning or an important shift in descriptive nuance, indicates that she practiced just such a wonderful simplicity. By scratching out the inessential, Dickinson produced more than "a few good pictures," such as the imagistic perfection of her description of the clematis just quoted, with all that vine's twining, clinging, and tensile properties fused in the single adjective "Electric." These same pictures were often unknowingly suggested by her "Dear Preceptor," Higginson himself. Again, there is no need to do extensive source hunting in Higginson's essays for the origin and evolution of individual Dickinson poems. It has long been known that "At Half-Past Three, a single Bird" (J 1084) takes its opening cue from a sentence in "Water-Lilies," and that "A Route of Evanescence" (J 1463) derives from his description of a hummingbird in the second paragraph of "The Life of Birds."[20] In his essay "Emily Dickinson's Letters," first published in the *Atlantic* in 1891 and later reprinted in *Carlyle's Laugh,* Higginson referred to this poem as "an exquisite little detached strain, every word a picture," adding that "nothing in literature, I am sure, so condenses into a few words that gorgeous atom of life and fire of which she here attempts the description" (*Carlyle's Laugh,* 285). Yet he never seems to have realized that it was his own word-painting that prompted this cameo performance, supplemented by the typically extravagant prose fragment he had quoted from a letter by Harriet Prescott Spofford, thinly disguised as "Harriet Rohan": "when a Humming-Bird, a winged drop of gorgeous sheen and gloss, a living gem, poising on his wings, thrust his dark, slender, honey-seeking bill into the white blossoms of a little bush beside my window, I should have thought it no such bad thing to be a bird" (*ODP*, 296–7).

When we remember that Dickinson tried to read every word that Higginson wrote, and that she revered his nature writings in particular as a secular scripture, one must simply accept his works as a fixture of her own well-furnished American Victorian sensibility. Just as she carried the singsong rhythms and fearsome folk images of Isaac Watts's hymns in her head, so did she mentally conduct a continuing dialogue with Higginson's high-style precepts and strenuous championship of elite culture.[21] So intimate was her knowledge of Higginson's prose that in their correspondence she often had to remind him that she was merely paraphrasing his own thoughts. Sometimes, as with "A Route of Evanescence," he missed the original referent altogether, and when in 1870 he recorded Dickinson's extraordinary declaration "I find ecstacy in living – the mere sense of living is joy enough" (*L* 2:474), he did not seem to recognize that she was restating his own contention in "Gymnastics" that "health finds joy in mere existence; daily breath and daily bread suffice" (*ODP*, 139). When she said that poetry was her only playmate and lamented after her father's death that he "never played," Higginson was supposed to remember his observation in "Saints and Their Bodies" that "We must not ignore the *play-impulse* in human nature, which, according to Schiller, is the foundation of all Art" (*ODP*, 22).

More important than individual descants, however, were the lessons that Higginson set for Dickinson as an aspiring nature writer and a silent partner of Lowell, Thoreau, James Elliot Cabot, Wilson Flagg, and other poet-naturalists (including Higginson himself) who contributed to the *Atlantic* in the 1850s and 1860s. These lessons were not only the catalogue of such as-yet-undescribed subjects as "the veery's carolling, the clover's scent, the glistening of the water, the waving wings of butterflies, the sunset tints, the floating clouds" listed in "The Procession of the Flowers" (*ODP*, 336). They were whole unrealized epics and chorales of nature. In "My Out-Door Study," Higginson wrote that

> time is a severe alembic of youthful joys, no doubt; we exhaust book after book, and leave Shakespeare unopened, we grow fastidious in men and women; all the rhetoric, all the logic, we fancy we have heard before; we have seen the pictures, we have listened

to the symphonies: but what has been done by all the art and literature of the world towards describing one summer day? The most exhausting effort brings us no nearer to it than to the blue sky which is its dome; our words are shot up against it like arrows, and fall back helpless. Literary amateurs go the tour of the globe to renew their stock of materials, when they do not yet know a bird or a bee or a blossom beside their homestead-door; and in the hour of their greatest success they have not an horizon to their life so large as that of yon boy in his punt. All that is purchasable in the capitals of the world is not to be weighed in comparison with the simple enjoyment that may be crowded into one hour of sunshine. What can place or power do here? "Who could be before me, though the palace of Caesar cracked and split with emperors, while I, sitting in silence on a cliff of Rhodes, watched the sun as he swung his golden censer athwart the heavens?" [*ODP*, 250–1]

Higginson later delighted in the fact that Dickinson told him, "When I lost the use of my eyes, it was a comfort to think that there were so few real books that I could easily find one to read me all of them," and that when she at last regained her sight, "she read Shakespeare, and thought to herself, 'Why is any other book needed?' " (*Carlyle's Laugh*, 274). Even the Shakespeare who wrote that "Summer's lease hath all too short a date" had not, however, attempted a full-length portrait of one entire summer's day, though Dickinson did in an unusually long poem that Thomas Johnson dates early in 1862:

> The Trees like Tassels – hit – and swung –
> There seemed to rise a Tune
> From Miniature Creatures
> Accompanying the Sun –
>
> Far Psalteries of Summer –
> Enamoring the Ear
> They never yet did satisfy –
> Remotest – when most fair
>
> The Sun shone whole at intervals –
> Then Half – then utter hid –
> As if Himself were optional
> And had Estates of Cloud
>
> Sufficient to enfold Him
> Eternally from view –
> Except it were a whim of His
> To let the Orchards grow –

A Bird sat careless on the fence –
One gossiped in the Lane
On silver matters charmed a Snake
Just winding round a Stone –

Bright Flowers slit a Calyx
And soared upon a Stem
Like Hindered Flags – Sweet hoisted –
With Spices – in the Hem –

'Twas more – I cannot mention –
How mean – to those that see –
Vandykes Delineation
Of Natures' – Summer Day!   [J 606]

It is significant that a good many of the poems that Dickinson enclosed with notes to Higginson dealt with what she here calls the "Far
Psalteries of Summer," emphasizing the season's symphonic or orches-
tral qualities. Higginson's own euphonious prose conveyed his sensuous
apprehension of the natural world, and in "The Procession of the
Flowers" he declared that "It is possible to dream of combinations of
syllables so delicious that all the dawning and decay of summer cannot
rival their perfection" (*ODP,* 337). He added, "To write them, were it
possible, would be to take rank with Nature, nor is there any other
method, even by music, for human art to reach so high." Literature,
then, would outstrip both music and painting as the queen of the arts
only when perfection in nature writing had been achieved. Dickinson
agreed that "continents of summer" and "firmaments of sun" (J 180)
would continue to foil courtly artists like Van Dyck even as she strove to
practice a humbler art that might still approach this impossible standard:

The One who could repeat the Summer day –
Were greater than itself – though He
Minutest of Mankind should be –

And He – could reproduce the Sun –
At period of going down –
The Lingering – and the Stain – I mean –

When Orient have been outgrown –
And Occident – become Unknown –
His Name – remain –   [J 307]

Here Dickinson's seemingly offhand and casual mention of the declining sun's "lingering" and "Stain" captures in a few masterful
strokes of word-painting the kind of effect that Higginson was groping

for when he quoted Walter Savage Landor's inflated rhetoric about the censer of the sun from the famous *Imaginary Conversations*. As sensitive as Higginson was to the nuances of language, he could not wholly comprehend Dickinson's sacramental attitude toward summer, and seems to have made no comment on "There came a Day at Summer's Full" when the poet sent it to him. Perhaps he was too fastidious to probe into what was obviously an open wound, and the complete scope of Dickinson's remarkable private mythology, combining nature worship, Platonic romance, and Calvinism, was after all unknown to him. He surely must have guessed from the beginning of their correspondence that her response to nature was as much "religious" as it was Transcendental. To Dickinson, her outdoor religion was a joyous heresy that poured new wine into the old bottles of the Calvinism that was her heritage, uniquely fulfilling Lowell's definition of Transcendentalism in his essay "Thoreau" as "simply a struggle for fresh air, in which, if the windows could not be opened, there was danger that panes would be broken, though painted with images of saints and martyrs" (*Study Windows*, 195)

It was the very orthodoxy of Emily Dickinson's nurture that lent such a sacramental intensity to her experience of nature, while Higginson's liberal upbringing permitted him an equally sympathetic but comparatively "mild" communion. To him the summer's day allured not because it provided an alternative to Calvinist exclusivity, but because it was a time when the ordinarily reserved New England climate was suddenly caught in flagrante delicto. It was Dickinson's genius, however, to fuse the erotic and the Calvinistic:

> One Joy of so much anguish
> Sweet nature has for me
> I shun it as I do Despair
> Or dear iniquity –
> Why Birds, a Summer morning
> Before the Quick of Day
> Should stab my ravished spirit
> With Dirks of Melody
> Is part of an inquiry
> That will receive reply
> When Flesh and Spirit sunder
> In Death's Immediately –   [J 1420]

Dickinson attempted to solve Higginson's problem, the problem that while the summer day was the most poetic and artistic of subjects, its essence seemed truly ineffable or inexpressible, by first becoming like a little child and bathing herself fully in the luxurious details of sight, sound, and scent that assaulted the doors of her human perception. Each of her poems on summer was his arrow of words shot at an unattainable target, a consciously absurd materialization of something impossibly ideal and ungraspable. Dickinson certainly matched Higginson in her purely sensual response to summer, but her religion of romance gave the summer day a whole new liturgical significance. The earthly paradise supplied all of the High Church ritual, all of that sacerdotal wealth of embroidered vestments, gleaming vessels, and heady incense, that Puritanism had denied her, reared as she was within the wintry confines of the New England meetinghouse:

> A something in a summer's Day
> As slow her flambeaux burn away
> Which solemnizes me.
>
> A something in a summer's noon –
> A depth – an Azure – a perfume –
> Transcending extasy.
>
> And still within a summer's night
> A something so transporting bright
> I clap my hands to see –
>
> Then vail my too inspecting face
> Lest such a subtle – shimmering grace
> Flutter too far for me –   [J 122]

In "The Procession of the Flowers," Higginson had warned:

> But, after all, the fascination of summer lies not in any details, however perfect, but in the sense of total wealth which summer gives. Wholly to enjoy this, one must give one's self passively to it, and not expect to reproduce it in words. We strive to picture heaven, when we are barely at the threshold of the inconceivable beauty of earth. [ODP, 335–6]

Although Higginson might doubt whether such feelings could be put into words and might not recognize the legitimacy of his pupil's efforts until after her death, in a number of poems Dickinson had already achieved, to her own satisfaction at least, the perfection of this impossible art:

> When Diamonds are a Legend,
> And Diadems – a Tale –
> I Brooch and Earrings for Myself,
> Do sow, and Raise for sale –

And tho' I'm scarce accounted,
My Art, a Summer Day – had Patrons –
Once – it was a Queen –
And once – a Butterfly –   [J 397]

IV

For Emily Dickinson, T. W. Higginson's nature essays in *Out-Door Papers* remained unmatched in their poetic quality. This is not to say that she did not also profoundly agree with the other essays in the book, which were mostly concerned with gymnastics and hygiene and which at first glance seem alien to the hothouse existence that we automatically associate with the life of the Amherst poet. For example, in "The Murder of the Innocents," a plea for doing away with the kind of deadening, rote education of young people that had given rise to such horrors as Charlotte Brontë's Lowood School in *Jane Eyre,* Higginson describes in detail the regimen of a fictional female seminary, "Dothegirls' Hall," based in turn on Dickens's infamous model in *Nicholas Nickleby.* This regimen includes eleven solid hours of study each day, while it allots only two hours to recreation, and it uncannily matches the actual description of Emily Dickinson's schedule at Mount Holyoke that she sent in a letter to Abiah Root in November of 1847 (*L* 1:54–5). The Dickinson who had to be taken home sick by her brother in the middle of the term, presumably because she had reacted to the religious and scholastic pressures of Mount Holyoke by going into a serious "decline," both psychic and physical, could well appreciate the polemics of Higginson's argument with his fictional dyspeptic, Dolorosus:

> To change the sweet privilege of childhood into weary days and restless nights, – to darken its pure associations, which for many are the sole light that ever brings them back from sin and despair to the heaven of their infancy, – to banish those reveries of innocent fancy which even noisy boyhood knows; and which are the appointed guardians of its purity before conscience wakes, – to abolish its moments of priceless idleness, saturated with sunshine, blissful, aimless moments, when every angel is near, – to bring insanity, once the terrible prerogative of maturer life, down into the summer region of childhood, with blight and ruin; – all this is the work of our folly, Dolorosus, of our miserable ambition to have our unconscious little ones begin, in their very infancy, the race of desperate ambition, which has, we admit, exhausted prematurely the lives of their parents. [101–2]

In Higginson's words in defense of an untrammeled childhood, we find some hint of why in her later years the defrauded Dickinson looked back with "rapture" on the daring of "losing my shoe in the Mud and going Home barefoot, wading for Cardinal flowers" (*L* 3:928–9), why she often used the persona of the "barefoot boy" in her nature poetry, and why she gleefully conspired with Austin's children against all the other "adults" in the two houses:

> So I pull my Stockings off
> Wading in the Water
> For the Disobedience' Sake
> Boy that lived for "or'ter"
>
> Went to Heaven perhaps at Death
> And perhaps he did'nt
> Moses was'nt fairly used –
> Ananias was'nt –   [J 1201]

Higginson, whose mother had been an easygoing Unitarian and who as a child had been allowed to play cards in the parlor on Sunday afternoons, was baptized as a liberal, confirmed as a freethinker, and ordained as a radical. He was never like Dickinson an outcast in his own family circle, nor did he have to put up with the religious pressures that blighted for latter-day Puritans the "summer region of childhood." Dickinson herself was one of those "extraordinary cases . . . who underwent great and prolonged trials and sorrows without especial religious consolation" that Higginson described in his 1910 essay "The Future Life."[22] To appropriate the categories William James elaborates in his *The Varieties of Religious Experience,* Emily Dickinson, with her manic-depressive swings from ecstasy to despair, was a perfect example of the "sick soul," whereas Higginson, with his extraordinary vigor, optimism, and natural sanity, was a perfect example of the "healthy-minded" individual.[23] It was this irrepressible healthy-mindedness, as well as his extraordinary response to nature, that elevated him in Dickinson's eyes to the role of savior as well as master. Dickinson herself declared more than once during their correspondence, extending over almost a quarter of the nineteenth century, that "of our greatest acts we are ignorant – You were not aware that you saved my Life. To thank you in person has been since then one of my few requests" (*L* 2:460).

How exactly did T. W. Higginson save Emily Dickinson's life? He did so not only by confirming her crisis conversion through the sanctifying graces of the earthly paradise, but also by his conscientious attention and unfailing courtesy. He consoled Dickinson for her personal losses as well as for her retreat from that great public world that he conspicuously represented. William James had written that "there are men who seem to have started in life with a bottle or two of champagne inscribed to their credit; whilst others seem to have been born close to the pain-threshold, which the slightest irritants fatally send them over" (*Varieties*, 117). Higginson drew upon that private stock of mental champagne and took the time to share it with Dickinson, even extending his sympathies to events that were seemingly trivial to others but momentous to her: "Carlo died . . . Would you instruct me now?" (*L* 2:449). His unceasing vitality was a natural inheritance, just as Emily Dickinson's sensitivity was by nature "morbid" and inclined toward valetudinarianism: her "fixed melancholy" at the age of sixteen, her temporary blindness during her thirties, and her later nervous collapse. How could the hearty Higginson, inured to dealing patiently with the quirks and crotchets of his own invalid wife, Mary Channing, neglect such subtle hints as Dickinson's pathetic confession of April twenty-fifth, 1862, "Your kindness claimed earlier gratitude – but I was ill – and write today, from my pillow" (*L* 2:404), or her clinical bulletin of early June 1864, "I was ill since September, and since April, in Boston, for a Physician's care" (*L* 2:431)?

Although Higginson was given little chance of surviving at birth, the unceasing devotion of his mother brought him through an initial period of extremely delicate health. By the time he was five Mrs. Higginson could remark in a letter, "We . . . have been quietly seated at our work . . . only interrupted by little Wentworth's rampant spirits before he went to bed" (*TWH*, 12). These same rampant spirits sustained Higginson for the next eighty-three years, in spite of the serious breakdown of his health during the Civil War, and he always blessed his mother for gifting him with the boon of extraordinary recuperative powers. As he wrote her when he reached his thirty-third year:

> My birthdays pass by almost uncounted, for I never feel any older; indeed in these last years I feel a sort of exuberance of life, and love of action and adventure, which seem more like 23 than 33. I think the one great possession of my life has been this sunny vigor of nature and unfailing animal spirits, which have carried me buoyantly over everything so far, and which I am sure I inherited from you. And many as are my other causes of gratitude, this seems the greatest. [*TWH*, 125]

In divinity school, Higginson had written in his journal, "I only felt assured that 'Despair! thy name is written on / The roll of common man!' was *not meant for a lesson for me*" (*TWH*, 72). The "sunny vigor of nature and unfailing animal spirits" that pervaded his personal life also characterized his literary pursuits. As Emerson had written, "The office of the scholar is to cheer, to raise, and to guide men by showing them facts amidst appearances" (*Works* 1:100). Emily Dickinson was not the only one who benefited from this kind of cheery guidance, since Higginson was the center of and rallying point for a remarkable group of women writers and poets, all of whom he actively sponsored, promoted, and tutored. Speaking of her life in provincial Newburyport, Harriet Prescott Spofford later remarked, "Mr. Higginson was like a great archangel to all of us then and there were so many of us! Coming into the humdrum life of the town, he was like someone from another star" (*TWH,* 95–6). In both public and private he expounded the encouraging Victorian doctrine that, as he put it, "each advance brings with it a new sorrow and a new joy, with the joy always in excess," and as gloomy and burdened an individual as the poet Edmund Clarence Stedman replied to one of Higginson's random "expression[s] of solicitude" during a season of uncommon personal and financial disaster:

> My Dear Higginson, – There *is* a good deal, say what you will, in "moral support." I have proved it during the last few weeks: 'twould have been hard to get through with them, but for just such words as yours. And I have had them in such abundance that, despite rather poor displays of human nature in a sample of mine own manufacture, I am less than ever a pessimist . . .
>
> We have suffered more, however, than the money-loss, bad as that is. And hence we are doubly grateful to those who, like yourself, send a cheery voice to us at just this time. [*Carlyle's Laugh,* 145]

Higginson reports that after the receipt of this letter "we had ample correspondence of a wholly literary and cheerful tone," and it is the word "cheerful" that becomes well-nigh a leitmotif of Higginson's biography, justifying the seemingly saccharine title of his valuable memoirs, *Cheerful Yesterdays.*[24] Higginson, in condescending to console the obscure Dickinson, stooped to conquer. But if there was some calculation involved on her side of this epistolary brother–sister relationship, a faint hope of achieving literary fame ("Could I make you and Austin– proud–sometime–a great way off–'twould give me taller feet," she had written to her sister-in-law in 1861 [*L* 2:380]), there was also a good deal of cold-blooded scientific curiosity on his. Even in his "Letter to a Young Contributor" he described the typical editor (himself) as "a bland and virtuous man" who had "educated his eye till it has become microscopic, like a naturalist's, and can classify nine out of ten specimens by one glance at a scale or a feather."[25] Higginson collected bizarre, unique, and intriguing acquaintances as eagerly as he had sought for rare examples of corals, starfishes, and sea urchins on the coast of the Azores in 1855. His passion for the vagaries of natural phenomena included the behavior of odd specimens of the family of man as well as those of the mollusca and lepidoptera.

V

From his boyhood on we find in Higginson's journals not only such entries as "caught a little green snake and afterwards killed and preserved it" or "skeletonizing a toad' (*TWH*, 28), but acute dissections of human curiosities like the Palfrey sisters of Cambridge, of whom he noted in 1844:

> Sarah languishes onward with the tremulous impetus of a forty-car freight train; Anna spins ahead like a lively young locomotive racing homeward, upsetting countless urchins (in white cravats) without mercy; and finally, after sundry jolts, bringing up breathlessly, with a smiling bump, against some impassable barrier, and starting thence again with scarce a respite. [*Letters and Journals*, 2]

It was precisely because he was such a dedicated amateur naturalist, a connoisseur of human nature as well as vegetable flora and fauna, that Higginson sustained his interest in Emily Dickinson over such a long period of time. She early appeared to him a rare species on the verge of total extinction, and it was no accident that he warned the readers of the first series of *Poems* that Dickinson's art was a wild growth lifted bodily from the Amherst humus: "In many cases these verses will seem to the reader like poetry torn up by the roots, with rain and dew and earth still clinging to them, giving a freshness and a fragrance not otherwise to be conveyed" (v–vi). Truly his elusive poetess seemed to be the last, diminutive flower of a fading Puritanism, a specimen eccentric in form and variety, intolerant of transplantation but with a lyric fragrance intoxicating almost beyond belief.

In his essay "April Days," first published in the *Atlantic* in April 1861 and later included in *Out-Door Papers,* Higginson characterized such wild flowers as the bloodroot and the Mayflower as representing "the aboriginal epoch of our history," conjuring up images of the native American and the Pilgrim settler. He noted that New England's wild flowers were all of a more delicate texture than coarser foreign importations, and that children showed their instinctive recognition of this delicacy by gathering the indigenous species rather than its naturalized neighbor. But now these original rarities, as shy and alluring as Pocahontas or as dainty as "Priscilla, the Puritan maiden," seemed doomed to extinction in the face of the onward march of nineteenth-century progress. Higginson lamented that

> there is something touching in the gradual retirement before civilization of these fragile aborigines. They do not wait for the actual brute contact of red bricks and curbstones, but they feel the danger miles away. The Indians called the low plantain "the white man's footstep"; and these shy creatures gradually disappear, the moment the red man gets beyond their hearing. Bigelow's delightful "Florula Bostoniensis" is becoming a series of epitaphs. Too well we know it, – those of us who in happy Cambridge childhood often gathered, almost within a stone's throw of Professor Agassiz's new Museum, the arethusa and the gentian, the cardinal-flower and the gaudy rhexia, – we who remember the last secret hiding-place of the rhodora in West Cambridge, of the yellow violet and the *Viola debilis* in Watertown, of the *Convallaria trifolia* near Fresh pond, of the *Hottonia* beyond Wellington's Hill, of the *Cornus florida* in West Roxbury, of the *Clintonia* and the dwarf ginseng in Brookline, – we who have found in its one chosen nook the sacred *Andromeda polyfolia* of Linnaeus. Now vanished almost or wholly from city suburbs, these fragile creatures still linger in the more rural parts of Massachusetts; but they are doomed everywhere, unconsciously, yet irresistibly, while others still more shy, as the *Linnaea,* the yellow *Cypripedium,* the early pink *Azalea,* and the delicate white *Corydalis* or "Duchman's breeches," are being chased into the very recesses of the Green and the White Mountains. [*ODP,* 234]

I have quoted this passage at length because in many respects Emily Dickinson, secreted in her chosen nook of Amherst, represented for Higginson another kind of sacred *Andromeda polyfolia* whose lance-shaped evergreen leaves both artfully concealed and closely protected the pendulous white bloom of her delicate flowering. The blossoms that Linnaeus found in Lapland signficantly reminded him of "a fine female complexion," and he described the dwarf beauty in poetic terms that deeply impressed the enthusiastic Higginson: "This plant is always fixed on some little turfy hillock in the midst of the swamps, just as Andromeda herself was chained to a rock in the sea, which bathed her feet as the fresh water does this plant . . . As the distressed virgin cast down her blushing face through excessive affliction, so does this rosy-colored flower hang its head, growing paler and paler until it withers away."[26] It is only necessary to note, in view of Dickinson's propensity for wearing white during her later years, that the American variety of *Andromeda* seldom achieved even the rose tint of its hardy Teutonic cousin. Indeed, it was equally if not more retiring in both its habits and its habitat.

Perishable native genius had retreated to the more rural parts of Massachusetts, though Higginson was still ready to seek it out with magnifying glass and collecting box. It is for this reason – his passion for exact description and classification – that we have the colonel's copious notes on his first interview with Dickinson, which record so many extraordinary facts that otherwise might have been lost to an equally curious posterity. A leaf of the poet's mind was pressed, as it were, into a specimen book much like the herbarium that Dickinson herself compiled, each specimen identified by its proper botanical Latin name.[27] There we may still view it today and wonder how many other unique species, now totally extinct, may have paralleled it.

In the beginning Dickinson was far from being the single item in Higginson's cabinet of native American curiosities. He went out of his way to call upon Whittier in 1849, to record his quaint Quaker dialect and antislavery conversation, just as he had sought out Henry Thoreau at his pencil factory in Concord, where he found the hermit of Walden Pond to be "a little bronzed spare man" whose ways "were more domestic and filial than one would suppose." In most cases Higginson attempted to be as precise about physical quirks and characteristics as he was about mental ones. When describing Emily Dickinson for his wife, Mary Channing, he noted "a step like a pattering child's in entry & in glided a little plain woman with two smooth bands of reddish hair & a face a little like Belle Dove's; not plainer – with no good feature." Dickinson's "manner" was "between Angie Tilton & Mr. Alcott – but thoroughly ingenuous and simple which they are not" (L 2:473). Belle Dove, Angie Tilton, and Bronson Alcott were previously classified specimens of human oddity that failed to provide exact analogues to the novelty that now stood in full glory at the feet of the collector. Higginson could not have been more intrigued had he, like similar explorers of his questing age, discovered a lily neglected by Linneas or found the source of the waters of the Blue Nile.

Because of his passion for exact classification, Higginson was just as interested in "physiognomy" – "The Visage of the Soul" (J 1311) – as was Dickinson herself, who cherished photographs of many of her correspondents. It is signficant that in his third letter to her he should have, as he later remembered, "written to ask for her picture, that I might form some impression of my enigmatical correspondent" (Carlyle's Laugh, 259). He received instead only the famous pen portrait so often quoted, but with his naturalist's eye, he always strove for the most complete physical description. As it was, he missed the symbolic significance of the day lily that Dickinson put in his hand at their first meeting, for the meaning of this emblem in the popular language of flowers was an unabashed "coquetry" (Burke, *Language and Poetry of Flowers,* 36). Higginson was almost as "photographic" if also less enthusiastic about his meeting with another hermetic New England poetess and sculptor, Anne Whitney. His formula, however, remained the same. "Here I am in a farmhouse," he wrote, again probably to Mary Channing,

> in the loveliest, greenest region of Watertown, on a by-road, next house but one above Mr. Cushing's and next to Miss Anne Whitney's . . . After my nap this afternoon, as I was beginning to write you . . . up came a message that Miss A. W. was below, so down I went. White dress and cape bonnet; face between Elizabeth Whittier and Susan Higginson: looking older than I expected. Her brother was with her, which made it less remarkable for her to call on me. She and I agreed on a walk, which we later took – a lovely walk through green lanes fringed with barberries to a beautiful great elm tree and some superb oaks. I really never saw such groups of trees. It was an elm tree with the vigor of an oak – a little marring its peculiar grace. A. W. is like her poems, in a less degree – spirited and decided and a little abrupt and odd, sometimes saying very condensed and graphic things, but with no grace, herein being unlike her poems. I don't know how she liked me; she said I was entirely unlike her expectations which I believe is uncommon for people to say, is n't it? She did not repel me, neither did she charm me . . . I took tea there afterwards and rode to a meeting and back with them this evening. [*Letters and Journals,* 115–16]

Anne Whitney, whatever her talent (she was later far more famous as a sculptor), fatally lacked Emily Dickinson's electric charm. Characteristically, Higginson seems here more interested in the surrounding vitality of nature and the sturdy vigor of the elm tree than he is in his sprightly poet, who appears to have been as unimpressed with him as he was with her. Once an item had been located, collected, and classified, Higginson usually lost interest in it, as he did after both his visits to Emily Dickinson, for each occasion seemed to initiate a new if temporary lapse in their correspondence. The second time, in 1873, he did not even bother to take notes. Dickinson became like the hepatica that Higginson "found in bloom at Mount Auburn for three successive years, on the twenty-seventh of March." Once the hiding place of this last of "the more delicate native tribes" had been located, (*ODP,* 231) some of the keenness of the quest was dissipated, and the rarity became almost commonplace. Dickinson, too, remained frustratingly obstinate about Higginson's attempts "to lead her in the direction of rules and traditions," although he confessed that he soon abandoned this course because "she interested me more in her – so to speak – unregenerate condition" (*Carlyle's Laugh,* 262).

Moreover, as if to prove her true native wildness, Dickinson absolutely refused to be transplanted into Higginson's more cultivated and cosmopolitan garden of bluestocking acquaintances. Indeed, because of his inherent vitalism he became at times somewhat annoyed at her pale ghostliness, and was prompted to write that "perhaps we should learn to love & cultivate these ruddy hues of life" (*L* 2:519–20). He pleaded with her to come to Boston, since "all ladies do," and wondered

> if it would be possible to lure you to the meetings on the 3rd of every month at Mrs. Sargent's 13 Chestnut St. at 10 A.M. – when somebody reads a paper & others talk or listen. Next Monday Mr. Emerson reads & then at 3 ½ P.M. there is a meeting of the Woman's Club at 3 Tremont Place, where I read a paper on the Greek goddesses. [*L* 2:462]

Like a marble Diana herself, Dickinson primly replied: "You speak kindly of seeing me. Could it please your convenience to come so far as Amherst I should be very glad, but I do not cross my Father's ground to any House or town" (*L* 2:460).

It was at such points that Higginson felt himself to be superfluous, and perhaps wished that his first letter in reply to Dickinson's request for an evaluation of her poetry had been his last. Certainly this initial response seems to have been designed as a polite and possibly terminal rejection, posing certain idle questions as to sources and influences, telling her that her verses definitely were not for publication, dissecting her meter and syntax, and generally deflating any immediate publishing expectations. Dickinson next spoke of Higginson's painful "surgery," though she also sent more examples of her work, as he requested. Perhaps his advice was to drop poetry altogether and, like Harriet Prescott Spofford, attempt prose fiction, for in a succeeding letter Dickinson thanked Higginson for his "justice" and talked of having been "bled." But she also asserted that she "could not drop the Bells whose jingling cooled my Tramp" (*L* 2:408). Yet Higginson's second letter was obviously much less formal and critical than his first, as his natural humanity – his unfailing "philanthropy," as Mary Channing referred to it – gained the upper hand and he tried to make amends for the pain he had inadvertently inflicted on this most sensitive of souls.

With this letter, he committed himself to Dickinson both as poetic preceptor and as spiritual counselor. It was as if he signed a bond or contract, swearing himself to an eternal friendship of blood brother-

hood, for Dickinson replied ecstatically, "Your letter gave no drunk-
eness, because I tasted Rum before," and "The 'hand you stretch me in
the Dark,' I put mine in, and turn away" (L 2:408–9). If it was not the
seal on a secret and mystic marriage of Daisy and Master, as some
critics have claimed, still this exchange did constitute a kind of oath of
fealty with high chivalric overtones, in which Higginson became the
protective knight and Dickinson the faithfully apprenticed squire. Whenever a definite break seemed imminent, Dickinson had but to touch on
Higginson's most sacred possession, his honor, and the correspondence
was soon renewed, with profuse apologies on his part. In this way the
Dickinson–Higginson relationship evolved to a stage far beyond these
early poses and postures, though it was precisely the quaint formality of
such conventions that seems to have sustained the friendship through
the erratic early years. At last, like old friends who take for granted
their mutual quirks and faults rather than debating or questioning them,
each gave as much as he took. As early as June of 1869 Higginson
wrote, for example:

> It is hard for me to understand how you can live so alone, with
> thoughts of such a quality coming up in you & even the compan-
> ionship of your dog withdrawn. Yet it isolates one anywhere to
> think beyond a certain point or have such luminous flashes as
> come to you – so perhaps the place does not make much differ-
> ence. [L 2:461]

In the same letter, he made his plea for Dickinson to come to Boston, though he closed by saying, "Write & tell me something in prose
or verse, & I will be less fastidious in future & willing to write clumsy
things, rather than none," which are the words of a man who is accommodating himself to circumstances rather than dictating conditions.
When Dickinson at last died in 1886 she had already become in Higginson's mind a legendary figure, a friend "who had put on immortality,
but who never really seemed to have taken it off." In his diary, with his
collector's flair and his usual botanical precision he described the funeral
"of that rare & strange creature, Emily Dickinson. The country exquisite, day perfect, & an atmosphere of its own, fine & strange about the
whole house & grounds – a more saintly & elevated 'House of Usher.'
The grass of the lawn full of buttercups [,] violets, & wild geranium; in
house a handful of pansies & another of lilies of valley on piano" (YH
2:474–5).

Whether there had been a curse on the house of Dickinson, as there
had been a taint of incestuous madness in the blood of Poe's unhappy
Roderick and Madeline, Higginson was never to know for sure.[28] All he

could do was to note sadly with a sigh that was partially that of a true friend and partially that of a genuine connoisseur of human oddities: "How large a portion of the people who have interested me have passed away" (*YH* 2:475).

Hans Frederik Gude, *Landscape: Norwegian Scenery, with Bears,* 1846. (Reproduction from the author's collection.)

Chapter 7

LONE LANDSCAPES

Dickinson, Ruskin, and Victorian Aesthetics

***

Ah! then, if mine had been the Painter's hand,
To express what then I saw; and add the gleam,
The light that never was, on sea or land,
The consecration, and the Poet's dream;
I would have planted thee, thou hoary Pile
Amid a world how different from this!
Beside a sea that could not cease to smile;
On tranquil land, beneath a sky of bliss.

William Wordsworth

It must be stated that, at this time, the public mind in America had been quickened in relation to art by the writings and teachings of Ruskin. Whatever may be said of the criticisms of works of art, ancient and modern, by this eminent writer, of his estimate of special genius, of his theories, hobbies, and idiosyncrasies, it is certain that he developed more interest in art in the United States than all other agencies put together. His remarkable word-painting, the theological bent of his mind, his ascetic temperament, his eccentricities, his moral injunctions, furnishing both pulpit and press with material for sermons, news, and gossip about art, making popular music on the three strings of the mental harp to which the public ear is sensitive, spread a knowledge of art among people who would not otherwise have given it a thought.

John Durand

Estranged from Beauty — none can be —
For Beauty is Infinity —
And power to be finite ceased
Before Identity was leased —

Emily Dickinson

Chance and circumstance dictated that Emily Dickinson's appreciation of nature be funneled through the genial lyricism of Thomas Wentworth Higginson rather than through the works of the more cosmic Ralph Waldo Emerson or more acerbic Henry David Thoreau. Al-

219

though she eagerly read and learned from these distinguished Transcendentalists, it was Higginson whom she knew face to face. He authored, in the form of the nature essays he published in the *Atlantic Monthly,* a convenient Baedeker that allowed her to explore those magic kingdoms which lay only as far as her own back door. Writing to Harriet Prescott Spofford in 1861, Higginson commented, "These essays on Nature delight me so infinitely that all other themes seem tiresome beside them; I am sure that I have never come so near to Nature as during the last year, and therefore never so truly and deeply lived; and sometimes I feel so Exalted in this nearness that it seems as if I never could sorrow any more" (*TWH,* 157–8).

Dickinson responded to these uplifted essays with equal exaltation, and she could say of her nature poems, as Higginson said of his prose, "I wrote from pure enjoyment, spending days and weeks on single sentences." Higginson's bright healthy-mindedness was like the sunlight in a typical Hudson River school landscape: It both sentimentalized and vivified the scene, making any shadows only an aesthetic device that added to the dramatic chiaroscuro of the whole. As Asher B. Durand explained in his influential *Letters on Landscape Painting,* published in his son John's journal the *Crayon* in 1855, "Sunshine is the joyous expression of Nature, the lovely smile that lights up all her beauty, so changing and adorning all it rests upon, as to seem itself creative."[1] In describing its effect, Durand conjured up a picture that was paralleled by passages in Higginson's "My Out-Door Study," Arthur Parton's *Woodland Scene,* or Durand's own canvases with titles like *In the Woods* or *Kindred Spirits.* "We are not liable to over-estimate the value of sunshine to the landscape," he wrote:

> By it all beauty is rendered more beautiful, and the ungainly made attractive . . . independent of its pictorial efficacy, it imparts a cheerful sentiment to the picture that all observers feel and enjoy; even the fearful darkness of storm and tempest is palliated and becomes agreeable, if but a gleam of sunshine enliven some corner of the scene; and, as it glides through the woven arches of the solemn forest, touching here and there some mossy trunk and pendant bough, and chequering the rich mould beneath with variegated gems, it cheers the silent gloom, and surprises us with the sudden presence of unlooked-for beauty. [Letter 6, April 4, 1855, 210]

Despite the transforming powers of sunshine and Transcendental optimism, the ungainly Dickinson sometimes thought of herself as an irredeemable "Only Kangaroo among the Beauty" (*L* 2:412), and she wrote nature poems that Higginson himself called "dark" (*L* 2:412).

There were some fearful eclipses of storm and tempest that no sun-beams could relieve, whether physical, mental, or painterly. It was not Higginson but the mighty John Ruskin who confirmed her in this apostasy from the religion of healthy-mindedness, for the religion of beauty that he preached was based in part upon an evangelical back-ground that was in many respects as intense and as excruciating as her own neo-Calvinist upbringing.[2] Developing a romantic typology that read the book of nature as a living fulfillment of the books of the Bible, Ruskin epitomized the successes and the failures of the descrip-tive or pictorial style that Henry James had execrated in the work of Spofford. His tumultous word-painting combined both art and criti-cism, and he was the transatlantic leader of a new elite culture that soon was taken up by all who thirsted for the living word of art's gospel of secular salvation.

   Not only did leading American aestheticians like Asher B. Durand appropriate Ruskin's authoritative vocabulary and ideas; provincial art collectors like Austin and Susan Dickinson bought his volumes, studied his dictums, and put into practice his pronouncements on the superior-ity of modern painters who, unlike many Old Masters, remained "true to nature."[3] Emily Dickinson could not help but be affected by such a cultural maelstrom, which was actively whirling next door in the form of the Amherst salon conducted by her sister-in-law, but again she did so in her own way and on her own terms. The budding poet who refused to see Emerson when he was staying only a few footsteps across the lawn was going to rely on her own powers of observation and cultivate her personal "original relation to the universe" before she quoted either a native saint or a foreign sage.[4]

I

Anyone who reads Dickinson's surviving poetry as well as her collected letters must immediately be struck by the uncommon intensity of her perception. Dickinson's sensibility quite simply was in large measure a visual one, and in her art of words she was to fulfill a prophecy that she made to Susan in 1854. Writing in a letter composed during late No-vember and early December of that year, Dickinson connected the reality of her loneliness with the possibility of its expression in some kind of tangible and visible art:

> Susie – it is a little thing to say how lone it is – anyone can do it, but to wear the loneness next your heart for weeks, when you sleep, and when you wake, ever missing something, *this,* all can-not say, and it baffles me. I would paint a portrait which would

bring the tears, had I canvass for it, and the scene should be—
solitude, and the figures—solitude—and the lights and shades, each
a solitude. I could fill a chamber with landscapes so lone, men
would pause and weep there; then haste grateful home, for a loved
one left. [*L* 1:310]

Like romanticism itself, Dickinson's vision is a paradoxical one, best
understood in terms of broad polarities like dark and light, real and
ideal, outer and inner. On the other hand, the portrait that Dickinson
would paint is abstract, emblematic, almost surreal, each individual
element obsessively becoming the same thing, inevitably bringing to a
modern reader's mind Salvador Dali's amorphous anatomies or his wet
watches stretched out along infinite lines of perspective. Yet to see
Dickinson's art in terms of a modernist aesthetic does her sensibility a
great disservice. Rather, the simplicity and stark abstraction of her images find more appropriate parallels in nineteenth-century emblem
books and other folk works, especially popular "sandpaper" drawings,
tonal renderings executed wholly in shades of black and gray.[5] Moreover, Dickinson here speaks of an inner landscape, a landscape of the
soul, and she personifies Solitude just as an emblematist might represent Hope as a young woman leaning on an anchor. In her poetry,
Eternity is a "Friend," (J 1684), the Infinite a "Guest," (J 1309), and
God a "portentous Neighbor" (J 1497). Such personification is oddly
disturbing and mannered, just as the folk form of Dickinson's art uneasily coexists with the often dense sophistication of its content. This
brings us again to Lévi-Strauss's concept of *bricolage* and Dickinson's
empathetic response to elite culture. For Dickinson had the uncanny
ability (that is to say, the genius) to compress, invert, domesticate, and
internalize the primary thought of her age in ways that, to use again
one of her own unique verbs, italicized the reality around her, thereby
both emphasizing and preserving it. Her interest in capturing and secur-
ing the visual residues of experience also reminds us of her reliance on
the portfolio tradition, which itself ran the gamut from formal studio
compositions to naive schoolgirl art.

   In the letter to Susan just quoted, Dickinson seems to make no
distinction between a portrait and a landscape, a portrait being a picture of a person and a landscape being the picture of a place. However, her own archaically romantic word "physiognomy" marries, in
a deep metaphysical sense, these two seemingly academic opposites. If
a place is a person, or possesses a personality, then a landscape can be
a portrait, and a portrait can be a landscape. Physiognomy becomes
the method of ascertaining the kind of personality expressed by a
particular place; from the physical features, the physiognomist (that is

to say, the romantic artist) intuits spiritual verities. Outer nature becomes a veil of phenomenality that demands constant watching by the
cautious observer:

> The Angle of a Landscape –
> That every time I wake –
> Between my Curtain and the Wall
> Upon an ample Crack –
>
> Like a Venetian – waiting –
> Accosts my open eye –
> Is just a Bough of Apples –
> Held slanting, in the Sky –
>
> The Pattern of a Chimney –
> The Forehead of a Hill –
> Sometimes – a Vane's Forefinger –
> But that's – Occasional –
>
> The Seasons – shift – my Picture –
> Upon my Emerald Bough,
> I wake – to find no – Emeralds –
> Then – Diamonds – which the Snow
>
> From Polar Caskets – fetched me –
> The Chimney – and the Hill –
> And just the Steeple's finger –
> These – never stir at all –   [J 375]

To Dickinson, the seasons are spiritual propmen who regularly shift
the stage scenery she can glimpse behind the protective veil of her
window "Curtain." A single "Crack" or rent in this veil is ample
enough for her oblique art, but for Nature it also provides a medium of
communication. Nature retains the power to conceal or reveal herself as
if by the means of a screening "Venetian blind"; in all and any events
she alone regulates the amount of available light and color; hence the
essential passivity of the artist, who is as much observed as observing.
Indeed, Dickinson is more passive patron than active artist, for though
she refers to "my picture," it is subject to a disconcerting series of
repaintings and revarnishings. Her duty remains to record the exact
details and to infer the spiritual significance of the canvas, almost oriental in its simplicity, that is set before her. Her task is prospective rather
than retrospective, and she studies the patterns and features of the landscape as the physiognomist would survey a visage, or the phrenologist
measure that prime indicator of intellect, the forehead, or the palmist
trace an individual destiny in the lines and contours of the hand. If the

hieroglyphic "Pattern" of a chimney suddenly takes on an occult meaning, or if the "Forefinger" of a weather vane points in some definite
direction, or the "Forehead" of the hill reveals some special knowledge,
such a communication remains essentially one-sided, since Nature has
merely changed her dress, not her substance. As Henry David Thoreau
wrote in *Walden,* appropriating Plutarch's image of the veiled Isis,
whose legend read, "I am whatever was, or is, or will be; and my veil
no mortal ever took up":[6]

> The oldest Egyptian or Hindoo philosopher raised a corner of the
> veil from the statue of the divinity; and still the trembling robe
> remains raised, and I gaze upon as fresh a glory as he did, since it
> was I in him that was then so bold, and it is he in me that now
> reviews the vision. No dust has settled on that robe; no time has
> elapsed since that divinity was revealed.[7]

Unlike Thoreau, Dickinson finds a slantwise view of Nature sufficient; she realizes the dangers of lifting the veil and remains satisfied
with an oblique angle of vision. Here her minimal art reflects Nature's
Yankee parsimony. What Henry James called "the spare, heavenward
finger of the New England meeting house"[8] is as much an emblem of
silence as it is a sign of faith. Again Dickinson's aesthetic is unique only
in form, not in theory, because this theory is a fundamental given of
nineteenth-century elite culture. Not only can her lone landscapes be
related to an international canon of judgment and taste like John Ruskin's *Modern Painters,* but, as we have seen, they can also be understood
in terms of the development of a native American romanticism like the
Hudson River school.

The best embodiment of Hudson River assumptions is Asher B.
Durand's *Letters on Landscape Painting,* which give the basic premises of
this romanticism that Ruskin in turn "Victorianized" through his sys-
temization of its chief principles.[9] James T. Flexner calls the *Letters* "one
of those rare documents that summarizes the spirit of a group and a
generation" (*That Wilder Image,* 72), but they are much more than that.
In the history of American aesthetics, they bear the same relationship to
the development of native painting as Ralph Waldo Emerson's "The
American Scholar" does to the progress of our intellectual thought,
serving as an artistic declaration of independence from old imitative
modes. Like Emerson, Durand reacted to the splendors of European
civilization by developing an even keener interest in, and appreciation
of, the American landscape. With Emily Dickinson, Durand regarded
Nature as a holy of holies that was to be approached only with impunity and a perfect confidence that one had gained such a privilege by a
long and priestly devotion to the ways of the Most High. As a natural

extension of the romantic theory of correspondences, Durand assumed
what Transcendentalists like Thoreau and Emerson assumed in such
works as *Walden* and "The Over-Soul": that the sensuous veil of nature
is but a protective covering over the naked creative spirit of the universe. Unlike them, however, Durand believed that it is wholly up to
the spirit to lift this veil and reveal glimpses of the all-creative power
that stirs perpetually beneath it. The artist's role is simply to remain
faithful, and, like the divine Raphael, to adore. "Where is the portrait-
painter," Durand asked in letter 4,

> having a just sense of his responsibilities, who has not often
> thrown down his brush in despair, after many fruitless attempts to
> express the soul that beams at times through the eye of beauty,
> and so with the yet more mysterious power of lofty intellect? And
> there is to be seen a corresponding soul and depth of expression in
> the beauty of landscape nature, which dignifies the Art that em-
> bodies it, and improves and elevates the mind that loves to con-
> template its pictorial image. [February 14, 1855, 98]

Landscape art as Durand conceived it was a contact point between
the Holy Spirit of God and the soul of man, a place where the trembling robe of absolute creative power and intellect could be actually
touched and felt. Since this power was an ever-volatile and changeable
one, the more the landscape artist aspired to fix on his canvas the most
elusive effects of Nature, the closer he came to approaching the mystery
of that "lofty intellect" that inspired, challenged, and allured him:

> To see the Summer Sky
> Is Poetry, though never in a Book it lie –
> True Poems flee –   [J 1472]

Nature in her restlessness became a mirror of the creative force of
God himself, and more particularly the specific atmosphere of a landscape view became a material correlative of the specific state of the
divine mind. This view in its turn produced a corresponding impression in the mind of the beholder. Atmosphere became the agent of
God's consciousness, the medium by which he expressed his own interior state and communicated it to man. As such, atmosphere – the intermediary realm between earth and sky, the human and heaven – also
became the agency by which the individual apprehended God. In his
fifth letter on landscape painting, Durand speaks of atmosphere as a
kind of usher or messenger of supreme potency. "When you shall have
acquired some proficiency in foreground material," he writes,

> your next step should be the study of the influence of atmo-
> sphere – the power which defines and measures space – an intangi-

ble agent, visible, yet without that material substance which belongs to imitable objects, in fact, an absolute nothing, yet of mighty influence. It is that which above all other agencies, carries us into the picture, instead of allowing us to be detained in front of it; not the door-keeper, but the grand usher and master of ceremonies, and conducting us through all the vestibules, chambers, and secret recesses of the great mansion, explaining, on the way, the meaning and purposes of all that is visible, and satisfying us that all is in its proper place. This, therefore, is an important personage, and no pains should be spared to make his acquaintance. [March 7, 1855, 146]

Here Durand employs a particularly Dickinsonian form of personification; Dickinson, contemplating a sunset that reveals the death of something inexpressible and sacred, sees the atmosphere and its cloud forms in Durand-like metaphors in a poem that Johnson dates about 1862:

> Departed – to the Judgment –
> A Mighty Afternoon –
> Great Clouds – like Ushers – leaning –
> Creation – looking on –
>
> The Flesh – Surrendered – Cancelled –
> The Bodiless – begun –
> Two Worlds – like Audiences – disperse –
> And leave the Soul – alone –   [J 524]

The state of the atmosphere at any given moment reflects the particular state of the God, Spirit, or Over-Soul that hovers beyond it. In the painting of the later Hudson River school, atmosphere becomes not simply a romantic glaze applied by the artist but the very "intangible" yet "visible" robe in which the deity conceals his spirit. Atmosphere is divinity's physical veil, and the only medium by which the artist can convey the ineffable mystery of his awesome subject. Durand's use of the word "expression" throughout the *Letters* is also important for an understanding of Dickinson's aesthetics. He often talks of capturing the mood of a landscape the way a portrait painter might speak of capturing the "likeness" of his subject. "Expression" corresponds once again to Emily Dickinson's idea of physiognomy, the skill of discerning spiritual character from physical features. The great test of the artist is if his canvas expresses the "effect" of a landscape, that quality of soul which animates, incarnates, and informs it.

This background may explain to some extent what Emily Dickinson meant when early in 1876 she sent to T. W. Higginson the cryptic message, "Nature is a Haunted House – but Art – a House that tries to be haunted" (*L* 2:554). Framed in dark romantic terms that converted the traditional temple of art into a private House of Usher, Dickinson's observation indicated that like the Hudson River painters, she saw it as the artist's task to capture the "likeness" or spirit or ghost that lurked within the Gothic castle of the landscape. The test of true poetry, as of true painting, was if the artist managed to "take" the likeness of this spiritual dimension as well as to present the merely physical outlines of a scene. Viewers then had to determine whether the finished work of art successfully expressed such an "effect" or not. Dickinson also recognized the paradox that Durand touched upon in his discussion of atmosphere as a veil or a medium, the fact that this mysterious agent or usher was most palpable at a distance and least tangible at close range. Rather than atmosphere, in a central poem Dickinson seized upon the allied element of water to express her apprehension of the elusive quality of nature's fluid hauntedness:

> What mystery pervades a well!
> The water lives so far –
> A neighbor from another world
> Residing in a jar
>
> Whose limit none have ever seen,
> But just his lid of glass –
> Like looking every time you please
> In an abyss's face!
>
> The grass does not appear afraid,
> I often wonder he
> Can stand so close and look so bold
> At what is awe to me.
>
> Related somehow they may be,
> The sedge stands next the sea –
> Where he is floorless
> And does no timidity betray
>
> But nature is a stranger yet;
> The ones that cite her most
> Have never passed her haunted house,
> Nor simplified her ghost.
>
> To pity those that know her not
> Is helped by the regret
> That those who know her, know her less
> The nearer her they get.   [J 1400]

What Dickinson calls the "ghost" in nature is what the Hudson River school meant by such equally elusive terms as "expression," "sentiment," and "effect." In "Nature" Emerson had written that "the noblest ministry of nature is to stand as the apparition of God," that "it is a perpetual effect" (*Works,* 1:62, 61). In his second letter on landscape painting, Durand says of the artist's long apprenticeship to the discipline of nature that "regarding the objects of your study, the intellect and feelings become elevated and purified, and in proportion as you acquire executive skill, your productions will, unawares, be combined with that undefinable quality recognized as sentiment or expression which distinguishes the true landscape from the mere sensual and *striking* picture"(January 17, 1855; 34).

Above all, the artist's highest goal was to capture the effect of that atmosphere which hung like a celestial veil between the heavenly throne of the deity and the earthly realm of the artist. One should not see nature as Claude or Salvator or even the founder of the Hudson River school, Thomas Cole, saw it, for "if abused and adulterated by the poisons of conventionalism, the result will be the corruption of veneration for, and faith in, the simple truths of Nature, which constitute the true Religion of Art, and the only safeguard against the inroads of heretical conventionalism . . . If you should ask me to define conventionalism," Durand added in his first letter, "I should say that it is the substitution of an easily expressed falsehood for a difficult truth" (January 3, 1855; 2). In "My Out-Door Study," T. W. Higginson had admiringly quoted Leslie's anecdote about " 'the most original landscape-painter he knew,' meaning Constable, that whenever he sat down in the fields to sketch, he endeavored to forget that he had ever seen a picture" (*ODP,* 27). Moreover, not only did Durand, the poet-naturalists, and the Hudson River school demand a fidelity to original open-air experience and local color, they required an equally intensive concentration on the effect of each individual moment, especially in regard to the diaphanous veil of mist and cloud. Durand wrote in his fifth letter on the expression of atmospheric space that

> the degrees of clearness and density, scarcely two successive days the same – local conditions of temperature – dryness and moisture – and many other causes, render anything like specific direction impracticable. I can do little more than urge on you the constant study of its magic power, daily and hourly, in all its changes, at times shortening, at others lengthening, the space before you; now permitting to be defined, in all its ruggedness, the precipice on the mountain side – and now transforming it to a fairy palace, and the solid mountain itself to a film of opal. [March 7, 1855, 146]

With that statement, Durand set the stage not only for the development of the native school of American painting, but also for the full acceptance of the aesthetics of that greatest of nineteenth-century defenders of "truthfulness to nature," John Ruskin. Ruskin's presence and even his extravagant rhetoric can be felt throughout the *Letters,* though Durand's stress on open-air experience and untutored development was fully a part of the American élan that produced Walt Whitman's *Leaves of Grass* the same year. As Roger Stein comments, "The ideas of the best American landscape painters of the period – Durand, Kensett, and others – sprang from the American Wordsworthian tradition . . . They read Ruskin later, and he corroborated and reinforced already existing ideas rather than showing them a new path" (*Ruskin,* 103). But Ruskin's acceptance of the book of nature as yet another living book of scripture and his forceful exposition of its great common types also prompted artists like Durand to declare boldly, as the latter did in his second letter, that the external world was "fraught with lessons of high and holy meaning, only surpassed by the light of revelation" (January 17, 1855, 34). Traditional Christian typology soon gave way to a romantic typology that made the heavens themselves into a constantly changing scripture, a whole Sistine Chapel ceiling painted in the sky.[10]

Ruskinian thought was the fruit of both natural theology, the pious heir of eighteenth-century rationalism that sought through scientific investigation to reconcile the book of nature with the books of the Bible, and the romantic theory of correspondences given weight and substance by the mystical works of Emanuel Swedenborg. Each mode of thought decisively linked the spirit of the landscape with the spirit of the human being. Although this romantic typology was developed at greatest length and at greatest depth by elite theorists such as Ruskin, in actuality it cut across the planes of folk, popular, and avant-garde cultures. The Neoplatonism of the Sentimental Love Religion fed and reinforced it, and popular piety and the learned attempt to reconcile science and religion, notably espoused by Edward Hitchcock, Amherst's most towering intellect in Emily Dickinson's youth, were its enthusiastic heralds (*LED* 2:342–51).

The hopeful intent of natural theology is perhaps best summed up by the orthodox Charles Wadsworth, who in his sermon "Retribution" declared that "we loose the scales from the adamantine scroll of geology, and lift the eye to the crystal tablet of astronomy, that we may study the sublime biography of our God" (*Sermons,* 89). Wadsworth's and Hitchcock's natural theology was in some respects only a halfway covenant with full-blown romantic typology, but the basis for its universal appeal can best be gauged by an undated clipping that appears on page 29 of Mary Warner's scrapbook, entitled "LITTLE MARY'S THOUGHT":

Little Mary had just come from the window, where she had been gazing out with great pleasure, and sat down on her little stool at her papa's feet. It was just at sunset; and a most glorious sunset it was. The western sky was mantled with clouds of the most gorgeous hues, upon which the little girl gazed with thoughtful pleasure.

"Papa," she said at length, "do you know what I think when I see those pretty clouds?"

"No; what do you think of them, Mary?"

"I always think they are God's veils. Doesn't he have beautiful veils, papa, to hide him from us?"

"True enough, little one," thought I; "the clouds which veil Him from our sight now are beautiful. There is a rainbow on them if we will see it; they shine with mercy and truth."

Was not that a pretty thought of little Mary's? And does it not remind you of the time when the veil shall be parted, and He "shall come with clouds, and every eye shall see Him."

Here, in naive and capsule form, is the germ or rather kernel of an aesthetic shared by Emily Dickinson and Asher B. Durand, by Charles Wadsworth and John Ruskin. In an ecstatic passage from his sermon "The Bright Side," Wadsworth preached from the pulpit what Little Mary had divined with the spontaneous eye of childhood. "For what are clouds," he asked, "but the curtains God gathers around the blinding splendors of His throne—the noiseless chariot of His love as He comes nearer to His children?" He continued:

"Clouds!" "clouds!" and not sunbeams, are unto finite vision the regalia of the Eternal one! Their dark side is toward us yet, lest we should be dazed and blinded by the uncreated splendor. But we know they are only the tremulous veil that falls between us and heaven. And how near, then, heaven is to us! Who talks of "a land afar off in its beauty?" [*Sermons*, 168–9]

Both darkening and privatizing "Little Mary's Thought," Dickinson wrote:

> Sunset that screens, reveals –
> Enhancing what we see
> By menaces of Amethyst
> And Moats of Mystery.   [J 1609]

And she condensed as well as gently satirized Charles Wadsworth's extravagant rhetorical emphasis on God's royal robes:

> Like Mighty Foot Lights – burned the Red
> At Bases of the Trees –

> The far Theatricals of Day –
> Exhibiting – to These –
>
> 'Twas Universe – that did applaud –
> While Chiefest – of the Crowd –
> Enabled by his Royal Dress –
> Myself distinguished God –   [J 595]

The syntax of this poem makes the viewer of the sunset ("Myself") almost as distinguished as God himself. In apprehending such divinity, Dickinson discovered a significance in her direct observation of the natural phenomena around her that was both confirmed and justified by her reading of Ruskin's *Modern Painters*.

II

It was Ruskin's task to elaborate as well as to systematize this cloud-borne romantic typology, bringing to a chaos of unrestrained subjective responses and wayward interpretations the authority of a secular pope. For example, in the first volume of *Modern Painters* Ruskin called for a new, serious, and concentrated look at the sky such as he believed had been achieved only by that dedicated modern master Turner. As for the skies of Old Masters like Claude Lorraine (so beloved of the Hudson River school's founder, Thomas Cole), they were "fixed, white, insipidities" (*MP* 1:237), mere masses of bravura brushstrokes.

> Where Poussin or Claude have three similar masses, nature has fifty pictures, made up of millions of minor thoughts – fifty aisles penetrating through angelic chapels to the Shechinah of the blue – fifty hollow ways among bewildered hills – each with their own nodding rocks, and cloven precipices, and radiant summits, and robing vapors, but all unlike each other, except in beauty, all bearing witness to the unwearied, exhaustless operation of the Infinite Mind. [235]

God clothed himself in the mystery of the cloud, and the sky was the perpetual radiation of his immortal glory, a "Shechinah" of blue light, to use the potent Hebraic term that Ruskin had borrowed from the Kabbalah. The sky was the robe of the deity, and when in volume 4 of *Modern Painters* Ruskin affirmed that it was atmosphere that acted, as Asher B. Durand pointed out in his *Letters,* as the "usher" to that great temple of the deity, he also happened naturally on the image that was central to the aesthetic thought of his century, the image of the veil. It is in chapter 5 of that fourth volume, entitled "Of Turnerian Mystery," that Ruskin explains the importance of atmosphere, because from his own acute observation he has at last realized just how rarely occurs the phenomenon of pure natural clarity. "Intense clearness," he writes, ". . . whether in the North after or before rain, or in some moments of twilight in the South, is always, as far as I am acquainted with natural phenomena, a *notable* thing." Hence "mist of some sort, or mirage, or confusion of light, or of cloud, are the general facts; the distance may vary in different climates at which the effects of mist begin, but they are always present; and therefore, in all probability it is meant that we should enjoy them" (68–9).

If mist then was preordained, it must have been preordained for a good reason, and that reason the pious Ruskin discovers in the idea that there are some things not meant for man's knowledge on this earth. There is more of intriguing mystery and beauty to this natural veiling of the deity than there would be in a purely naked and clairvoyant revelation. Ruskin describes "Turnerian mystery" as the technique of reproducing the natural veil of mist, cloud, and mirage, of "the right of being obscure," since "noble mystery differs from ignoble, in being a veil thrown between us and something definite, known, and substantial; but the ignoble mystery is a veil cast before chaos, the studious concealment of Nothing" (73). Ultimately there is not only a mystery of cloud and atmosphere but also "the mystery of clearness itself" (80). As he explains:

> In an Italian twilight, when, sixty or eighty miles away, the ridge of the Western Alps rises in its dark and serrated blue against the crystalline vermilion, there is still unsearchableness, but an un-searchableness without cloud or concealment, – an infinite unknown, but no sense of any veil or interference between us and it: we are separated from it not by any anger or storm, not by any vain and fading vapor, but only the deep infinity of the thing itself . . . Probably the right conclusion is that the clear and cloudy mysteries are alike noble; but that the beauty of the wreaths of frost mist, folded over banks of greensward deep in dew, and of the purple clouds of evening, and the wreaths of fitful vapor gliding through groves of pine, and irised around the pillars of waterfalls, is more or less typical of the kind of joy which we should take in the imperfect knowledge granted to the earthly life, while the serene and cloudless mysteries set forth that belonging to the redeemed life. But of one thing I am well assured, that so far as the clouds are regarded, not as concealing the truth of other things, but as themselves true and separate creations, they are not usually beheld by us with enough honor; we have too great veneration for cloudlessness. [80–1]

Here at last we return full circle to the aesthetic conciousness of
Emily Dickinson and her own conservative concept of the necessity of
the veil. Her attitude toward the landscape embodies precisely this approach to the two noble mysteries of obscurity and of clarity. Dickinson, like Ruskin, believes that nature can never really be stripped
naked, save by an unskillful or faithless artist, and even then the result
would have to be caricature rather than the capturing of a true likeness,
effect, sentiment, or expression. The landscape always remains mysterious, it is always a "Haunted House," and the artist's corresponding
duty is to seek out the hidden ghost and invest his own art with the
secret spirit or character of a physical scene. But Dickinson, too, revered the cloudy over the cloudless mysteries:

> The thought beneath so slight a film –
> Is more distinctly seen –
> As laces just reveal the surge –
> Or Mists – the Appenine –   [J 210]

Dickinson was tantalized by the "unsearchableness" of natural
phenomena, yet her concept of the earthly paradise as a holy of holies
precluded her consideration of it as a thing to be coldly analyzed, since
such an act would be profanation, a sacrilege tantamount to the dissection of an archangel. As skilled as Ruskin in the natural sciences – at
least in astronomy and botany, if not in geology – Dickinson also tried
to reconcile her acute observation of natural phenomena with her reverent attitude toward the subject matter of her study. Nature was fully as
much a scripture as the Old or New Testaments, and both books were
written in languages that required expertise as well as inspiration, a
knowledge of the letter as well as of the spirit, to translate into intelligi-
bility. Otherwise the natural world became merely an auction house
where mystery was sold to the highest bidder:

> A transport one cannot contain
> May yet, a transport be –
> Though God forbid it lift the lid –
> Unto it's Extasy!
>
> A Diagram – of Rapture!
> A sixpence at a Show –
> With Holy Ghosts in Cages!
> The *Universe* would go!   [J 184]

From her Calvinist background, Dickinson drew upon a time-tested
method of biblical typology in order to accomplish her accommodation
of Genesis to geology, just as Ruskin did when, in discussing the death

of Moses, he wrote of "that other Holy of Holies, of which the mountain peaks were the altars, and the mountain clouds the veil, the firmament of his Father's dwelling" (*MP* 4:379). To those who approached
them in the right manner, mountains were not threatening slag heaps or
gloomy piles of rock, but rather communion tables on which the sacramental gifts of the deity were freely offered, and their hovering mists
were but the visible emanations of God's perpetual glory. "Serene and
cloudless mysteries," as Ruskin said of the unclothed Alps, were the
type of the world to come, the redeemed and perfected life, and for
Emily Dickinson, who saw the fleecy train of clouds as an actual procession of the saints, or a visible map of the provinces of heaven (J 7),
the lifting of this intermediary veil of atmosphere revealed only deeper
and more unsearchable infinities:

> Our lives are Swiss –
> So still – so Cool –
> Till some odd afternoon
> The Alps neglect their Curtains
> And we look farther on!
>
> *Italy* stands the other side!
> While like a guard between –
> The solemn Alps –
> The siren Alps
> Forever intervene!   [J 80]

The romantic typology of this Pisgah view is exactly the same as in
those other poems which deal with her explanation of the ostensible
symbol of the veil: that there are veils that will be removed only by the
passage from life to death, and that there might always remain some
ultimate, impenetrable mysteries. To be sure, as we have seen, some
surprises also will be in order:

> Of all the Souls that stand create –
> I have elected – One –
> When Sense from Spirit – files away –
> And Subterfuge – is done –
> When that which is – and that which was –
> Apart – intrinsic – stand –
> And this brief *Drama in the flesh* –
> Is shifted – like a Sand –
> When figures show their royal Front –
> And Mists – are carved away,
> Behold the Atom – I preferred –
> To all the lists of Clay!   [J 664]

Until then, Emily Dickinson believed with Ruskin that a veiled, cloudy, or obscure knowledge was preferable to the shattering experience of a complete face-to-face revelation. The human should perceive a nobility in the concealment of the ultimate, Ruskin had written, "rejoicing that the kindly veil is spread where the untempered light might have scorched us, or the infinite clearness wearied" (*MP* 4:69). Too much revelation could burn human consciousness to a crisp:

> Had I not seen the Sun
> I could have borne the shade
> But light a newer Wilderness
> My Wilderness has made –   [J 1233]

The same conservatism produced Dickinson's testimony about the painful experience of entering by accident into a natural holy of holies in "No man saw awe" (J 1733), for her accommodation to the sublimity of unattainable mystery was not without its pain. Like Ruskin she possessed a naturally analytical mind that prompted her to focus on the physical and the sensational as a means of warding off, for a time, the metaphysical, which too often threatened to overwhelm her completely with its numinous power. Her response to awe was simply to continue breathing and apply her strategy of physiognomy even to the momentous experience of glimpsing God unveiled and then living to tell about it. The immediate danger was not death but rather engulfment by madness, for the price of absolute vision was to be rendered unable to express what had been actually seen and touched, to become unintelligible oneself. When she explored this veiled and unsearchable quality of the most high, and merged it with her private mythology and her equivocal relationship to an equally aloof, tantalizing Phoebus, Alpine peaks could suddenly become positively cruel in their superciliousness:

> In lands I never saw – they say
> Immortal Alps look down –
> Whose Bonnets touch the firmament –
> Whose Sandals touch the town –
>
> Meek at whose everlasting feet
> A Myriad Daisy play –
> Which, Sir, are you and which am I
> Upon an August day?   [J 124]

Concealing mists and vapors sometimes froze into an adamantine barrier rather than condensing into an alluring medium:

> Ah, Teneriffe!
> Retreating Mountain!
> Purples of Ages – pause for *you* –

Sunset – reviews her Sapphire Regiment –
Day – drops you her Red Adieu!

Still – Clad in your Mail of ices –
Thigh of Granite – and thew – of Steel –
Heedless – alike – of pomp – or parting

Ah, Teneriffe!
I'm kneeling – still –   [J 666]

Dickinson's solution to the problem of the veiled mountains and
siren Alps of consciousness was that familiar one which we have already seen gradually working itself out in her life and in her art. She
wrapped her inner as well as her outer life more and more in what
Higginson called a "fiery mist" of mystery (L 2:461), a mail of gauze
and tulle made up of her retreat to the firmament of her father's house,
where she spun the fragile rainbow webs of her poetry. Added to this
veiling was her development of a philosophy of deprivation that regarded the unattainable, the unconsummated, and the unrevealed as the
teleology of such a life and such an art. Dickinson's poetry became a
poetry of revelation only in the sense Shelley had suggested in his
famous "Defense" of that art: that the poet's duty was to lift one veil
while replacing it with another. With the sunset, the poet had to
"screen" in order to "reveal." Dickinson, like Turner as Ruskin saw
him, claimed the right of being obscure, of telling all the truth but also
telling it from a mystifyingly different angle of perception (J 1129).

III

To Ruskin the divine and supernatural light made possible by his new
religion of beauty could be obtained only by a dedicated study of nature
as well as Scripture. One now had to know the new testament of
science as well as Old Testament Hebrew in order to comprehend the
Word, for the physical landscape was the point of living contact between the mind of man and the passions of God. Even Charles Wadsworth affirmed that "every thing, from the flower of the field to the
stars of the firmament, are God's thoughts and feelings made manifest," that "He is working out His own moral character in material
forms" (Sermons, 89). Here is where one sacred language touched
another; gazing at the ever-changing cloud forms, which were the
chariots of God, was to apprehend the active imagination of his constant creation, fragmentation, and reconstitution of the elements air,
fire, earth, and water. It was in this sense Ruskin also found nature to
be sentient with the living spirit of the godhead. The veil of the firma-

ment was not simply a witness to God's presence. It was an expression of God's will, even a revelation of his interior life, since the consanguinity between the nature of the human and the nature of the deity implied that they shared a similarity of substance as well as a similarity of form. In one magnificent passage of typological word-painting, Ruskin summed up the consequences of his literal belief that through the agency or "ordinance" of the atmosphere, the world was charged with the grandeur of God:

> This, I believe, is the ordinance of the firmament; and it seems to me that in the midst of the material nearness of these heavens God means us to acknowledge His own immediate presence as visiting, judging, and blessing us. "The earth shook, the heavens also dropped, at the presence of God." "He doth set His bow in the cloud," and thus renews, in the sound of every drooping swathe of rain, his promises of everlasting love. "In them hath he set a *tabernacle* for the sun"; whose burning ball, which without the firmament would be seen as an intolerable and scorching circle in the blackness of vacuity, is by that firmament surrounded with gorgeous service, and tempered by mediatorial ministries; by the firmament of clouds the golden pavement is spread for his chariot wheels at morning; by the firmament of clouds the purple veil is closed at evening round the sanctuary of his rest; by the mists of the firmament his implacable light is divided, and its separated fierceness appeased into the soft blue that fills the depth of distance with its bloom, and the flush with which the mountains burn as they drink the overflowing of the dayspring. And in this tabernacling of the unendurable sun with men, through the shadows of the firmament, God would seem to set forth the stooping of His own majesty to men, upon the *throne* of the firmament. As the Creator of all the worlds, and the Inhabiter of eternity, we cannot behold him; but as the Judge of the earth and the Preserver of men, those heavens are indeed His dwelling-place. "Swear not, neither by heaven, for it is God's throne; nor by the earth, for it is his footstool." And all those passings to and fro of fruitful shower and grateful shade, and all those visions of silver palaces built about the horizon, and voices of moaning winds and threatening thunders, and glories of colored robes and cloven ray, are but to deepen in our hearts the acceptance, and distinctness, and dearness of the simple words, "Our Father." [*MP* 4:87–8]

Emily Dickinson never came to quite this accommodation with the Father, but as we have seen, she certainly could perceive his awesome power, and in Ruskin's ecstasy at the glories of ministering cloud forms we come closest to the sentiment that inspired many of her landscape poems, especially those dealing with the effects of the rising and the setting sun, tabernacled in the shadows of the firmament:

> The Day came slow – till Five o'clock –
> Then sprang before the Hills
> Like Hindered Rubies – or the Light
> A sudden Musket – spills –
>
> The Purple could not keep the East –
> The Sunrise shook abroad
> Like Breadths of Topaz – packed a Night –
> The Lady just unrolled –
>
> The Happy Winds – their Timbrels took –
> The Birds – in docile Rows
> Arranged themselves around their Prince
> The Wind – is Prince of Those –
>
> The Orchard sparkled like a Jew –
> How mighty 'twas – to be
> A Guest in this stupendous place –
> The Parlor – of the Day –   [J 304]

Here Dickinson domesticates the royal splendor of Ruskin's lofty imagery, yet like him she realizes that different "ghosts" – holy and otherwise – haunted the house of nature, different spirits dwelt in the tabernacle of the sky at different moments in the course of the mystic day. Ruskin's lyrical exegesis of Genesis was a means of synthesizing the real and the ideal, just as Hudson River school artists like Durand concluded that the closest, most exacting open-air study of nature was a form of worshipping God, or poet-naturalists such as Thoreau and Higginson decided that the most economical yet accurate description of nature would raise language itself to its highest possible level of communication. The method employed by all of these artists was an acute attentiveness and obedience to the ways of natural phenomena, a scientific recording of the minute particulars of nature without any destructive autopsy of its wholeness. Only in this way would one capture through sentiment, effect, or expression the creative spirit that hovered just beyond both the earthly and the heavenly veils.

Such was the glittering theurgy of correspondences that lay behind the search for a romantic typology. In practice, however, and especially in Dickinson's domestication of Ruskinian aesthetics, the terms of this typology were skewed, inverted, and obscured by its merging with a private mythology of the self. As we have seen, Dickinson Gothicized the entire relation among art, the artist, and nature, while the terrible doubleness of her passion for Phoebus, her personal sun-god, made him into an elusive and sometimes indifferent deity. The capricious playfulness of the Calvinist Father was transferred to Dickinson's personal election to a Sentimental Love Religion, and though nature remained a haunted house, one never knew if it were inhabited by a savior, a monster, or—most frightening—nobody at all. Ruskin had written that there was judgment in the storm cloud and blessing in the sunbeam, but in the landscape of the inner life, these categories could become terribly perverted and twisted. Sometimes the result was a negative crisis conversion to unbelief:

> There's a Certain Slant of light,
> Winter Afternoons—
> That oppresses, like the Heft
> Of Cathedral Tunes—
>
> Heavenly Hurt, it gives us—
> We can find no scar,
> But internal difference,
> Where the Meanings, are—
>
> None may teach it—Any—
> 'Tis the Seal Despair—
> An imperial affliction
> Sent us of the Air—
>
> When it comes, the Landscape listens—
> Shadows—hold their breath—
> When it goes, 'tis like the Distance
> On the look of Death—   [J 258]

The oppressive light of this poem acts as both penetrating spear and murderous blunt instrument; consequently, Dickinson suffers internal scourging, crucifixion, and death, with no immediate hope of resurrection. If, like Saint Thomas, we ask to examine her wounds, we must first examine our own faith, for they are totally spiritual and interior. The synesthetic word "heft" also reminds us that one favorite medieval punishment for heresy or the defiance of authority was to have the victim slowly pressed to death (as was done with the unfortunate Giles Cory of the Salem witchcraft trials). Here Dickinson is as passive as the fly sealed in amber, but she is also eternally covenanted to despair; the exquisite pain of her melodious martyrdom is expressed by the oxymoronic terms "Heavenly Hurt" and "imperial affliction."

This cold Pentecost that numbs rather than inflames descends upon her not from the Father or the Holy Ghost but from "the Air," a lofty pun signifying the complete vaporization of the Son, "heir" to the kingdom, the power, and the glory. Consequently, time and nature are both suspended, since there can be no correspondence between the inner and the outer at psychic degree zero. One of the ancient forms of judgment rendered by a coroner's jury was "Death by the visitation of God," and we can paraphrase our own postmortem of this poem as "Despair by the Visitation of Nothing." It records another one of those "dangerous" moments "when the meaning goes out of things and Life stands straight – and punctual – and yet no signal comes" (L 3:919). As the soul is drained away, so does romantic typology crumble, for in this most lone of Dickinson's lone landscapes, all sacred events are swallowed up in what Emerson called "the apocalypse of the mind" (*Works* 1:48).

Yet even in "There's a Certain Slant of light," Dickinson has proceeded according to the strictest canons of romantic aesthetics; she has fixed exactly in her art the specific spiritual state of particular natural phenomena at a precise moment in time. What is important is not that her approach has changed, but rather that the subject matter has shifted, and shifted menacingly. Durand had urged his young pupil to a "constant study" of the "magic power" of light and atmosphere, observing it "daily and hourly, in all its changes," and in her bleak winter landscape of the soul Dickinson did exactly this, though through the different medium of words. When in England Durand had been mightily impressed with Constable's sketches of cloud forms, "with notes on the backs stating the hour of the day, direction of the wind, and kind of weather,"[11] whereas Ruskin was so confident of Turner's ability to capture these same effects that he included a meteorological chart of that artist's sky studies in *Modern Painters* (1:267–9).

In any individual poem, Dickinson likewise concentrated the mental weather of a complex psychic, spiritual, and emotional experience into a single moment of intense apprehension. Her private mythology invested twenty-four hours with the significance of a lifetime, expanding it to a passion drama that measured the progress of the soul just as sundials measured the rise and fall of the sun. The term for the wedge-shaped piece of metal that casts a shadow on a sundial is "gnomon," a word that recalls Dickinson's fondness for the Greek root meaning judge or interpreter; in "There's a Certain Slant of light" we know that time stops precisely because "Shadows – hold their breath" and no longer register the sun's onward march. Depending upon her own mood and circumstances and her placement within the four quadrants of the mystic day – dawn, noon, sunset, and midnight – Dickinson could rejoice in what lay before her, luxuriate in the ecstasy of the

present moment, or view a future phase with mingled hope and fear.
At each stage her close observation remained critically acute, and like
Turner she carried out her strategy of physiognomy by noting the most
minute gradations of the changing veil of color, cloud, light, and image. Of the resurrection of the lord of day she could write:

> I'll tell you how the Sun rose –
> A Ribbon at a time –
> The Steeples swam in Amethyst –
> The news, like Squirrels, ran –
> The Hills untied their Bonnets –
> The Bobolinks – begun –
> Then I said softly to myself –
> "That must have been the Sun"!   [J 318]

Here Dickinson's study from nature is as soft and as delicate as the
sunrise itself. At the high noon of midsummer, however, as in "There
came a Day at Summer's full" (J 322), Dickinson's ecstatic communion
with the landscape entailed a certain tension or pang of agony, because
she realized that this moment of perfect equilibrium could not possibly
last, that it must soon give way to the yellow ripeness of the afternoon,
and finally to the bloody sacrifice of sunset. At the fall of day she
remained just as attentive as she had been at sunrise, yet now she was
fully conscious of the increase of pain and loss that, as a Victorian artist,
she was obliged to keep under rigid control:

> Bound – a trouble –
> And lives can bear it!
> Limit – how deep a bleeding go!
> So – many – drops of vital scarlet –
> Deal with the soul
> As with Algebra!

> Tell it the Ages – to a cypher –
> And it will ache – contented – on –
> Sing – at it's pain – as any Workman –
> Notching the fall of the Even Sun!   [J 269]

Dickinson's "cypher" was of course her art, in which she secreted
the pain of her physical emotional reaction while adapting it to the
character of that ghost or spirit who inhabited the evening landscape.
The "Algebra" of the soul that she mentions is but another term for her
strategy of physiognomy. When she concentrated on the purely personal and subjective, this algebra could tend toward cosmic abstraction:

> Pain – expands the Time –
> Ages coil within

The minute Circumference
Of a single Brain –

Pain contracts – the Time –
Occupied with Shot
Gammuts of Eternities
Are as they were not –   [J 967]

Dickinson's final strange landscape was herself. She too was haunted,
she too sometimes found in the infinite planar recessions of consciousness not a brooding Holy Ghost, but a prowling Jack the Ripper against
which the body vainly "bolts the Door" (J 670). Or even worse, she
was seized by an utter, paralyzing emptiness. Everything that Ruskin
wrote about the veil of earth, water, and air, Dickinson internalized and
applied to what Poe significantly called "the veil of the soul."[12] Art was
the reproduction of this veil or drapery in all its changefulness, at a
particular moment in time. Dickinson's poetry of the moment, like her
commitment to romantic love, could produce "A Quartz contentment,
like a stone" (J 341), or cause excruciating pain, or engender an oceanic
softness and serenity. In contrast to her hard, almost brutal inscapes of
loneliness, Dickinson was fully capable of finding in the veiled outer
landscape benediction as well as malediction:

The Mountains stood in Haze –
The Valleys stopped below
And went or waited as they liked
The River and the Sky.

At leisure was the Sun –
His interests of Fire
A little from remark withdrawn –
The Twilight spoke the Spire,

So soft upon the Scene
The Act of Evening fell
We felt how neighborly a Thing
Was the Invisible.   [J 1278]

Here Dickinson's painterly method approaches that of the native
American school called luminism, in which, as Barbara Novak writes,
"time stops, and the moment is locked in place," while "the emanat-
ing light can also draw the senses in an intoxication of feeling."[13] But
whether Dickinson was seeking to define the spirit in that landscape or
the spirit in herself, she practiced what Americans from their reading
of Ruskin and popular digests of his thought considered to be a Pre-
Raphaelite realism. "The term Pre-Raphaelite," Novak observes, was

"often rather broadly used in American criticism at mid-century," yet it "always implied careful detail" (*Nature and Culture,* 250). The Pre-Raphaelites were a group composed of differing personalities and divergent aims, linked loosely together under the banner of fashionable medievalism, but Americans were most impressed with their naturalism, their uncomprising literalism of fact. In her Preface to *Oldtown Folks,* Harriet Beecher Stowe declared to her "Gentle reader," "My studies for this object have been Pre-Raphaelite, – taken from real characters, real scenes, and real incidents. And some of those things in the story which may appear most romantic and like fiction are simple renderings and applications of facts" (47).

Dickinson's landscape poems, whether dark or light, inner or outer, deal with just such an emphasized reality. The glare of this kind of precise rendering, in which "they almost paint even separate hairs," was too much for Nathaniel Hawthorne, who thought that the Pre-Raphaelite pictures he saw on exhibit in Manchester in July of 1857 were "like unripe fruit." Characteristically, he thought that "they leave out some medium – some enchantment that should intervene, and keep the subject from pressing so baldly and harshly upon the spectator's eyeballs. With the most lifelike reproduction, there is no illusion." He added, "I think if a semi-obscurity were thrown over the picture, after finishing it to this nicety, it might bring it nearer to Nature."[14] But what semi-obscurity or painterly chiaroscuro could mute the harsh truth of

> The last Night that She lived
> It was a Common Night
> Except the Dying – this to Us
> Made Nature different
>
> We noticed smallest things –
> Things overlooked before
> By this great light upon our Minds
> Italicized – as 'twere.
>
> As We went out and in
> Between Her final Room
> And Rooms where Those to be alive
> Tomorrow were, a Blame
>
> That Others could exist
> While She must finish quite
> A Jealousy for Her arose
> So nearly infinite –

We waited while She passed –
It was a narrow time –
Too jostled were Our Souls to speak
At length the notice came.

She mentioned, and forgot –
Then lightly as a Reed
Bent to the Water, struggled scarce –
Consented, and was dead –

And we – We placed the Hair –
And drew the Head erect –
And then an awful leisure was
Belief to regulate –   [J 1100]

Dickinson, according to Ruskin's precepts, was again being "true to nature," the dramatically different nature of emotional trauma. Her psychic landscape was italicized by the bolt of lightning that set all in bold and brutal relief. Referring to the death of Higginson's baby after the receipt of a memoir from the grieved father, Dickinson wrote, "These sudden intimacies with Immortality, are expanse – not Peace – as Lightning at our feet, instills a foreign Landscape" (L 3:661).

IV

As Ruskin had suggested, the typology of the storm cloud, especially when combined with lightning, signified a ministration of God's judgment, one that Ruskin was later to amplify in his great polemic "The Storm-Cloud of the Nineteenth-Century" (1884). In volume 5 of *Modern Painters,* however, Ruskin personified the storm cloud as "The Angel of the Sea," resurrecting the old Greek myths of generation and invoking the terrible names of the Gorgons and Medusa in order to image its destructive power. Even so, he included a magnificent word-painting to illustrate the immediacy of this dark angel's judgment:

The approach of trial-storm, hurricane-storm, is indeed in its vastness as the clouds of the softer rain. But it is not slow nor horizontal, but swift and steep: swift with the passion of ravenous winds; steep as slope of some dark, hollowed hill. The fronting clouds come leaning forward, one thrusting the other aside, or on; impatient, ponderous, impendent, like globes of rock tossed of Titans – Ossa on Olympus – but hurled forward all, in one wave of cloud lava – cloud whose throat is as a sepulchre. Fierce behind them rages the oblique wrath of the rain, white as ashes, dense as showers of driven steel; the pillars of it full of ghastly life; Rain-

Furies, shrieking as they fly; – scourging, as with whips and scor-
pions; – the earth ringing and trembling under them, heaven wail-
ing wildly, the trees stooped blindly down, covering their faces,
quivering in every leaf with horror, ruin of their branches flying
by them like black stubble. [137–8]

To Dickinson the sudden judgment of storm and lightning reveals
new internal as well as external landscapes:

> The Soul's distinct connection
> With immortality
> Is best disclosed by Danger
> Or quick Calamity –
>
> As Lightning on a Landscape
> Exhibits Sheets of Place –
> Not yet suspected – but for Flash –
> And Click – and Suddenness.   [J 974]

The flash of lightning is exactly that kind of blinding glare which
equalizes all objects, including human ones. Yet if the storm is "judgment" in Ruskinian terms, then its result can be salvation as well as
damnation. As Dickinson makes plain in her poetry, this awesome
conjunction of fear and of hope results first and foremost in a hell of
anticipation, since the thunderstorm is simply "prospective" of the
sound of the last trumpet when the final separation of the Elect from
the damned will be made manifest:

> There came a Wind like a Bugle –
> It quivered through the Grass
> And a Green Chill upon the Heat
> So ominous did pass
> We barred the Windows and the Doors
> As from an Emerald Ghost –
> The Doom's electric Moccasin
> That very instant passed –
> On a strange Mob of panting Trees
> And Fences fled away
> And Rivers where the Houses ran
> Those looked that lived – that Day –
> The Bell within the steeple wild
> The flying tidings told –
> How much can come
> And much can go,
> And yet abide the World!   [J 1593]

Though for Ruskin only pagan horrors could body forth the primeval wrath of the storm, that wrath still belonged to the biblical God. Jehovah used a Greek weapon to enforce his will, since "the Angel of the Sea has also another message, – in the 'great rain of his strength,' rain of trial, sweeping away ill-set foundations. Then his robe is not spread softly over the whole heaven, as a veil, but sweeps back from his shoulders, ponderous, oblique, terrible – leaving his sword-arm free" (*MP* 5:137). Ruskin named the "Angel of the Lightning" after Chrysaor, "wielder of the golden sword" sprung from the blood of Medusa; Dickinson domesticated it to "The Doom's electric Moccasin," converting the snaking locks of a classical monster into an aboriginal American menace. Like Spofford's Indian Devil the word "moccasin" suggests an amalgam both of natural evil (poisonous snake) and human depravity (savage stealth).

The truth of Dickinson's poems is the wisdom of a survivor rather than the didactic pronouncements of one of the saved. It is a spare, ambiguous wisdom that we see again in such late nineteenth-century narratives as Stephen Crane's "The Open Boat," but most immediately, it is also a wisdom based upon an intense, concentrated observation. Her strategy of physiognomy still leaves the spiritual facts (if any) to be inferred from the physical features, lest the corresponding metaphysical truth overwhelm and totally engulf the frail consciousness of the observer:

> Tell all the Truth but tell it slant –
> Success in Circuit lies
> Too bright for our infirm Delight
> The Truth's superb surprise
> As lightning to the Children eased
> With explanation kind
> The Truth must dazzle gradually
> Or every man be blind –   [J 1129]

Such were the dangers of dealing with the unveiled mysteries of the sublime. The paradox was that as the veil of mist and atmosphere was dissipated by the "Angel of the Sea," only "unsearchable" vacuity was exposed. Thunderstorms countered Dickinson's belief that we actually see best through a cushioning screen of mist and cloud. When Nature herself withdrew that cloud to a great height, and firmly separated the earth from the heavens, Dickinson's strategy of physiognomy became more and more difficult, the character of the landscape more and more anonymous. For the clouds that veiled God's face did not always shine with the rainbows of mercy and truth as affirmed in "Little Mary's Thought":

A Cap of Lead across the sky
Was tight and surly drawn
We could not find the mighty Face
The Figure was withdrawn —

A Chill came up as from a shaft
Our noon became a well
A Thunder storm combines the charms
Of Winter and of Hell   [J 1649]

Since a thunderstorm turned day into night by its power of blackness, it also upset Dickinson's typology of the mystic day, substituting the hell of midnight for the heaven of noontide. At the same time, since the storm cloud was a manifestation of the sublime, marrying "transport" to fear, Dickinson enjoyed a peculiar kind of ecstasy or giddy heightening of consciousness in the anticipation of impending meteorological doom:

The Symptom of the Gale —
The Second of Dismay —
Between it's Rumor and it's Face —
Is almost Revelry —

The Houses firmer root —
The Heavens cannot be found —
The Upper Surfaces of things
Take covert in the Ground —

The Mem'ry of the Sun
Not Any can recall —
Although by Nature's sterling Watch
So scant an interval —

And when the Noise is caught
And Nature looks around —
"We dreamed it"? She interrogates —
"Good Morning" — We propound?   [J 1327]

Dickinson here focuses not so much on extremes of calm or storminess as rather on the individual seconds between the gale's approach and its consummation. "Nature's sterling Watch" may run according to Greenwich time, but psychologically the storm's seconds are the ticking of a meteorological time bomb. Like the storm described by Mark Twain in *Life on the Mississippi,* such tempests "produced effects which enchanted the eyes and set electric ecstacies of mixed delight and apprehension shivering along every nerve in the body in an unintermittent procession."[15] As Dickinson writes in another poem, to be struck by lightning merely takes away the "Power to perceive His Process / With Vitality," (J 925). To continue as a prisoner of the storm combines an exquisite anticipation with a Kierkegaardian dread:

> These are the Nights that Beetles love –
> From Eminence remote
> Drives ponderous perpendicular
> His figure intimate
> The terror of the Children
> The merriment of men
> Depositing his Thunder
> He hoists abroad again –
> A bomb upon the Ceiling
> Is an improving thing –
> It keeps the nerves progressive
> Conjecture flourishing –
> Too dear the Summer evening
> Without discreet alarm –
> Supplied by Entomology
> With it's remaining charm   [J 1128]

Confronted with the summer thunderstorm's "ponderous perpendicular" of lightning and the explosive "Bomb upon the Ceiling" that is its thunder, which any moment might bring the entire house down upon her head, Dickinson takes a wryly pragmatic approach. The thunderstorm becomes a lesson in Victorian self-improvement – "It keeps the nerves progressive" – and ironically stimulates the imagination. The only sign of Dickinson's "alarm" is her discreet but intensive pursuit of entomology, for, since the storm is taking place at night, she cannot practice her usual strategy of physiognomy in the dark. Therefore she turns to the classification of those beetles who love such nights. These beetles are concrete symptoms of the approaching storm, its accompanying Furies that Dickinson attempts to transmute into Eumenides by a determined use of the apotropaisms of science. Whether they prove to be June beetles, lightning bugs, or grave-loving scarabs, such insects are also natural objects that must be delineated as precisely as possible by the steady hand of the artist, lest the interior bomb of her consciousness burst under unbearable pressure. Attentiveness and obedience – the attentiveness and obedience of a Pre-Raphaelite or poet-naturalist – are once again necessary in dealing with these volatile phenomena. For the power of the storm is even more threatening when it prowls under cover of darkness:

The Lightning is a yellow Fork
From Tables in the sky
By inadvertent fingers dropt
The awful Cutlery

Of mansions never quite disclosed
And never quite concealed
The Apparatus of the Dark
To ignorance revealed.   [J 1173]

Such a violent revelation or rending of the natural protective veil of
the atmosphere upsets all categories. Like Turner's rendering of the
poor shepherd struck dead by a lightning bolt at Stonehenge, a scene
vividly described by Ruskin in the first volume of *Modern Painters* (260–
1), one might oneself end up as the dainty morsel sliced to pieces by
such clumsy and "awful Cutlery." To flee is impossible, since the only
ones safe from such force are those who have already yielded to it:

The Clouds their Backs together laid
The North begun to push
The Forests galloped till they fell
The Lightning played like mice

The Thunder crumbled like a stuff
How good to be in Tombs
Where Nature's Temper cannot reach
Nor missile ever comes   [J 1172]

In the tomb, judgment has already taken place. Far worse is the internalization of storm, the constant presence of the "Emerald Ghost" that
haunts from within:

It struck me – every Day –
The Lightning was as new
As if the Cloud that instant slit
And let the Fire through –

It burned Me – in the Night –
It Blistered to My Dream –
It sickened fresh upon my sight –
With every Morn that came –

I thought that Storm – was brief –
The Maddest – quickest by –
But Nature lost the Date of This –
And left it in the Sky –   [J 362]

V

In all of Dickinson's poems about the terror of thunder and lightning, the most fearsome of her lone landscapes, we are inevitably drawn back to the facts of material culture, to the people as well as to the things that were a part of her life. When Dickinson was only three years old, she was taken by her Aunt Lavinia Norcross while "mother Dickinson" and her new baby, Emily's sister Vinny, were ill. Aunt Norcross vividly describes what overtook her and her niece on their journey back to Monson, Massachusetts, in May of 1833:

> Just after we passed Mr. Clapps – it thundered more & the thunder & lightning increased – Elizabeth [Emily] called it *the fire* – the time the rain wind & darkness came we were along in those pine woods – the thunder echoed – I will confess that I felt rather bad – tho' I was wonderfully supported – the horse when the rain came with such fury shook his head & galloped on – did not like it much – it soon grew lighter, but continued to rain some & the thunder & lightning continued also – We tho't if we stopped we should not get home that night – Elizabeth felt inclined to be frightened some – she said "Do take me to my mother" But I covered her face all under my cloak to protect her & took care that she did not get wet much – I was truly thankful on her account & on my own when we reached home – [*YH* 1:20–1]

Such a traumatic experience seems to have conditioned poems written as early as "Through lane it lay – thro' bramble" (J 9), where "The lightning's poinards" gleam in a Gothic recreation of the old ballad of "The Babes in the Wood," as well as the late apprehensions of the stormy sublime we have just been considering. In Dickinson's aesthetic there was always a Pre-Raphaelite concreteness behind the elusive symbology of her verse. Likewise, her domestication of a romantic typology found a material stimulus in the remarkable collection of American and European paintings assembled by her brother, Austin, and her sister-in-law, Susan. To her, as she wrote to Samuel Bowles and his wife, "Sue's Drawing Room" was a type of "Jerusalem," both the sacred earthly city and the holy heavenly one (*L* 2:334), since Dickinson had only to cross the path from the Homestead to the Evergreens to be ushered into an elite temple of art that reflected the collecting habits and assumptions of her entire century. For while the taste of the Austin Dickinsons was decidedly eclectic, it was solidly Pre-Raphaelite in its reverence for fact and unabashedly romantic in its preference for landscapes that featured mountains, lakes, and all manner of diaphanous atmospheric effects.

Their American paintings illustrating the Hudson River aesthetic articulated by Asher B. Durand, besides the relatively late *Woodland Scene,* by Arthur Parton, discussed and reproduced in Chapter 6, included *Sunset with Cows* (1856), by John F. Kensett; *Autumn Evening in the White Hills* (1858), by Sanford R. Gifford; *Sea in Fog,* signed "Cook" but listed as coming "from the studio of William Trost Richards"; and a large work called *Ruffled Grouse* or *Prairie Hens* (1859), by an artist named Hill, who may be one of two brothers well known as American disciples of Pre-Raphaelitism.[16] A small luminist work called *Painting of a Mullein* signifies its American origins by its focus on this hardy wild flower growing next to a large boulder set in a meadow near the tranquil sea.[17] There is an equally detailed nature study of wild wood violets in watercolor, and a sweeping mountain vista, listed in the inventories as either *Scene in the Alps* or *Scene in the Cumberland Mountains,* by Jacobus N. Stakenbourgh, a Dutch-born landscapist who exhibited American views at the Pennsylvania Academy in 1850 and 1852. Landscapes by other foreign-born artists include the huge (42 **b** 36) *Landscape: Norwegian Scenery, with Bears* (1846), by Hans Frederik Gude (see the illustration at the opening of this chapter); *Alpine Landscape,* by Gottfried Johann Pulian; and the lively and colorful *Habitant Farm: Winter* (1857), by the popular Canadian genre painter Cornelius Krieghoff.[18] Later additions to the Dickinson collection were a small Barbizon school work entitled *Harvest Scene,* C. H. Shearer's tonalist *Winter Scene with Fox* of 1882, and L. C. Fish's *Blue Jays and Chestnut Leaves,* a pastel dated 1875 and done in a stylized manner that owes much to the Victorian vogue for Japanese prints.

Both Austin and Susan Dickinson began collecting art early in their married life, since the Kensett *Sunset* bears Susan's name in pencil on the back of the stretchers, and it was she who was responsible for the purchase of the Arthur Parton *Woodland Scene* ("*Oaks at Old Shokan*"). Later both Susan and her daughter, Martha Dickinson Bianchi, would acquire various Italian works during their grand tours of Europe, but just as Emily Dickinson was part and parcel of the second generation of American high romantics, so did her aesthetic taste relate most directly to the paintings bought by her brother Austin during the flush decade of the 1850s (see Appendix B, "Austin Dickinson as Connoisseur"). Perhaps the most typical and meaningful of thse landscapes is the *Autumn Evening in the White Hills* by Sanford R. Gifford, a masterpiece of luminist quiescence and calm with its muted tints, mirrored lake surface, and light veilings of mist.[19] The prose simulacra of this painting might be passages from Thoreau's *Walden* or Dickinson's own "The Mountains stood in Haze," which combines a botanical realism and Pre-Raphaelite exactness of detail with a delicate feeling for the numinous, of "how neighborly a Thing" the "Invisible" can become. This thinning of the veil of atmosphere to the point where a luminous presence seems to suffuse the very air itself was also captured by Dickinson's mentor, T. W. Higginson, through the medium of his own word-painting in the second paragraph of "My Out-Door Study":

> The wood are hazy, as if the warm sunbeams had melted in among the interstices of the foliage and spread a soft film throughout the whole. The sky seems to reflect the water, and the water the sky; both are roseate with color, both are darkened with clouds . . . The wooded islands are poised upon the lake, each belted with a paler tint of softer wave. The air seems fine and palpitating; the drop of an oar in a distant rowlock, the sound of a hammer on a dismantled boat, pass into some region of mist and shadows, and form a metronome for delicious dreams. [*ODP*, 250]

But there is no need to match every painting owned by the Dickinson family with some relevant literary passage or even with specific poems by Emily Dickinson, though such exercises as her sprightly portrait of the blue jay in "No Brigadier throughout the Year" (J 1561) would seem to cry out for comparison with L. C. Fish's bold pastel. Rather, the age itself – its art, its aesthetics, its mode of seeing – is the only real source of Dickinson's remarkable domestication of an elaborate romantic typology and a Ruskinian truth to nature. When this romantic age "went up to heaven," in Emerson's phrase, Dickinson's poems preserved its close observations in the unique medium of her verse, to puzzle and to startle readers of the 1890s and after who had long turned from the native scene to imported artistic standards.

This very shift is reflected in the evolution of Austin Dickinson's own collection, which records the gradual demise of the Hudson River school and the growing dominance of European art, like that of the Düsseldorf and Barbizon schools. Paradoxically, it was the seership of Ruskin himself and the American desire for a Pre-Raphaelite realism that undermined the popularity of the atmospheric painting practiced by Durand and his followers. The Civil War brought this crisis of taste to a head, as it did the extravagance of the Azarian school and Dickinson's own private mythology of passion. In his biography of his father, John Durand wrote, "The eclipse of American art may be said to begin with the establishment of the Düsseldorf Gallery in New York in 1849, a gallery which owes its existence to Mr. John G. Boker, a resident in Dusseldorf for twenty years, and afterwards Prussian counsul in the city of New York" (*Asher B. Durand*, 192).

Boker was a shrewd entrepreneur who succeeded in transporting the products of a provincial German school, centered in Düsseldorf, to an aesthetically naive America. Acting in response to the revolutionary upheavals of 1848 and a consequent depression of the foreign art market, Boker brought his collection of Düsseldorf paintings to a stable, new rich, art-hungry clientele. The Düsseldorf school itself was calculated to appeal to a pious and solidly middle-class taste; it was the purely aesthetic corollary of that staid, domestic furniture style that has come to be known as Biedermeier. The most famous product of that school was Leutze's monumental *Washington Crossing the Delaware* (1850), for Düsseldorf artists specialized in the kind of history painting that made history itself into a costume drama. Peasant life, scenes of touching incident, and gloomy medieval landscapes were also a forte of the Düsseldorfers, whose city soon became a northern mecca for young Americans in search of picturesque subject matter and firm academic training.[20]

In their conservative and homely "moral" qualities, the paintings of the Düsseldorf school made aesthetic meaning obvious and available to anybody with a gift for anecdote. In its technical proficiency, the style appealed to those who demanded that a painting be a highly finished work of art, that it demonstrate that the artist had taken some time with the composition and had labored long and deliberately over it. Düsseldorf products appealed to those who marveled at rocks so real that one could reach out and touch them, at encounters so touching and tender that one could weep aloud over them. The cosmopolitan critic James Jackson Jarves, who tried to judge every painting on which his dyspeptic eye lighted by the objective standards set by the Old Masters and the subjective standards set by Ruskin's nobility of intent, dismissed the offerings of Germany in his *The Art-Idea* of 1864 as "of the Dryasdust order," as "the ballast of modern art, keeping it from premature flights, or being too much swayed by imagination and impulse."[21]

I would not devote so much attention to the Düsseldorf school and the influential Düsseldorf Gallery, were it not for the fact that Austin Dickinson was one of those Americans whose taste was decisively converted to the virtues of foreign painting by the success of John Boker's grand enterprise. Austin's *Landscape: Norwegian Scenery, with Bears,* by Gude, was purchased at the auction of the Düsseldorf Gallery that took place on December nineteenth, 1862. Art had become not merely a hobby but a way of life with Austin, especially as he felt himself more and more stifled by a provincial existence in Amherst and suffocated by an increasingly unsatisfactory marriage. A year before the auction, Susan Dickinson wrote in a Christmas note to Samuel Bowles: "Austin came home [from New York] in a feverish excitement over pictures –

utterly worn out with his passion – The real fact of the matter is his desire and half plan for three of the Dusseldorf collection – He is fascinated with the longing, and I advise him to get them. I have not seen him so convulsed with excitement 'since the days when he went gypsying' " (*YH* 2:41). Besides the Gude, Austin bought two paintings by Pulian that were offered by the gallery, the small *Alpine Landscape* that still remains at the Evergreens and the larger *Scene Near Dresden* that he willed to his mistress, Mabel Loomis Todd, at his death in 1895. Whatever caustic critics like James Jackson Jarves might say against the Düsseldorf school, it succeeded by out-Ruskinizing the Ruskinians in its thoughtful rendering of the real and its grasping for the ideal. In the "Historical Sketch of the Düsseldorf School of Art" that serves as a preface to a sumptuous catalogue published in 1863, entitled *Gems from the Düsseldorf Gallery,* in which all of Austin Dickinson's purchases are photographically reproduced, the anonymous historian assures us that

> the characteristics of the School are, perfect fidelity to nature, in form, color, and expression; minuteness in detail, delicacy of finish, and perfectness in rendering the *language* of every subject. All this implies the most exclusive study; for, the licenses and extravagances of genius once discarded, nothing except the power of truthfullness is left. But, though their ordinances are so severe, no formality, no coldness, nor barrenness, can attach to the School. The great variety in the paintings which form this collection, shows that the loftiest and the lowliest subjects alike are rendered with success; history, allegory, landscape, fruit, animals, humor and pathos, piety and enthusiasm, poetry and passion – all have their most noble and exquisite interpretation. No art-collection in this country ever embraced more excellence in the way of diversity of subject.[22]

The catalogue description of Pulian's *Scene Near Dresden* stresses the liveliness of this genre, or story-telling, piece – "The busy women washing their clothes in the running stream; the young urchins, driving into the brook yon flock of geese," and so on – while it sets the stamp of Ruskinian truth and received authority on the result: "There is a truth to nature in the whole of this picture that cannot be excelled, and which has earned for its author, the unqualified praise, of both artist and connoisseur." The use of the term "author" is significant, for these paintings were meant to be "read" in expressly literary terms. How Emily Dickinson might have read Gude's *Landscape: Norwegian Scenery, with Bears,* which became the central jewel of her brother's own private collection, is indicated from a review first published in the *New York*

Albion and subsequently reprinted in the various catalogues of the gallery. This "gem of the whole gallery," the reviewer wrote,

> represents "Norwegian Scenery, with bears painted after nature."
> The eye looks up a torrent forming a succession of waterfalls, to a
> mountain of considerable elevation that rises in the background.
> Heatherly plants and stunted fir-trees show the soil and climate –
> nor is the rocky scene one of particularly striking character. But
> the treatment is masterly. The aerial perspective, the vapor from
> the falling water, the quiet tone of the foreground, the sense of
> solitude befitting the scene, despite Bruin, and a pathway running
> upwards by the stream – here is a combination of excellence that
> makes up a very perfect picture. As for the bears, they are in the
> Catalogue, and they are in the picture, and they figure less con-
> spicuously in the latter than in the former, not sitting palpably for
> their portraits, but regularly toned in – one sucking his paws, the
> other eyeing his shadow on the path, and both mere sketches – so
> that without the hint, you might almost stumble over them. This
> admirable work of art is of large cabinet size. We trust no one will
> hurry past it.[23]

Disagreeing with the *Albion* critic, the cataloguer of *Gems from the Düsseldorf Gallery* thought that "the two bears . . . add to the feeling of loneliness and grandeur which pervades the scene," and he appended to his catalogue a sentimental poem by William Denton, beginning:

> *My* pictures are landscapes, unfading and true,
> Each set in a frame of magnificent blue;
> The *Master* who painted retouches them still,
> No mark of *His* pencil but tells of *His skill*
> Each moment they change, and new beauties unfold:
> Now tinted with lead, and then burnished like gold.

The poem signified that Gude's scenery and God's scenery were for all practical purposes the same. Even more appropriate were the verses that were attached to an almost identical picture by the same artist, another mountainous *Norwegian Landscape* with a "sense of solitude." In this case, a work by Charles Cotton from *Dana's Household Book of Poetry* was chosen to gloss the scene's romantic typology:

> Dear solitude, the soul's best friend,
>   That man acquainted with himself doth make,
> And all his Maker's wonders to intend.
>   With thee I here converse at will. And would

> be glad to do so still,
>   For it is thou alone that keep'st the soul
> awake.[24]

In volume 4 of *Modern Painters* Ruskin warned his readers against a
monkish withdrawal to the "Hill solitudes" (383), but the New England nun Emily Dickinson kept her soul awake by creating her own
landscapes, both inner and outer. In gazing at such scenes as those
portrayed by Gude, where "the immense forests of hardy firs, the lofty
mountains, a-down which we see the torrents rushing with impetuous
force, the cold gray sky . . . most faithfully portray the features of a
northern landscape, where solitude reigns paramount" (*Gems from the
Düsseldorf*) how could she help but see her own long-projected portrait
of solitude made manifest?

> There is a solitude of space
> A solitude of sea
> A solitude of death, but these
> Society shall be
> Compared with that profounder site
> That polar privacy
> A soul admitted to itself—
> Finite Infinity.   [J 1695]

If the lofty, snow-capped mountain was Master and she herself was
like one of the lonely, insignificant bears, overwhelmed by the grandeur of nature as well as obscured by its own shadow, the strength of
Dickinson's romantic passion still matched the cold mountain torrent
that rushed "with impetuous force" down the glacial slope. Gude's
painting preserved in its icy grandeur the private mythology that fixed
her own life after the 1860s and its tumultuous inner Civil War, until
her late encounter with Judge Lord melted the snows and brought a
second spring to her nordic hibernation. Whatever stimulus Dickinson
might have received from her brother's purchases in the postbellum
world of nouveau riche collectors, it was the paintings he bought in the
1850s and early 1860s that, like her reading during that period, remained fixed on the marble shelf of her mind. Not only a deliberate
primitivist but also a proud chauvinist, she was wedded to New England romance and would not change her homespun folk verse forms,
like Mary Moody's shroud, no matter what new and daring thoughts
might come to wear it. In this she was as steadfast a patriot as one could
wish, and just as her white dress was symbolic of her white election to
stainless passion, so did the stars and stripes of the Union become her
personal oriflamme:

My country need not change her gown,
Her triple suit as sweet
As when 'twas cut at Lexington,
And first pronounced "a fit."   [J 1511]

Even T. W. Higginson began to purchase darker French Barbizon works in the late 1860s, turning away from his earlier glorification of a pristine and sun-drenched American nature.[25] Like Whittier's Barbara Frietchie, Dickinson stuck to her nativist loyalties, and just as steadfast was her strategy of physiognomy, which diagnosed the soul's condition, expressed in the landscape or in the self, at a particular instant of time, place, and psychic experience. For Dickinson as for her century, the education of the soul became the highest aim of art or life, and once again Ruskin can help to define for us this other dimension of meaning. In volume 5 of *Modern Painters,* Ruskin struggled with the correspondences among nature, God, and the soul. In a brilliant chapter entitled "The Dark Mirror," he came at last to Dickinson's conclusion that, when compared to the inward absolute, the outward means – art itself – was in some ways a superfluous endeavor. Speaking of the usefulness of painting, Ruskin was still forced to admit that

all the purposes of good which we saw that the beauty of nature could accomplish, may be better fulfilled by the meanest of her realities than by the brightest of imitations. For prolonged entertainment, no picture can be compared with the wealth of interest which may be found in the herbage of the poorest field, or blossoms of the narrowest copse. As suggestive of supernatural power, the passing away of a fitful rain-cloud, or opening of dawn, are in their change and mystery more pregnant than any pictures. A child would, I suppose, receive a religious lesson from a flower more willingly than from a print of one, and might be taught to understand the nineteenth Psalm, on a starry night, better than by diagrams of the constellations. [193]

Emily Dickinson fully agreed with this contention when she wrote:

I would not paint – a picture
I'd rather be the One
It's bright impossibility
To dwell – delicious – on –
And wonder how the fingers feel
Whose rare – celestial – stir –
Evokes so sweet a Torment –
Such sumptuous – Despair –

I would not talk, like Cornets —
I'd rather be the One
Raised softly to the Ceilings —
And out, and easy on —
Through Villages of Ether —
Myself endued Ballon
By but a lip of Metal —
The pier to my Pontoon —

Nor would I be a Poet —
It's finer — own the Ear —
Enamored — impotent — content —
The License to revere,
A privilege so awful
What would the Dower be,
Had I the Art to stun myself
With Bolts of Melody!   [J 505]

It was this emphasis on experience, on Platonic experience, that led Dickinson to think of her poetry as a "gauze" or "film" that was the ultimate veil of the self, a fabric as useless as a discarded cocoon once that self had achieved circumference or passed beyond mortality. For this reason she left instructions that all her papers be destroyed, and it was only because of the Yankee stubbornness of her sister, Lavinia, who preserved the poetry in order to provide material for a "modest" memorial tribute, that we today possess the corporeal remains of her art. Yet even in so chilling a dress rehearsal of her own demise as "Because I could not stop for Death," Dickinson notes the drama of the "Setting Sun" at the very time — or not-time — when she is realizing that her tippet, the necessary veil of her art, is of "tulle," the flimsiest of substances. That the sun was a type of Phoebus, her Christ-like love, only partly explains her close observation of this drama, which became the justification for her private mythology, her Platonic passion, and her whole amazing art.

Chapter 8

THE ART OF PEACE
Dickinson, Sunsets, and the Sublime

---

*The perfection of culture is not rebellion but peace; only when it has
realized a deep moral stillness has it really reached its end.*

Walter Pater

*Keep to the conventional, and you have something which all have
seen even if they disapprove; copy Nature, and her colors make art
appear incredible. If you could paint the sunset before your window
as gorgeous as it is, your picture would be hooted from the walls of
the exhibition.*

T. W. Higginson

*To pile like Thunder to it's close
Then crumble grand away
While Everything created hid
This—would be Poetry—*

*Or Love—the two coeval come—
We both and neither prove—
Experience either and consume—
For None see God and live—*

Emily Dickinson

In his "Vision of the Last Judgment," the eighteenth-century poet,
painter, and mystic William Blake put into personal and anecdotal form
an idea that we have seen taken up by elite nineteenth-century culture
and further domesticated by Emily Dickinson. "When the sun rises,"
he asked rhetorically, "do you not see a round disk of fire somewhat
like a Guinea?" "O no no," he answered; "I see an Innumerable company of the Heavenly host crying, 'Holy, Holy, Holy is the Lord God
Almighty.' " For as he explained, "I question not my Corporeal or
Vegetative Eye any more than I would Question a Window concerning
a Sight. I look thro' it & not with it."[1] Dickinson too looked through
visionary lenses at the *Sanctus* that was the rising and setting of the sun,

John F. Kensett, *Sunset with Cows*, 1856. (By permission of Mary L. Hampson.)

but she looked as well with the personal mythology that she had distilled from her surrounding culture. To William Blake the sun was a constant symbol of the imagination; to Dickinson as to Ruskin and to Little Mary (of "Little Mary's Thought" in the Warner scrapbook), it was a living representation of the deity. For the Amherst poet this deity resolved into the Phoebus-Apollo who was Master, as she tempered a public romantic typology with the passionate allegory of a private love religion. Yet the same paradox that applied to Christian concepts of an unsearchable Jehovah worried this symbolism. How could one confront the godhead unveiled? how could one stare into the naked sun without going blind?

A host of Old Testament images of the veil, mainly centered around the figure of Moses and the building of the tabernacle in the wilderness, confirmed the harsh injunction that challenged Dickinson in both "To pile like Thunder to it's close" (J 1247) and "No man saw awe" (J1733) that "None see God and live−".[2] Yet the latter poem ends with the suggestion that, as for Moses, an unveiled vision of the sublime is a true human possibility:

> "Am not consumed," old Moses wrote,
> "Yet saw him face to face" −
> That very physiognomy
> I am convinced was this

Dickinson's physiognomic solution to facing the *Mysterium tremendum* of the sublime involved a two-pronged strategy. Whether this sublimity was imaged by the pagan veiled Isis or by the Old Testament God robed in a pillar of fire or an unconsumed burning bush, one could survive only by concealing the mystery through veils of one's own. If the sublime chose to unveil itself even partially, attentiveness and obedience were in order, for the most exact description of the phenomenon that human art could accomplish was dictated by the prevailing romantic theory of correspondences. But this art itself had to remain sacred rather than profane, and the only way to achieve such sanctity was to preserve the mystery from prying eyes, eyes that, as Blake had said, were "Vegetative" rather than visionary. Sunset, which itself screened as much as it revealed (J 1609), was the perfect natural expression of this kind of sublimity, since it was a mundane event that still allowed direct contact with some higher power. Sometimes the sun set unveiled, in a blazing clarity of undimmed glory, but more often it went to its rest obscured by marvelous cloud forms and color tones − what Little Mary had called "God's veils." As we shall see, Dickinson was not alone in her sun worship, which formed another kind of *bricolage* that united folk, popular, and elite levels of culture. As always, she preferred to cover and conceal rather than to lift the robe of either God or goddess, for to her, as to the visionary American painter Elihu Vedder, "Isis unveiled would be Isis dead."[3]

I

At the most traditional or folk level, the actions of the sun were intimately bound up with the life of man through their regulation of the life of nature. "Red sun in the morning / Sailor's warning / Red sun at night, / Sailor's delight." The romantic movement sought to see beyond this purely utilitarian view, and we have noted the symbolic importance of sunlight in the allied romantic genres of T. W. Higginson's nature essays and the landscape paintings of Asher B. Durand and the Hudson River school. In an article called "Sunsets" in the *Crayon* for September of 1855, W. Sylvester begins by noting the difference between the poetic and quotidian views of this phenomenon. He writes that "the cool promenade or the red promise of a to-morrow which rejoices some and depresses others, according to the leadings of their respective interests as involved in the weather, are the sum and substance of the enjoyment given by the daily marvel which attends the withdrawal of light." He then asserts, "It is not that every sunset is a brilliant or a gorgeous one, but every one is marvellous."[4] In the letter in which Emily Dickinson wrote to her sister-in-law of her wish to fill a chamber with landscapes so lone that men would pause and weep at them, she made a similar matter-of-fact observation about the sunset, one that seems at first purely meteorological. "Today has been a fair day," she wrote, "very still and blue. Tonight, the crimson children are playing in the West, and tomorrow will be colder. In all I number you. I want to think of you, each hour in the day. What you are saying – doing – I want to walk with you, as seeing yet unseen" (*L* 1:310).

As her concluding choice of words and phrases ("number," "walk with you," "seeing yet unseen," echoing many New Testament Scripture passages) attests, Dickinson found the sunset prophetic not only of external but of internal weather. She was to focus more and more intently on that subject which she quaintly personifies here, a mundane apocalypse that for her was to take on a myriad of revelatory meanings. Even the ordinarily placid and equilibrating Emerson could wax rhapsodic over the sunset in his early "Nature," and ask of it the questions that Dickinson was to ask over and over again. "Not less excellent," he writes in the segment of his essay subtitled "Beauty,"

> except for our less susceptibility in the afternoon, was the charm, last evening, of a January sunset. The western clouds divided and

subdivided themselves into pink flakes modulated with tints of unspeakable softness, and the air had so much life and sweetness that it was a pain to come within doors. What was it that nature would say? Was there no meaning in the live repose of the valley behind the mill, and which Homer or Shakespeare could not re- form for me in words? The leafless trees become spires of flame in the sunset, with the blue east for their background, and the stars of the dead calices of flowers, and every withered red stem and stubble rimed with frost, contribute something to the mute mu- sic. [*Works* 1:17–18]

Emerson's description of the sunset here is photoerotic, almost Tur- neresque in its analysis of the pink flakes and tints of sky, but as her private mythology developed Dickinson saw in the same scene the quickening or fading of a living pulse. To her the "live repose" in the landscape that Emerson fleetingly glimpsed became evidence of a being possessing consciousness as well as color. At the same time it tested her strategy of physiognomy to the limits, for this intimidating quarry sometimes converted the pursuer into the pursued, the analyst into the analysand, the hunter into the hunted:

> An ignorance a Sunset
> Confer upon the Eye –
> Of Territory – Color –
> Circumference – Decay –
>
> It's Amber Revelation
> Exhilirate – Debase –
> Omnipotence' inspection
> Of Our inferior face –
>
> And when the solemn features
> Confirm – in Victory –
> We start – as if detected
> In Immortality –   [J 552]

At the distance of well over a hundred years, it must be admitted that sunsets, like mountains, had a much greater significance for the nine- teenth century than they do for our less earthbound age, dazzled by moonwalkers and dedicated to instant information storage and retrieval. Speaking of the modern usurpation of the natural by the artificial, Susan Sontag has written: "Photographs create the beautiful – and – over the generations of picture-making – use it up. Certain glories of nature, for example, have been all but abandoned to the indefatigable attention of amateur camera buffs. The image-surfeited are likely to find sunsets corny; they now look, alas, too much like photographs."[5]

Emily Dickinson was never surfeited by the sunset; her own sensibility and perception had to serve as a Daguerrean apparatus to capture the daily passion drama of the sun's decline and death. Against Sontag's expression of modernist ennui, which relegates the sunset to the categories of kitsch or camp, or Göethe's famous remark that even the greatest sunset becomes boring after three-quarters of an hour, we can set Thoreau's passionate romantic affirmation in his journal for January seventh, 1852:

> We never tire of the drama of sunset. I go forth each afternoon and look into the west a quarter of an hour before sunset, with fresh curiosity, to see what new picture will be painted there, what new panorama exhibited, what new dissolving views. Can Washington Street or Broadway show anything as good? Every day a new picture is painted and framed, held up for half an hour, in such lights as the Great Artist chooses, and then withdrawn, and the curtain falls.[6]

Not only did Emily Dickinson's room in her father's house in Amherst face west, but she had a superb and unimpeded view of the Pelham Hills from the cupola that topped the whole mansion. MacGregor Jenkins, who knew her when he was a child, writes: "She had a habit of standing in rapt attention as if she were listening to something very faint and far off. We children often saw her at sunset, standing at the kitchen window, peering through a vista in the trees to the western sky, – her proud little head thrown back, her eyes raised and one hand held characteristically before her."[7] No matter what her vantage point, from the very bulk of Dickinson's sunset poems it would appear that she regarded the daily observance of the setting sun as an almost holy duty, an obligatory vespers. For Emily Dickinson, the sunset was a common revelation of a supreme mystery, a time when the still, small voice of God was all but audible, or synesthetically translated into a new language of color and cloud. To this New England nun sunset was the canonical hour when the secret of that Holy Ghost who lay beyond the landscape was literally closest to the earth. The problem was to capture the effect or character of this ghost through the haunted medium of one's art. The spirit did not always appear even when the poet abandoned the claustrophobic kitchen for the open-air temple of nature:

> The Sun kept stooping – stooping – low!
> The Hills to meet him rose!
> On his side, what Transaction!
> On their side, what Repose!

Deeper and deeper grew the stain
Upon the window pane –
Thicker and thicker stood the feet
Until the Tyrian

Was crowded dense with Armies –
So gay, so Brigadier –
That *I* felt martial stirrings
Who once the Cockade wore –

Charged, from my chimney corner –
But Nobody was there!   [J 152]

Dickinson as an artist here remains confined, shut off from a full experience of the sunset by staying inside rather than outside and keeping to her chimney corner, behind her sheltering pane of glass, until it is too late to enjoy a full communion with the secret of the evening sky. The more Dickinson held herself back from an open-air apprehension of the glories of sunset, the more brutal and threatening the meaning of this phenomenon became. At its worst – the poet's or the artist's psychic worst as well, a complete lack of the bond or "transaction" of faith – the setting of the sun was only a sign of the continued indifference of an aloof Calvinist God, a Blakean "Nobodaddy" rather than an elusive "Nobody":

The Sunset stopped on Cottages
Where Sunset hence must be
For treason not of His, but Life's,
Gone Westerly, Today –

The Sunset stopped on Cottages
Where Morning just begun –
What difference, after all, Thou mak'st
Thou supercilious Sun?   [J 950]

The treason was not nature's but that of "Life," the life of some beloved friend, which had ended abruptly, and entered the west of eternity. Dickinson's pessimism here is a rarity in her sunset poems, though it also indicates that she was less sanguine than Ruskin about the landscape's always keeping some metaphysical secret from our eyes. To Dickinson, the ghost in nature was a capricious spirit, often an outright poltergeist who jested and played with the sublime laws of romantic correspondence as a child would with its toys. The fact that this spirit might be but another manifestation of the Father also linked his machinations with the tricks and ambushes of the dread cat-god, but only obliquely, for the particular spirit of the sunset was more an androgynous god of beauty than a brutal god of wrath. This divine hermaphrodite demanded the faithfulness of the devoted artist rather than the sacrifice of the writhing souls of the damned. The feminized "juggler" that Dickinson saw in the fiery western sky was but another alternative to the grim, patriarchal deity whom she had been forced to worship out of fear as a young girl, holding no hope of election:

> Blazing in Gold and quenching in Purple
> Leaping like Leopards to the Sky
> Then at the feet of the old Horizon
> Laying her spotted Face to die
> Stooping as low as the Otter's Window
> Touching the Roof and tinting the Barn
> Kissing her Bonnet to the Meadow
> And the Juggler of Day is gone   [J 228]

Significantly, although Dickinson does employ the image of feline stealthiness and power here, the sunset's energetic spring belongs not so much to Harriet Prescott Spofford's Indian Devil as to Thoreau's unpredictable "Nature, lying all around, with such beauty, and such affection for her children, as the leopard."[8] The ambiguous genie of the sun more often appears as a masculine Phaeton or Phoebus-Apollo, but his chariot of fire as imaged in the clouds of the lower heaven is definitely feminine, often domestic:

> She sweeps with many-colored Brooms –
> And leaves the Shreds behind –
> Oh Housewife in the Evening West –
> Come back, and dust the Pond!
>
> You dropped a Purple Ravelling in –
> You dropped an Amber thread –
> And now you've littered all the East
> With Duds of Emerald!
>
> And still, she plies her spotted Brooms,
> And still the Aprons fly,
> Till Brooms fade softly into stars –
> And then I come away –   [J 219]

The sun at its most furious and secretive was a privateer who buried his treasure in the western sky. The artist, as a witness to this covert act, had then to decide her own poetic strategy before the dangerous freebooter sailed away, or discovered the presence of the hapless intruder:

I never told the buried gold
Upon the hill – that lies –
I saw the sun – his plunder done
Crouch low to guard his prize.

He stood as near
As stood you here –
A pace had been between –
Did but a snake bisect the brake
My life had forfeit been.

That was a wondrous booty –
I hope 'twas honest gained.
Those were the fairest ingots
That ever kissed the spade!

Whether to keep the secret –
Whether to reveal –
Whether as I ponder
"Kidd" will sudden sail –

Could a shrewd advise me
We might e'en divide –
Should a shrewd betray me –
Atropos decide!   [J 11]

In a letter to Master written about 1858, Dickinson lamented, "I wish that I were great, like Mr. Michael Angelo, and could paint for you," because only then could she successfully give expression to "what the lips in the West, say, when the sun goes down" (L 2:333). The problem of whether to keep the secret of the treasure of sunset or whether to reveal it was the problem of art itself. The "shrewd" in this sense is actually the reader of the poem or the viewer of the picture that attempts to depict the sunset landscape. If the finished work of art is not "true" – if it hides too much, or reveals too much – the artist is effectively dead, betrayed by a false trust in skill, and consequently the work of art, or treasure map, is a failure. If the artist succeeds, artist and patron can divide between them the spoils of the aesthetic adventure.

Like Asher B. Durand, or Turner as John Ruskin viewed him, Dickinson devised an aesthetic strategy that captured the ghost or likeness of the sunset by an imaginative fidelity to the exact conditions of what she saw before her, in the open air, aided by a long attentiveness and obedience to the ways of natural phenomena and an informed understanding of their physical processes. Each of her sunset poems was a "sketch" or "study from nature" that tried to be as faithful as possible to particular conditions of local character and color without sacrificing the imaginative quality that separated an effective composition from a mere servile imitation. Depending upon the mutability of the phenomenon, the artist sometimes produced only a quick rendering in broad, impressionistic strokes:

> A slash of Blue –
> A sweep of Gray –
> Some scarlet patches on the way,
> Compose an Evening Sky –   [J 204]

While Nature perfected her composition, the artist might be left with a few color notes. "Waste not your time, therefore, on *broad sketches* in color; such only can be useful to the mature artist, as suggestive rather than representative," Asher B. Durand warned in his third letter on landscape painting in the *Crayon* (January 31, 1855, 66); in the next he outlined the high but not impossible discipline that characterized such maturity. Long practice was necessary to see nature truly, for

> the poet sees in nature more than mere matter of fact, yet he does not see more than is there, nor what another may not see when *he* points it out. His is only a more perfect exercise of perception, just as the drapery of a fine statue is seen by the common eye, and pronounced beautiful, and the enlightened observer also pronounces it beautiful; but the one ascribes it to the graceful folding, the other to its expression of the figure beneath, but neither sees more or less in quantity than the other, but with unequal degrees of completeness, in perception. [February 14, 1855; 98]

If old masters like Michaelangelo or Raphael, who looked on nature "with childlike affection and religious reverence, ever watchful that no careless or presumptuous touch should mar its fair proportions," and so "saw through the sensuous veil" (February 14, 1855, 98), could not always capture such fleeting expressions of soul, what hope was there for the rank amateur? Yet Dickinson could attempt a full-length portrait of art's common failure to achieve the ideal, even as she cunningly displayed her own virtuoso skill with glowing pigments, dissolving views, and a panoramic canvas:

> How the old Mountains drip with Sunset
> How the Hemlocks burn –
> How the Dun Brake is draped in Cinder
> By the Wizard Sun –
>
> How the old Steeples hand the Scarlet
> Till the Ball is full –

Have I the lip of the Flamingo
That I dare to tell?

Then, how the fire ebbs like Billows –
Touching all the Grass
With a departing – sapphire – feature –
As a Duchess passed –

How a small Dusk crawls on the Village
Till the Houses blot
And the odd Flambeau, no men carry
Glimmer on the Street –

How it is Night – in Nest and Kennel –
And where was the Wood –
Just a Dome of Abyss is Bowing
Into Solitude –

These are the Visions flitted Guido –
Titian – never told –
Domenichino dropped his pencil –
Paralyzed, with Gold –   [J 291]

Thus did she both transcend and parody Durand's lament, also in
letter 4: "Where is the portrait-painter, having a just sense of his re-
sponsibilities, who has not often thrown down his brush in despair,
after many fruitless attempts to express the soul that beams through the
eye of beauty, and so with the yet more mysterious power of lofty
intellect?" (98).

II

In his article in the *Crayon,* Sylvester had urged an intense study of both
the color tones and the significance of sunset. The transition of color in
even the dullest was "exquisitely beautiful," even

the cold, wet, stormy, cloud-drifting skies of the September equi-
noctial, when the only change is that from the warm greys of
daylight to the sepulchral gloom of the lightless scud which floats
across the pale green or yellow grey sky; and, so monotonous,
there is an impressiveness in the very monotony, in the cold, joy-
less shutting down of the heavens, which, to one whose temperament admits of its right perception, or who feels it to be an emblem
of life darkened down and veiled from all the brightness of the
future, is freighted with a deeper meaning than any sky streaming
and flaming with gold and scarlet, can have. ["Sunsets," 191]

One who possessed just such a staying power and receptive temperament was Emily Dickinson, for though she may have thought that as an artist she had often failed to capture the likeness of the mutable face that was hidden in the glory of the sunset, she succeeded admirably in reproducing the changing colors, subtle or intense, of the evening sky. She noted every minute gradation of hue and tone that could be discerned in the changing veil of the atmosphere, and here again she was perfectly in accord with Ruskinian methods and Ruskin's own technique of brilliant word-painting. In volume 1 of *Modern Painters* Ruskin had written of the phenomenon of cloud color that "if you watch for the next sunset," there is "no single part or portion of the whole sky which has not in itself variety of color enough for a separate picture, and yet no single part which is like another, or which has not some peculiar source of beauty, and some peculiar arrangement of color of its own" (224–5).

Even to capture these subtleties of tone was something of a triumph, and as we have seen, Dickinson's landscape poetry was a special kind of artistic "Algebra" that dealt with the limits of the individual soul as well as with the unknowns of the earthly paradise. "Notching the Fall of the Even Sun" (J 269) was the greatest challenge of her art, and Dickinson joined both the Hudson River school painters and poet-naturalists like Higginson and Thoreau in trying to set down through a purely physical medium the spiritual resonances of sunset. Thoreau, who never tired of the drama of sunset, appropriately enough filled his own journals with lengthy descriptions of "The far Theatricals of Day." On July tenth, 1851, he wrote (using a domestic metaphor that would have appealed to Dickinson, who imagined the day as a well-furnished "Parlor" [J 304]) a typical description of this living panorama:

A gorgeous sunset after rain, with horizontal bars of clouds, red sashes to the western window, barry clouds hanging like a curtain over the window of the west, damask . . . How many times I have seen this kind of sunset – the most gorgeous sight in na-ture! . . . Now between two stupendous mountains of the low stratum under the evening red, clothed in a slightly rosaceous amber light, through a magnificent gorge, far, far away, as per-chance may occur in pictures of the Spanish coast viewed from the Mediterranean, I see a city, the eternal streets no traveller has trod, over whose pavements the horses of the sun have already hurried, some Salamanca of the imagination. But it lasts only for a moment, for now the changing light has wrought such changes in it that I see the resemblance no longer. [Journals 2:295–6]

The very evanescence and protean quality of the sunset sky made it the ultimate subject for high romantic art, which did not have the benefit of high-speed color film or split-second exposures. In January of 1852, while viewing the cloud forms and cloud colors of the evening sky, Thoreau wrote: "In the west, were flitting mother-o'-pearl clouds which change their loose-textured form and melt rapidly away, never any so fast, even while I write. Before I can complete this sentence, I look up and they are gone, like smoke or rather the steam from the engine in the winter air" (3:186). Rather than throw down her pencil, Dickinson, too, cherished the Platonic attempt to reproduce such microscopic color changes as a kind of crystalline discipline of the soul. For no matter what the ultimate chances of success, the theory of correspondences in which Ruskin, Thoreau, and Dickinson all believed assumed that the spectrum of nature and the spectrum of spirit were identical. Moreover, the landscape of the soul was as various and diverse a phenomenon as external reality, though unlike Thoreau, Dickinson felt that the final lifting of the veil would occur only after death. Therefore she prized the ungraspable as a pledge or token of the high fulfillment of her private heaven:

> The Tint I cannot take—is best—
> The Color too remote
> That I could show it in Bazaar—
> A Guinea at a sight—
>
> The fine—impalpable Array—
> That swaggers on the eye
> Like Cleopatra's Company—
> Repeated—in the sky—
>
> The Moments of Dominion
> That happen on the Soul
> And leave with a Discontent
> Too exquisite—to tell—
>
> The eager look—on Landscapes—
> As if they just repressed
> Some Secret—that was pushing
> Like Chariots—in the Vest—
>
> The Pleading of the Summer—
> That other Prank—of Snow—
> That Cushions Mystery with Tulle,
> For fear the Squirrels—know.
>
> Their Graspless manners—mock us—
> Until the Cheated Eye
> Shuts arrogantly—in the Grave—
> Another way—to see—   [J 627]

All of the aspects of nineteenth-century landscape painting that we have discussed surface in this poem, but cast into Dickinson's particular local terms and metaphors. Her duty as a landscapist is to capture the "likeness" of the sunset, to try her best to express those ineffable tints and contours that compose the evening sky at any given moment. Like Durand and Ruskin, Dickinson believes that nature is haunted or sentient, for at the setting of the sun the landscape seems to wear an "eager look" and hint at some impartation of a superior wisdom beyond that of a mundanely material or merely physical sort. The veil of the deity or creative spirit is now as close as it can come to the earthly realm of the human, as the sun rests its mighty force on the horizon line itself. Yet the very impalpable quality of this golden hieroglyph is enhanced by its untranslatable quality; the best the artist can do is to transfer the secret to another medium, the medium of art. Thus the secret is both screened and revealed anew in the successful work of art, as Dickinson follows out in practice Shelley's definition of poetry as the replacement of one veil with another.

To be truly "faithful" to the mystery of the landscape the artist must "express" it rather than solve it, and here all of Dickinson's conservative attitudes toward nature as an inviolable holy of holies prevail, along with all the strictures on a profane "lifting of the veil" that we have already explored. Veil enhances veil, and the medium of words or paint, if it is really true to nature, like a fall of new snow cushions the mystery with a "Tulle" or poetic gauze rather than laying it bare for profane and probing vegetative eyes. True "seeing" – authentic clair-voyance – will be achieved only after death, as Dickinson's submerged but familiar reference to 1 Cor. 2:9 ("Eye hath not seen, nor ear heard, neither have entered into the heart of man, the things which God hath prepared for them that love him") indicates. Here the cloudy rather than the cloudless mysteries abide. Even in heaven there will remain those veils which cannot be removed, lest the beholder be dazzled by a destroying "Excessive Bright." The sunset, then, is a curious amalgam of triumph and defeat, an experience that robs as much as it bestows. One cannot *tell* it, one can only reproduce its features as faithfully and as humbly as possible, hoping that the effect, character, or likeness of the hidden spirit will be evoked by corresponding poem or painting:

> If this is "fading"
> Oh let me immediately "fade"!
> If this is "dying"
> Bury me, in such a shroud of red!
> If this is "sleep,"
> On such a night

> How proud to shut the eye!
> Good Evening, gentle Fellow men!
> *Peacock* presumes to die! [J 120]

Dickinson's romantic strategy of physiognomy required that an artist be faithful to the real as a means of glimpsing the ideal – the ghost in the haunted house of nature – so that spirit could be in turn represented by an expressive, "haunted" art. Hence the Pre-Raphaelite quality of so many of her sunset poems, matched by Thoreau's increasingly precise attention to the coloristic fact of atmospheric change. A journal entry dated July twenty-third, 1852, describing a sunset that seems like "a splendid map, where the fancy can trace islands, continents, and cities beyond compare" (4:249), is in fact a lengthy and detailed word-painting in which Thoreau uses the sharp palette knife of pure scientific observation rather than the flexible tubes and bladders of Transcendental empathy. Yet the American Thoreau remains just as "poetic" as the English Turner in so answering John Ruskin's magisterial taunt in the chapter of *Modern Painters* he entitled "Of the Open Sky": "Who saw the dance of the dead clouds when the sunlight left them last night, and the west wind blew them before it like withered leaves?" (1:205). Thoreau's minute attentiveness and obedience to exact time and exact hue satisfied not only a Ruskinian truth to nature but also accepted Hudson River practice as enunciated by Asher B. Durand, who in his eighth letter on landscape painting asked with equal rhetorical extravagance, "Who has ever seen the glowing sun-light or transparent silvery atmosphere too servilely imitated?" (March 21, 1855, 355).

Here Durand praised sunset clouds as containing "every intermediate gradation and contrast within the range of human perception" (355). Hence Dickinson's attempt to fix in words the almost imperceptible fading of tone into tone:

> Of Yellow was the outer Sky
> In Yellower Yellow hewn
> Till Saffron in Vermillion slid
> Whose seam could not be shewn – [J 1676]

The genius of the artist who succeeded at this Herculean task was equally indefinable:

> These held their Wick above the West –
> Till when the Red declined –
> Or how the Amber aided it –
> Defied to be defined –
>
> Then waned without disparagement
> In a dissembling Hue

That would not let the Eye decide
Did it abide or no – [J 1390]

The sunset was an ultimate blending of opposites. To romantics like Dickinson and Wordsworth, it imparted (as the latter wrote in "Tintern Abbey") "a sense sublime / Of something far more deeply interfused / Whose dwelling is the light of setting suns" (*Works,* 104), but to orthodox believers such metamorphic transitions of color and cloud were merely emblems of the passage from earth to heaven.[9] This view is nicely illustrated by an anonymous poem entitled "The Golden Sunset," included on page 16 of Mary Warner's scrapbook, which itself mixes the reflective calm of a well-known American luminist landscape like Fitz Hugh Lane's *Brace's Rock* with the obligatory piety of the sentimental vision:

The golden sea its mirror spreads
   Beneath the golden skies,
And but a narrow strip between
   Of land and shadow lies.

The cloud-like rocks, the rock-like clouds,
   Dissolved in glory float,
And, midway of the radiant flood,
   Hangs silently the boat.

The sea is but another sky,
   The sky a sea as well,
And which the earth, and which the heavens
   The eye can scarcely tell.

So when for us life's evening hour
   Soft fading shall descend,
May glory, born of earth and heaven,
   The earth and heavens blend;

Flooded with peace the spirits float,
   With silent rapture glow,
Till where earth ends and heaven begins,
   The soul shall scarcely know.

Because of the ambiguity of her transforming passion for Phoebus, the sunset for Dickinson means war as well as peace, and to capture its ghost in word-painting entails both a crown of triumph and a crown of thorns. The sunset and its governing spirits tempt and tantalize the artist by trailing their gorgeous veils in the dust, yet the artist takes her psychic life in her hands if she dares to clutch at them. This dangerous "glory" is strengthened by a romantic typology that makes the sunset into a crucifixion, a deposition, and an entombment. The sunset is a magnificent outpouring of the lifeblood of the Redeemer, a descent into darkness that symbolizes all manner of halfway states between death and resurrection, living faith and holy dying, triumph and tragedy. Sunset is both God's betrayal of his own golden son and the fulfillment of the Father's promise of redemption; it is the equivocal "crowning glory" of a martyr who, nailed to a cross that sardonically proclaims that he is an earthly monarch, is actually king of a spiritual realm beyond all earthly sight. Similarly, the dawn is a type of the Resurrection, of the rolling away of the great stone from the tomb of the night. Sometimes, in her faithfulness to the daily passion of Christ-Phoebus, Dickinson is one of the few witnesses at both these mighty events that blend sacred history with natural history:

> The Sun went down – no Man looked on –
> The Earth and I, alone,
> Were present at the Majesty –
> He triumphed, and went on –
>
> The Sun went up – no Man looked on –
> The Earth and I and One
> A nameless Bird – a Stranger
> Were Witness for the Crown –   [J 1079]

Because she is such a steadfast disciple, and because she has established a truly consanguineous relationship with the martyrdom of nature's lord and master, the sun, Dickinson is also able to share in the gaudy glories of his divine passion as well as in his wrenching pain and despair:

> The Day that I was crowned
> Was like the other Days –
> Until the Coronation came –
> And then – 'twas Otherwise –
>
> As Carbon in the Coal
> And Carbon in the Gem
> Are One – and yet the former
> Were dull for Diadem –
>
> I rose, and all was plain –
> But when the Day declined
> Myself and It, in Majesty
> Were equally – adorned –

> The Grace that I – was chose –
> To Me – surpassed the Crown
> That was the Witness for the Grace –
> 'Twas even that 'twas Mine –   [J 356]

Dickinson well knew that to create a diamond from a coal required tremendous heat and pressure, a literal crucifixion of the substance, and that such a brilliant "Majesty" was as painful as it was ultimately irrelevant. To possess the grace, or be possessed by it, was enough, and no exterior signs or symbols, no glittering gems or diamond tiaras, were needed. Only those who were fully intimate with nature could understand the passion of the sun as a participatory ritual rather than a mere meteorological conflict of color and cloud:

> There's the Battle of Burgoyne –
> Over, every Day,
> By the Time that Man and Beast
> Put their work away
> "Sunset" sounds majestic –
> But that solemn War
> Could you comprehend it
> You would chastened stare –   [J 1174]

Dickinson's empathy with the slow death of the martyred sun could, depending upon mood, achieve as well a Claudian calm and repose:

> Look back on Time, with kindly eyes –
> He doubtless did his best –
> How softly sinks that trembling sun
> In Human Nature's West –   [J 1478]

Sunset for Emily Dickinson was not a profane event but a sacred experience. When the sun was masculine and Christ-like, the day itself became the sun's mother, a Mary who stood as a sometimes agonized, sometimes ecstatic witness of her child's birth, death, entombment, and resurrection. The sun moved through the sky in a royal progress that was reminiscent of Christ's ministry on earth, making of twenty-four ordinary units of time a sacred book of hours that I have already called the mystic day. It is this sense of the sun's regulation of time, nature, emotion, and art that effectively unites folk, popular, and elite levels, making Dickinson's poetry a complete yet unique expression of her rich American Victorian culture.

III

Rebecca Patterson has delineated the broad outlines of this aspect of Emily Dickinson's private mythology in her chapter of *Emily Dickinson's Imagery* entitled "The Cardinal Points." "In brief," she writes, Dickinson

> associates each quarter of the compass with its traditional time of day and season of the year, assigns it a color, or colors, and usually an element, and equips it with a certain range of emotional significance; she has also two symbolic movements of the sun corresponding to her North-South and East-West divisions. On this double axis she has suspended literally hundreds of poems, many of them interlocking with scores of other symbol clusters, and the whole producing a notable economy of allusion and effect within a tightly organized corpus. Indeed, it is not too much to say that by means of these interconnected symbol clusters she has effectually organized her emotions and experience and unified the poetry of her major period, making of it a more respectable body of work than the faulty and too often trivial fragments in which it is customarily presented. [181]

This symbolism is not unique to the Amherst poet, for in many respects it is similar to the fourfold universe of William Blake's prophetic books, especially *The Four Zoas,* a cosmology most fully expressed in his sacred city of art, Golgonooza. As S. Foster Damon has written, Blake's conception is "psychological, not Ptolemaic or Copernican," and the same thing can be said of Dickinson's mystic day, which also deals with emotional time, inner space, and seasons of the soul.[10] There was a stimulus for the development of such an elaborate map of consciousness in Emerson's suggestion in "Nature" that "the dawn is my Assyria; the sunset and moonrise my Paphos, and unimaginable realms of faerie; broad noon shall be my England of the senses and the understanding; the night shall be my Germany of mystic philosophy and dreams" (*Works* 1:17). But to use Patterson's phrase, Dickinson was a "naive symbolist" who based her myths on felt experience rather than on ready-made constructs.[11] Whereas Patterson stresses the spatial aspects of this myth, "The Cardinal Points," I am here more concerned with its temporal dimension, the mystic day that compressed "Eternity in an hour" (see Appendix C, "The mystic day").

Like most romantics, Dickinson was obsessed with the idea of time. As Georges Poulet writes, "All her spiritual life and all her poetry are comprehended only in the determination given them by two initial moments, one of which is contradicted by the other, a moment in which one possesses eternity and a moment when one loses it" (*Human Time,* 346). The mystic day was a means of solving this dilemma by merging these two moments and collapsing time into eternity, though such a method of necessity brought with it infinite agony or infinite ecstacy, depending on one's placement in the houses of her transcendent zodiac. For the day, like Dickinson's bed, had four corners with four guardian angels or evangels: sunrise, noon, sunset, and midnight. It began with the east as Mecca and ended with the west as Golgotha; noon was the equivocal midpoint and high tide of light; midnight its eerie, equally magical doppelgänger, or twin of darkness. Noon was a realm of luminous white magic and midnight a domain of sinister black magic, a true "witching hour." Since Dickinson collapsed time into a sundial rather than into a clock, each specific time of day was haunted by its own particular holy ghost. Similarly, sunrise stood for the promise of spring; noon for the fulfillment of summer; sunset for the reluctant, bittersweet harvest time of autumn; and night for the long keeping time of winter. The latter season could be either cold and despairing or warm and hopeful, depending upon one's psychic placement inside or outside the magic circle of faith. Night was finally the ultimate mystery, the mystery of eternity, even more veiled than the public execution of sunset, which remained an experience open to participation or "witness" by the living. Eternity, however, was experienced only through death, and so night was Christ's season in hell, just as morning was his youth, and noon his manhood.

The allegorical imagination that inspired Thomas Cole surely did not die with him, for the spirit of such series as *The Course of Empire* (1836) and *The Voyage of Life* (1840) lived on in the very personal and much more elaborate correspondences that Dickinson made of her passion of the mystic day. The secret of sunset could, depending upon what followed it, be either apocalyptic or millennial, either a complete denial or a glorious confirmation of the suffering that had gone before. If dawn followed, as the mythology of the day assured the believer it would, then resurrection and redemption were secure: if it did not, there was only the eternal abyss and limbo of those who mourned without hope. This is why Dickinson studied the death of the sun with as much intensity as she brought to the scanning of the dying faces of her friends, relatives, and loved ones: Was there some sign, some ghost behind the veil of this phenomenon that could indicate to her with any finality the ultimate destiny of the immortal soul? As a passionate observer, Dickinson is preternaturally attuned to any hint of meaning in the landscape, and she is especially wary of the slightest indication of treachery or betrayal in the two solstices (noon, midnight) and the two equinoxes (sunrise, sunset) that compose the mystic day. The sun is a Keats for her, flushed with creative fever in a frenzy before he dies; day is the faithful Severn who holds the dying poet in his arms. But when the sun is Christ and day is the Mater Dolorosa, the sunset becomes not only romance but ritual.

Dickinson attempts to understand this ritual by coming to terms with the sumptuous, transient, and tantalizing language of color and cloud forms in which it is clothed, just as the priest changes the color of his vestments in accord with the rubric of the liturgical year. The likeness of the sunset, the ghost or spirit that presides over this private mass, is an intensely meaningful but ultimately unknowable combination of that hope and fear which, as Blake had affirmed, were the components of absolute vision:

> Fairer through Fading – as the Day
> Into the Darkness dips away –
> Half Her Complexion of the Sun –
> Hindering – Haunting – Perishing –
>
> Rallies Her Glow, like a dying Friend –
> Teazing with glittering Amend –
> Only to aggravate the Dark
> Through an expiring – perfect – look –   [J 938]

The strategy of physiognomy is once again not to allow the emotion of reading the face of nature to overwhelm the artist; rather, it is to discipline perception by the intellect and transfer the visionary to the more controlled medium of art. Dickinson's sunset poems and indeed her landscape poetry in general are attempts to render the experience of an experience, filtered through the creative and selective imagination of the engaged artist. This artist could never really compete with the creative spirit, deity, or Holy Ghost who continually formed, informed, and unformed the physical lineaments of the landscape, but she could make that spirit more immediate and tangible by capturing its "likeness" in a portrait study from nature. Ruskin had affirmed that "the cloud, or firmament . . . signifies the ministration of the heavens to man" (*MP* 5:322), and as Barbara Novak writes of Hudson River aesthetics, "The rapid changes of light at such times were faithfully observed and recorded, then placed at the service of a devotional idea – the sky itself as the vessel of spirit" (*Nature and Culture,* 98).

The rapidity and transience of the phenomenon of sunset required that the artist capture its essence as well as merely contemplate it, that he utilize, to employ Coleridge's terms, both fancy and imagination. Sometimes the changes took place so fast that only fancy could be called upon, leaving the lingering glow of recollection in tranquillity to gather about half-finished images. Therefore, in his description of the sunset of July twenty-third, 1852, Thoreau likened the sky to "a splendid map, where the fancy can trace islands, continents, and cities beyond compare" (*Journals* 4:249) whereas in that of July tenth, 1851, he glimpsed a "Salamanca of the imagination" (2:296). The sunset sky could variously be compared to a mountain range, a cityscape, a battle, an ocean, or a fleet of Spanish galleons, depending upon the depth and range of the artist's fancy. Indeed, such instant imagism was the only means by which a poet-naturalist deprived of palette and brush could fix in words the fleeting subject of his study. Yet as Gerald Wilkinson has noted about Turner's early sketches, especially of sunset, a single line can recall an entire moment of vision,[12] and we have Thoreau's own testimony of December tenth, 1856, that

> It is remarkable how suggestive the slightest drawing as a memento of things seen. For a few years past I have been accustomed to make a rude sketch in my journal of plants, ice and various natural phenomena, and though the fullest accompanying description may fail to recall my experience, these rude outline drawings do not fail to carry me back to that time and scene. It is as if I saw the same thing again, and I may again attempt to describe it in words if I choose.[13]

Dickinson's penchant for "rude outline drawings" in her poems dealing with the volatile shapes of clouds recalls the portfolio tradition and its pictorial roots. Again, Dickinson domesticates this kind of vapory shorthand in ways that make Hamlet's camels, weasels, and whales seem pedestrian. In an unfinished sunset poem of about 1884, she uses a startling image that translates Phaeton's chariot into a folk metaphor drawn from the contemporary paraphernalia of teamsters and wagoners:

> The Sun in reining to the West
> Makes not as much of sound
> As Cart of man in road below
> Adroitly turning round
> That Whiffletree of Amethyst   [J 1636]

An undated sketch combines the deer park and the linen closet, and may owe something to the Currier and Ives view of Windsor Castle that hung in her bedroom:

> A curious Cloud surprised the Sky,
> 'Twas like a sheet with Horns;
> The sheet was Blue –

The Antlers Gray –
It almost touched the Lawns.

So low it leaned – then statelier drew –
And trailed like robes away;
A Queen adown a satin aisle,
Had not the majesty.   [J 1710]

And an apocalyptic vision of about 1877 centers on the deadly flower so
favored by Pre-Raphaelites like Dante Gabriel Rosetti:

It was a quiet seeming Day –
There was no harm in earth or sky –
Till with the setting sun
There strayed an accidental Red
A Strolling Hue, one would have said
To westward of the Town –

But when the Earth began to jar
And Houses vanished with a roar
And Human Nature hid
We comprehended by the Awe
As those that Dissolution saw
The Poppy in the Cloud   [J 1419]

Like Ruskin in her cloud worship, Dickinson realized that it was the
artist's chief duty to capture the fleeting image of such divine ministers
and messengers. She had only herself to blame if she did not jot down
the outline of these majestic phenomena:

A Cloud withdrew from the Sky
Superior Glory be
But that Cloud and it's Auxiliaries
Are forever lost to me

Had I but further scanned
Had I secured the Glow
In an Hermetic Memory
It had availed me now.

Never to pass the Angel
With a glance and a Bow
Till I am firm in Heaven
Is my intention now.   [J 895]

An early poem compares retreating storm clouds to "listless Ele-
phants" straggling down "Horizons" (J 194), but Dickinson's genius in
using this device of fanciful imagism to secure a "Hermetic Memory"

of the sunset can best be gauged if we recall the painting *Sunset with Cows* (1857) by the noted Hudson River artist John F. Kensett, owned by Susan Dickinson (see the illustration at the beginning of this chapter). This highly but subtly colored work is far different from the barren coast scenes and pungent seascapes that would make Kensett one of the most popular artists of the 1860s and 1870s, allying him to the stripped-down gestalt of American luminism. As John K. Howat comments about a similar view, *The Genesee River* of 1871, "The subject matter—cows in a river with elms—was a staple of painters of the period" (*Kensett,* fig. 44), and though it is obviously based on Dutch models, *Sunset with Cows* still conveys the pastoral calm and soft aerial benediction that were characteristic of the best early Hudson River school manner. In a poem written about 1862, Dickinson boldly applies the convention to the sky itself and transfers Kensett's cows momentarily to the realm of cloud, as natural art surpasses human artifice:

> They called me to the Window, for
> " 'Twas Sunset"—Some one said—
> I only saw a Sapphire Farm—
> And just a Single Herd—
>
> Of Opal Cattle—feeding far
> Upon so vain a Hill—
> As even while I looked—dissolved—
> Nor Cattle were—nor Soil—
>
> But in their stead—a Sea—displayed—
> And Ships—of such a size
> As Crew of Mountains—could afford—
> And Decks—to seat the skies—
>
> This—too—the Showman rubbed away—
> And when I looked again—
> Nor Farm—nor Opal Herd—was there—
> Nor Mediterranean—   [J 628]

Both early and late in her career, the sea is a favorite image for roughing in the outline of the evening sky, just as Thoreau sees in sunset a Mediterranean coast scene, and the anonymous author of "The Golden Sunset" claims that "The sea is but another sky / The sky a sea as well." In a sketch that Johnson dates about 1861, Dickinson captures a fantastic display of color with an equally fantastic mixture of her own human ultramarine and floral chrome yellow:

> Where Ships of Purple—gently toss—
> On Seas of Daffodil—

> Fantastic Sailors – Mingle –
> And then – the Wharf is still! [J 265]

A more finished composition follows, which succeeds through oriental floats and tints of watercolor rather than the thick impasto of oils:

> This – is the land – the Sunset washes –
> These – are the Banks of the Yellow Sea –
> Where it rose – or whither it rushes –
> These – are the Western Mystery!
>
> Night after Night
> Her purple traffic
> Strews the landing with Opal bales –
> Merchantmen – poise upon Horizons –
> Dip – and Vanish like Orioles! [J 266]

The meaning of the mysterious cargo delivered by sunset's busy commerce became evident only after Dickinson had transformed her secret passion for Phoebus into a sacramental passion for nature and buttressed it with her private mythology of the mystic day. A sketch written about 1884 employs the familiar marine imagery, but now connects it with a redemptive vision that anticipates the ambiguous dynamics of the execution scene in Melville's *Billy Budd:*

> A Sloop of Amber slips away
> Upon an Ether Sea,
> And wrecks in Peace a Purple Tar,
> The Son of Ecstacy – [J 1622]

Yet Dickinson's technique here is also far more hard-edged than her earlier sweeps and splashes of pigment, a reminder that the poem is contemporary with the symbolist movement,[14] and the decadence of color and even of sentiment almost matches Mallarmé's:

> . . . des galères d'or, belles comme des cygnes,
> Sur un fleuve de pourpre de parfums dormir
> En berçant l'éclair fauve et riche de leurs lignes
> Dans un grand nonchaloir chargé de souvenir![15]

Mallarmé, too, made the connection between autumn and sunset that Dickinson had devised as part of her morphology of the mystic day, in which the seasons of an entire year were collapsed into twenty-four hours, as the hope of an entire life could be coiled into the compass of a single moment. To the French poet, however, the sunset harbored only the sure promise of destruction and the womblike ignorance of the Dark Ages. Not for him was the fragile hope of future ecstasies that was so much a part of Dickinson's experience of the linked analogies between the death of the year and the death of the sun. Yet Mallarmé's reverie in his "Plainte d'automne" defines a major dimension of the sunset's meaning for Dickinson, especially when he admits that his favorite season is "the last languid days of summer that immediately precede autumn" and his favorite hour is "when the sun rests before disappearing, with beams of yellow copper on the grey walls and of red copper on the window panes." He adds that "in the same way, the literature, from which my spirit asks pleasure, will be the dying poetry of the last instants of Rome, as long as it does not, however, breathe in any way the rejuvenating approach of the barbarians or stammer the childish Latin of the first Christian proses" (*Mallarmé*, 119–20).

Dickinson's sun, in spite of his awesome splendor, was not only the dying Apollo but the crucified Christ. Even so, she expressed a preference for decline and fall that was very much of her time:

> I'd rather recollect a setting
> Than own a rising sun
> Though one is beautiful forgetting –
> And true the other one.
>
> Because in going is a Drama
> Staying cannot confer
> To die divinely once a Twilight –
> Than wane is easier –   [J 1349]

Of Turner, Ruskin had written in *Modern Painters:* "His own favorite light is not Æglé, but Hesperid Æglé. Fading of the last rays of the sunset. Faint breathing of the sorrow of night" (5:332). Ruskin attributes Turner's obsession with these dying shades in part to historical context; his youth was blasted by the rise of Napoleon, which produced a European holocaust "that turned sunsets into blood" (5:296). Like Turner's burning skies, the colors of the most significant Dickinson sunset poems are not the pale pastels of the decadence but the rich, sacrificial blood reds of battle and Victorian magentas of martyrdom. Here we should pause to remember that magenta was a new color in the nineteenth century, derived from a coal-tar dye, "discovered in the year of the battle of *Magenta* (1859), and named for its bloodiness."[16] Furthermore, in his history *Painting in America,* E. P. Richardson writes that because of the discovery of these new chemical colors,

> After 1856 a series of sharp new reds and purples flared upon the artist's palette. Mauve was quickly followed by magenta and cobalt violet (1859) and cobalt yellow (about 1861). In the next few

years most of the ancient mineral colors and practically all the organic colors gave way to new synthetic products. Some of these proved to be fugitive and quickly faded, others blackened in chemical combinations with other pigments, but all were new, brilliant, and irresistibly tempting to the artist's eye.[17]

The discovery of the coal-tar dyes paralleled the extravagant word-painting and photoeroticism of the Azarian school, and though in her poetic vocabulary the conservative Dickinson remained faithful to the tried and true, unfading organic pigments – tyrian (from shellfish), brazil (from a South American wood), cochineal (from insects) – we have already seen her lavish use of the literary equivalent of cobalt yellow and violet in her sunset poems. The explosion of synthetic color during the 1860s meant that atmospheric effects impossible even for Turner could now be captured on canvas; among the results were such hot cadmium extravaganzas as Frederic Church's famous *Twilight in the Wilderness* of 1860. In 1864 James Jackson Jarves complained bitterly that "we are undergoing a virulent epidemic of sunsets," and in his devastating 1865 *North American Review* attack on Spofford's *Azarian,* Henry James condemned "these clever conceits, this keen eye for the superficial picturesque, this inborn love of bric-à-brac and sunsets." Yet both James and Jarves failed to acknowledge that the pyrotechnic display of red employed by Spofford, Church, and Dickinson was but a natural outgrowth of John Ruskin's sermon on the romantic typology of this central color. In the final volume of *Modern Painters,* Ruskin instructed his readers that "the peculiar innovation of Turner was the perfection of the color chord by means of *scarlet,*" for "other painters had rendered the golden tones, and the blue tones, of sky; Titian, especially, the last, in perfectness. But none had dared to paint, none seem to have seen, the scarlet and purple" (5:317). In his subsequent discussion of Turner's momentous discovery of "the scarlet *shadow*" of cloud forms, Ruskin also touched upon the typological meaning inherent in Turner's – and also Church's and Dickinson's – repeated pursuit of the extremes of such colors: "Now, this scarlet color," Ruskin expounded

> – or pure red, intensified by expression of light, – is, of all the three primitive colors, that which is most distinctive. Yellow is of the nature of simple light; blue, connected with simple shade; but red is entirely an abstract color. It is red to which the color-blind are blind, as if to show us that it was not necessary merely for the service or comfort of man, but that there was a special gift or teaching in this color. Observe, further, that it is this color which the sunbeams take in passing through the *earth's atmosphere*. The

rose of dawn and sunset is the hue of rays passing close over the earth. It is also concentrated in the blood of man. [316–17]

Time and space prevented Ruskin from fully following out, by citing biblical chapter and verse, "the mystical connection between life and love, set forth in that Hebrew system of sacrificial religion to which we may trace most of the received ideas respecting sanctity, consecration, and purification." He could only suggest that "scarlet, used with the hyssop, in the Levitical law, is the great sanctifying element of visible beauty inseparably connected with purity and life," and he admonished that if his readers examined earnestly "the original sources from which our heedless popular language regarding the washing away of sins has been borrowed," they would find that the bloody "fountain in which sins are indeed to be washed away, is that of love, not of agony" (5:317–22). In her chapter entitled "Emily Dickinson's Palette," Rebecca Patterson reminds us that "the most striking characteristic of the poet's color system [is] this very insistence upon red and the different shades, including purple, that she sometimes identified with blood" (*Emily Dickinson's Imagery,* 114). For Ruskin, "the very sign in heaven itself which, truly understood, is the type of love, was to Turner the type of death. The scarlet of the clouds was his symbol of destruction. In his mind it was the color of blood" (*MP* 5:336). To Dickinson, the red of the sunset was just such an ambiguous, inextricable commingling of love and death, triumph and defeat, exhilaration and abasement. Since the life of the landscape and the life of the artist were, at the highest moments, consanguineous, the sunset was a shared sacrifice or fading away of the lifeblood, a ritual drama that combined in its primal scarlet the elements of sanctification, consecration, purification, and atonement:

> Whole Gulfs – of Red, and Fleets – of Red –
> And Crews – of solid Blood –
> Did place about the West – Tonight –
> As 'twere specific Ground –
>
> And They – appointed Creatures –
> In Authorized Arrays –
> Due – promptly – as a Drama –
> That bows – and disappears –   [J 658]

The season of autumn, the dying time of the year, was marked by a similar explosion of sacrificial crimson:

> The name – of it – is "Autumn" –
> The hue – of it – is Blood –

An Artery – upon the Hill –
A vein – along the Road –

Great Globules – in the Alleys –
And Oh, the Shower of Stain –
When Winds – upset the Basin –
And spill the Scarlet Rain –

It sprinkles Bonnets – far below –
It gathers ruddy Pools –
Then – eddies like a Rose – away –
Upon Vermillion Wheels –   [J 656]

Emily Dickinson's palette, if not her specific subject or interpretation, was Turneresque and Ruskinian, though her depiction of the gory
brilliance of a New England fall reminds us that some autumnal Hudson River landscapes, when first exhibited in England, drew the criticism that there was far too much of a gaudy redness in the foliage. But
the artist in fact was only being faithful to the peculiar local color of his
native land. Jasper Cropsey, a noted member of the school, whose
massive *Sunset on the Hudson* combined a blazing sky with what Flexner
calls a "cacophonous use of autumn color" (*That Wilder Image,* 275),
even had a bunch of American leaves sent across the waters to validate
the accuracy of his palette. It was also natural to see in the slaughter of
the sun a landscape of "solemn War," a "Battle of Burgoyne." T. W.
Higginson fleshed out this imagery in a late ghost story he called "The
Haunted Window":

Returning . . . by the stage-coach, we drove from Tiverton, the
whole length of the island, under one of those wild and wonderful
skies which give, better than anything in nature, the effect of a
field of battle. The heavens were filled with ten thousand separate
masses of cloud, varying in shade from palest gray to iron-black,
borne rapidly to and fro by upper and lower currents of opposing
wind. They seemed to be charging, retreating, breaking, recom-
bining, with puffs of what seemed smoke, and a few wan sun-
beams sometimes striking through for fire. Wherever the eye
turned, there appeared some flying fragment not seen before; and
yet in an hour this noiseless Antietam grew still, and a settled
leaden film overspread the sky, yielding only to some level lines
of light where the sun went down.[18]

John Ruskin's word-painting was contagious, though Higginson
chose to do his sunset in luminist tonalities of black and gray rather
than employ the magentas of martyrdom so beloved by Dickinson. To

Ruskin's "primitive" triumvirate of yellow, blue, and red, however, Dickinson (because of the special fourfold structure of the mystic day) added a pure white or neutral tone, thereby linking her private mythology to Herman Melville's "colorless, all-color of atheism" as expressed by Ishmael in his terror-filled chapter "The Whiteness of the Whale." In doing so, she gave a final and unique turn of the screw to her appropriation of this common romantic symbolism, but not before stuggling with the problems of scientific classification of the sublime that also inform the grand "anatomy" that is *Moby-Dick*.

IV

Dickinson's unique "black light" stood for the dark night of the soul that followed the detonation of sunset or preceded the rosy flush of dawn. Night was necessarily black, yet because it could harbor hope and faith as well as doubt and despair, it became either the sum of all colors or the complete negation of them:

> The Red – Blaze – is the Morning –
> The Violet – is Noon –
> The Yellow – Day – is falling –
> And after that – is none –
>
> But Miles of Sparks – at Evening –
> Reveal the Width that burned –
> The Territory Argent – that
> Never yet – consumed –   [J 469]

The "color" of night – of imprisonment, of New England, of Winter – was the heraldic hue of "Argent," a silver or snow-white field upon which any meaningful figure could be emblazoned by whatever recording angels still existed in this dour realm. Yet Dickinson sought most in her sunset poetry to express not the polarities of her mythology but rather their compromise, the mystery of their organicism. The sunset was ultimately not to be analyzed, only "arrested" or apprehended, and then presented in the veiled medium of words or paint. In perhaps the most inclusive of her sunset poems, Emily Dickinson expressed her conviction that the ghost or spirit that presided over the death of the day demanded the exercise of the imagination as well as the fancy. In this case the color of reverie or recollection in tranquillity became an equally inseparable mixture of blue tinged with red and silver, a "firmamental" lilac or crowning "royal purple":

> The Lilac is an ancient shrub
> But ancienter than that

The Firmamental Lilac
Upon the Hill tonight –
The Sun subsiding on his Course
Bequeaths this final Plant
To Contemplation – not to Touch –
The Flower of Occident.
Of one Corolla is the West –
The Calyx is the Earth –
The capsules burnished Seeds the Stars
The Scientist of Faith
His research has but just begun –
Above his synthesis
The Flora unimpeachable
To Time's Analysis –
"Eye hath not seen" may possibly
Be current with the Blind
But let not Revelation
By theses be detained –   [J 1241]

This poem is a remarkable example of that close botanical, meteorological, or geological attention to detail linking together the three related nineteenth-century modes of thought that I have already touched
on: the writings of the American poet-naturalists, the paintings of the
Hudson River school, and the aesthetics of John Ruskin. To Dickinson,
the great amateur of sunsets, what is seen hovering upon the western
hills is imaged (and preserved) as an immense floral specimen, a blossom related to that most persistent and characteristic of New England
exotics, the lilac. The crucifixion that is implicit in the romantic typology of sunset is here subsumed by Dickinson's study of the overwhelming, passional color of the scene. To analyze this phenomenon,
in fact, would itself be a kind of crucifixion of her subject by the
devoted artist, who can only admire and try her skill in her chosen
medium of poetic reproduction. As Emerson wrote in "Nature" of a
similar visionary moment, "The beauty that shimmers in the yellow
afternoons of October, who ever could clutch it? Go forth to find it and
it is gone; 't is only a mirage as you look from the windows of diligence" (Works 1:19). Dickinson's "windows of diligence," like those of
Durand, Thoreau, Turner, and Ruskin, are the materials of her art,
mastered by a long training and intimacy with nature. She uses the
highly technical botanical terms of "Corolla" and "Calyx" in order to
express as precisely as possible the fanciful image that first presents
itself to her. In painting with words the bursting bloom of the sunset,
she may capture as well its presiding "ghost," and some of the meaning

of its hidden secret or prophecy. Where in his description of the January sunset in "Nature" Emerson had noted with Pre-Raphaelite accuracy the "stars of the dead calices of flowers" around him, touched by flame and frost (*Works* 1:18), Dickinson transfers this image to the firmament itself, elaborating, multiplying, and cosmicizing it.

The danger once again is so concentrated an intellectual approach that the butterfly may be crushed in the hands of the student, or the flower crumbled when it is plucked for the collecting box. Here the discipline that Ruskin speaks of in his Preface to the second edition of *Modern Painters,* volume 1, comes into play: the difference between the botanist's knowledge of plant life and that of the great poet or painter is that

> the one counts the stamens, and affixes a name, and is content; the other observes every character of the plant's color and form; considering each of its attributes as an element of expression, he seizes on its lines of grace or energy, rigidity or repose; notes the feebleness or the vigor, the serenity or tremulousness of its hues; observes its local habits, its love or fear of peculiar places, its nourishment or destruction by particular influences; he associates it in his mind with all the features of the situations it inhabits, and the ministering agencies necessary to its support. Thenceforward the flower is to him a living creature, with histories written on its leaves, and passions breathing in its motion (*MP* 1:xxxv–xxxvi).

Even the conservative Charles Wadsworth, in his sermon entitled "Songs in the Night," thundered that the age was "an era of cold, material, skeptical philosophy. We have quenched the fire in the bush, that we may achieve its botany; and we have classified the star of Bethlehem with the meteors, because of our astronomy; and would walk Zionward rather lighted by Gideon's lamps of conflict than cheered by David's harp of victory" (*Sermons,* 45). Emerson also condemned this skeptical approach to pure natural history when he wrote in his essay "Beauty" in *The Conduct of Life* that

> the bird is not in its ounces and inches, but in its relations to nature; and the skin and skeleton you show men is not more a heron than a heap of ashes or a bottle of gases into which his body has been reduced, is Dante or Washington. The naturalist is led *from* the road by the whole distance of his fancied advance. The boy had juster views when he gazed at the shells on the beach or the flowers in the meadow, unable to call them by their names, than the man in the pride of his nomenclature . . . Chemistry takes to pieces, but it does not construct. Alchemy, which sought

to transmute one element into another, to prolong life, to arm
with power, – that was in the right direction. [*Works* 6:281–2]

Echoing both Ruskin and Wadsworth in " 'Arcturus' is his other
name – " (J 70), Dickinson also encapsulated Emerson's sentiment in
appropriately chemical or alchemical terms when she wrote:

> Banish Air from Air –
> Divide Light if you dare –
> They'll meet
> Whiles Cubes in a Drop
> Or Pellets of Shape
> Fit.
> Films cannot annul
> Odors return whole
> Force Flame
> And with a Blonde push
> Over your impotence
> Flits Steam.   [J 854]

The profane scientist who cast nature into a crucible and attempted to
force its secrets by the fire of intellect alone would soon find that he
was impotent to capture the elusive ghost, spirit, essence, or "steam"
that flitted into new forms above his dead and blackened residues. It
was this same spirit that inhabited and animated the landscape, a spirit
whose own method was one of synthesis, of spheres and cubes that
melted into whole and inseparably transmuted entities. If the artist was
to practice the method of nature as part of her strategy of physiognomy
(another one of those supposedly outmoded sciences that actually was
in "the right direction" for both Emerson and Dickinson), then her
study must be a living anatomy rather than a deadly dissection:

> A science – so the Savans say,
> "Comparative Anatomy" –
> By which a single bone –
> Is made a secret to unfold
> Of some rare tenant of the mold,
> Else perished in the stone –
>
> So to the eye prospective led,
> This meekest flower of the mead
> Upon a winter's day,
> Stands representative in gold
> Of Rose and Lily, manifold,
> And countless Butterfly!   [J 100]

The wisdom that applied to the "meekest flower of the mead" also held for the gigantic lilac-blossom of the sunset. Dickinson's botanical terms were a means only of placing or fixing the specimen, not of destroying it. Rising above analysis, the artist had to be a "Scientist of Faith" whose science was the living anatomy of the sunset and whose faith was that the sunset was "prospective," that it stood for more than itself. Just as the lilac hue of this transcendent sunset was an indecipherable synthesis or blend of other colors, so was the artist's approach one of balance and fusion. For a state in which the cloudy mysteries must prevail, the revelation of this scene was enough for Dickinson. In this world, at least, the sunset was the closest that the human could come unto the divine. A kingly purple proved to be the most fitting trophy in Dickinson's royal hunt of the sun.

In Dickinson's private mythology of the mystic day, there was only one other state or condition that matched the time of sunset in its aura of mystery and veiled revelation. This was the occurrence of the northern lights, a brilliant but constantly changing veil of color that overspread the void of the night as the stain of the dying sun did that of day's end.[19] The sun in all its variety of atmospheric veils – mist, haze, fog, and cloud – was replaced at nighttime by a host of walpurgisnacht entities, among which were the moon, the stars, meteors, and the aurora borealis. Of these "lamps" the northern lights were the most hopeful ministers, for they shone forth in the iridescence of a magical fire, a consuming Wagnerian love-death. Like the great curtains of color in Frederic Church's *Aurora Borealis* of 1865, they were a sign that, even in the midst of potential darkness and engulfment, a cold, pure, elusive hope stood burning, a vestal flame of the almost forgotten faith in dawn and resurrection. The northern lights revealed a spirit or a ghost that was entirely unique, a deity who inspired paradoxically fervent yet coldly crystalline dreams of fulfillment:

> The Sunrise runs for Both –
> The East – Her Purple Troth
> Keeps with the Hill –
> The Noon unwinds Her Blue
> Till One Breadth cover Two –
> Remotest – still –
>
> Nor does the Night forget
> A Lamp for Each – to set –
> Wicks wide away –
> The North – Her blazing Sign
> Erects in Iodine –
> Till Both – can see –

> The Midnight's Dusky Arms
> Clasp Hemispheres, and Homes
> And so
> Upon her Bosom – One –
> And One upon her Hem –
> Both lie –   [J 710]

The northern lights too provided a synthesis, but it was a dark communion of souls involved in death or dream. Night was the climax of the cloudy mysteries of doubt – the entombment of Phoebus – as dawn was the fulfillment of the cloudless mysteries of redemption – his resurrection. The frigid blaze of the northern lights was the only consolation for those too terrified to keep the faith. Like the sunset, the aurora borealis could confirm the prophecy of heavenly reunion that was engendered at summer's full, the high solstice of the season of love. It became not a false dawn but a kindly light that led to the triumph of belief, strengthening the resolve of the poor in spirit:

> Of Bronze – and Blaze –
> The North – Tonight –
> So adequate – it forms –
> So preconcerted with itself
> So distant – to alarms –
> An unconcern so sovreign
> To Universe, or me –
> Infects my simple spirit
> With Taints of Majesty –
> Till I take vaster attitudes –
> And strut upon my stem –
> Disdaining Men, and Oxygen,
> For Arrogance of them –
>
> My Splendors, are Menagerie –
> But their Completeless Show
> Will entertain the Centuries
> When I, am long ago,
> An Island in dishonored Grass –
> Whom none but Beetles – know.   [J 290]

The sunset, with the northern lights, was only one of the splendors of the mystic day, but Dickinson took some pride in realizing that if she could but once capture the true "effect" of this phenomena, her art would be as permanent and "firmamental" as the incredibly difficult and elusive subjects that she chose to depict. Sunrise, noon, and midnight were all important stations on the *via crucis* that she traveled every day, but sunset was the most important, because most prophetic, of her private appassionata. One might even compare the depth of her attachment and her truly consanguineous relation to the mystery of the dying, bleeding sun to what was said of the death of George Inness, that great Hudson River artist equally attracted to sunset scenes. Inness was a Swedenborgian, a mystic who believed in a theory of correspondence among the look of a landscape, the mind of God, and the soul of man. He was another romantic artist who placed the capturing of effect above all, and whose pictures, as his son, George Inness, Jr., noted in his biography, "breathed forth the poetic side of all he saw, but his special interest was for the elusive beauties of lights and shades, of atmospheric conditions, and for the rich, full, throbbing life of earth and sky." It was equally prophetic and appropriate that he should have died with the sun itself as his companion. As George Inness, Jr., wrote of his father's passing:

> Late on the afternoon of August 3 [1894] he suggested to my mother that they take a drive, and that while she was dressing he would stroll about and look at the sunset. He went out to a point where he could best see the flaming sky, which was unusually beautiful that evening. A sunset had always moved him to the deepest emotions, and as he gazed he was filled with an ecstacy too profound, a pain too exquisite, for the frail earthly body. Just as the big red ball went down below the horizon he threw his hands into the air and exclaimed, "My God! ah, how beautiful!" and fell stretched on the ground.[20]

As melodramatic as this incident may seem to us today, it is an entirely appropriate analogue to the sensibility of an Emily Dickinson who could write, after a similarly long and intensive study of the evening sky:

> The Sun kept setting – setting – still
> No Hue of Afternoon –
> Upon the Village I perceived –
> From House to House 'twas Noon –
>
> The Dusk kept dropping – dropping – still
> No Dew upon the Grass –
> But only on my Forehead stopped –
> And wandered in my Face –
>
> My Feet kept drowsing – drowsing – still
> My fingers were awake –
> Yet why so little sound – Myself
> Unto my Seeming – make?

How well I knew the Light before –
I could not see it now –
'Tis Dying – I am doing – but
I'm not afraid to know –   [J 692]

CODA

Sunset was the ultimate dress rehearsal for death, and in focusing on it
the fundamental question that Dickinson, Ruskin, and the Hudson
River school were asking, in spite of the monumentality of their aesthetics, was not "What is the nature of art" but rather "What shall I do
to be saved?" In Ruskin's chapter in *Modern Painters* entitled "The Dark
Mirror," where the critic finally abjures art for nature, he does so from
an increasing humanist motivation that soon was to lead him into those
very paths of reform already trodden by the most active of the New
England Transcendentalists. Art alone cannot save, unless it is tied to
specifically human concerns: the salvation of the soul through a redemption of the general quality of life. Ruskin at last arrives very nearly
at Emerson's position, especially when he admits that "in these books
of mine, their distinctive character, as essays on art, is their bringing
everything to a root in human passion or human hope" (5:196). "Fra-
grant tissue of flowers, golden circles of cloud," he writes, "are only
fair when they meet the fondness of human thoughts, and glorify human visions of heaven." Moreover, "the essential connection of the
power of landscape with human emotion is not less certain, because in
many impressive pictures the link is slight or local. That the connection
should exist at a single point is all that we need" (197). This connection,
as I have before stated, is fundamentally a connection of soul with soul
and spirit with spirit. But in "The Dark Mirror," Ruskin also makes an
open declaration of the massive change in emphasis that has been occurring throughout the five volumes of *Modern Painters,* the shift of his
thought from an interest in theology to an interest in psychology.

In a willful attempt at accommodating himself to the dark glass of self,
Ruskin entitles the final chapter of *Modern Painters* "Peace," yet the
whole thrust of his last volume is a restlessness, a frustration, and a
growing despair at the condition of man in the nineteenth century. The
best he can do is to find, through his aesthetics and his steadily enfeebled
Christianity, some kind of justification through works, though his confession is eventually to be one of life without hope.[21] The book of nature
is superseded by the even more mysterious leaves of the book of self:

"But this poor miserable Me! Is *this,* then, all the book I have got
to read about God in?" Yes, truly so. No other book, nor frag-

ment of book, than that, will you ever find;—no velvet-bound
missal, nor frankincensed manuscript;—nothing hieroglyphic nor
cuneiform, papyrus and pryamid are alike silent on this matter;—
nothing in the clouds above, nor in the earth beneath. That flesh-
bound volume is the only revelation that is, that was, or that can
be. In that is the image of God painted; in that is the law of God
written; in that is the promise of God revealed. Know thyself; for
through thyself only thou canst know God.

Through the glass, darkly. But except through the glass, in no
wise. [5:200]

Since the Puritans, American thinkers and artists had been studying
the book of the self as intensively as they looked for images and shadows of divine things in the revelations of landscape. What they had
discovered was a truth that Ruskin came to only too late, when the
mirror of his individual being had already been fatally clouded by the
lengthening shadow of madness. For if as Poe had suggested, the soul
too was a veil, then the lifting of this veil had as dire consequences as
the rending of the natural mantle of the atmosphere, or the parting of
the film of matter that covered the spirit of visible creation. The human
soul itself was capable of hauntedness; it had its peculiar genii and local
spirits—invisible, intangible, elusive, beneficent, or sinister—as did the
closets of the general house of nature. Dickinson surely could join with
Ruskin in hoping that the ultimate reward of the anguish of art was, if
not faith, a deep abiding peace. "Another kind of peace I look for than
this, though I hear it said of me that I am hopeless" (*MP* 5:351), he
wrote, and she who had also often been deemed "hopeless" replied:

> The Martyr Poets—did not tell—
> But wrought their Pang in syllable—
> That when their mortal name be numb—
> Their mortal fate—encourage Some—
> The Martyr Painters—never spoke—
> Bequeathing—rather—to their Work—
> That when their conscious fingers cease—
> Some seek in Art—the Art of Peace—   [J 544]

Ruskin announced in "The Dark Mirror" that "all the power of
nature depends on subjection to the human soul," that "man is the sun
of the world; more than the real sun. The fire of his wonderful heart is
the only light and heat worth gauge or measure. Where he is, are the
tropics: where he is not, the ice-world" (*MP* 5:200–1). Emily Dickinson, however, had already tested this assertion and rejected it. For she
knew from experience that within the soul itself were the possibilities of

a tropical paradise or a polar world of despair, with glacial mountain ranges composing infinitely lone landscapes. If in her late poetry Dickinson still sought the light, it was because she had already struggled with the darkness that was soon to overwhelm the unfortunate Ruskin. That light, like that darkness, was internal as well as external, an illumination defined by one of her favorite lines from Wordsworth, his "Elegiac Stanzas, suggested by a Picture of Peele Castle, in a Storm, painted by Sir George Beaumont."[22] Its meaning had been perfectly explicated by none other than Emerson himself, for in his essay "Beauty," Emerson wrote: "Wordsworth rightly speaks of 'a light that never was on sea or land,' meaning that it was supplied by the observer" (*Works* 6:303). It was just such an observer that Emily Dickinson became. For whether she gloried in the Red Deeps of sunset or traversed the wintry wastelands of the self, her inward eye remained steadfastly, obediently open, keeping her soul both alive and awake. This was the final secret of her art, of her peace, and of her greatness.

Martha Dickinson Bianchi, ca. 1935. (By permission of Mary L. Hampson.)

THE BOOKS OF REVELATION
by
Martha Dickinson Bianchi

═══════════════

Author's note: This piece was later incorporated into Bianchi's unpublished "Life" of her aunt, but it was originally a separate essay, composed sometime in the 1930s. The epigraph is taken from a letter written by Dickinson to Maria Whitney in the spring of 1883. In Johnson's edition the full quotation reads "I am glad you have an hour for books, those enthralling friends, the immortalities, perhaps each may pre-receive. 'And I saw the Heavens opened' " (*L* 3:771). I have silently corrected a few slight errors of spelling and punctuation.

> *"Books – those enthralling friends – the immortalities perhaps each may perceive. 'And I saw the Heavens opened.' "*

That "chamber facing West" where Emily Dickinson lived for the most part her remote interior life, had four windows open to the sun and moon, beside her own sky path, short-cut to Infinity. Her only writing desk was a small mahogany table, eighteen inches square, with a drawer deep enough to take in her ink-bottle, paper and pen – awaiting further peradventure. The external paraphernalia of a literary woman were entirely lacking. No clutter of detail interrupted her flight when she took off from that bare table top, with a sheet of "commercial note" paper from her father's law office or a page of her own favorite "Quadrille" for wings.

On a narrow white mantel shelf nearby stood the books that surrounded her life; not those she oftenest referred to in her letters, but an intimate few, aloof in their relation to her. There is no desecration in turning them over, for – like her own Bee – Emily has dined on the honey of each flower and flown on – leaving only the shadow of her passing.

None of this particular group was published later than 1860; and, quite apart from the authors in her father's library, or her own frequently professed favorites, they preserve a distinct eloquence of their time and subjective influence upon her.

Aside from even her well-known devotions a few varied volumes stood apart – do now – half a century after her death – still hoarding their peculiar import to her between their faded covers.

The oldest of them is "Ranthorpe: or a Poet's First Struggles," published in 1847. (Ward and Lock, 158, Fleet Street, London, according to the cover, and Chapman and Hall, 186, Strand, London, on the title page.) The book is anonymous; but written in pencil on the title page, in an unknown hand, is "By G. W. Lewes, Author of Life of Göthe," – of sharper interest to Emily for its association with George Eliot beyond a doubt – though the two quotations on the title page must have arrested her:

> "J'avis entrepris une lutte insensée; je combattais la misère avec ma plume.
>
> H. de Balzac."

and

> "Wie verfährt die Natur, um Hohes und Niedres im Menschen Zu verbinden? Sie stellt Eitelkeit zwischen hinein!
>
> Göthe."

According to the Preface, the story was written five years before it was published, and it is keyed in the exaggerated pitch of romance of its time. Open where one will there are exclamations of frantic remorse, unrestrained suffering, despondency, despair.

> "Ring the bell," said Florence, "Miss Churchill has fainted."
> "Fainted" – he replied in a hollow tone, – "She is dead – I have killed her."

How could any young writer save herself from such contagion of unbridled sentimental outpourings as ensue? Yet however Emily may have been moved as she read, she never wavered from her own tense habit of expression.

It was an era of sacrificial heroines. They outshone all happier women by the expression of divinely borne torment on their colorless brows. They were noble, – it shone out around them to the extinction of their rivals. They drew apart not only from the impression created by the hectic language describing them, but from their author's ideal, – emerging on the last page dazzling in all the virtues imagination exalts.

The hero, Percy Ranthorpe, "author of the Poet's Heart," is divinely handsome. "Apollo himself is not more fascinating." Not only is he "the supreme writer in albums, but the first waltzer in London." When the sufferings of a young poet overtake him, "the Eumenides goad him to despair!" Bitterness, agitation, mockery of the world consume him, and the unhappy heroine meets him with palpitating heart, and he rests his aching head upon her bosom.

As for this wretched being, later spurned, her pallid lips move – but no word comes from them, the blood leaves her ashen cheek; and withdrawing from the world she lives in her painting of scenes from Nature, with a huge St. Bernard dog as her only companion.

The chapter entitled, "Isola in her Retreat," is headed by a line from Shelley:

"The pleasure that is in sorrow is sweeter than
the pleasure of pleasure itself."

In Emily's copy a page is turned down at Lewes' development of the theme that the tendency to dwell on grief is greater in women than in men; firstly because of their greater sensibility, and secondly because of the monotony of their lives. His philosophy of suffering recalls the cruelties of life which Byron "poured in splendid verse to draw down the admiration and pity of all Europe." Lewes' heroine, Isola, expounds these truths to a later unwelcome suitor. That "Art alone enshrines the sadness of the world," is her conclusion, which evaporates when the long parted lovers do at last meet, and it is "in a burst of rapture with which they clasp each other in wild embrace." Only after "many a giddy faintness, many a sick despondency" Ranthorpe is then able to look calmly on the path before him.

When Emily Dickinson put the book down, what impression did the profound advice of Richter, quoted by Lewes, – "The first thing to be conquered in grief is the pleasure we feel in indulging it," – leave with her? All of that turned down page may signify an impression that was exceptional, as Emily never marked her books in any way.

"The Life of Jean Paul" (Frederick Richter), published in its period, was handed back and forth between Emily, Sue, and Austin, and could not have failed to tinge their thought, for the time being at least, with its extreme and exalted German sentiment. This was the Werther period, of course, when every youth was infected with the sentimentality so widely familiar to all lovers of Heine. There are many passages Emily may well have assimilated, though the markings are Susan's and her name is on the title page.

Neither Shelley nor Byron were ever conspicuous in Emily's preference, nor did Keats more than once come into any remembered mention; but Lewes' quotations and reference may have explained her interest in a book published later, which belongs to this exclusive little group: "Recollections of the Last Days of Byron and Shelley," by E. J. Trelawney, prefaced by Shelley's words which were to become so prophetic of Emily Dickinson's own case:

"No living Poet ever arrived at the fulness of his fame. The jury which sits in judgement upon a Poet, belonging as he does to all Time, must be composed of his peers; it must be impanelled by Time from the selectest of the wise of many generations."

Emily's name is written inside by Sue's hand, and a plain card on which Emily herself wrote *Emily* is inserted at the page where again Shelley's epitaph from Shakespeare is quoted:

"Nothing of him that doth fade,
But doth suffer a sea change
Into something rich and strange."

But carefully as the old brown Ticknor and Fields copy, published in 1859, has been cherished, there is no certainty that Emily placed it where it was first noticed. It was all so long ago.

Emily did write her own name in "The Mill on the Floss," contrary to precedent, for whatever her friends did, she herself kept her books free of any sign of proprietorship. Not even "The Tenant of Wildfell Hall" or "Wuthering Heights" bear witness of her ownership, her dislike of "living aloud" perhaps withholding her.

No one who knew Emily in life could ever forget her tenderness for Maggie Tulliver, whose adoration for her only brother Tom paralleled the deep affection between Emily and her only brother Austin. And as for Aunt Glegg and Aunt Pullett, their shrewd sayings were household words with her, deliciously spicing all sorts of domestic situations – from bonnet-crowns to morals. Through Emily the River Floss and those who dwelt beside it became of almost magical memory – unlike scene and actors of any other novel – to the niece and nephew who grew up under her spell. A mere mention of "the Red Deeps" associated with the ill-fated love of Maggie and Philip Wakem never failed to bring a haunted look to her face – as if she recalled the pain of an actual cruelty to those she had loved.

It was this same old green copy of "The Mill on the Floss" that led her to ask Susan for Thomas à Kempis' "Imitation of Christ" – the book Maggie Tulliver relied upon that last night of agonized uncertainty between Love and Duty – before the flooding river put an end to all that forever. Contrast the realism of the stern moralist of 1860 with the hysterical crises of Ranthorpe of 1847, as George Eliot tells how Maggie alone in the wild storm of rain and wind waited for the light:

"She sat quite still far into the night with no impulse to change her attitude, without active force enough even for the mental act of prayer – only waiting for the light that would surely come again. The words that were marked by a quiet hand in the little old book that she had long ago learned by heart rushed over her lips–'I have received the Cross–I have received it from Thy hand; and I will bear it till death, as Thou hast laid it upon me. I will bear it till death–O God! if my life is to be long, let me live to bless and comfort'–At that moment Maggie felt a startling sensation of sudden cold about her knees and feet–it was water flowing under her. She started up; the stream was flowing under the door. She was not bewildered for an instant; she knew it was the flood."

Emily's copy of Thomas à Kempis was published in 1857 by "John Henry and James Parker, Oxford and Strands 377, London,–A New Edition." The pages are framed with double lines of red, and the black cover is ornamented on the back with two gilt clasp-like designs and the sides are stamped with imitations of heavy hinges such as appear on old leather books of the Renaissance.

Between pages 188 and 189 is a bit of twisted tissue paper grey with age. On these pages are enumerated all that should be undertaken cheerfully for the love of God, with the assurance that "These help to virtue; these are the trial of a novice in Christ; these frame the Heavenly Crown."

Could Emily's accomplished cheerfulness, unfailing demeanor in her daily life, be related in any remote degree to the pattern set by this holy Preceptor? In certain moods she would likely have tossed up the crown for the immediate earthly gift withheld her. In such moments she was quite capable of the same brand of spiritual ribaldry of a Quarles or Dr. Donne. But in her prevailing spirit of mysticism she is not inconceivable as raising her brow to receive that angelic certifying.

That her soul had a guest has never been doubted, though she had committed herself to Time in her lines:

> Time feels so vast
> That were it not for Immortality
> I fear me this circumference
> Engros my Finity.

But there *was* Eternity–staring her in the face when the enamouring of Time and her own mental adventures slowed down.

The last of these faded books of revelation is the "Romance of Abelard and Heloise" by G. S. Wight (translator of Cousin's "History of Philosophy") published in 1853. From the brown wrapping paper in which it came to her Emily has cut the address and pasted it on the fly leaf:

Emily Dickinson
Amherst
Massachusetts.

The masculine writing of the sender is bold, and unidentified with that of the family friends. Between pages 134 and 5 a red clover, "that purple democrat," "flower that Bees prefer," has stained the page without losing its own color, and at page 200 a torn corner of notebook paper is still tucked in the binding.

The historic story is a familiar classic: Abelard, the greatest scholar of all Europe in the Middle Ages, founder of a movement that triumphed with Martin Luther after the martyrdom of Huss and how many more; Heloise, the greatest of her sex, with whom began the first step toward the enfranchisement of women; – the greatest man and greatest woman of the twelfth century – "who were brought by fortune into romantic relations with each other and as lovers possess for each one of us an extraordinary interest."

The words of Abelard in these epistles to Heloise are white flame. The Priest to his "spouse in God" burns the phrases of mere human men to ashes. Before such, Emily Dickinson was not one to shrivel or perish, rather to arise and soar.

Heloise so well sustained her part in their correspondence that her questions in theology drew from him the sermons he dedicated to her, as well as the hymns he composed for her.

A victim of jealousy, envy and persecution, Abelard entered the Abbey of St. Denis a few days after Heloise had taken the veil at Agenteuil, – the most brilliant thinker of all Europe and the most learned woman set apart for one life by veil and cowl. Yet if these famous French victims of conviction were externally removed, did they not serve the same altar? At the close of the Canonical hour the Sisters were accustomed to offer for Abelard a special supplication to the Lord, and he urges them to further formulas for his preservation from his enemies. Their cloister was consecrated to the Paraclete, – that is to say the Comforter, – and especially adorned by that name; and there, after Abelard had withdrawn to the Abbey of St. Gildas, Heloise was transferred as Abbess, and there he bids her live – "Live, you and your Sisters, and remember me as in Christ." She is his "inseparable companion," to whom he writes, "You who transcend even men, and who have exchanged the malediction of Eve for the benediction of Mary, – what profanation if those sacred hands which now are employed in turning the holy pages were condemned to the vulgar cares which are the lot of women!"

Again, he expounds to her, "whatever pertains to you I do not regard as foreign to myself," though inviting always her recollection that she is the Spouse of Christ, in whose name he feels they have been reserved for some great purpose in His honor, – though, like Emily, Heloise seems only to want a small corner in Heaven.

United in their religious obligations imposed upon them hour by hour, season by season, "their romance has so established itself in glory that it has traditionally maintained its splendor for five hundred years."

Their love letters purified by Catholic incense must have been indeed a foreign fragrance in the Puritan chamber where Emily Dickinson, in the long silences of summer days or by the light of her small glass kerosene lamp in the white nights of Winter, read "how others strove."

And if, like them, the Actual Presence became confused with the absent-presence, in such spirit abstractions would it have been strange or blameworthy?

And it was perhaps looking up from their letters that she wrote her own –

> Read, sweet, how others strove,
> Till we are stouter;
> What they renounced,
> Till we are less afraid;
> How many times they bore
> The faithful witness,
> Till we are helped
> As if a kingdom cared!
>
> Read then of faith
> That shone above the fagot;
> Clear strains of hymn
> The river could not drown;
> Brave names of men
> And celestial women,
> Passed out of record
> Into renown!

Austin Dickinson, ca. 1870. (By permission of Mary L. Hampson.)

Appendix B

AUSTIN DICKINSON AS CONNOISSEUR

It was the strange fate of the Dickinson family that longings and desires frustrated in one generation worked themselves out to violent extremes in the next. Samuel Fowler Dickinson bankrupted himself by helping to found Amherst College. In reaction his son Edward dedicated himself wholly to business and a single-minded pursuit of the Protestant ethic in order to reestablish the family fortune. That he triumphantly accomplished this goal is symbolized by his purchase of the old Homestead on Main Street in 1855. In turn his son, Austin Dickinson, was induced to give up plans for a new life in Detroit by an offer of a partnership in Edward's thriving law firm and also by the lure of a baronial mansion that was built to order by his father on a next-door lot. It is important to realize that this grandiose Italian villa, done in the latest style of cottage architecture, remained the property of Edward Dickinson until 1868, for it was only then that circumstances forced Austin to buy the house he had been living in since 1857. The explanation for this arrangement is a tangled one, but it allows us to understand the seeming intrusion of the Newman family into Dickinson affairs.

Mark Newman was Edward Dickinson's brother-in-law, owner of a very successful publishing business in Brooklyn; when he died in 1852 he orphaned five children, a son and four daughters. As Jay Leyda writes, "Newman's publishing house had brought him a substantial fortune, but he left the bulk of it to the American Home Missionary Society; there was still plenty for each of the children, but the son, Mark, was so disgruntled by the terms of the will that he left home and his relatives never heard from him again" (*YH* 1:lxiv). Edward Dickinson was eventually appointed trustee of the Newman estate and guardian of the daughters, who were parceled out to live with various relatives until 1858, when Clara and Anna joined Austin and Susan Dickinson at the Evergreens. Clara resided there until her marriage in 1869, and Anna remained for fourteen years. The years 1857 and 1868 were periods of deep crisis for Edward Dickinson, a methodical man who made an inventory of his credits and debits every January from 1850 almost until his death in 1874.[1] Significantly there are *two* inventories for 1857: In the somewhat scrambled first one his assets amount to $24,035 and his debts to $9,251.79; in the much neater second one his assets have jumped to $40,370, but his debts have also ballooned to $17,030. In spite of Edward Dickinson's assiduous business practices and his speculations in such enterprises as the Sunderland Bridge, the Union Bank, and Michigan land bonds, the items that most suddenly helped to swell his assets were a reevaluation of the Homestead from $3,000 to $10,000 and the addition of the "W. A. Dickinson place" at an assessment of $5,500. On the debit side, the increase is accounted for by an item in the amount of $6,000 silently ascribed to the "Newman Estate." There is still $4,000 owed on the "Sam. E. Mack House," another name for the Dickinson Homestead, for which he originally paid $10,000, so the facts seem fairly clear.

Even a shrewd and ambitious country lawyer could not make enough capital to buy one substantial estate in 1855 and build another in 1857. Village gossip itself noted the squire's newfound prosperity. Writing about the "flourishing condition" of Amherst to her brother in New York, Mrs. Elizabeth Hammun commented on December seventh, 1856, "Edward Dickinson Esq has Bought General Macks place and has made great repares it is now one of the most pleasant places in Amherst it Cost him I understood over five thousands to repair it it is a Splendid House and everything about the House is the same" (*YH* 1:339). Such splendiferous display, however, was not totally the reward of a determined Protestant ethic. As executor of the Newman trust, Edward Dickinson loaned himself a sum substantial enough both to renovate his own home and to construct a new one for his son (ostensibly for the use of the Newman sisters), with enough left over to make some fresh investments while shoring up what he termed his "unproductive property." By 1859 the debt owed the Newman estate had grown to $10,425; in 1863 it was $13,000; in 1868 it was "about $13,600." Edward tried to whittle down his debt over the years, but the estate obviously became a convenient sinking fund into which he easily could dip when some extraordinary expense loomed on the horizon.

In 1868 Sara Newman had married Dr. J. Anson Bates of Baltimore, and in 1869 Clara Newman married Sydney Turner of Norwich, Connecticut. Some hard reckoning finally had to be made, and so in Edward Dickinson's personal inventories for January of 1868 and 1869 we find listed under his assets $3,000 "Due from Austin on his house." The hurriedly handwritten bond for the deed to the Evergreens is also dated January 1, 1868, and it reveals that for "the sum of three thousand dollars valuable consideration, and natural love & affection," Edward Dickinson sold to Austin Dickinson "a certain lot or parcel of land situated in the centre of said town of Amherst & now occupied by same Wm. Austin as his homestead containing one hundred & six rods, more or less, bounded East on my homestead which was conveyed to me by Samuel E. Mack, North and Southwest, on Luke Sweetser, and South on Main Street." Austin was further obligated to pay his father this $3,000 within two years, "with interest annually theron," while Edward was to deliver to him "a good & sufficient deed of the premises above described."[2]

Inventories made after 1869 are missing until we reach that of 1873, which is written in a curt, shaky, and abbreviated form. Although Edward was not to die until June of 1874, this was probably the last inventory that he made, since it bears annotations initialed by Austin and was the closest thing to a will that his father left: This leading lawyer unaccountably died intestate. It does not even carry the customary dateline of "January." Although no value is assigned to "Homestead and land," and Austin still owes him $3,000, the value of Edward's "cash & stocks" has now shrunk to $17,875, less a debt of $3,700 owed to a party named Brownell. There appear to be two separate debts of $9,000 each, but the writing is almost indecipherable and the sums are not even added up. They seem again to refer to Michigan land bonds and may contain the names "Anna" and "Sara." Significantly, Jay Leyda notes that Anna Newman was the last of Edward's nieces to marry and that her wedding to George H. Carleton of Haverhill on June third, 1874, was "the last social occasion attended by her guardian, Edward Dickinson, two weeks before his death" (*YH* 1:lxiv). That death occurred after a sudden attack of apoplexy.

The mysteries of Edward Dickinson's finances – how he could be worth over $40,000 in 1857 and only $17,000 in 1873 – might be explained by transferences of capital to trusts set up for his children. But his estate could just as well have been eaten up by the debts he contracted to his brother-in-law's estate, an estate with which (even judging charitably) he seems to have played fast and loose. A note by Austin Dickinson on the 1873 inventory indicates that the Brownell debt was in part liquidated by notes his father held in the amount of $4,000; and other holdings may have been similarly forfeited. Yet Austin still obtained ownership of the Evergreens at a price far below its stated value of $5,500. Certainly Edward appears to have augmented the Dickinsons at the expense of the Newmans, and this may explain something of his tight-lipped, emotionally repressed nature; the eventual breakdown of his health; and his melancholy, morose religious disposition. It is an odd fact that he did not join the First Church of Amherst until 1850, when he was forty-seven years old, even though he "had been long under conviction" (*YH* 1:178). Could his later dealings have led him to doubt this early conversion experience, and have shaken his faith in his own sainthood? As late as May 1873, Edward made what Leyda calls "a private contract" with the Calvinist Jehovah, signing his name to a paper that reads, "I hereby give myself to god." This testament of acceptance was found in his wallet only after his death (*YH* 2:200). Perhaps Edward Dickinson could make such a contract only because he had at last discharged to his own satisfaction all of his debts: financial, psychological, and spiritual.

How much Austin Dickinson knew of his father's financial dealings with the Newmans is a moot point, for both men were involved in many complicated real estate transactions. There is a warranty deed dated April sixth, 1864, in which Edward as "Trustee under the last will & testament of Mark H. Newman late of Brooklyn" conveys to his son a piece of land one rod in width on the east side of the Newman house at the center of Amherst, for a consideration of $25. Certainly Austin must have learned something of the situation in 1868, when he had to purchase the Evergreens outright, and he could have pieced together the whole story after Edward's death from the inventories his father had preserved. If Austin had been privy to the full extent of his father's indebtedness in the early 1860s, one doubts that he would have spent so much money on fine horses and expensive paintings. But a showplace like the Evergreens had to be appropriately furnished, and Susan Dickinson spent a good deal of her own dowry on its appointments,[2] as a long and detailed bill dated March twenty-eighth, 1856, from the Boston firm of Doe, Hazelton and Company, "Importers and Manufacturers of Drawing Room, Parlor and Chamber Furniture," proves. It is in the amount of $888.03 for such items as an oak sideboard, a black walnut corner whatnot, and a Gothic chair of the same precious and highly prized wood so beloved by the Victorians. We also remember that it was Susan who purchased the Kensett *Sunset with Cows* and the Arthur Parton *Woodland Scene: Oaks at Old Shokan*.

The furnishings of the Evergreens were in stark contrast to those of the Homestead, where Edward Dickinson's taste concentrated on large, serviceable pieces of mahogany veneer in the American Empire style, solid early Federal and painted Hitchcock chairs, and a series of pious prints illustrating the story of "The Prodigal Son." These decorated the parlor of the Homestead, which T. W. Higginson found "dark & cool & stiffish" (*YH* 2:151), and they became oddly prophetic of Austin Dickinson's life of wasted talents and compensatory spending sprees. Although Austin would throw himself down in front of the fire in his library grate and exclaim, "My thousand dollar picture!" in time he nearly bankrupted himself by his continuing hunger for fine as opposed to natural art. His daughter reminisced that "Austin's passion for pictures kept him without some other comforts, for he could not resist them; and once, after spirited bidding at a picture sale in New York, he was being carried beyond his depth, when a stranger whispered to him 'Excuse me, Sir, but do you know you are bidding against A. T. Stewart's agent?' " (FF, 126–7). As Bianchi observes, "It must have been a shock to the young country lawyer, but it was entirely characteristic of him," for A. T. Stewart at his death in 1876 was considered to be the richest man in America, as well as famed as one of the first millionaire collectors of foreign art.

Austin could not resist even street vendors and wandering artists, noting in his diary on July 5th, 1884, that he "bought a water color of some one at the door this P M for $20.00" (YH 2:425). Gradually abandoning the quietism and lyricism of the early Hudson River school, he became more and more attracted to the coloristic and anecdotal products of fashionable European masters, with their high "finish" and academic correctness. As Bianchi writes:

> Forever allured by color and all that was daring and gorgeous in art, he began to take us children from the time we were very young to New York and Boston to store our memories for the future. Great actors like Booth, Sarah Bernhardt in "Camille," Calvé singing "Carmen," as well as preachers like Dr. Gordon at the Old South in Boston and Phillips Brooks at Trinity at the height of their powers – all belonged to the gallery he was providing us; and in pictures, not only those of the best American painters, but notable English, French, and Dutch importations, far less taken for granted in those days, and such exotics as Munkacsy's "Christ before Pilate," and the famous "Russian Wedding." [FF, 125]

Back in orthodox Amherst, this "gallery" surely would have been considered scandalous viewing for the innocent eyes of children, but in Boston or New York Austin could play the aesthete and the cosmopolite with impunity. His taste was now for those melodramatic and theatrical products that had been pioneered in America by the Düsseldorf school and that were to clog the international art market at the end of the century, just as French impressionism and a radical return to the primitive were to destroy such conventionalisms in their own turn. Entranced by this glorious never-never land of flaming color, high drama, and glaring sentiment, Austin could even forget his mundane duties as a concerned father, a struggling lawyer, a disgruntled husband, and an unwilling pillar of Amherst society. His daughter remembered that oblivious of fatigue or hunger himself at such happy times, he was unconsciously intolerant of it in us, and we did our best not to remind him we were tired or had gone without luncheon into the late afternoon. Once he forgot me entirely for several hours, and went on to another gallery in his rapt absorption, hurrying back later much disturbed, his anxiety and remorse changing to pleasure as he found me curled up in front of a marine by Percy Moran, quite contented by the great sea on his canvas. [*FF*, 125]

Austin became a willing client of that new class of professional art dealers who came into being with the foundation of the Düsseldorf Gallery and who were to dictate the taste of the nouveau riche in the boom years of unbounded conspicuous consumption that followed the Civil War. Indeed, in his unchecked mania for fine horses and high art, he seems almost like the sybaritic connoisseur parodied by Oliver Wendell Holmes in his satirical poem "Contentment":

> I would not have the horse I drive
>> So fast that folks must stop and stare;
> An easy gait – two, forty-five –
>> Suits me; I do not care; –
> Perhaps, for just a *single spurt*
> Some seconds less would do no hurt.

> Of pictures, I should like to own
>> Titians and Raphaels, three or four, –
> I love so much their style and tone, –
>> One Turner, and no more,
> (A landscape, – foreground golden dirt, –
> The sunshine painted with a squirt.)   [*Works*, 171]

Surely, as the example of his bidding against A. T. Stewart's agent illustrates, Austin was often out of his depth and out of his class. Between his family's social extravagance and his own extensive expenditures on this private passion for paintings, he appears almost to have worked himself to death, fulfilling a supressed suicidal or self-destructive longing that otherwise cropped up in his wild and reckless horsemanship. "Austin loved excitement," his daughter commented, "and liked to drive down the Main Street from his law office with his horse going at racing speed, reins lying loose, turning in on one wheel at the old gate, and never slackening the pace till the flaring nostrils of the proud animal hit the carriage-house door." (*FF*, 129–30). Although this behavior is rationalized as "a bit of domestic circus for Emily's special benefit, should she chance to be near the window, where her hand seldom failed its flash of salute" (130), Bianchi still expressed some relief that "nothing ever did happen." "He loved to do what he called 'shave hairs,' " she remarks of her father, and reports that his only comment "when besought not to risk quite such close chances" was, "It steadies my nerves" (130).

What his sister Emily channeled into the volcanic passion of her poetic art as a whole, Austin Dickinson expressed in an active taste for expensive paintings and self-contrived hairbreadth escapes. "A symptom of Cavalier tendencies in a Puritan setting," Bianchi called it (*FF,* 130). Yet because they both shared "the extravagant qualities of the Dickinson nature" (124) as well as a thirst for aesthetic and cultural excitement, Austin also shared the depths of his passion for art with that sister who cultivated her own even more private one of poetry. "He was so familiarly known at the New York galleries of Shaus and Goupil," Bianchi writes,

> whose place in the art world was later filled by Knoedler, that they often telegraphed him to come down and see a new treasure before it was out on public sale. When he actually did buy a painting and get it home, he sometimes kept it upstairs in the guest-room with the door shut for weeks before showing it to his father, whose taste in art ran – or rather walked – to steel engravings, and who might well consider such doings of Austin extravagant, if not unduly fanciful. Of course, when he was ready, Sue and Emily were the first to peep at each one, propped up against a chair to catch the best light. A picture in itself, those three standing there, Austin and Sue flushed and excited, Emily revelling in a new emotion of color as she gazed. [126]

Austin's increasing taste for foreign art is indicated not only by his early interest in the Düsseldorf school but by such volumes as the lavishly illustrated *The Galleries of Munich,* by E. Holloway (Dresden: A. H. Paine, n.d.); *The London Art Journal* (London: George Virtue, 1852); and *The Masterpieces of French Art* (Philadelphia: Gebbie, 1883) that are still in the parlor of the Evergreens; these were the coffee-table books of their time. Among the prints hanging throughout the house are a small engraving of Turner's view of Lake Lucerne (London: Henry Graves, 1854); the large *Vaches à l'breuvoir* painted by August Bonheur and engraved by Paul Giradet (New York: M. Knoedler; Paris: Goupil, 1874); another Giradet engraving of *Le Saltimbanque* by Louis Knaus (New York: Knoedler; Paris: Goupil, 1865); and two typically sentimental subjects by Landseer, *The Forrester's Family,* engraved by Thomas L. Atkinson (London: Henry Graves; Paris: Goupil; 1854), and *The Lost Sheep,* engraved by Thomas Landseer (London: Henry Graves, n.d.). Austin's changing tastes and his close connection to the New York galleries parallel a wider shift in American elite culture outlined by John Durand, who writes that

> this great influx of foreign art could not have occurred without a corresponding expansion of wealth at home. Beginning in the East, the wave of wealth rolled onward to the Pacific. Through the profits of mines, railway enterprises, and cattle-raising, it ran mountain high. A new generation of energetic men indifferent to Eastern ideals spring up, and, carving new outlets for the expediture of their fortunes as well as new criterions of social distinction, find these in the adoption of a taste for art. Western millionaires begin to buy French pictures right and left. Entering the markets of New York and Paris, they vie with each other and with their Eastern rivals in seeing who could pay dearest for recognised masterpieces. Other agencies help this *furore* along. Picture-dealers, exercising the most influence, find in foreign art a gold-mine. Realising profits of one, two, and three hundred percent on the works that pass through their hands, they serve as intermediaries between patron and artist, and keep the interest at fever heat. The Press push on a cause equally fertile in new items and sensational phenomena. Native students, finding foreign art in the ascendent, abandon original perceptions and imitate the methods and aims of a foreign school. Add to this the one-sided admiration of this or that French "Master" whose life and career offer romantic episodes, ludicrously exaggerated in the eyes of those familiar with the facts, and we have a remarkable combination of influences which fully explain the disappearance of local art – like houses and bridges swept away in a mountain torrent. [*Asher B. Durand,* 194–5]

Austin Dickinson came from old Yankee stock, but he was fully caught up in the materialism of the Gilded Age that Durand sketches here. Yet his fever for art appears to have burned itself out soon after Mabel Loomis Todd arrived in Amherst on August thirty-first, 1881, when another long-smoldering flame was ignited. One of Austin's last purchases was probably the *Winter Scene with Fox* painted by C. H. Shearer in 1882, in which the high finish and minute sense of detail so characteristic of his Pre-Raphaelite leanings of the 1850s and 1860s have wholly given way to a soft, painterly, and moody tonalism. On September eleventh, 1882, Austin and Mabel crossed the "Rubicon" and passed over into the forbidden territory of an illicit love affair that was to last until Austin's death in 1895 (*LED* 1:196).

Another generation of Dickinsons was to take up the thirst for collecting, as Martha Dickinson Bianchi filled whatever wall space was left
in the Evergreens with souvenirs from her European tours, especially
prints and paintings that reflected the new vogue for Italian primitives
and the great artists of the High Renaissance. Walter Pater and Bernard
Berenson ruled where once John Ruskin had held undisputed sway.
Austin Dickinson's collection would become a testament to the "eclipse
of the American school, not yet at an end," so lamented by John
Durand in the biography of his father that was published only a year
before Austin's death (*Asher B. Durand,* 196). Two items in that collection, however, would be sacrificed to the new passion that devoured
Austin Dickinson's thwarted energies in his last decade. For by terms of
his will dated November third, 1887, Austin left to Mrs. Mabel Loomis
Todd "the engraving in my parlor called 'The Night Watch' and the
larger of the two oil paintings by Perlion [*sic*] called a scene near
Dresden."[3]

With the Dickinsons – as ever – art, life, and romance were indissolu-
bly linked together.

Emily Dickinson, ca. 1848. On the back of a reproduction of this daguerreotype of her aunt, Martha Dickinson Bianchi wrote in October of 1931, "My
distinct recollection of her was fuller and softer of face, with her hair loosely
arranged in a little brown velvet net. The expression was never rigid – as this
picture indicates, but sweet, absorbed, vivacious according to her mood and
with far more humor." (By permission of the Trustees of Amherst College.)

DICKINSON'S MYSTIC DAY

This zodiac of lights, this tent of dropping clouds, this striped coat of climates, this fourfold year.

Ralph Waldo Emerson

Sun cycle	Sunrise	Noon	Sunset	Midnight
Cardinal points	East	South	West	North
Seasonal cycle	Spring	Summer	Fall	Winter
Human cycle	Birth & re-birth	Maturation	Death	Burial & "Eternity"
Christian cycle	Resurrection (Easter)	Ministry & Communion (Sermon on the Mount)	Crowning & Crucifixion (Good Friday)	Entombment (Holy Saturday)
Spiritual cycle	Hope	Faith	Passion & prophecy	Doubt
Psychological cycle	Expectation	Love	Trial & separation	Endurance & deprivation
Color cycle	Amethyst & yellow (dawn)	Blue & violet (summer haze)	Red, purple, & yellow (autumn leaves)	White (snow)
Floral cycle	Jonquil & crocus	Rose	Gentian	Hemlock (evergreen)
Geographical cycle	Switzerland, the Alps	Italy, the Indies	China/Asia	New England
Illumination	Morning light	Full sun	Twilight	Aurora borealis (northern lights)
Religious cycle	Conviction & awakening	Conversion & "grace"	Sanctification & justification	Repentance and purgation

NOTES

APOLOGIA

1 Austin Warren, "Emily Dickinson" (1957), in Richard Sewall, ed., *Emily Dickinson: A Collection of Critical Essays* (Englewood Cliffs, N.J.: Prentice-Hall, 1963), 109.

2 T. S. Eliot, "Tradition and the Individual Talent," in Eliot, *The Sacred Wood* (1920; New York: Barnes & Noble, 1960), 53.

3 See Philippe Ariès, *The Hour of Our Death,* trans. Helen Weaver (New York: Knopf, 1981); and Roland Barthes, *Camera Lucida: Reflections on Photography,* trans. Richard Howard (New York: Hill & Wang, 1981).

4 Henry James, "Honoré Daumier," in James, *The Painter's Eye: Notes and Essays on the Visual Arts,* sel. and ed. by John L. Sweeney (Cambridge: Harvard University Press, 1956), 238.

5 Charles Eliot Norton, in the *Nation,* September 6, 1866, reprinted in Herman Melville, *Battle-Pieces and Aspects of the War,* ed. Sidney Kaplan (Amherst: University of Massachusetts Press, 1972), xxxvii–xxxviii.

6 See my essay, "Emily Dickinson and the Occult," *Prairie Schooner* 51 (Winter 1977/78): 345–57; and R. Laurence Moore, *In Search of White Crows: Spiritualism, Parapsychology, and American Culture* (New York: Oxford University Press, 1977). See especially Moore's chap. 4, "The Medium and her Message," 102–29. For a discussion of the poet as spiritualist medium, see Oliver Wendell Holmes, "Exotics" (1875), reprinted in Holmes, *The Autocrat's Miscellanies,* ed. Albert Mordell (New York: Twayne, 1959), 141–2.

7 Preface to Emily Dickinson, *Poems,* eds. Mabel Loomis Todd and T. W. Higginson (Boston: Roberts Bros., 1890), iii. See also Higginson's "An Open Portfolio," *Christian Union* 42 (September 25, 1890):392–3, reprinted in Caesar R. Blake and Carlton F. Wells, eds., *The Recognition of Emily Dickinson: Selected Criticism since 1890* (Ann Arbor: University of Michigan Press, 1968), 3–10.

8 Ralph Waldo Emerson, "New Poetry," in Emerson, *Uncollected Writings: Essays, Addresses, Poems, Reviews and Letters,* ed. Charles C. Bigelow (New York: Lamb, 1912), 139, first published in the *Dial* (October 1840):220–32.

9   See the section on albums in Katherine Morrison McClinton, *Antiques of American Childhood* (New York: Clarkson N. Potter, 1970), 124–34.

10   Justin Kaplan observes that "the tendriled cover design of *Leaves of Grass,* and the germ of Whitman's title as well, may have been borrowed from . . . *Fern Leaves from Fanny's Portfolio*" (*Walt Whitman: A Life* [New York: Simon & Schuster, 1980], 216).

11   Charlotte Brontë, *Jane Eyre* (1847; New York: Modern Library, 1950), 133, 135.

12   Oliver Wendell Holmes, *The Professor at the Breakfast-Table; with the Story of Iris* (Boston: Ticknor & Fields, 1860), 284, 286. That Dickinson was early familiar with Holmes's *Poems* is proved by an 1849 copy inscribed to her by James Kimball, who formed part of a reading group to which the young Dickinson belonged. In his *Emily Dickinson's Reading, 1836–1886* (Cambridge: Harvard University Press, 1966), Jack L. Capps maintains that these poems "failed to impress her, and she appears to have given Holmes little attention other than her reading of his biography of Emerson, published the year before she died" (120). Yet in an unpublished life of her aunt, entitled "Emily Dickinson: Her Life, Lineage, and Legacy," written with Alfred Leet Hampson and now at the Evergreens, Martha Dickinson Bianchi draws attention (p. 371) – as does Leyda (*YH* 2:132) – to a cutting from Holmes's sentimental class poem entitled "Joe and Bill," sent to her mother, Susan, by Emily at some unspecified date. Dickinson would have followed Holmes's "Breakfast-Table Series" in the pages of the *Atlantic,* and though there was little in his neoclassical verse forms for her to imitate, his anticlerical, enlightened, and ameliorative stance must have appealed to her immensely. For a suggestive source study focusing on *Elsie Venner* (1861), see Alice Hall Petry, "The Ophidian Image in Holmes and Dickinson," *American Literature* 54 (December 1982): 598–601.

13   This phrase was applied to Harriet Prescott Spofford in a contemporary *New York Times* review of her work. See Elizabeth K. Halbeisen, *Harriet Prescott Spofford* (Philadelphia: University of Pennsylvania Press, 1935), 1. On Spofford and Dickinson, see my essay " 'I Must Have Died at Ten Minutes Past One': Posthumous Reverie in Harriet Prescott Spofford's 'The Amber Gods,' " in Howard Kerr, John W. Crowley, and Charles L. Crow, eds., *The Haunted Dusk: American Supernatural Fiction, 1820–1920* (Athens: University of Georgia Press, 1983), 99–119; and Chapters 5 and 6 of this study.

14   Sidney E. Lind sees a source for this poem in Nathaniel Hawthorne's "The Old Manse" (1846), but the date of its composition as given by Johnson (1866) places it much closer to the work of Holmes. See Sidney E. Lind, "Emily Dickinson's 'Further in Summer than the Birds' and Hawthorne's 'The Old Manse,' " *American Literature* 39 (May 1967):163–9.

15   See R. W. Franklin, ed., *The Manuscript Books of Emily Dickinson,* 2 vols. (Cambridge: Harvard University Press, 1981) 1:ix–xxii.

16   William H. Shurr, *The Marriage of Emily Dickinson: A Study of the Fascicles* (Lexington: University of Kentucky Press, 1983).

17 Jonathan Holstein, *American Pieced Quilts* (New York: Viking Press, 1972), 7–8. See also chap. 6, "The Skilled Hand, The Practiced Eye," in Holstein's excellent survey, *The Pieced Quilt: An American Design Tradition* (Greenwich, Conn.: New York Graphic Society, 1973), 113–27. In *MW* (1858–9), Harriet Beecher Stowe refers to the arrangement of the "rainbow shapes and quaint traceries" of patchwork as one of the "few . . . fine arts" (436) practiced by New England women. See my Chapter 3 for a discussion of this work. Dickinson equates her poetry with the "humblest Patchwork" in J 618.

18 See George Monteiro, "The One and Many Emily Dickinsons," *American Literary Realism* 7 (Spring 1974):137–41.

19 John Updike, *Hugging the Shore: Essays and Criticism* (New York: Knopf, 1983), 547.

20 See David Porter, *Dickinson: The Modern Idiom* (Cambridge: Harvard University Press, 1981), especially chap. 2, "Strangely Abstracted Images," 25–36.

21 For the title of this apologia and for many ideas about alternative models of unity in the visual arts, I am endebted to William C. Seitz's pioneering study, *The Art of Assemblage* (Garden City, N.Y.: Doubleday, 1961).

1. KEEPSAKES

1 Ralph Waldo Emerson, "Nature," in *The Complete Works of R. W. Emerson,* ed. Edward Waldo Emerson (Boston: Houghton Mifflin, 1904) 1:35.

2 Walter Pater, *Studies in the History of the Renaissance* (London: Macmillan, 1873), 38.

3 The most recent example of this type of criticism is Karl Keller, *Only Kangeroo among the Beauty: Emily Dickinson and America* (Baltimore: Johns Hopkins University Press, 1979).

4 See Leslie Fiedler, *Love and Death in the American Novel* (New York: Dell, 1966), especially chap. 2, "The Novel's Audience and the Sentimental Love Religion."

5 C. S. Lewis, *The Screwtape Letters* (New York: Macmillan, 1943), 129.

6 Henry Glassie, "Folk Art," in Richard M. Dorson, ed., *Folklore and Folklife: An Introduction* (Chicago: University of Chicago Press, 1972), 258.

7 Claude Lévi-Strauss calls this process *bricolage*. See Glassie, "Folk Art," p. 260; and Chapter 5 of this study. For a case study of a modern "offspring produced from a melding of folk and popular material culture traits," see Stephen A. Cole, "The Vernacular Group of L. L. Bean: Toward a New Definition in American Material Culture," *Journal of American Culture* 2 (Fall 1979):193–209.

8 See Richard B. Sewall, *The Lyman Letters: New Light on Emily Dickinson and Her Family* (Amherst: University of Massachusetts Press, 1965), 33–7. See also Jonathan Morse, "Emily Dickinson and the Spasmodic School: A Note on T. W. Higginson's Esthetics," *New England Quarterly* 50 (September 1977): 505–10; and Chapter 3 of this study.

9 In his memoir entitled *Yankee Bookseller* (Boston: Houghton Mifflin, 1937),

Charles E. Goodspeed notes that Burnham's originally occupied part of the basement of the Old South Meeting House, and describes it as "a dark labyrinth of alleys, to be visited only by the light of a candle." He adds that "many of the books were covered with the dust of years which made a general examination of the shelves impossible, and, indeed, the visitor was not expected to attempt it. If he came with a definite want he would be served, as there was some arrangement of the stock which was familiar to the attendants." (27–8).

10   Elizabeth Oakes Smith, *The Sinless Child, and Other Poems,* ed. John Keese (New York: Wiley & Putnam, 1843), 39–40.

11   David Higgins, *Portrait of Emily Dickinson: The Poet and Her Prose* (New Brunswick, N.J.: Rutgers University Press, 1967), 12–13.

12   See Susan H. Dickinson, "Magnetic Visitors" (1892), *Amherst* 33 (Spring 1981):8–15, 27. Susan herself was named for a once-celebrated friend of her mother's, the pious Mrs. Susan Huntington. See Benjamin B. Wisner, *Memoirs of the Late Mrs. Susan Huntington of Boston, Mass.* (Boston: Crocker & Brewster, 1826).

13   T. W. Higginson, "Emily Dickinson," in Higginson, *Carlyle's Laugh and Other Surprises* (Boston: Houghton Mifflin, 1909), 273.

14   Sandra M. Gilbert and Susan Gubar, *The Madwoman in the Attic: The Woman Writer and the Nineteenth-Century Literary Imagination* (New Haven, Conn.: Yale University Press, 1979), 584.

15   *LED* 2:673. "Hugh Conway" was the pseudonym of the popular author Frederick John Fargus. The title of his book was appropriated by Dickinson for the famous last lines written to her Norcross cousins (*L* 3:1046) and by Madame Bianchi for the legend on her aunt's tombstone.

16   *Letters and Journals of Thomas Wentworth Higginson, 1846–1906,* ed. Mary Thacher Higginson (Boston: Houghton Mifflin, 1921), 115.

17   Twain had begun to take aim at the "sweet drapery" of the Mount Auburn school as early as 1870, when he wrote a satirical sketch entitled "Post-Mortem Poetry." See *The Complete Humorous Sketches and Tales of Mark Twain,* ed. Charles Neider (New York: Hanover House, 1961), 152. Julia Moore was the author of the notorious *Sentimental Song Book* (1870) and is identified as the original of Emmeline Grangerford by Walter Blair in *Mark Twain and Huck Finn* (Berkeley: University of California Press, 1960), 210–13. During his residence in Hartford, however, Twain could hardly have avoided contact with the memory of that city's own most famous mortuary poetess, Lydia H. Sigourney (1781–1865), author of obituary verses on demand. Sigourney was often called "The American Hemans" by her admirers because her poem entitled "Death of an Infant" was mistakenly attributed to this equally popular and equally morbid British poet often ranked with Keats, Shelley, and Wordsworth during the nineteenth century. See Gordon S. Haight, *Mrs. Sigourney: The Sweet Singer of Hartford* (New Haven: Yale University Press, 1930), 78–9. Emily Dickinson never mentioned Sigourney, though one of the books given to her by her father, *Wild Flowers Drawn and Colored from Nature* (New York, 1859), contained

an introduction by Sigourney. Likewise, she never mentioned Hemans, though one of her most intimate correspondents and the man most often nominated as the great love of her life, the Reverend Charles Wordsworth, out-eulogized the eulogists by himself writing an ode "On the Death of Mrs. Hemans" – as, of course, did Sigourney. For the fictional examples mentioned in the text, see Mary Wilkins Freeman, "A Poetess," in Freeman, *A New England Nun and Other Stories* (New York: Harper & Bros., 1897); and William Faulkner, *Absalom, Absalom!* (New York: Modern Library, 1936).

18 I am indebted to George Monteiro for this suggestion.

19 S. L. Clemens, "An Adventure of Huckleberry Finn: With an Account of the Famous Grangerford–Sheperdson Feud," *Century Magazine* 29 (December 1884):268–78. Although there are five illustrations by E. W. Kemble accompanying this section, none have to do with Emmeline Grangerford. The book version includes two, one being her unfinished mortuary drawing, the other an illustration of a scene in her "Ode to Stephen Dowling Bots, Dec'd."

20 S. L. Clemens, *Adventures of Huckleberry Finn,* ed. Hamlin Hill (San Francisco: Chandler, 1962), 139–40. This is a facsimile of the first edition.

21 See George Monteiro and Barton L. St. Armand, "The Experienced Emblem: A study of Emily Dickinson's Poetry," in Jack Salzman, ed., *Prospects,* vol. 6. (New York: Burt Franklin, 1981), 186–280.

22 This scrapbook is now the property of Amherst College and is part of the items on exhibit at the Dickinson Homestead.

23 For an example of this method, see Miriam Baker Finkelstein, "Emily Dickinson and the Practice of Poetry" (Ph.D. diss., State University of New York at Stony Brook, 1970).

24 See John Livingston Lowes, *The Road to Xanadu: A Study in the Ways of the Imagination* (Boston: Houghton Mifflin, 1927).

25 *YH* 1:lxxviii. For other sources on the Warner–Crowell Family, see William Lyman Cowles, "Speech at the Unveiling of a Portrait of E. P. Crowell, December 18, 1912," MS, Amherst College Archives; "Old Amherst House Filled with Color," *Springfield Sunday Union and Republican,* June 23, 1935, 9A; Annie L. Crowell, "Emily Dickinson," *Mt. Holyoke Alumni Quarterly* 29 (February 1946):129–30; and Jane C. Crowell, "I Have a Missing Friend," in Crowell, *Guests in Eden* (New York: Zeta Chapter, Phi Delta Gamma, 1946), 6–9. Jane Crowell sums up the Dickinson–Warner–Crowell relationship when she states that "for about one hundred years the two families were closely associated" (6). Aaron Warner, Mary's father, was an ordained minister who sometimes preached in the Congregational Church. In a letter to Sue written September 26, 1858, Dickinson wrote: "I attended church early in the day. Professor Warner preached. Subject – 'little drops of dew' " (*L* 2:340).

26 Most items in the scrapbook date from the 1850s, although Mary Warner Crowell added a group of clippings from the early 1870s, mostly juvenile

tales and poems, probably for her own children's use and instruction. This scrapbook is now at the Evergreens and is used with the kind permission of Mrs. Mary L. Hampson.

27 The original "Song of Nature" appeared in the *Atlantic* 5 (January 1860):18– 20. Although published anonymously, it was in fact by Ralph Waldo Emerson (*Works* 9:244–7). An oracular, cosmic, and somewhat bombastic production, this poem has been called "the crown of Emerson's evolutionary humanism, making a synthesis of ancient fable and modern science" (Carl F. Strauch, "The Sources of Emerson's 'Song of Nature,' " *Harvard Library Bulletin* 9 [Autumn 1955]:300). The final stanzas of the parodic scrapbook "Song," which describe Nature as a "first-rate cook" who brews an elemental punch and the poet as the one who dresses her in an "apron," may have inspired Dickinson's 1877 picture of Nature "in an Opal Apron, / Mixing fresher Air" (J 1397).

28 See the chapter entitled "Fairy Painting" in Jeremy Maas, *Victorian Painters* (London: Barrie & Rockliff, 1969), 148–61; and Patricia Allderidge, *Richard Dadd* (New York: St. Martin's Press, 1974).

29 In an article entitled "The Spider" in *Parley's Magazine,* a periodical that Edward Dickinson subscribed to in 1838 but that his children were probably familiar with long before that date, we read: "It often happens that the wind, or the broom of the house-maid, destroys in a minute the labor of a Spider's life time" (no. 14, pt. 3 [September 14, 1833], 12). There is another article called "The Spider" in no. 21, pt. 4 (December 21, 1833), 47–48.

30 "Sophistries" is a variant for "Boundaries" in line 12. Hereafter variants noted by Johnson will be silently interpolated into the texts of individual Dickinson poems.

31 *The Poems of Edward Taylor,* ed. Donald E. Stanford, foreword by Louis L. Martz (New Haven, Conn.: Yale University Press, 1960), 464–5.

32 Jonathan Edwards, *Representative Selections,* ed. Clarence H. Faust and Thomas H. Johnson (New York: Hill & Wang, 1962), 152.

33 *The Poetical Works of Mary Howitt* (Boston: Phillips, Sampson, 1854), 140. Carl Ray Woodring, in his *Victorian Samplers: William and Mary Howitt* (Lawrence: University of Kansas Press, 1952), notes the sexual overtones of "The Spider and the Fly" (34). *Parley's Magazine* is rich in anecdotes of threatening spiders and gorgeous butterflies. See, for example, "The Butterfly's Complaint," vol. 8 (May 1840):159.

34 When it was published in the *Springfield Republican,* "Safe in their Alabaster Chambers" was datelined "Pelham Hill, June, 1861" (J, note to 216). One must assume that this information emphasizes not only the "open-air" character of the poem as a true "sketch from nature," but its superior moral stance as well, since the Pelham Hills look down on Amherst. Moreover, Dickinson's ironic reference in the text to Matt. 5:5 ("Blessed are the meek: for they shall inherit the earth"), signals that this is her version of "The Sermon on the Mount" as well as an elegy written above and about, rather than actually in, a New England country churchyard.

35 Nathaniel Hawthorne, *The Scarlet Letter,* ed. Hyatt H. Waggoner and George Monteiro (San Francisco: Chandler, 1968), 98.

2. DARK PARADE

1   Mary Warner Crowell to Susan Gilbert Dickinson, March 17, 1896, November 30, 1883, the Evergreens, Amherst, Mass.

2   *The Poems of Maria Lowell,* ed. Hope J. Vernon (Providence, R.I.: Brown University Press, 1963), 45–7.

3   Ann Douglas, *The Feminization of American Culture* (New York: Knopf, 1970), 208.

4   For a full exploration of this motif, see William E. Bridges, "The Family Circle in American Verse: The Rise and Fall of an Image" (Ph.D. diss., Brown University, 1963). 66.

5   William Wordsworth, *Poetical Works,* ed. Thomas Hutchinson and Ernest DeSelincourt (London: Oxford University Press, 1965), 66.

6   Lydia H. Sigourney, *Gleanings* (Hartford: Brown & Gross, 1860), 153. The figure of the praying Samuel was a favorite mortuary sculpture for children's graves and a prominent feature of most American nineteenth-century monument catalogs. For examples of the type, see Edmund V. Gillon, Jr., *Victorian Cemetery Art* (New York: Dover, 1972), 66, 76–7, 112.

7   Ann Douglas Wood, "Mrs. Sigourney and the Sensibility of the Inner Space," *New England Quarterly* 45 (June 1972):163–4.

8   My interpretation of mourning iconography is based largely on the work of Anita Schorsch. See her introduction ("The Story of Mourning Art") to *Mourning Becomes America: Mourning Art in the New Nation* (Philadelphia: William Penn Memorial Museum, 1976) and her articles entitled "Mourning Art: A Neoclassical Reflection in America," *American Art Journal* 8 (May 1976):4–15, and "A Key to the Kingdom: The Iconography of a Mourning Picture," *Winterthur Portfolio* 14 (Spring 1979):41–71. See also Laverne Muto, "A Feminist Art – The American Memorial Picture," *Art Journal* 37 (Summer 1976):352–8; Jane C. Nylander, "Some Print Sources of New England Schoolgirl Art," *Antiques* 110 (August 1976):292–301; and Linda DePauw and Conover Hunt, *"Remember the Ladies": Women in America, 1750–1815* (New York: Viking Press, 1976). For an excellent selection of mass-produced mourning prints, see Martha V. Pike and Janice Gray Armstrong, *A Time to Mourn: Expressions of Grief in Nineteenth-Century America* (New York: The Museums at Stony Brook, 1980), 160–2.

9   See James Steven Curl, *The Victorian Celebration of Death* (Detroit: Partridge Press, 1972); James J. Farrell, *Inventing the American Way of Death, 1830–1920* (Philadelphia: Temple University Press, 1980); and Ronald Slusarenko, "Necrotexture: The Underground Population Explosion and Its Impact on Cemetery Design," *Landscape Architecture* 60 (July 1970):297–300. On the popularity of rural cemeteries, see Douglas, *Feminization,* 208–13, 372 n.19; for studies of this important cultural movement, see espe-

cially Stanley French, "The Cemetery as a Cultural Institution: The Estab-
lishment of the 'Rural' Cemetery Movement," *American Quarterly* 26
(March 1974):37–59, and Blanche Linden, "Death and the Garden: The
Cult of the Melancholy and the 'Rural' Cemetery," 2 vols. (Ph.D. diss.,
Harvard University, 1981).

10   See David E. Stannard, *The Puritan Way of Death: A Study in Religion,
     Culture and Social Change* (New York: Oxford University Press, 1977).

11   Lydia H. Sigourney, *Letters to Mothers* (Hartford, Conn.: Hudson & Skin-
     ner, 1838), 207.

12   For a pictorial representation of the sinless child as guilding star, see S. P.
     Mount's "A Portrait of Camille" (1868), reproduced on p. 77 of Pike and
     Armstrong, *A Time to Mourn*. Included in the portrait of the recently
     deceased child are a watch pointing to the time of her birth, a disembodied
     face hovering in the clouds, and the morning star in the distance.

13   For the emblematic origins of Dickinson's imagery, see Monteiro and St.
     Armand, "The Experienced Emblem," 196–204.

14   Lydia H. Sigourney, *Poems* (New York: Leavitt & Allen, 1856), 33.

15   William Cullen Bryant, *Poetical Works* (New York: Appleton, 1879), p. 21–
     3. This important poem blends romantic feeling with neoclassical stoicism;
     its title, which translates as "A View of Death," emphasizes the high
     survey of a landscape prospect that characterizes Dickinson's "The Sleep-
     ing" as originally published in the *Springfield Republican*. For a similar
     perspective, see "When we stand on the top of Things" (J 242).

16   See Thomas H. Johnson, *Emily Dickinson: An Interpretive Biography* (New
     York: Atheneum, 1972), 206–7.

17   See Nancy Lee Beaty, *The Craft of Dying: The Literary Tradition of the Ars
     Moriendi in England* (New Haven, Conn.: Yale University Press, 1970).

18   Sigourney's death occurred on June 10, 1865. See Lydia H. Sigourney,
     Letters of Life (New York: Appleton, 1866), 413. This autobiography was
     completed by her daughter, Mary, who in 1855 had married the Reverend
     Francis T. Russell, pastor of St. Mark's Church, New Britain, Conn.

19   *The Complete Poetical Works of Thomas Hood,* ed. Walter Jerrold (London:
     Oxford University Press, 1906), 444. Jerrold notes that this poem was
     published in August 1831 and was supposed to have been based on the
     death of the poet's sister.

20   Lydia H. Sigourney, *The Weeping Willow* (Hartford, Conn.: H. S. Parsons,
     1850), 8.

21   For a view of Victorian death rituals as a necessary process of socialization,
     see John Kucich, "Death Worship among the Victorians: The Old Curios-
     ity Shop" *PMLA* 95 (January 1980):58–70.

22   John Morley, *Death, Heaven and the Victorians* (Pittsburgh: University of
     Pittsburgh Press, 1971), 91.

23   See Robert W. Habenstein and William M. Lamers, *The History of American
     Funeral Directing* (Milwaukee, Wis.: Bulfin Printers, 1962), especially chap.
     8, "Through the Ice-Age in Embalming," 311–52.

24   *Reports of the Committee of Arrangements of the Common Council of New York*

of the Obsequies in Memory of the Hon. Henry Clay (New York: McSpedon & Baker, 1852), 23–4. Emily Dickinson's father, Edward Dickinson, owned a copy of a similar memorial volume, *Obituary Addresses on the Occasion of the Death of the Hon. Daniel Webster . . .* (Washington, D.C.: Robert Armstrong, 1853), inscribed to him by the Honorable George T. Davis of Greenfield, Mass., who delivered the first obituary address before the U.S. Senate. The binding features a sarcophagus stamped in gold.

25 Hunt's "Georgiana" is from *The Amaranth; or, Token of Remembrance* (Boston: Phillips & Sampson, 1846), 310. The other two quotations are from W. C. Whitcomb, ed., *The Early Dead; or, Transplanted Flowers* (Worcester: Henry J. Howland, 1857), 55, 140–1.

26 Washington Irving, *The Sketch Book of Geoffrey Crayon, Gent.* (1819; New York: New American Library, 1961), 142. Irving's antiquarian study of English funeral customs had an important influence on the development of the popular gospel of consolation. For another Dickinson poem where the coffin is a "house" with its own special "key" see "I am alive–I guess" (J 470). Nehemiah Adams explicates the meaning of such a unique mortuary keepsake in his *Agnes and the Little Key* (Boston: Ticknor & Fields, 1863), when he writes: "It is an emblem and pledge of reopening. We use keys not merely to lock up. You seem to have regarded this key as a seal upon the stone. This is true, but also think of it as an emblem and a pledge of re-admission . . . The little key is a token of possession" (64). This quotation is from the revised eighth edition of the work originally entitled *Agnes and the Key of Her Little Coffin* (1857).

27 As early as 1871, Amherst was well stocked with caskets of all tastes and types. In a small booklet entitled *The Attractions of Amherst* (Amherst: Henry M. McCloud, 1871), Addington D. Welch writes that on a visit to Marsh and Son's Furniture and Coffin Warehouse he examined "a casket of rare design" that was "just the nicest thing of the kind we have ever seen. It is a folding casket, which on being opened and laid out flat looks like a satin bed." Welch adds that "there is no look of the 'coffin' about it, and it robs death of much that is disagreeable. Few people like to remember a dear one in his coffin; on the one they showed us, the occupant looks more like a person lying asleep" (10–11).

28 Although Dickinson wrote Higginson in December 1879, "Of Poe, I know too little to think" (L 2:649), the little that she did know was undoubtedly "Annabel Lee." On June 13, 1858, Joseph Lyman quoted some "rare and delicate touches" he found in a letter recently received from Emily Dickinson. In one of them she wrote, "The 'Kingdom by the Sea' never alters, Joseph, but the children do," a clear reference to Poe's

> I was a child, and she was a child,
> In this kingdom by the sea

See Sewall, *Lyman Letters*, 52; and Poe's *Poems*, ed. T. O. Mabbott (Cambridge: Harvard University Press, 1969), 477.

In a section of George and Samuel Duffield's *The Burial of The Dead:*

A Pastor's Complete Hand-Book for Funeral Services (New York: Funk and Wagnalls, 1885) entitled "Indications of Actual Death," we read that the first signs of death are like those of approaching sleep after deep weariness, but far stronger. At the same time a cold sweat is often perceptible on the face and limbs . . . The senses one by one are enfeebled, perhaps extinguished. First the sight fails; spots and flakes appear before the eye . . . the countenances of friends are but imperfectly distinguished; the candle held closely shines as if through a thick mist; darkness comes on" (73).

29 Jay Leyda, "Miss Emily's Maggie," *New World Writing # 3* (New York: New American Library, 1953), 266–7.

30 Elizabeth Longford, *Queen Victoria: Born to Succeed* (New York: Harper & Row, 1964), 562. The body of Victoria was attired in a white dress, lace wedding veil, and white widow's cap (ibid., 563). For a deathbed portrait of the Queen in this attire, see Morley, *Death,* fig. 57. The "tulle" mentioned in "Because I could not stop for Death" (J 712) was another favorite material for wedding veils.

31 The other was an example of schoolgirl art painted by her mother (reproduced in *LED* 1:facing p. 77). Both items are mentioned in an inventory of the contents of the Evergreens made by Martha Dickinson Bianchi in 1923 as having hung in "Emily's room," and both are now at Harvard.

32 *FF,* 61. In Stowe's *Old-town Folks* (ed. Henry F. May [Cambridge: Harvard University Press, 1966]), Sam Lawson, "The Village Do-Nothing," who helps with the laying out of the dead, remarks: "I was at Parson Rider's funeral, down to Wrentham. He was laid out in white flannel." (81). See Chapter 3 for a discussion of this work.

33 Lydia H. Sigourney, *Select Poems* (Philadelphia: Frederick W. Greenough, 1838), 24–5.

34 See L. Burke, *The Illustrated Language and Poetry of Flowers* (New York: Routledge, n.d.), 61, 35, 28. That Dickinson was familiar with the language of flowers but that Master was not can be inferred from a letter she sent about 1858: "You ask me what my flowers said – then they were disobedient – I gave them messages" (L 2:333). Lydia Sigourney edited a similar volume of these "floral emblems" entitled *The Voice of Flowers* (1846). The only major work of American fiction in which this flower code appears is Herman Melville's *Mardi* (1849).

35 Martha Dickinson Bianchi, *The Life and Letters of Emily Dickinson* (Boston: Houghton Mifflin, 1924), 102.

36 Mark Girouard, *The Victorian Country House* (New Haven, Conn.: Yale University Press, 1979), 116–7.

37 *The Complete Poems of Emily Brontë,* ed. Philip Henderson (London: Folio Society, 1951), 247. This was popularly known as "Emily Brontë's Last Poem," on the basis of information supplied by her sister Charlotte, but Henderson notes that it is dated "January 2, 1846" and that Emily worked on other projects before her death on December 19, 1848 (281).

3. KINDRED SPIRITS

1 Northrop Frye defines "private mythology" as a poet's "own spectroscopic band or peculiar formation of symbols" in *Fables of Identity* (New York: Harcourt, Brace & World, 1963), 11.

2 Orlando Williams Wight, *The Romance of Abelard and Heloise* (New York: Appleton, 1853), 9–10. According to information in the *National Cyclopaedia of American Biography*, Orlando Williams Wight was a physician and author born at Centerville, N.Y., February 19, 1824. He attended Westfield Academy and Rochester Collegiate Institute, and for a time taught Latin, Greek, and mathematics. In 1847 he went to New York City, where he studied theology and was ordained a Universalist minister, although he apparently never really considered himself of any denomination. He spent a year in Europe in 1853, after which he returned and took a medical degree at Long Island College Hospital. He started a practice in Milwaukee and in 1874 was named surgeon-general for Wisconsin, becoming health officer for Milwaukee in 1878 and for Detroit in 1882. Somewhere in between he picked up A.M. and LL.D. degrees from Yale. He died in Detroit, October 19, 1888. Besides his *Abelard and Heloise*, his publications included *The Philosophy of Sir William Hamilton* (1853), a translation of Victor Cousin's *History of Modern Philosophy* (1852), miscellaneous pieces on Pascal and Balzac, and a translation (with Mary L. Booth) of Henry Martin's *History of France* (1863).

3 For a succinct treatment of the candidates proposed by various critics and biographers, see the section entitled "Biography" by James Woodress in "Emily Dickinson," in Robert A. Rees and Earl N. Harbert, eds., *Fifteen American Authors before 1900* (Madison: University of Wisconsin Press, 1971), 146–50. In *The Hidden Life of Emily Dickinson* (New York: Simon & Schuster, 1971), John Evangelist Walsh suggests that Otis Phillips Lord was the original recipient of the Master letters (185–202). A recent addition to this list is a distant cousin, Richard Salter Storrs Dickinson, nominated by Dorothy Waugh in *Emily Dickinson's Beloved: A Surmise* (New York: Vantage Press, 1976).

4 That "Saxon" was a code-word for her lover is demonstrated by "Many a phrase has the English language" (J 276), with its closing lines "Say it again, Saxon! / Hush – Only to me!" See also *L* 2:374, where Dickinson declares that "The love of the Plantagenet is my only apology." Most critics have taken her statement to T. W. Higginson of June 7, 1862, that "I have no Saxon, now" to refer to an inability to write poetry, when actually it is a cryptic allusion to her absent lover.

5 See Millicent Todd Bingham, *Emily Dickinson: A Revelation* (New York: Harper & Bros., 1954), 1–2.

6 See Oliver Wendell Holmes, *Poetical Works* (Boston: Houghton Mifflin, 1890), 172–4.

7 Timothy Titcomb [Josiah Gilbert Holland], *Letters to the Joneses* (New York: Scribner, 1864), 14. Jay Leyda notes that these letters were originally

published in the *Springfield Republican* (*YH* 2:81). Dickinson herself would have glimpsed some self-satire in letters 15, "To Miss Felicia Hemans Jones – Concerning her strong desire to become an authoress," and letter 21, "To Diogones Jones – Concerning his disposition to avoid society."

8   For an excellent discussion of the development and decline of the New Divinity, see Douglas, *Feminization,* 121–64. For a historial survey, see Frank Hugh Foster, *A Genetic History of New England Theology* (Chicago: University of Chicago Press, 1907). The formidable Mary Lyon, preceptress of Mount Holyoke Female Seminary during Dickinson's stay there, had grimly written to her own mother on July 21, 1821, "Should any cherish a false hope, should any lay their foundation in the sand, almost as easily might the dead be raised, as such be rescued from eternal destruction." See Edward Hitchcock, *The Power of Christian Benevolence Illustrated in the Life and Labors of Mary Lyon* (Northampton, Mass.: Hopkins, Bridgman, 1852), 19–23.

9   Jonathan Edwards, "A Divine and Supernatural Light," in *Representative Selections,* 104–5.

10   "If I am the Devil's child, I will live then from the Devil" (Emerson, "Self-Reliance," in *Works* 2:52).

11   *The Minister's Wooing* was serialized in the *Atlantic Monthly* beginning in December 1858, and we know that Dickinson was an avid reader of this journal, to which her sister-in-law, Susan, subscribed. The editors of Dickinson's *Letters* have ascribed her fondness for the image of "Ancestor's Brocades" (*L* 2:420) to her reading of George Eliot's *Mill on the Floss,* but the same figure can be found in *MW* (559) and *Oldtown Folks* (94). The former also mentions "full ruffles of old Mechlin lace" (560), and "Mechlin" is another favorite term with Dickinson (see J 274, J 374, J 1423). Gilbert and Gubar note a convincing source for "One need not be a Chamber – to be Haunted" (J 670) in *Uncle Tom's Cabin* (*Madwoman,* 624). After the success of this 1852 work, Stowe sometimes summered in Amherst and was a guest of Susan Dickinson's at the Evergreens. Among the Dickinson books at Harvard are Susan's copies of Stowe's *Agnes of Sorrento, The Pearl of Orr's Island,* and *Uncle Tom's Cabin.*

Although dealing with the same mythic substratum deposited by a glacial New England Calvinism, *Oldtown Folks* is separated from *The Minister's Wooing* not only by a gulf of ten years, but by the cultural chasm of the Civil War. Stowe's earlier work is in fact more millennial than retrospective; the later novel increasingly isolates the real from the ideal, the antiquarian from the utopian, and the individual from the communal. The result is, as Stowe herself observed of *Oldtown Folks,* that "under all the drollery that is to be found in it, this book will be found to have in it the depths of the most solemn tragedy of life." (quoted, from Stowe to James T. Fields, August 16, 1868, by May in his Introduction to *Oldtown Folks,* 30). Its tone is one not of joyful amelioration but, as in Frost's "Oven Bird," of a sad perplexity engendered by the problem of "what to make of a diminished thing," that thing being postbellum New England culture.

12 Gail Parker, *The Oven Birds* (Garden City, N.Y.: Doubleday, 1972), 13.

13 On Catharine Beecher's struggle against orthodoxy see Martha Bacon's chapter, "Miss Beecher in Hell," in her *Puritan Promenade* (Boston: Houghton Mifflin, 1964), 73–93; and Kathryn Kish Sklar, *Catharine Beecher: A Study in American Domesticity* (New Haven, Conn.: Yale University Press, 1973). See also May's Introduction to *Oldtown Folks,* 3–43.

14 Nathaniel Hawthorne, *The Blithedale Romance and Fanshaw,* ed. Fredson Bowers (Columbus: Ohio State University Press, 1964), 121–2.

15 See Nina Baym, *Women's Fiction: A Guide to Novels by and about Women in America, 1820–1870* (Ithaca, N.Y.: Cornell University Press, 1978).

16 Daniel Aaron, *The Unwritten War: American Writers and the Civil War* (New York: Knopf, 1973), 355.

17 Elizabeth Stuart Phelps, *Chapters from a Life* (Boston: Houghton Mifflin, 1896), 97.

18 See John Cody, *After Great Pain: The Inner Life of Emily Dickinson* (Cambridge: Harvard University Press, 1971).

19 Julia Ward Howe, "Battle Hymn of the Republic," *Atlantic Monthly* 9 (February 1862):145.

20 Herman Melville, "A Utilitarian View of the Monitor's Fight," in Melville, *Selected Poems,* ed. Hennig Cohen (Garden City, N.Y.: Doubleday, 1964), 17.

21 See Habenstein and Lamers, *American Funeral Directing,* 324 and passim.

22 In 1876 Stowe wrote of the Confederate War Memorial in Savannah, Georgia, that "the veiled figure with the fingers on the lip is the fittest emblem for a monument that perpetuates the memory of strife among brothers" (quoted by Edward Wagenknecht, *Harriet Beecher Stowe: The Known and the Unknown* [New York: Oxford University Press, 1965], 183).

23 For Dickinson's use of Tennyson's "Charge of the Light Brigade," see Curtis Dahl, " 'To Fight Aloud' and 'The Charge of the Light Brigade': Dickinson on Tennyson," *New England Quarterly* 52, (March 1979):94–9.

24 William Augustus Stearns, *Adjutant Stearns* (Boston: Sabbath School Society, 1862), 155. There are two copies of this work among the Dickinson books at Harvard. One is bound in green cloth with a gold tooled design; the other is inscribed "Master Edward Dickinson from Dr. Stearns, Amherst College, 21 July, 1874." For more recent information see Phyllis Lehrer, "Frazar Stearns: A Young Man with a Promise," *Amherst Record,* May 5, 1982, 15–16.

25 Compare Walt Whitman's softening of these marmoreal conventions in his "Ashes of Soldiers":

> Perfume therefore my chant, O love, immortal love,
> Give me to bathe the memories of all dead soldiers,
> Shroud them, embalm them, cover them over with tender pride.
> > *Leaves of Grass and Selected Poems,* ed. Sculley Bradley
> > (New York: Holt, Rinehart & Winston, 1965), 401–2.

26 The full quotation is from 2 Cor. 5:1: "For we know that if our earthly house of this tabernacle were dissolved, we have a building of God, an

house not made with hands, eternal in the heavens." For Dickinson's use of this verse, see *L* 2:321, 323, 552; *L* 3:797. Helen Hunt Jackson has a long nature poem entitled "My House was not made with Hands," the idea for which she probably got from Dickinson. See Helen Hunt Jackson, *Poems* (Boston: Little, Brown, 1898), 147–50.

4. PARADISE DEFERRED

See Helen Sootin Smith, Introduction to Elizabeth Stuart Phelps, *The Gates Ajar* (Cambridge: Harvard University Press, 1964), v–xxxiv. For an analysis of *Gates* as the apotheosis of traditional consolation literature, see Ann Douglas, "Heaven Our Home: Consolation Literature in the Northern United States, 1830–1889," *American Quarterly* 26 (December 1974):496–515. Howard Kerr considers *Gates* as a specimen of spiritualistic fiction in *Mediums, and Spirit-Rappers, and Roaring Radicals: Spiritualism in American Literature, 1850–1900* (Urbana: University of Illinois Press, 1972), 108–9. On Phelps's role as reformer and feminist, see not only her *Chapters from a Life* but Mary Angela Bennett, *Elizabeth Stuart Phelps* (Philadelphia: University of Pennsylvania Press, 1939); and Christine Stansell, "Elizabeth Stuart Phelps: A Study in Female Rebellion," in Lee R. Edwards, Mary Heath, and Lisa Baskin, eds., *Woman: An Issue* (Boston: Little, Brown, 1972), 239–56. For a criticism of the ideas expressed in this chapter, see Robin R. Fast, " 'The One Thing Needful': Dickinson's Dilemma of Home and Heaven," *ESQ* 27 (Third Quarter 1981):157–69.

2   Elizabeth Stuart Phelps, *Austin Phelps: A Memoir* (New York: Scribner, 1891), 176–7. Austin Phelps himself wrote a best-selling treatise on prayer entitled *The Still Hour; or, Communion with God* (Boston: Gould & Lincoln, 1859). He was also the editor, along with Edwards Park and Lowell Mason, of *The Sabbath Hymn Book* (New York: Mason Bros., 1858). Edward Dickinson owned five copies of this work, some of which were richly bound in brown and black morocco, with the owner's name stamped in gold on the front cover.

3   Walsh's *Hidden Life* has this supposed plagiarism as its main thesis.

4   For an earlier autobiographical fiction recounting the anguish of this event, see Elizabeth Stuart Phelps, "A Sacrifice Consumed," *Harper's New Monthly Magazine* 28 (January 1864):235–40.

5   See George M. Fredrickson, *The Inner Civil War: Northern Intellectuals and the Crisis of the Union* (New York: Harper & Row, 1965).

6   The exact personal relationship between Dickinson and Phelps remains circumstantial. Dickinson's "Dear Preceptor," T. W. Higginson, was acquainted with Phelps and may have suggested Dickinson as a contributor to the *Woman's Journal,* which Phelps edited. Indeed, he once declared that if Shakespeare had been living in the nineteenth century, he would have been a subscriber and probably a contributor as well. In 1872 Dickinson wrote Louise Norcross about an importunate "Miss P" who requested her "to aid the world by my chirrup more." Dickinson declined, and "Miss P"

never replied; Dickinson was prompted to comment that "she might have been offended, or perhaps is extricating humanity from some hopeless ditch." The editors of Dickinson's letters suggest that "the Miss P may be Elizabeth Stuart Phelps," who was well known for her involvement in temperance and other reform movements (L 2:500). Leyda considered the connection significant enough to note that a copy of *Gates* was placed in Amherst's Circulating Library, according to the *Amherst Record* of April 26, 1871 (*YH* 2:173). The relatively late date of the accession can perhaps be explained by the strict orthodoxy of Amherst public opinion. There is more definite evidence that Emily Dickinson was acquainted with the works of the elder Elizabeth Stuart Phelps, though she would also have encountered the daughter's short fictions as they appeared anonymously in the pages of the *Atlantic Monthly*. In February of 1855, a Mrs. James Brown presented to Lavinia and Emily Dickinson a gift edition of *The Last Leaf from Sunnyside* as a memento of the sisters' stay in Washington, D.C., where their father was for a short time U.S. representative for Massachusetts. This work contained the posthumous writings of "H. Trusta," penname of the elder Elizabeth Phelps, with a memoir by her husband, Austin. This copy is now in the Jones Library, Amherst.

7 Richard Chase, for example, writes of Dickinson that "she would not be of great eminence, surely, if her reputation depended solely on her love poems. They are weakened almost throughout by the inadequacies of her private system of imagery, her word-magic, and the general view of life that went with these tendencies" (*Emily Dickinson* [1951; Westport, Conn: Greenwood Press, 1973], 242–3). William R. Sherwood provides an extensive discussion of Dickinson's love poems in *Circumference and Circumstance: Stages in the Mind and Art of Emily Dickinson* (New York: Columbia University Press, 1968), but he relates their imagery to the conventions of the Puritan tradition, arguing that the poet underwent a conversion from "a love that is ecstatic, defiant, liberating, ennobling, and banal" to an "experience of divine forgiveness which both Emily Dickinson and her Puritan ancestors designated 'grace' " (84). For another view of Dickinson's orthodoxy see David R. Williams, " 'This Consciousness That Is Aware': Emily Dickinson in the Wilderness of the Mind," *Soundings* 66 (Fall 1983):360–81.

8 Charles Beecher, *Spiritual Manifestations* (Boston: Lee & Shepard, 1879), 32.

9 Charles Wadsworth, *Sermons* (Philadelphia: Presbyterian Publishing Co., 1882), 202. For an early exploration of Dickinson's debt to Wadsworth, see Mary Elizabeth Barbot, "Emily Dickinson Parallels," *New England Quarterly* 14 (December 1941):689–96. Leyda also includes a good number of extracts from Wadsworth's work in his *Years and Hours*. Wadsworth's sermons are intensely psychological, and filled with the colorful word-painting of the period. They are moody, manic-depressive meditations on inner torments and spiritual ecstasies, violently anti-Darwinian and passionately orthodox.

10 Perhaps the most famous expression of this idea was Longfellow's "Resignation," "Written in the autumn of 1848, after the death of his little

daughter Fanny." There seems small doubt that Dickinson knew this poem, for Longfellow's stanza 5 affirms:

> She is not dead, – the child of our affection, –
> But gone unto that school
> Where she no longer needs our poor protection,
> And Christ himself doth rule.

[*Works,* intro. by George Monteiro (Boston: Houghton Mifflin, 1975), 107]

Dickinson writes:

> I shall know why – when Time is over –
> And I have ceased to wonder why –
> Christ will explain each separate anguish
> In the fair schoolroom of the sky –   [J 193]

11 Dickinson is referring to 2 Kings 2:24, where the prophet Elisha is mocked by children: "And he turned back, and looked on them, and cursed them in the name of the Lord. And there came forth two she-bears out of the wood, and tare forty and two children of them." Watts's *Divine Songs for Children* renders this version of the Scripture story in "Against Scoffing and Calling Names," *Poetical Works* (London: C. Cooke, n.d.), 223. Watts's gory rendition of an already violent incident would have been made even more vivid in Dickinson's mind by the fact that American editions of Watts's *Divine Songs* were sometimes embellished with wood-cuts of this scene. See, for example, *Songs, Divine and Moral* (Philadelphia: H. Peck & Thomas Bliss, n.d. [ca. 1830]), 101.

12 Frank E. Manuel and Fritzie P. Manuel, "Sketch for a Natural History of Paradise," in Clifford Geertz, ed., *Myth, Symbol, and Culture* (New York: Norton, 1974), 106. Quoting Van Oosterzee's *Christian Dogmatics,* George and Samuel Duffield in *The Burial of the Dead* describe "The Intermediate State" in the following terms: "On the death of the body the departing spirit is transported into a condition which, in the light of the Gospel, can just as little be conceived of as one of unconscious sleep, as one of already completed happiness or misery. Rather must it be looked upon as a state of self-consciousness and of preliminary retribution, but, at the same time, one of gradual transition to a great final decision – a transition experienced in a world of spirits, in whose various circles Salvation or Perdition is determined above all by the inner state of each." (81).

13 Edgar Allan Poe, *Complete Works,* ed. James A. Harrison (New York: Crowell, 1902) 2:615.

14 Mark Twain, *Extract from Captain Stormfield's Visit to Heaven* (New York: Harper & Bros., 1909), 87. Later contributions to this genre of celestial satire would include Charles Erskine Scott Wood, *Heavenly Discourse* (1927) and Marc Connelly, *The Green Pastures* (1930). For a dissenting view of the relation between Phelps and Twain, see Robert A. Rees, " 'Captain Stormfield's Visit to Heaven' and *The Gates Ajar,*" *English Language Notes* 7 (March 1970):197–202. For an affirmative one, see Jay Martin, "Ghostly

Rentals, Ghostly Purchases: Haunted Imaginations in James, Twain, and Bellamy," in Kerr, Crowley, and Crow, *The Haunted Dusk*, 123–31. Ray B. Browne reviews the relevant sources and documents in *Mark Twain's Quarrel with Heaven* (New Haven, Conn.: College and University Press, 1970). For a twentieth-century neo-orthodox fantasy of a material heaven, which owes much to Hawthorne's "The Celestial Railroad," see C. S. Lewis, *The Great Divorce* (New York: Macmillan, 1946).

15   See Richard Wilbur, "Sumptuous Destitution" (1960), in Sewall, *Critical Essays*, 127–36; and George Monteiro, *"Love & Fame, or What's a Heaven For?* Emily Dickinson's Teleology," *New England Quarterly* 51 (March 1978):105–13.

16   For an analysis of some similar hymns of the period that "reflect the increasing stress on Christ's love and God's mercy," see Barbara Welter, "The Feminization of American Religion: 1800–1860," in Mary S. Hartman and Lois Banner, eds., *Clio's Consciousness Raised: New Perspectives on the History of Women* (New York: Harper & Row, 1974), 141–3. Many of Watts's late seventeenth-century and early eighteenth-century hymns also stress an erotic relationship to Christ. Here are some representative stanzas from *The Psalms, Hymns, and Spiritual Songs of the Rev. Isaac Watts, D.D., to Which Are Added Select Hymns from Other Authors*, edited by Samuel Worcester, "Professor of Rhetoric at Amherst College" (Boston: Crocker & Brewster, 1839):

> Jesus, the vision of thy face
> Hath overpowering charms!
> Scarce shall I feel death's cold embrace,
> If Christ be in my arms.   [Hymn 19, bk. 1]

> Now, through the veil of flesh I see,
> With eyes of love he looks on me;
> Now, in gospel's clearest glass,
> He shows the beauties of his face.   [Hymn 69, bk. 1]

> The op'ning heavens around me shine,
> With beams of sacred bliss;
> While Jesus shows his heart is mine,
> And whispers I am his.   [Hymn 54, bk. 2]

17   Mary Warner's scrapbook, 18–19, from *Putnam's Monthly Magazine* 7 (April 1856):420–7. The name of the salvific woman is Anne Harrison, who pines away for the young Cyrus Field, but refuses to marry him because he is skeptical and unconverted. Converted at last in the Ohio wilderness, Field returns homes, only to find Anne dead from an epidemic fever caught while ministering to the poor. He learns that on her deathbed she "sent for my mother, and told her to say she had loved me to the last, and should look for me in heaven." Consequently Field is called to the ministry, but never marries, anticipating a final reunion with Anne in paradise.

18 For an extensive discussion of the metaphor of the house in Dickinson's poetry, see Jean McClure Mudge, *Emily Dickinson and the Image of Home* (Amherst: University of Massachusetts Press, 1975).

19 Lydia Sigourney, whose own marriage was troubled, expressed the same idea of the rigidity of the marriage bond in her poem "The Bride," who girds on "The harness, which the ministry of Death / Alone unlooseth, but whose fearful power / May stamp the sentence of Eternity." (*Selected Poems*, 255). We should also remember that in Mormon usage, to give a woman in marriage was rendered by the verb "to seal." Dickinson's private love religion has strong affinities to the Perfectionism represented by Mormon doctrine. As Welter notes, "Women could legitimately claim that Mormonism recognized their importance more than any other religion because it tied them to their husbands for all time and eternity" ("Feminization," 150).

20 Eugene Crowell, *The Spirit World: Its Inhabitants, Nature and Philosophy* (Boston: Colby & Rich, 1880), 70.

21 Twain is referring to the pastor of Brooklyn's Central Presbyterian Church, T. DeWitt Talmage, who "attracted swarms of people with his racy narrative accounts of vice and degradation in the seamy sections of the city" (David S. Reynolds, "From Doctrine to Narrative: The Rise of Pulpit Storytelling in America," *American Quarterly* 32 [Winter 1980]:494). Yet as Reynolds remarks, it was Dwight L. Moody, Talmage's equally colorful contemporary, who preached a "famous sermon on Heaven (1876), which sold more than 425,000 copies in pamphlet form by 1900." This sermon "contained eight successive stories, making spiritual regeneration dependent on mawkish anecdote rather than on doctrinal exposition" (496). Reynolds is too hard on Moody, who did not write down his sermons but allowed them to be transcribed and edited by others. This is what happened with his sermon on heaven, which is actually the main butt of Twain's satire. In a new revised edition of this sermon published in 1880 we find the original of Twain's exhaltation of Sir Richard Duffer, for Moody asserts that "Paul, the humble tent-maker, will have a higher seat in heaven than the best and greatest soverign that ever ruled the earth. If the Czar should meet John Bunyan, the poor tinker up in heaven, he no doubt would find him the greater man" (D. L. Moody, *Heaven: Where It Is, Its Inhabitants, and How to Get There* [Chicago: F. H. Revell, 1884], 54–5).

22 A similarly stratified heaven was also envisioned by Queen Victoria in the preamble to her last will and testament, dated October 25, 1897:

> I die in peace with all fully aware of my many faults relying with confidence on the love, mercy and goodness of my Heavenly Father and His Blessed son & earnestly trusting to be reunited to my beloved Husband, my dearest Mother, my beloved Children and 3 dear sons-in-law. – And all who have been very near & dearest to me on earth.
>
> Also I hope to meet those who have so faithfully & so devotedly

served me especially good John Brown and good Annie Macdonald who I trusted would help to lay my remains in my coffin & to see me placed next to my dearly beloved Husband in the mausoleum at Frogmore.

As Louis Auchinchoss observes, "One notes the hierarchical propriety. The servants, even the beloved Gillie, Brown, must wait for the second paragraph" (*Persons of Consequence: Queen Victoria and Her Circle* [New York: Random House, 1974], 23).

23 Robert Browning, *The Ring and the Book* (1868–9; New York: Norton, 1961), 278. An 1869 edition of this work published in Boston, which bears the autograph of Susan Dickinson and has many passages marked in pencil by Emily, is now in the Dickinson collection at Harvard.

24 See also John Maass, *The Glorious Enterprise: The Centennial Exhibition of 1876 and H. J. Schwarzmann, Architect-in-Chief* (New York: American Life Foundation, 1973), fig. 44. A photograph of the staircase hall of Lutton Hoo, plate 190 in Clive Aslet's *The Last Country Houses* (New Haven, Conn: Yale University Press, 1982), reveals that this statue ended up as part of "the magnificent art collection" (322) of Lutton Hoo's owner, the diamond millionaire Sir Julius Wernher.

25 Susan Chitty, *The Beast and the Monk: A Life of Charles Kingsley* (New York: Mason/Charter, 1975), 17, 77. This sentiment was of course not peculiar to the oversexed Kingsley. As Barbara Welter notes in "The Feminization of American Religion," the founder of the Oneida community, John Humphrey Noyes, "went so far in identifying the sex act with Perfectionism as to assert that sexual intercourse was practiced in heaven" (149).

5. AMERICAN GROTESQUE

1 In *This Was a Poet: A Critical Biography of Emily Dickinson* (New York: Scribner, 1938), George F. Whicher writes that "no one who . . . reads the poems metrically" can deny that Dickinson was "orthodox in her choice of meters, except in a very small number of poems" (240). For confirmation of this conclusion, see Thomas Johnson's discussion of Dickinson and hymnology in his *Interpretive Biography*, 84–100; and Martha Winburn England, "Emily Dickinson and Isaac Watts," in M. W. England and John Sparrow, *Hymns Unbidden: Donne, Herbert, Blake, Emily Dickinson and the Hymnographers* (New York: New York Public Library, 1966), 113–47. England observes that "Amherst was in the heart of a Watts enclave" (113).

2 Lucy Larcom, *A New England Girlhood (Outlined From Memory)* (Boston: Houghton Mifflin, 1889), 58, 68.

3 *Alice in Wonderland,* chap. 2, in *The Annotated Alice,* intro. and notes by Martin Gardner (New York: Clarkson N. Potter, 1960), 38–9.

4 On the genesis of this work, and continuing New England controversies about acceptable anthologies of Watts's hymns, see Sandra S. Sizer, *Gospel*

Hymns and Social Religion: The Rhetoric of Nineteenth-Century Revivalism (Philadelphia: Temple University Press, 1978), 67 and passim.

5 William Austin Dickinson, "Representative Men of the Parish, Church Buildings and Finances," in *An Historical Review: One Hundred and Fiftieth Anniversary of the First Church of Christ in Amherst, Massachusetts* (Amherst: Amherst Record, 1890), 56–7.

6 Hymn 538 in Asahel Nettleton, *Village Hymns for Social Worship* (Hartford, Conn.: Goodwin, 1824), 434, and hymns 447 and 100 in Worcester's *Watts and Select,* 755, 435. One must also acknowledge the influence on Dickinson of later compilations and anthologies such as her father's standard hymnal, Park, Phelps, and Mason's *Sabbath Hymn Book* of 1858. Book 14 of this edition (pp. 763–812) is entitled "Selections for Chanting" and presents representative psalms, gospel passages, and prayers marked with a special notation of bars and dashes that may have great relevance for the idiosyncratic punctuation of Dickinson's poems.

7 See my essay "Emily Dickinson's 'Babes in the Wood': A Ballad Reborn," *Journal of American Folklore* 90 (October–December 1977):430–41, for a case study of this process. See also Albert B. Friedman, *The Ballad Revival* (Chicago: University of College Press, 1961), 344–5; and Marianne Thalmann, *The Romantic Fairy-Tale: Seeds of Surrealism,* trans. Mary Corcoran (Ann Arbor: University of Michigan Press, 1964).

8 See Frances Bzowski, " 'Half-Child, Half-Heroine': Emily Dickinson's Use of Traditional Female Archetypes," *ESQ* 29 (Third Quarter 1983):154–69. Bzowski argues that even this submissive archetype is in fact deeply subversive of patriarchal authority, since "at the quivering moment of sexual awareness," such heroines "achieve a union with Christ rather than an earthly marriage," thus choosing "real death" over the "legal death" of conventional bourgeois contractual relationships (155).

9 Martha Gilbert Dickinson, *The Cathedral and Other Poems* (New York: Scribner, Sons, 1901), 9.

10 It is reproduced in color in *Masterpieces of American Primitive Painting,* intro. by Albert Ten Eyck Gardner (New York: American Federation of Arts, 1961), 97, and on the cover of *Art News* 53 (July–August 1954).

11 William Carlos Williams, "Painting in the American Grain," *Art News* 53 (July–August 1954):55.

12 Donald B. Kuspit, "American Folk Art: The Practical Vision," *Art in America* 68 (September 1980):96. See also C. K. Dewhurst, B. MacDowell, and M. MacDowell, *Artists in Aprons: Folk Art by American Women* (New York: Dutton, 1979).

13 See Vivian Pollak, "Emily Dickinson's Valentines," *American Quarterly* 26 (March 1974):60–78.

14 See George Monteiro, "Dickinson's 'I never lost as much but twice,' " *Explicator* 30 (September 1971):item 7.

15 Albert Gelpi, *Emily Dickinson: The Mind of the Poet* (Cambridge: Harvard University Press, 1965), 37.

16 Michael Wigglesworth, "The Day of Doom," in Harrison T. Meserole,

ed., *Seventeenth-Century American Poetry* (Garden City, N.Y.: Doubleday, 1968), 102.

17 The portrait is in some respects oddly prophetic of the children's later destinies. The determined Lavinia holds the tablet with the cat; Emily (wearing an enigmatic smile) clutches a moss rose on an open book depicting flowers, either a gift book or a botanical guide, or a book on the language of flowers; and the Byronic Austin stands in front of a ruined pillar wreathed in honeysuckle. In the language of flowers, the moss rose stands for "Confession of Love" and the honeysuckle connotes "The colour of my fate" (Burke, *Language and Poetry of Flowers*, 53, 28). A stormy background seems to hint at trouble ahead for all three. Phoebe Lloyd points out ("Posthumous Mourning Portraiture," in Pike and Armstrong, *A Time to Mourn*, 71–89) that cut flower, keepsake book, and fragile vine (not to mention approaching storm and broken column) are conventional emblems of death usually present only in mourning portraits, the child subjects of which were already deceased.

18 In her unpublished "Life" of her aunt, Bianchi writes that Elisha Kane's *Arctic Explorations in Search of Sir John Franklin* became Edward Dickinson's "prime favorite" piece of travel literature "when published in 1857." The two-volume edition of the work, with Edward Dickinson's autograph, is now at Harvard. His fondness for Kane's chilly narrative was obviously a shared family joke.

19 Bill to Lavinia Dickinson from F. O. Curtiss, Dealer in New and Creamery Milk and Cream, Amherst, Mass., July 5, 1897, the Evergreens. Curtiss delivered 93½ quarts of milk at $0.05 a quart from April 1 to July, for a total price of $4.67.

20 Martha Dickinson Bianchi, Introduction to Emily Dickinson, *The Single Hound: Poems of a Lifetime* (Boston: Little, Brown, 1915), xii.

21 Robert Browning, "Caliban upon Setebos," in Browning, *Poems, 1833–1865* (London: Cassell, 1910), 592.

22 Susan Huntington Dickinson, "Harriet Prescott's Early Work," *Springfield Sunday Republican,* February 1, 1903, 19. This article is datelined "Roma, Italia, January, 1903" and signed "S.H.D." Fragments of Emily Dickinson's letter were presented as verbatim comments by Bianchi in *FF*, 28, but because of the lack of a full text, the letter was omitted by Thomas Johnson in his standard edition of the *Letters*. Leyda notes Bianchi's citations in *YH* 2:6, though he speculates that Emily Dickinson was referring to Spofford's tale "The Amber Gods" rather than to "Circumstance." For an exploration of the significance of the latter story in Dickinson's work, see my essay " 'I Must Have Died at Ten Minutes Past One.' "

23 See Anna Mary Wells, *Dear Preceptor: The Life and Times of Thomas Wentworth Higginson* (Boston: Houghton, Mifflin, 1963), 114–15; and the discussion of Spofford's works in Chapter 6 of this study.

24 William Dean Howells, "A Reminiscent Introduction," in *The Great Modern American Stories: An Anthology* (New York: Boni & Liveright, 1920), vii.

eds., *Artists of the Nineteenth Century* (Boston: Osgood, 1879) 2:164–5. The Dickinsons bought their *Woodland Scene* a year before the publication of this work, in which it is noted that Parton's "Sycamores in Old Shokan" is "in the possession of Amherst College" (164). In a letter of November 12, 1980, Sean B. Tarpey, Curatorial Assistant at the Mead Art Museum, Amherst College, informed me that "there is no record of this work ever being in the collection." However, in the inventory of the Evergreens that she made in 1923, Martha Dickinson Bianchi mentioned among the paintings hanging in the East Parlor one entitled "Oaks at Old Shoken [*sic*], by Arthur Parton." Since Tarpey also writes that "the records of early loans to the museum are far from complete," this painting may have been on loan to Amherst College when Clement and Hutton compiled their data, or the Dickinsons may simply have used Amherst College as a convenient cover to protect their privacy. Shokan is described in the *Columbia Lippincott Gazetteer of the World* as a "resort village, Ulster Co., SE N.Y., in the Catskills, on Ashokan Reservoir, 12 mi. WNW of Kingston."

20 Mary Elizabeth Barbot notes the source for "At Half-Past Three, a single Bird" in "Emily Dickinson Parallels" 693, and Hyatt Waggoner that for "A Route of Evanescence" in *American Poets: From the Puritans to the Present* (Boston: Houghton Mifflin, 1968), 672.

21 About mid-July of 1867, Dickinson wrote to Higginson: "Bringing still my 'plea for *Culture,*' Would it teach me now?" (*L* 2:457). Thomas Johnson reads this as a plaintive request to renew their lapsed correspondence, but he also notes that Dickinson refers to Higginson's essay entitled "A Plea for Culture," first published in the January 1867 *Atlantic* and later collected in *Atlantic Essays* (Boston: Osgood, 1871).

22 T. W. Higginson, "The Future Life," in Higginson, *In After Days: Thoughts on the Future Life* (New York: Harper & Bros., 1910), 139–40.

23 See William James, *The Varieties of Religious Experience* (1902; New York: New American Library, 1964).

24 T. W. Higginson, *Cheerful Yesterdays* (Boston: Houghton Mifflin, 1878). The title was taken from Wordsworth's *The Excursion,* bk. 7:

> A man he sees of cheerful yesterdays
> And confident tomorrows.

25 T. W. Higginson, "A Letter to a Young Contributor," in Higginson, *Atlantic Essays,* 73.

26 Linnaeus, quoted by Neltje Blanchan in *Nature's Garden: An Aid to Knowledge of Our Wild Flowers and Their Insect Visitors* (New York: Doubleday, Page, 1901), 235.

27 Richard Sewall comments that "the herbarium shows a fine sense of composition, as well as a concern for precise Latin nomenclature" (*LED* 1:86 n. 8). This herbarium is now at Harvard. For reproductions of some of its pages, see the endpapers of vol. 1 of *LED*.

28 Higginson's real blindness was to the religious pressures that contributed to

25 Harriet Prescott Spofford, *The Amber Gods and Other Stories* (Boston: Ticknor & Fields, 1863), 157–8. For the use of a similar motif in Gothic fiction, probably based in part on Spofford's work, see Ambrose Bierce, "The Eyes of the Panther," in *Ghost and Horror Stories of Ambrose Bierce,* ed. E. F. Bleiler (New York: Dover, 1964), 105–13. Josephine Pollitt gives a synopsis of "Circumstance" in *Emily Dickinson: The Background of Her Poetry* (New York: Harper & Bros., 1930), 177–82, but she dismisses it as an influence on the poet. There are episodes involving confrontations with mountain lions both in J. F. Cooper's *The Pioneers* (1822) and in C. B. Brown's *Edgar Huntly* (1799). In a travel essay published in 1852, Jacob Abbot relates an anecdote about a panther who once attacked a servant in a convent and instead of killing him outright, "began to play with him as a cat plays with a mouse which she has succeeded in making her prey" ("Memoirs of the Holy Land," *Harper's New Monthly Magazine* 512 [August 1852]:302).

26 C. S. Lewis, *A Grief Observed* (Greenwich, Conn.: Seabury Press, 1963), 32.

27 On the nature of the hymn as a special form of nineteenth-century consolation literature, see Douglas, *Feminization,* 213–20.

28 Theodore Parker, "A Discourse of the Transient and Permanent in Christianity," in Perry Miller, ed., *The American Transcendentalists* (Garden City: Doubleday, 1957), 125.

29 The phrase is William James's: He distinguished between a "block" (deterministic) and an "open" (nondeterministic) universe.

30 Georges Poulet, *Studies in Human Time* (Baltimore: Johns Hopkins Press, 1970), 346.

31 Millicent Todd Bingham, *Ancestor's Brocades: The Literary Début of Emily Dickinson* (New York: Harper & Bros., 1945), 29.

6. THE EARTHLY PARADISE

1 On Higginson's sponsorship of other women writers, see Wells, *Dear Preceptor.* These included Dickinson's close friend and correspondent Helen Hunt Jackson. See also *LED* 2:532–92.

2 T. W. Higginson, "The Decline of the Sentimental," *Independent* 39 (November 3, 1887):1. In the autumn of 1853, Dickinson wrote to Dr. and Mrs. Josiah Holland, "I wrote to you last week, but thought you would laugh at me, and call me sentimental, so I kept my letter for 'Adolphus Hawkins, Esq.'" (*L* 1:264). The editors remind us that "Adolphus Hawkins, in Longfellow's prose romance *Kavanagh,* is a character whose writings satirize the effusions of the village poet." This is Dickinson's first consciously "literary" letter to survive, anticipating the virtual *petits poèmes en prose* that are her later epistles.

3 Henry James, review of *Azarian,* by Harriet Prescott [Spofford], *North American Review* 100 (January 1865):270. Such was the effect of James's review on Spofford that she did not publish another book until 1871, when

a collection of anecdotes, folklore, and local history entitled *New England Legends* appeared. He notes, for example: "If the dictionary were a palette of colors, and a goose-quill a brush, Miss Prescott would be a very clever painter. But as words possess a certain inherent dignity, value, and independence . . . her pictures are invariably incoherent and meaningless" (270).

4 T. W. Higginson, review of *Azarian, Atlantic Monthly* 14 (October 1864):515.

5 Rebecca Patterson, *Emily Dickinson's Imagery*, ed. Margaret H. Freeman (Amherst: University of Massachusetts Press, 1979), 115.

6 See n. 8, Chapter 1. There is ample evidence from Dickinson's letters that she was an admirer of that eclectic school of romantic poets pejoratively dubbed "spasmodic" by its sharpest critics. Moreover, there is abundant proof in Richard Sewall's *Lyman Letters* that Dickinson's circle of young friends in the mid-1850s were all infused with enthusiasm for the spasmodics. Joseph Lyman makes repeated references in his letters to Tennyson's *Maud* (1855) and James O. Bailey's Faustian epic poem *Festus* of 1839 (33–6), both considered to be masterpieces of the new spasmodic school. See also Mark A. Weinstein, *William Edmonstoune Aytoun and the Spasmodic Controversy* (New Haven, Conn.: Yale University Press, 1968). *Aurora Leigh,* beloved by both Dickinson and Phelps, was considered to be the culmination of the mode. As Jerome Hamilton Buckley notes, it "throbbed with a spasmodic faith in the poet's mission and the sanctity of subjective impulse" (*The Victorian Temper* [New York: Vintage Books, 1964], 62).

7 Harriet Prescott Spofford, *Sir Rohan's Ghost: A Romance* (Boston: J. E. Tilton, 1860), 86–7.

8 Harriet Prescott Spofford, "Pomegranate Flower and Apple Blossoms," *Harper's Bazaar* 25 (June 4, 1892):450–1.

9 Fred Lewis Pattee, *The Development of the American Short Story* (New York: Harper & Bros., 1923), 163.

10 In her unpublished "Life" of Emily Dickinson, Martha Dickinson Bianchi states: "It was in 1862 that Emily's literary philandering with Colonel Thomas Wentworth Higginson began through a stray note of admiration from her for his article in the 'Atlantic Monthly,' 'The Procession of the Flowers,' sent over to her by Sue" (468), and "when Colonel Higginson's article, 'The Procession of the Flowers' appeared in the *Atlantic* Sue ran over with it to Emily the hour it arrived. They read it together and apart, and frequently went back to it" (529–30). Certainly "Letter to a Young Contributor" was not the only Higginson essay that spoke directly to Emily Dickinson's taste and needs. Although "The Procession of the Flowers," published in the December 1862 issue of the *Atlantic,* was not the first piece to elicit the poet's admiration, her response to it was representative of her attachment to Higginson's work, as Bianchi's reminiscence of Dickinson family tradition attests.

11 See James Russell Lowell, *My Study Windows* (Boston: Houghton Mifflin, 1892). Dickinson presented an 1872 copy of this book to her sister-in-law,

an indication of how highly she esteemed it. Sometime in 1869 Dickinson wrote to Louise Norcross that she had "Read Mr. Lowell's [A Good Word for] *Winter,*" and commented, "One does not often meet anything so perfect" (L 2:466).

12 *Thoreau: The Major Essays,* ed. Jeffrey L. Duncan (New York: Dutton, 1972), 1.

13 William Ellery Channing, *Thoreau: The Poet-Naturalist* (Boston: Roberts Bros., 1873).

14 On the basis of a relineated pencil draft written at the same time, Thomas H. Johnson accords this utterance the status of a poem:

Paradise is of the option.
Whosoever will
Own in Eden notwithstanding
Adam and Repeal.   [J 1069]

15 Nathaniel Hawthorne, "Buds and Bird Voices," in Hawthorne, *Mosses from an Old Manse* (Boston: Houghton Mifflin, 1884), 175.

16 Walt Whitman, quoted by F. O. Matthiessen, *American Renaissance: Art and Expression in the Age of Emerson and Whitman* (New York: Oxford University Press, 1941), 626.

17 T. W. Higginson, *The Afternoon Landscape: Poems and Translations* (New York: Longmans, Green, 1889).

18 On Durand, see James Thomas Flexner, *That Wilder Image, The Painting of America's Native School from Thomas Cole to Winslow Homer* (New York: Bonanza Books, 1962); Barbara Novak, *American Painting of the Nineteenth Century* (New York: Praeger, 1969); and David B. Lawall, *A. B. Durand, 1796–1886* (Montclair, N.J.: Montclair Art Museum, 1971).

19 In the case of the Parton landscape that executes in paint the mood of Higginson's "Out-Door Study," we must credit Susan Dickinson and her daughter, Martha, rather than the possessive Austin, whose passion for collecting had somewhat abated by this time (see Appendix B, "Austin Dickinson as connoisseur"). A letter from a close Dickinson acquaintance, Henry E. Hills, written to his absent wife on March 21, 1878, mentions that "Mrs. D[ickinson] & Mattie will come first of week after next," and then adds, "They have a new picture by Arthur Parton a Landscape trees cattle & water Mother and all delighted with their picture" (YH 2:290). Arthur Parton and his younger brother Ernest carried on the arcadian tradition of quiescent Hudson River landscape painting established by Thomas Cole and perfected by Durand. Born in 1842, Arthur Parton was elected an associate of the National Academy in 1872. His brother studied with him for two years, but otherwise received no formal training. The work of both men reflects the intensification of the familiar that marked the later phase of Hudson River practice, though Arthur was also much influenced by English Pre-Raphaelite and French Barbizon techniques. He did many landscapes in the Adirondacks and the Catskills and became a full academician in 1884. See Clara E. Clement and Laurence Hutton,

Dickinson's manic-depressiveness. Although he was an ordained minister, he wrote in *Cheerful Yesterdays,* "Greatly to my bliss, I escaped almost absolutely all those rigors of the old New England theology which have darkened the lives of so many. I never heard of the Five Points of Calvinism until maturity; never was converted, never experienced religion. We were expected to read the New Testament, but there was nothing enforced about the Old, and were as fortunate as a little girl I have since known, who was sure that there could be no such place as hell, because their minister had never mentioned it"(35).

7. LONE LANDSCAPES

1   Asher B. Durand, *Letters on Landscape Painting,* letter 6, *Crayon* 1 (April 4, 1855):209.

2   On Ruskin's life, see the excellent short study by John D. Rosenberg, *The Darkening Glass: A Portrait of Ruskin's Genius* (New York: Columbia University Press, 1961); and on the evolution of his critical theory, see George P. Landow, *The Aesthetic and Critical Theories of John Ruskin* (Princeton, N.J.: Princeton University Press, 1971).

3   I take seriously Dickinson's confession to Higginson in her second letter to him, of April 25, 1862, that the first among her prose masters was John Ruskin (*L* 2:404). Among the Ruskin volumes owned by Susan and Austin Dickinson were the 1860 anthology *Precious Thoughts, Sesame and Lilies* (1865), *The Stones of Venice* (1860), and another anthology entitled *The True and the Beautiful* (1868). See "Handlist of Books Found in the Home of Emily Dickinson" (Harvard, 1951). There are no extant copies of *Modern Painters,* but as a faithful reader of the *Atlantic Monthly,* Dickinson would have read William Stillman's enthusiastic review of the fifth volume of *Modern Painters* in vol. 6 (August 1860), where he commented that "the first volume of 'Modern Painters', was, as every body will remember, one of the sensational books of the time, and fell upon the public opinion of the day like a thunderbolt from a clear sky" (239). Higginson gently criticized Ruskin in "My Out-Door Study" for "taking rather the artist's view of Nature, selecting the available bits and dealing rather patronizingly with the whole" (*ODP,* 259), and in "Literature as an Art" he lamented, "What glorious gift of heaven would have been the style of Ruskin, for instance, could he but have contained himself, and put forth only half his strength, instead of always planting, in the words of Old Fuller, 'a piece of ordnance to batter down an aspen-leaf'!" (*Atlantic Essays,* 39). Yet in "A Letter to a Young Contributor," he cited the graduate of Oxford as a stylistic authority: "And as Ruskin says of painting that it is in the perfection and precision of the instantaneous line that the claim to immortality is made, so it is easy to see that a phrase may outweigh a library" (*Atlantic Essays,* 75). It is significant that he ended his Preface to the first series of Dickinson's *Poems* with a quotation from Ruskin ("No weight nor mass nor beauty of execution can outweigh one grain or fragment of thought") as a means of

defending Dickinson's "extraordinary grasp and insight, uttered with an uneven vigor, sometimes exasperating, seemingly wayward, but really unsought and inevitable" (vi).

4   See George F. Whicher, "Uriel in Amherst," *Amherst Graduates' Quarterly* 23 (August 1934):286–8; and Susan Dickinson, "Magnetic Visitors," 12–13. Emily Dickinson's only comment on Emerson's 1857 visit to the Evergreens was the note she afterward sent to Susan, "It must have been as if he had come from where dreams are born!" (Bianchi, *Life and Letters,* 82; *FF,* 137–9).

5   See, for example, figs. 216, 217, 218, and 219 of "American Primitives" in the *Kennedy Quarterly* 10 (December 1970):148–9. The catalogue description of these items reads: "The art of 'sandpaper drawing' flourished in the middle of the nineteenth century as a successor to 'Grecian drawing,' with commercial sandpaper used in place of millboard or artists' board prepared with a fine covering of marble dust. Powdered, non-greasy crayons or powdered lead dust was then applied with stomps, chamois, or various other instruments. The technique lent itself particularly to black and white drawings, and the strong contrasts of light and shade, combined with the light overall sparkle of the surface, often produced extremely effective results" (169). For an illustration of a paint box and implements for monochromatic painting, see figs. 127 and 128 in Nina Fletcher Little, *Neat and Tidy: Boxes and Their Contents Used in Early America* (New York: Dutton, 1980), 122–3.

6   Plutarch, "Of Isis and Osiris, or of the Ancient Religion and Philosophy of Egypt," in *Plutarch's Morals,* ed. William W. Goodwin (Boston: Little, Brown, 1870) 4:72. This is a reprint of the well-known English translation "by Several Hands" first published in London in 1684–94. Significantly, the 1870 reprint features an introduction by Emerson, which takes note of Plutarch's "vast popularity" in modern times and compares him with Goethe, Montaigne, and Hume (1:ix–xxiv). Dickinson was familiar with a popular work that quoted this esoteric source, Thomas Moore's Egyptian romance *The Epicurean* (1827), which she read in 1848 (*L* 1:66). This latter work is filled with heady references to veiled apparitions and the "dark, awful," and "mighty" veils of temples and sanctuaries; the veiled Isis with her cryptic inscription serves as an introduction to the hero's mystery-initiation beneath a pyramid situated in the Alexandrian Necropolis. Moore even footnotes Plutarch in the original Greek in order to validate his hero's observation, "At Sais I was present during [the] Festival of Lamps, and read, by the blaze of innumerable lights, those sublime words on the temple of Neitha: 'I am all that ever has been, that is, and that will be, and no man hath ever lifted my veil' " (*The Epicurean, a Tale and Alciphron, a Poem* [London: John Macrone, 1839], 25, 215 n).

7   Henry David Thoreau, *Walden; or, Life in the Woods* (1854; New York: Holt, Rinehart & Winston, 1966), 81.

8   Henry James, *The Bostonians* (1886; Indianapolis: Bobbs-Merrill, 1976), 165.

9   See Roger B. Stein, *John Ruskin and Aesthetic Thought in America, 1840–1900* (Cambridge: Harvard University Press, 1967).

10 I owe this concept to David C. Huntington, who has made a similar observation in two places. In *The Landscapes of Frederic Edwin Church: Vision of an American Era* (New York: Braziller, 1966), he writes: "A plate in *Modern Painters* seems to illustrate the point. A spectacular dawn over the Lombard Apennines appears to have struck Ruskin as a natural metaphor of the Sistine Ceiling, a sky Michelangelo might have painted had he been a nineteenth-century Englishman" (79). Huntington reiterates this point in "Church and Luminism: Light for America's Elect," in John Wilmerding, ed., *American Light: The Luminist Movement, 1850–1875* (Washington, D.C.: National Gallery of Art, 1980), where he notes that Ruskin did not specify that his illustration be taken as a correlative of Michelangelo's masterpiece, but that in his "evocation of the Sistine ceiling in the alpine sky" he was "simply confirming habits of religious imagination that were ingrained in romantic Christian consciousness" (175). Huntington uses the term "natural typology" (ibid., 180) for the process of transference that I call "romantic typology."

11 John Durand, *The Life and Times of Asher B. Durand* (1894; New York: Da Capo Press, 1970), 151.

12 In one of his "Marginalia," Poe writes, "Were I called upon to define, very briefly, the term 'Art,' I should call it 'the reproduction of what the senses perceive in Nature through the veil of the soul' " (*Works* 16:164).

13 Novak, *American Painting of the Nineteenth Century*, 97, 99. See also her *Nature and Culture: American Landscape Painting, 1825–1875* (New York: Oxford University Press, 1980), 38–44.

14 Nathaniel Hawthorne, *The English Notebooks*, ed. Randall Stewart (London: Oxford University Press, 1941), 550.

15 Mark Twain, *Life on the Mississippi* (Boston: James R. Osgood, 1883), 502. The first part of the quotation notes that "the thunder-peals were constant and deafening; explosion followed explosion with but inconsequential intervals between, and the reports grew steadily sharper and higher-keyed, and more trying to the ear."

16 My attribution and titling of these paintings is based largely upon the entries in an inventory taken by Susan Dickinson of the contents of the Evergreens soon after Austin Dickinson's death in 1895 and upon the diary-inventory made by Martha Dickinson Bianchi in 1923. In some cases these entries are vague or even misleading (Bianchi lists *Autumn Evening in the White Hills* as "Lake at Daybreak" by "Swayne Gifford," another American painter, when the back of the canvas reveals true title, date, and artist), but for the most part they accurately reflect the facts of family acquisitions and provenances. Where signatures are illegible and information in the inventories is lacking, I have omitted attribution, save when physical evidence seems trustworthy, as in the case of the Kensett *Sunset with Cows,* where the name "Kensett" is written in pencil on the back stretchers. This painting, reproduced as a frontispiece to Chapter 8, is similar in technique

and composition to others of this period in the artist's development. See, for example, his *Scene on the Delaware* of 1856, reproduced on p. 23 of John K. Howat, *John Frederick Kensett, 1816–1872* (New York: American Federation of Arts, 1968). For biographical information on the individual artists, see such standard works as Clement and Hutton, *Artists of the Nineteenth Century*. On the Hill brothers, John William and John Henry, and the entire American absorption in Pre-Raphaelitism, see David Howard Dickason, *The Daring Young Men: The Story of the American Pre-Raphaelites* (Bloomington: Indiana University Press, 1953).

17 This work is dated September 1867 and appears to be signed by "W. Mory"; it is, in any event, in the Ruskinian vein of open-air "study from nature." For the significance of the mullein as an American nativist emblem, see Thomas Cole's *Black Birds on Mullen Stalks* (1836), reproduced in Ellwood C. Parry III, "Thomas Cole's Ideas for Mr. Reed's Doors," *American Art Journal* 12, (Summer 1980):38; and Henry Inman's *Mumble the Peg* (1842), in Novak, *Nature and Culture,* fig. 53, p. 102.

18 On Gude and Pulian, see the works on the Düsseldorf school cited in subsequent notes and the biographical entries in *Allgemeines Lexikon der Bildenden Künstler* (Leipzeg, 1922) and *Die Düsseldorfer Malerschule* (Düsseldorf, 1969). On Krieghoff, see Hugues de Jouvancourt, *Cornelius Krieghoff* (Toronto: Musson, 1971); and J. Russell Harper, *Krieghoff* (Toronto: University of Toronto Press, 1979).

19 For a list of similar subjects by Gifford, see *A Memorial Catalogue of the Paintings of Sanford Robinson Gifford, N.A., with a Biographical and Critical Essay by John F. Weir* (New York: Metropolitan Museum of Art, 1881). Comparable examples of like subject-matter and painterly technique are *Mount Mansfield* (1859), *Landscape and Cow* (1859), and *In the Green Mountains* (ca. 1861), reproduced as figs. 16, 17, and 19 in Nicolai Cikovsky, *Sanford Robinson Gifford* (Austin: University of Texas Press, 1971); and *Mount Washington from Saco* (ca. 1854), reproduced as fig. 110 on p. 98 of Donald D. Keys, *The White Mountains: Place and Perceptions* (Durham, N.H.: University of New Hampshire Art Galleries, 1980).

20 On the rise and fall of the Düsseldorf Gallery see R. L. Stehle, "The Düsseldorf Gallery of New York," *New York Historical Society Quarterly* 58 (October 1974):305–15. On the influence of the Düsseldorf school on American artists, see Donelson F. Hoope's essay in *The Düsseldorf Academy and the Americans* (Atlanta: High Museum of Art, 1972), 19–34; and *American Artists in Düsseldorf: 1840–1865* (Framingham, Mass.: Danforth Museum, 1982).

21 James Jackson Jarves, *The Art-Idea,* ed. Benjamin Rowland, Jr. (1864; Cambridge: Harvard University Press, 1960), 27. Susan Dickinson owned a first edition of this work. Jarves's fervent Ruskinianism was another avenue by which elite ideas could have been absorbed by the poet who lived next door to the rich library housed in the Evergreens.

22 *Gems from the Düsseldorf Gallery, Photographed from the Original Pictures by A. A. Turner and Reproduced (for the First Time) under the Superintendence of*

B. Frosham (New York: Appleton, 1863), 28. This sumptuous folio is not among the books found at the Evergreens, though the Dickinsons must have been familiar with it, since they owned a slightly reduced framed reproduction drawn from it, *Winter Scene* by G. Saal.

23 *Catalogue of a Private Collection of Paintings and Original Drawings by Artists of the Düsseldorf Academy of Fine Arts* (New York: G. F. Nesbitt, 1858), 35–6. *Catalogue of Paintings from the Düsseldorf Academy of Fine Arts* (New York: Cosmopolitan Art Association, ca. 1857) contains the "Historical Sketch" reprinted in *Gems from the Düsseldorf Gallery* (3–5) and the same description of *Landscape: Norwegian Scenery, with Bears* (8), though here the painting is numbered 48. An article in the *Crayon* 3 (January 1856), discussing a painting by Gude in the collection of John Wolfe, refers to him as "the painter of the famous bear landscape." Another ecstatic description in the 1858 *Catalogue* reflects Gude's appeal to contemporary connoisseurs brought up on a diet of Ruskinian truthfulness to nature: "What a beautiful representation of Nature in her wildest moods is Gude's 'Norwegian Scenery, with Bears.' How palpable the clear atmosphere beyond the mountain tops! How rich the color! How bold and broad the general effect, and yet with what nicety the details are finished, even to the torrent's spray, the rocks and fern leaves!" (33–4).

24 The conjunction of Denton and Cotton in a "reading" of Gude's landscapes by a contemporary is suggestive. William Denton (1823–83) was an American radical reformer, a freethinking Transcendentalist who sought direct communion with nature without the intermediary of church or Scripture. The quotation used in the catalogue comes from a long poem entitled "My Fortune," which declares: "God's palace is mine, with its high dome of blue / Its curtains, the clouds, with the light peeping through" (*Poems for Reformers* [1856; Cleveland: Vanguard Office, 1859], 72–3). This book was reissued (again at the author's own expense) as *Radical Rymes* in 1871. In Denton's active conviction that nature was the only true scripture, and man the only true prophet, we can observe the fruits of the Transcendental revolt begun by Emerson in his 1836 "Nature." Charles Cotton (1630–87) was on the other hand an ardent Royalist and archetypal Cavalier poet, a friend of Izaak Walton. The lines from *Dana's Household Book* excerpted by the cataloguer are from a poem called "The Retirement: Stanzas Irreguliers" dedicated to Walton and included by him in the fifth edition (1676) of *The Compleat Angler*. Although Cotton was definitely not a Metaphysical but a lover of neoclassic and Restoration verse forms, he was proud of his father's association with Donne and preserved a contemplative strain in these particular lines. See *Poems of Charles Cotton, 1630–1687*, ed. John Beresford (New York: Boni & Liveright, 1923), 46, 405. In the contemporary choice of Denton and Cotton as glosses, we see a typical *bricolage* of the seventeenth century and the nineteenth, the archaic and the avant-garde, the inwardly contemplative and the outwardly Transcendental. It is also significant that Cotton's nature poems were admired by Lamb, Wordsworth, and Coleridge and praised for their

simplicity and sincerity. Compare Dickinson's combination of romantic rebellion with her own form of archaic but direct "irregular stanzas."

25 Peter Bermingham, *American Art in the Barbizon Mood* (Washington: Smithsonian Institution Press, 1975), 36.

8. THE ART OF PEACE

1 William Blake, "A Vision of the Last Judgment," in *The Complete Writings of William Blake, with Variant Readings,* ed. Geoffrey Keynes (London: Oxford University Press, 1966), 617.

2 See Exod., especially 3:1–6 (the burning bush); 13:21–2 (the pillars of cloud and fire); 24:15–18 (the glory of God in a cloud); and 26:31–4 (the veil of the tabernacle). For a face-to-face confrontation with the godhead similar to Dickinson's and employing the same biblical imagery, see Helen Hunt Jackson's "Showbread" (*Poems,* 96).

3 Elihu Vedder, *The Digressions of V* (Boston: Houghton Mifflin, 1910), 451. About the year 1880 Dickinson wrote to Judge Lord, "I dreamed last week that you had died – and one had carved a statue of you and I was asked to unvail it – and I said what I had not done in Life I would not in death when your loved eyes could not forgive" (*L* 3:663–4).

4 W. Sylvester, "Sunsets," *Crayon* 2 (September 26, 1855):191. The entire essay encapsulates an important romantic taxonomy of "three distinct types of sunsets": the scud or rain cloud, which is "the most powerful in its effect on the mind"; the cirrus, which is "remarkable for repose, purity and delicacy of color"; and the cloudless, which is paradoxically "the least interesting and most poetical." It is obvious from his scientific attitude, his rhapsodic word-paintings, and his rapt quotations from Wordsworth that Sylvester has been reading Ruskin. For some of the earliest recorded folk wisdom linking the sunset with weather prognostication, see Matt. 16:2–3.

5 Susan Sontag, *On Photography* (New York: Farrar, Straus & Giroux, 1978), 85.

6 *The Journal of Henry David Thoreau,* ed. Bradford Torrey and Francis H. Allen, 14 vols. (1906; Boston: Houghton Mifflin, 1949) 3:179.

7 MacGregor Jenkins, *Emily Dickinson: Friend and Neighbor* (Boston: Little, Brown, 1939), 37.

8 H. D. Thoreau, "Walking," in *Major Essays,* 218.

9 This orthodox typological significance of sunset is also explicated by Edward Hitchcock in his *Religious Lectures on Peculiar Phenomena in the Four Seasons* (Amherst: J. S. & C. Adams, 1850). Here is a selection from Hitchcock's chapter "The Triumphal Arch of Summer": "Contemplate now the rainbow of the evening, or rather of the setting sun, and you have a beautiful emblem of hopes, temporal and eternal, that are true and will become reality. And a striking difference between these hopes and such as will perish lies in the fact, that they follow, instead of preceding, the storms of life. After the clouds and the darkness, and it may be tempests of affliction, and disappointment have passed by, God impresses upon those

who have endured them the tokens of his approbation and favor, and gives them a bright earnest of happier days: it may be on earth, but assuredly in heaven" (71–2).

10 S. Foster Damon, *A Blake Dictionary: The Ideas and Symbols of William Blake* (Providence, R.I.: Brown University Press, 1965), 142. See Damon's complete entries on "The Four Zoas" (142–5) and "Golgonooza" (162–5).

11 For a modern psychological interpretation of this fourfold paradigm, see Jung's discussion of the mysteries of the Cabiri, who "represent the four cardinal points and the four seasons, as well as the four colours and the four elements" ("The History and Psychology of a Natural Symbol," in Jung, *Psychology and Religion: West and East,* trans. R. F. C. Hull [New York: Pantheon Books, 1958], 64–105).

12 See Gerald Wilkinson, *Turner's Early Sketchbooks* (New York: Watson-Guptil, 1972), 94–5.

13 *Journals* 9:174–5. For some examples of these sketches see those of witch hazel for February 9, 1852 (3:292); river reflections for April 11, 1852 (3:403); and "short clouds, horizontal and parallel to one another, each straight and dark below with a slight cumulus resting on it," for April 10, 1852 (3:396).

14 See Charles Anderson, *Emily Dickinson's Poetry: Stairway of Surprise* (New York: Holt, Rinehart & Winston, 1960), 91–2.

15 Stephane Mallarmé, "Les Fenêtres," in *Mallarmé,* ed. Anthony Hartley (Baltimore: Penguin Books, 1965), 18. For more sunset imagery similar to that of Dickinson and Thoreau, but strained through an urban symbolist consciousness, see Baudelaire's prose poem "Le Crépuscle du soir," published in his *Le Spleen de Paris* (1867; Paris: Georges Crès, 1917), 96.

17 E. P. Richardson, *Painting in America: The Story of 450 Years* (New York: Crowell, 1956), 219.

18 T. W. Higginson, *Oldport Days* (Boston: J. R. Osgood, 1873), 78–9. In January 1874 Dickinson wrote to Higginson: "I was re-reading 'Oldport.' Largest last, like Nature" (*L* 2:518).

19 Emily Dickinson was not the only family member to be captivated by meteorological effects like sunsets, Dr. Hitchcock's remarkable rainbow, and the aurora borealis. In a letter to Austin written on October 1, 1851, in which she notes sadly that "Martha and I were talking of you the other night, how we wished you were here to see the autumn sun set and walk and talk with us among the fading leaves," she also reports: "There was quite an excitement in the village Monday evening. We were all startled by a violent church bell ringing, and thinking of nothing but fire, rushed out in the street to see. The sky was a beautiful red, bordering on a crimson, and rays of a gold pink color were constantly shooting off from a kind of sun in the centre. People were alarmed at this beautiful Phenomenon, supposing that fires somewhere were *coloring the sky.* The exhibition lasted for nearly 15 minutes, and the streets were full of people wondering and admiring. Father happened to see it among the very first and rang the bell *himself* to call attention to it. You will have a full account from the pen of

Mr Trumbell, whom I have not a doubt, was seen with a large lead pencil, noting down the sky at the time of it's highest glory" (*L* 1:139). Leyda excerpts part of J. R. Trumbell's account of this "beautiful Phenomenon" published in the *Hampshire and Franklin Express* on October 3: "AURORA BOREALIS. – One of the most splendid displays of this kind we remember ever to have witnessed, was visible on Monday night . . . The rays converged at the zenith and extended over the concave above like folds of crimson attached to the center by a ring" (*YH* 1:214).

It is interesting to observe that while Dickinson was more attuned to the remarkable colorism of this event, Trumbell was more concerned with fixing a fanciful image in his reader's mind. Later Dickinson would learn to combine both techniques in her own meteorological shorthand, but she was conditioned to study such events not only by her father's Puritan attention to signs and wonders (matched by the fervent natural theology of Edward Hitchcock) but by such lyrics as the following, which appeared in *Parley's Magazine* 8 (1840):136. This song, "Aurora Borealis," originally published with music, was furnished by Lowell Mason, "Professor in the Boston Academy of Music":

> See the Northern light! the Northern light!
> To the zenith of the skies,
> How the glowing columns rise!
> Brightly gleaming, Brightly gleaming, Brightly gleaming,
> Through the veil of the night.

> See the Northern light! the Northern light!
> See the dark clouds round the base,
> Brilliant streaks from place to place,
> Ever changing, Ever changing, Ever changing,
> Now 'tis dim, now bright.

> See the Northern light! the Northern light!
> Like the dawning day it shines,
> Shooting stream from stream combines,
> Brightly gleaming, Brightly gleaming, Brightly gleaming
> Through the veil of the night.

> See the Northern light! the Northern light!
> Plainly telling He is great
> Who did all its beams create
> Never changing, Never changing, Never changing
> Source of life and light.

Mason was coeditor, with Austin Phelps and Edwards Park, of *The Sabbath Hymn Book* (1858), Edward Dickinson's favorite hymnal. He was also the composer of the music for the famous "Missionary Hymn" beginning "From Greenland's icy mountains," whose lyrics were written in 1819 by the English bishop of Calcutta, Reginald Heber.

20 George Inness, Jr., *Life, Art and Letters of George Inness*, intro. by Elliott Daingerfield (New York: Century, 1917), 209.

21 See George Landow's chapter "Ruskin's Religious Belief," in *Aesthetic and Critical Theories*, 241–317.

22 *Works*, 452–3. See the passage from this poem already quoted as an epigraph to Chapter 7. There are only three quotations from Wordsworth in Emily Dickinson's surviving letters. One is from "We Are Seven," but the other two fasten on "the light that never was on sea or land" from "Elegiac Stanzas." The first is an altered version of the lines and the second an exact quotation (see *L* 2:449, 510). In an 1872 essay called "French Pictures in Boston," Henry James declared that Wordsworth's mysterious light "is simply the light of the mind" (*The Painter's Eye*, 47).

APPENDIX B. AUSTIN DICKINSON AS CONNOISSEUR

1 MS inventories, 1850–69, 1873, the Evergreens. Other documents cited in the text are from the same source.

2 The notion that Susan Gilbert was a *poor* orphan girl is dispelled by a letter that she wrote sometime in August of 1855 to her two wealthy brothers (Dwight and Frank) in Michigan. It is quoted on pp. 347–8 of Bianchi and Hampson's unpublished "Emily Dickinson: Her Life, Lineage, and Legacy," and gives some insight into the heady days of her engagement, which included the renovation of the Homestead and the building of the Evergreens:

> My dear Brothers
>
> One day has passed since the reception of your letter and I almost feel this morning as if I could never answer it, – not from lack of feeling but expression. You must know that such a generous present would quite melt my heart and dizzy my brain, and in such a state what can one say?
>
> The tears have hardly been out of my eyes since the letter came, not alone for the pleasure of being the executive of five thousand dollars but also the love and tenderness that prompted it.
>
> Whenever I have thought of my future plans I have never felt any solicitude for I knew from the past that it would be your pleasure to bestow enough to furnish my home, wherever it might be, comfortably and tastefully, but I never dreamed of such a present as you have given me and can hardly realize it. May God bless you here for your love for us and give you a crown in heaven! I have many and almost unclouded anticipations of a sweet home and they are heightened by the prospect of all the essentials and luxuries even, taste can suggest. Austin's plans are now definite, as he is writing you, though they have resulted differently from our previously formed expectations, we are both very happy in them and hope they may strike you as pleasantly.

Austin's Father has overruled all objections to remaining here; even tho' it has been something of a sacrifice for Austin's spirit and rather a struggle with his preconceived ideas, I feel satisfied that in the end it will be best and he will be fully rewarded. He goes into partnership with his Father the 1st of June. (1855)

Mr. Dickinson is fitting up the old Mack house very handsomely for himself and in the course of the Summer, Austin will have a pleasant house in process of erection on the lot West (of that place). For the sake of going at once into our own home, all complete, we have decided to defer our marriage until another Spring and that will give me no more time than I want to prepare for house keeping. As soon as Austin's house plan is regularly drawn, I will send it to you. It will not be a great castle but when we get it all fixed, if you do not say it is pleasant and perfect, then I am mistaken. Won't I be proud to get you an oyster supper some cold night? Don't speak of it, it makes me too happy. Oh my brothers, if you knew the happiness you have given me! I hope you will not think me foolishly happy. I am not. I believe I know what life is and even now my joyous anticipations are chastened by the recollections and sorrows of the past. "The knowledge that entereth in through suffering" we all know something about speaks of the one who has been taken from us.

3   Certified copy of last will and testament of William A. Dickinson, Amherst, copy dated Northampton, Mass., September 13, 1895, the Evergreens. Millicent Todd Bingham, daughter of Mabel Loomis Todd, writes that "by terms of his will Mr. Dickinson bequeathed to Mrs. Todd two large framed pictures, an oil painting of a landscape near Dresden, by Johann Gottfried Pulian, and an engraving of lions at the ruins of Persepolis, both in my possession" (*Ancestor's Brocades,* 332 n. 2). A large engraving of lions at the ruins of Persepolis is also at the Evergreens. Austin may have purchased another copy of it for his inamorata while still living, since the written will specifies only the Pulian and the Rembrandt.

INDEX